FATAL INFLUENCE

THE IMPACT OF IRELAND ON BRITISH POLITICS
1920–1925

KEVIN MATTHEWS

Published by the
UNIVERSITY COLLEGE DUBLIN PRESS
PREAS CHOLÁISTE OLLSCOILE BHAILE ÁTHA CLIATH

2004

First published 2004 by
UNIVERSITY COLLEGE DUBLIN PRESS
Newman House 86 St Stephen's Green, Dublin 2, Ireland
www.ucdpress.ie

© Kevin Matthews 2004

ISBN 1 904558 06 2 hardback
ISBN 1 904558 05 4 paperback

CIP data available from the British Library

*The right of Kevin Matthews to be identified as the author of this work
has been asserted by him*

Typeset in Ireland in Adobe Caslon and Bodoni Oldstyle
by Elaine Shiels, Bantry, Co. Cork
Text design by Lyn Davies
Printed in England on acid-free paper
by MPG Books Ltd, Bodmin,
Cornwall

For my mother
Florence May Matthews
and to the memory of
my father
Charles Benjamin Matthews

*

'Ireland is indeed a fatal influence in British politics.'

AUSTEN CHAMBERLAIN TO IVY CHAMBERLAIN
31 JULY 1924

Contents

Illustrations

Maps

A note on terminology, citations and abbreviations

Works on Anglo-Irish history follow a number of different, sometimes contradictory rules when referring to governments, political parties, and organisations. Here, the terms 'Northern Ireland' and 'Ulster' are used interchangeably when referring to the six-county state. In the same way, after 1921 'Ireland' and 'Irish' are used interchangeably with 'Free State' and 'Free Stater' to refer to the 26-county state.

Although the British Conservative Party was still officially the 'Unionist Party', it and its supporters are referred to as 'Conservative' or 'Tory' throughout; the latter term is not employed in any derogatory sense. The term 'Unionist' is reserved for the Northern Ireland government and the supporters of partition, while 'Nationalist' has been employed as a generic term to refer to supporters of Irish independence and reunification, whether they lived in the North or the South. 'Imperial' is used interchangeably with 'British' as this was the fashion of the time.

£1 for the following years was equivalent in 2001 to the amount in brackets: 1920 (£23.92); 1921 (£30.26); 1922 (£37.09); 1923 (£35.90); 1924 (£35.63); 1925 (£36.28) (data from Economic History Services). A request of £160,000 for Ulster's Special Constabulary in 1922 is roughly £5.8 million today.

For the sake of brevity, secondary sources are given a full citation only on first reference. Thereafter, the source is cited by the author's last name and an abbreviated title. Unless otherwise noted, portions of quotations are emphasised or contain irregular spellings only when this is the case in the original text.

A number of abbreviations are used in the footnotes and, occasionally, in the text. These abbreviations are listed below. Northern Ireland government documents are prefaced with PRONI (Public Record Office of Northern Ireland) to distinguish them from British government records.

Abbreviations

AC	Austen Chamberlain Papers
AJB-B	Arthur James Balfour Papers, British Library
AJB-S	Arthur James Balfour Papers, Scottish National Archives
Annual Register	*The Annual Register: A Review of Public Events at Home and Abroad: 1920–1925*
BBK	Lord Beaverbrook Papers
BL	Andrew Bonar Law Papers
C	Conclusions of British Cabinet meetings and conferences
CAB	Cabinet Papers
CJ	Records created or inherited by the Northern Ireland Office
Cmd	Command Papers
CO	Colonial Office Papers
Comp IV–V	Gilbert's Companion series of printed documents
CP	Cabinet Paper
CSC	Clementine Spencer Churchill Papers
Dáil Deb	*Dáil Éireann Debates*
Dáil Deb I	*Minutes of the First Dáil Éireann*
Dáil Deb II	*Private Sess. Minutes of the Second Dáil, Private Sessions*
Dáil Treaty Deb	*Dáil Treaty Debates*
DE	Dáil Éireann Papers
DFA	Department of Foreign Affairs Papers, Irish Free State
DO	Dominions Office Papers
D/T	Department of the Taoiseach Papers
EB	Ernest Blythe Papers
EC Min	Executive Council Minutes (Irish Free State)
EM-NLI	Eoin MacNeill Papers, National Library of Ireland
EM-UCD	Eoin MacNeill Papers, University College Dublin Archives
FIN	Department of Finance, Government of Northern Ireland
HC Deb	*Parliamentary Debates. Hansard House of Commons, Fifth Series*
HL Deb	*Parliamentary Debates. Hansard House of Lords, Fifth Series*
HHW	Henry Wilson Papers
HNKY	Maurice Hankey Diaries
HO	Home Office Papers
IBC	Irish Boundary Commission

IO	India Office Papers
IUA	Irish Unionist Alliance Papers
JDPF	John French Papers
JHC	J. H. Collins Papers
JRM	James Ramsay MacDonald Papers
LC	Leaders Conference – minutes of meetings and committee reports of the Conservative Shadow Cabinet
LG	David Lloyd George Papers
MP	Member of Parliament
NC	Neville Chamberlain Papers
NEBB	North-Eastern Boundary Bureau Papers
NI HC Deb	*Parliamentary Debates. Northern Ireland House of Commons, First Series*
NUA	National Unionist Association Papers
PG	Provisional Government of Ireland Papers
PGI	Provisional Government of Ireland Committee Papers (British Cabinet)
PM	Department of Prime Minister's Correspondence (Government of Northern Ireland)
PR	Proportional Representation
PREM	Records of the Prime Minister's Office (United Kingdom)
PRO	Public Record Office, London
PRONI	Public Record Office of Northern Ireland
RF	Richard Feetham Papers
RM	Richard Mulcahy Papers
RUC	Royal Ulster Constabulary
S(4)	4th Marquess of Salisbury Papers
SB	Stanley Baldwin Papers
S.F.(B) and (C)	British Cabinet documents related to the Irish negotiations
SFM	Sinn Féin Standing Committee Minutes
T	Treasury Papers
TD	Teachtaí Dála – Member of Dáil Éireann
TJ	Tom Jones Papers
UUC	Ulster Unionist Council
W-E	Sir Laming Worthington-Evans Papers
WO	War Office
WSC	Winston Spencer Churchill Papers

Preface

Like most such books, this volume bears only one name as its author. But, in truth, it is the work of many hands. What originally was a study of the independence leader, Michael Collins, expanded as I found myself questioning long-held assumptions about the Irish partition. Stranger still was Ireland's omission from the story of a turning point in twentieth-century British politics. My aim is to place the Irish Question within the broader context of that story and to show how each affected the other. While the judgments here are mine alone, many people contributed to the making of this book. To the extent that what you find between these pages is informative and, dare I even hope, enjoyable to read, the credit for that accomplishment is theirs as much as it is mine.

This book draws heavily from a doctoral thesis written while I was at the London School of Economics and Political Science. Even before that, Jack Murray, Holly Buchanan, Jennifer Fromer, and the Rev. Canon William C. Neuroth generously assisted me in gathering the initial material on which this book is based. Later, while working in the Dublin archives, I was welcomed into the homes of the Cummins and Malone families; I owe a special debt of gratitude to Sister Ailbe Cosgrove and the women of St Caral Convent, Bethany Hostel, who allowed me to stay with them during a final visit to Ireland. For much of my time in London, I lived with Andrew and Jane Walker. They saw me through a number of difficult situations; we started as acquaintances and became friends for life.

Many people have been extraordinarily kind and generous with their time. Among them, the late Michael Collins, nephew of his famous namesake, shared a number of insights about his uncle and steered me away from several errors in my early research. My thanks also go to the Viscount Davidson for allowing me to quote from the unpublished correspondence of Joan Davidson and Stanley Baldwin, and to his son-in-law, Richard Oldfield, who invited me to stay at his home, Sittingbourne, so that I could examine the letters.

This study is based on extensive research in the archives of Great Britain, Ireland, and Northern Ireland. I wish to thank the University of London's Central Research Fund and the Royal Historical Society for providing assistance which enabled me to undertake this work. My thanks also go to the London School of Economics' Student Union Hardship Fund and to the History Department of Northern Kentucky University for a Professional Development Award.

The staffs of all of the research institutes and libraries that I visited were unfailingly kind and often went out of their way to assist me. In particular, I would like to express my gratitude to the staff of the House of Lords Record Office, especially to Katharine Bligh; the Rev. Father Ignatius Fennessey, OFM, of the Franciscan Library, Killiney; Dr J. Graham Jones, of the National Library of Wales; Robin Harcourt Williams, Hatfield House; and Godfrey Waller, supervisor of the manuscripts department at Cambridge University Library. Thanks to the intervention of Ann McVeigh, Grace McGrath, and Ian Montgomery of the Public Record Office of Northern Ireland it was possible for me to examine and obtain permission to quote from documents only recently opened to the public.

I am deeply grateful to the many copyright holders who have granted me permission to quote from the letters, diaries, and other documents that I have researched. These holders include: Virginia Brand (H. H. Asquith papers); Earl Baldwin; Earl Balfour; Lady Juliet Townshend (Lord Birkenhead papers); Valerie Scriven (Austen Chamberlain papers); James Lloyd (Neville Chamberlain papers); Professor A. K. S. Lambton (Cecil of Chelwood papers); Mary Bennett (H. A. L. Fisher papers); Sir Erskine William Gladstone; John Grigg; Sara Morrison (Walter Long papers); Alan Maclean; the Mulcahy Trust; Lord Salisbury (4th Marquess of Salisbury and Baron Quickswood papers); the Earl of Selborne; Brian Dingwall (Lady Spender's diary); the Office of the First and Deputy First Minister, Northern Ireland (Sir Wilfrid Spender papers); and Verily Anderson Paget (Viscount Templewood papers).

The British Library's Oriental and India Office Collections has kindly allowed me to quote from papers held in its archive. Quotations from the Strachey papers are reprinted courtesy of *The Spectator*. I also wish to thank the Clerk of Records for permission to quote from papers in the custody of the House of Lords Record Office; the Trustees of the Imperial War Museum for permission to quote from Sir Henry Wilson's papers; and the London School of Economics for permission to quote from the Passfield and Piercy papers, Copyright © London School of Economics and Political Science, 1923–5. I am also grateful to David Jobbins, assistant editor of the *Round Table*, for permission to quote from that journal and from the Lionel Curtis papers.

Quotations from the Churchill papers have been reproduced with permission of Curtis Brown Ltd, London on behalf of Winston S. Churchill. Copyright © Winston S. Churchill. I would also like to thank the Lady Soames for allowing me to research Lady (Clementine) Churchill's papers. References to Sir Maurice Hankey's diaries have been made thanks to the Master, Fellows and Scholars of Churchill College, Cambridge. Quotations from the Tom Jones papers are made by permission of the National Library of Wales. I also wish to thank the staff of the Public Record Office at Kew for their help with my research and in answering my queries regarding Crown Copyright. I am also indebted to the staff of the Bodleian Library, Oxford, with special thanks to Jill Spellman, and to Conservative Central Office for permission to quote from National Unionist Association documents.

The staff at the National Archives of Ireland were extraordinarily kind, and I wish to thank the Director for permission to quote from papers held at that archive. I am equally indebted to the staff of the National Library of Ireland and to the staff of Trinity College, Dublin, Library, especially Stuart Ó Seanóir, for their advice and assistance. I also owe a debt of gratitude to Seamus Helferty of University College Dublin Archives. Lastly, in this regard, I would like to offer a word of gratitude to the Deputy Keeper of the Records, the Public Record Office of Northern Ireland for permission to quote from documents held at that archive and, also to the depositor of the Craigavon papers for permission to quote from Lady Craig's diary and Sir James Craig's papers, as well as to the Ulster Unionist Council for permission to quote from that organisation's papers.

I have made a good faith effort to contact the present copyright holders of all of the papers quoted in this book. If contact was not made with a present copyright holder, I hope that he or she will excuse me, and I also apologise to anyone who has not been properly credited.

Dr Anthony Howe and John Barnes of the LSE, my former boss, and friend, James A. Haught at the *Charleston* (W.Va.) *Gazette*, and Dr Cynthia DeMarcus Manson of Southern University at Baton Rouge read drafts of my work at various stages, as did Ronald Brennan who also assisted me with the Biographical Notes. I am indebted to them for their advice, as I am for the same reason to Dr W. Michael Ryan and Dr Jeffrey C. Williams of Northern Kentucky University.

While I was at the LSE, the administrative secretaries of the Department of International History – Pat Christopher, Mary McCormick, Brigid Spillane, and Susanne Umerski – were generous with their time, their expertise, and with their friendship. All of the research and much of the writing of this book was accomplished using a laptop computer that was given to me by Leah Kay Matthews, my steadfast and generous twin sister. At the same time, without the help and guidance and, again, friendship of Larry Ward, and of Carole Simpson and Joanne Bourne of the LSE, it would have been impossible for me to put this technology to its best use. The support of all four of these people was absolutely crucial.

Not least, I wish to thank my supervisor at the LSE, Professor David Stevenson. His advice was invariably accurate, his criticism as constructive as it was kind, and his encouragement unfailingly generous. Most importantly, he allowed me to go my own way, to chart my own course, and for that I shall always be grateful.

I also owe a word of appreciation to Stephen Hannon for his rendering of the maps in this book and to Frank Mack who helped with the reproduction of several of the photographs used here. The other prints were obtained by Barbara Mennell, my editor. Throughout, she has been both understanding and patient, and it is a blessing to work with her.

Of all these debts, there is none greater than the one I owe to Andrea Heatley, my wife. She is my editor of first resort, reading and re-reading the drafts of these chapters and making invaluable suggestions on the manuscript. More than anyone else, she has been with me every step of the way.

Finally, I wish to thank my mother, Florence Matthews. Over many years, and through many hard times, she has never once lost faith in me, and for that there are no words to express my gratitude, except to say that it is eternal. It is for this reason that this book is dedicated, in part, to her.

KEVIN MATTHEWS
Washington, DC
December 2003

A DAMNABLE LEGACY

St Patrick came to see the land
From which the snakes he'd banished
'What's this across my path?' he cried,
'I thought they all had vanished.'

A monstrous serpent squirmed around
From Antrim Glens to Derry;
'Bad luck to it,' a Southern said,
'Shure, isn't that the boundary.'[1]

———

One mid-summer's morning in June 1923, a motorcade sped along the back roads of Northern Ireland bound for the Irish frontier. The excursion had been organised by Stephen Tallents, Britain's representative in the province. Two guests accompanied Tallents on his tour of the boundary: Sir Wilfrid Spender, secretary to the Northern Ireland Cabinet, and Spender's wife, Lilian.[2]

'[O]ur route corkscrewed about in the most bewildering manner', Lady Spender wrote in her diary. Not wanting to stray into Free State territory, the party took 'innumerable by-roads in order to avoid crossing the Border' but were often frustrated, as happened at Clady, where 'here again the Boundary was an imaginary line across the middle of the river bridge'.

To Sir Wilfrid, who had served in the Ulster Division during the First World War, the boundary 'reminded him more than anything else' of the Western Front, 'complete with blockhouses, sandbags, barbed wire' and trenches – most of which 'we have cut . . . wherever the roads cross the Border'. Lady Spender tried looking beyond these barriers toward the 'beautiful wild country', but found she could not. 'The beautiful blue mountains of Donegal', she wrote

1   '"The Boundary Serpent" by "Turf Clod"', *Derry Sentinel*, ? Dec. 1925, RF, 7/1, ff. 42.
2   Tallents to Anderson, 22 June 1923, HO 317/68.

stood up in the west, cut off from us, alas, by this tragic state of civil war. It gave one a strange feeling to see a country so unnaturally and ungeographically divided – like seeing a living creature cut in two.[3]

Despite its seeming permanence – despite the trenches, the blockhouses, the customs huts – few on either side of this, the only international land border in the British Isles, believed that a boundary so unnatural and ungeographical could long survive. And for good reason. The boundary travelled by Tallents and the Spenders was the result of the 1920 Government of Ireland Act and its creation of two Irish governments: one for the 26 counties of south, west, and northwest Ireland, and another for the six northeastern counties of Ulster. Although the 1920 Act temporarily divided the island, its 'ultimate aim', according to its creators, 'was a united Ireland with a separate Parliament of its own, bound by the closest ties to Great Britain'.[4]

Even before the 1920 Act reached the Statute Book few believed that 'such an artificial creation' would be the government's 'last word' on Ireland.[5] And they were right. A year later the 1920 Act was supplanted by the Irish Treaty, creating one government for the whole of Ireland, including the six partitioned Ulster counties, and granting to it 'the same constitutional status' in the British empire as the dominions of Canada, Australia, New Zealand, and South Africa.[6] But what this first article of the Treaty gave in the way of Irish unity was taken back by a series of clauses beginning with Article 11, which temporarily suspended the new government's jurisdiction over the six counties. There then followed what one of the Treaty's framers later admitted were its 'elements of dynamite': Article 12.[7] The first half of this article gave Ulster's government the choice of opting out of the new Irish dominion for good. In that case, the terms of the 1920 Act would remain in place so far as Northern Ireland was concerned. But if Northern Ireland opted out,

a Commission consisting of three persons, one to be appointed by the Government of the Irish Free State, one to be appointed by the Government of Northern Ireland, and one who shall be Chairman, to be appointed by the British Government, shall determine, in accordance with the wishes of the inhabitants, so far as may be

---

3   Lady Spender's diary, 25 June 1923, D/1633/2/26.

4   C 10 (19), 3 Dec. 1919, CAB 23/18. Unity remained the legislation's stated aim. 'The Act', Irish Chief Secretary Sir Hamar Greenwood told Parliament, 'provides for the political unity of Ireland'. See *HC Deb*, vol. 138, col. 647, 21 Feb. 1921.

5   Hoare to Lord Midleton, 9 Nov. 1920, Templewood Papers, 1: 12 (18). Anti-Partition League to Lloyd George, 13 Mar. 1920, Lothian Papers, GD 40/17/79.

6   Cmd 1560: *Articles of Agreement for a Treaty Between Great Britain and Ireland*, 1921, Sess. II, i, 75, Article 1. The Treaty is reprinted in Appendix II.

7   The speaker was Lord Birkenhead. See *HL Deb*, vol. 62, col. 1232, 9 Dec. 1925.

compatible with economic and geographic conditions, the boundaries between Northern Ireland and the rest of Ireland, and for the purposes of the Government of Ireland Act of 1920, and of this instrument, the boundary of Northern Ireland shall be such as may be determined by such Commission.[8]

For the Treaty's critics, Article 12 immediately became the focal point of controversy. Former Conservative Party leader Andrew Bonar Law called it his one 'serious objection' to the agreement.[9] Whether the Commission was empowered to make only minor readjustments to the border, or whether it had the right to transfer whole counties from North to South was a matter of hot dispute. Changes, though, there would be. As one Ulster Unionist MP put it, by the time the Boundary Commission was finished the six counties would be 'so cut up and mutilated that we shall no longer be masters in our own house'. It would mean the end of partition and the reunification of Ireland.[10]

But the boundary that Lady Spender saw in 1923 did not change. Eighteen months later the Boundary Commission's award was suppressed just as it was about to be released. All of the politicians had been wrong, except one. From the moment the boundaries of his new state were challenged, Northern Ireland Prime Minister Sir James Craig told his followers that there would no concessions to anyone. 'What we have', Craig declared, 'we hold'.[11]

* * *

There, it has been said, the story ends. Writing many years after the fact, A. J. P. Taylor memorably explained that with the 1921 Treaty, British Prime Minister David Lloyd George had not merely answered the Irish Question for 'good or ill'; he had magically 'conjured it out of existence'.[12] Historians find Taylor's imagery seductive and for the most part have been content to echo his verdict. Lloyd George, one wrote, 'for good or ill, effectively settled the "Irish Question" as generations of British people had understood it', and this, another noted, explains the 'quickly diminishing importance of the Irish question . . . in British domestic politics' after the Treaty was signed.[13]

---

8   Ibid., Article 12.
9   *HC Deb*, vol. 149, col. 203, 15 Dec. 1921.
10 Ibid., col. 56–7, 14 Dec. 1921.
11 *NI HC Deb*, vol. 2, col. 598, 23 May 1922.
12 A. J. P. Taylor, *English History: 1914–1945* (Oxford, 1965), pp. 161, 236.
13 K. O. Morgan, 'Lloyd George and the Irish', in R. Blake, Introduction, *Ireland After the Union: Proceedings of the Second Joint Meeting of the Royal Irish Academy and the British Academy, London, 1986* (London, 1989), p. 83. S. Lawlor, *Britain and Ireland: 1914–1923* (Dublin, 1983), p. 154. 'Except for a brief flare-up in 1922', writes Michael Kinnear, 'the Irish question was now shelved until the 1970s'. See *The Fall of Lloyd George: The Political Crisis of 1922* (London, 1973), p. 15. D. G. Boyce writes that Ireland

Certainly, British politicians were ready to turn their backs on Ireland. Their wish was granted when, in 1923, most discussion of Irish affairs in Parliament was ruled out of order by the Speaker of the House of Commons. A year later this ban was further extended so that MPs could not raise 'any matters of administration for which a Minister in Northern Ireland is responsible'.[14]

Out of sight, the Irish problem was left to fester. As a government White Paper explained in 1973, 'the uncomfortable lessons of history provided every inducement to the Government in London to keep Northern Ireland out of United Kingdom politics'. This code of silence extended to every level and branch of government. Civil servants soon learned that they 'would get little thanks in Whitehall or Westminster' if they forced ministers and MPs to look too closely into Britain's attic; the door was to be kept closed and bolted shut.[15]

Nor were the men who were supposed to have solved the Irish riddle particularly inclined to talk about their handiwork. Winston Churchill excepted, their recollections (along with an authorised biography of Lord Birkenhead) are singularly uninformative when it comes to the Coalition's handling of the Irish Question.[16] This seeming lack of interest has proved contagious, and their biographers have also largely disregarded Ireland once the Treaty negotiations are dealt with.[17]

13 *cont.* played a major role 'for the last time with its departure from the centre of the British political stage in 1922'. See *The Irish Question and British Politics: 1886–1986* (London, 1988), p. 31.

14 *HC Deb*, vol. 162, cols 2246–7, 19 Apr. 1923; vol. 171, cols 549–50, 19 Mar. 1924.

15 Cmnd. 5460: *Royal Commission on the Constitution, 1969–1973* [The Kilbrandon Report] (London, 1973), para. 1303.

16 See, e.g., D. Lloyd George, *Is It Peace?* (London, 1923), pp. 267–75. A. Chamberlain, *Down The Years* (London, 1935), pp. 144–50. Ephesian [pseud. Bechhofer Roberts], *Lord Birkenhead* (London, 1926), pp. 85–8. Churchill, characteristically, took the opposite approach. See *The World Crisis*, vol. v: *The Aftermath* (New York, 1929), pp. 289–372.

17 John Campbell makes only passing reference to the troubles the Irish Treaty caused Birkenhead's political career. See *F. E. Smith: First Earl of Birkenhead* (London, 1983), pp. 601, 603, 650. Nor does he address Lloyd George's flirtation with the Irish issue in 1924 in *Lloyd George: The Goat in the Wilderness, 1922–31* (London, 1977). The same is true of Peter Rowland's *David Lloyd George* (New York, 1975); of Charles Petrie's *The Life and Letters of the Right Hon. Sir Austen Chamberlain*, vol. II (London, 1940); and David Dutton's *Austen Chamberlain: Gentleman in Politics* (Bolton, England, 1985). Catherine Shannon, in *Arthur J. Balfour and Ireland: 1874–1922* (Washington, 1988), p. 279, notes that Balfour sought to influence the Boundary Commission's deliberations but does not explore his actions. Martin Gilbert, in *Winston S. Churchill*, vol. v: *1922–1939* (London, 1976) devotes only a page and a half to Churchill's role in the 1925 Boundary Commission crisis. See pp. 137–8. This is difficult to explain given that in *Winston Churchill – Companion V*, Part I (London, 1979) his selection of documents demonstrates the importance of Ireland in Churchill's post-Coalition political comeback. See pp. 151–2, 172–4, 183–97, 203–4, 389–90, 469, 591–3, 603–17. For recent examples, see G. Best, *Churchill: A Study in Greatness* (London, 2001); and R. Jenkins, *Churchill: A Biography* (New York, 2001).

Yet, nearly two years after the fall of the Lloyd George Coalition, Herbert Asquith rose in the House of Commons to warn the British people that they were 'confronted with precisely the same problem' that had taken them to the brink of civil war in the summer of 1914.[18] The Irish Question, an issue that had dominated British politics for the better part of 40 years, had not been conjured away. Magic is, after all, based on illusion, and so was the notion that Lloyd George had made the Irish Troubles disappear. Instead, the problem was distilled to what was and perhaps still is its intractable core, the 'central and almost insuperable difficulty' of Anglo-Irish relations: 'the question of Ulster'.[19]

The issue at hand in 1924 was the same as in 1914 and in 1921. As Asquith told the Commons, the Irish dispute 'centred, as it centres now, mainly or exclusively upon the position of the two counties of Tyrone and Fermanagh'.[20] With their Nationalist majorities, these two counties symbolised the larger issue at stake. Both Ulster Unionists and Irish Nationalists passionately believed that on the outcome of this struggle hung Ireland's future as a united or a divided country.[21] It is revealing that in the aftermath of the First World War an official in Dublin Castle called Fermanagh and Tyrone the 'Alsace-Lorraine' of the Irish Question.[22]

Because the most contentious element in the Irish dispute – the future of Northern Ireland – was not settled, it returned to haunt Britain's leaders, and it did so just as they were caught up in 'a revolution in English politics' as profound as any which had been experienced in nearly a hundred years.[23] By the end of this revolution, the Liberals would be eclipsed as the leading party of the left. In their place, Labour under Ramsay MacDonald joined with the Conservatives under Stanley Baldwin to re-establish Britain's two-party political system. This reformation was the outcome of a period of extraordinary upheaval. In the space of just three years, there were four governments and three general elections. Nothing was certain, and for a time it seemed just as possible that the Conservatives not the Liberals would be consigned to electoral oblivion.[24]

18   *HC Deb*, vol. 177, col. 46, 30 Sept. 1924.

19   'His Conscience Must be Clear', *New Statesman*, 5 Nov. 1921. According to R. W. G. Carter and A. J. Parker, ed., *Ireland: Contemporary Perspectives on a Land and its People* (London, 1989), p. 3, Ireland's partition created 'an island under stress'.

20   *HC Deb*, vol. 177, cols 46, 30 Sept. 1924. Also, see Churchill's speech, *HC Deb*, vol. 150, col. 1270–1, 16 Feb. 1922; Craig's address in *NI HC Deb*, vol. 2, cols 1151–2, 7 Dec. 1922; and CP 503 (25), 3 Dec. 1925, CAB 27/295.

21   See, e.g., Michael Collins's speech in 'Sinn Fein and Ulster', *The Times*, 5 Sept. 1921. For the Unionist view, see 'Saving the Conference', *The Observer*, 6 Nov. 1921.

22   Sturgis diary, 14 Nov. 1921, PRO 30/59/5. The Franco-German dispute over Alsace-Lorraine helped to bring about the 1914–1918 conflict.

23   *The Annual Register: A Review of Public Events at Home and Abroad, 1924* (London, 1925), p. 8.

24   M. Cowling, *The Impact of Labour: 1920–1924* (Cambridge, 1971), pp. 419–21.

When it was signed, the Irish Treaty had 'almost unanimous approval' and was hailed as the 'crowning achievement' not only of the Coalition government of Liberals and Conservatives, but of Lloyd George's career.[25] A scant three years later, its Ulster clauses were being condemned as 'one of the damnable legacies of Lloyd Georgeism'. The rebuke, though made by a Labour newspaper, could just as easily have rolled off the lips of most Conservatives.[26] In the midst of Britain's political turmoil, the Tories in particular feared being trapped in the Irish 'cul-de-sac'.[27] Baldwin spoke for many public figures, certainly for most Conservatives, when he warned Craig at a particularly delicate moment: 'I do not want the Irish conflict revived in the House of Commons in any shape or form if it can justly be avoided.'[28]

Revived, though, it would be, inspiring hope for Lloyd George's political resurrection, hastening the downfall of Labour's first government and, throughout, threatening Baldwin's reconstruction of the Conservative Party as he attempted to reunite those Tories who had supported the Lloyd George Coalition with those who had destroyed it. Even after the Conservatives' overwhelming electoral victory in 1924, another year would elapse before the inter-war generation of British politicians could safely say that the Irish Question had been put behind them. As Churchill reminded fellow MPs in 1925, 'only a year ago this boundary question very nearly became a disastrous and dominating issue in our political life'.[29]

The aim of this work is to set these attempts to answer the Irish Question within the wider context of the revolution then taking place in British politics. Specifically, it means to show how the 'answer' devised by Lloyd George and his Coalition partners was constructed and then dismantled largely because of this revolution.[30]

The construction began with the Government of Ireland Act and, when that proved to be insufficient, was completed with the Treaty of 1921. In neither instance, however, was Lloyd George primarily concerned with the Irish

---

25 'Towards Irish Peace', *The Times*; and 'The New Peace', *Manchester Guardian*, both 8 Dec. 1921. 'A Free State', *Pall Mall and Globe*; and 'Real Hope', *Daily Herald*, both 7 Dec. 1921.

26 'Ulster Boundary Crisis', *Daily Herald*, 29 Apr. 1924. Neville to Ida Chamberlain, 3 Aug. 1924, NC 18/1/446.

27 See, e.g., Wood to Baldwin, 10 Sept. 1924, Halifax Papers, A4.410/14/1.

28 Baldwin to Craig, 14 Jan. 1924, SB vol. 101, ff. 197–8.

29 *HC Deb*, vol. 189, col. 360, 8 Dec. 1925.

30 This point has been made elsewhere but seldom explored in detail. See, e.g., G. J. Hand, *Report of the Irish Boundary Commission: 1925* (Shannon, 1969), p. viii. Paul Canning's *British Policy Towards Ireland: 1921–1941* (Oxford, 1985) takes a broad look at many of the issues specifically addressed in this study.

conflict. His chief ambition was to reorganise the Coalition as a political party in its own right. These plans came unstuck in part because Lloyd George failed to settle the question of Ulster, and within a year his government fell.

In its place, a new set of politicians came to the fore with a very different agenda. This was bound to affect those parts of the Irish settlement that were yet to be implemented. The rest of this narrative examines how the Treaty's inducements for Irish unity were dismantled, indeed how they were reversed in Northern Ireland's favour, as Coalition politics gave way to a return to the traditional two-party system.

When considering whether or not the Treaty's negotiators seriously attempted to resolve the Ulster Question, other studies have focused almost exclusively on the Boundary Commission.[31] In fact, the Treaty contained a series of interrelated and self-reinforcing clauses in Articles 11 to 15 which were designed to bring about 'the eventual establishment of a Parliament for the whole of Ireland'.[32] These clauses were themselves linked to other parts of the agreement which gave the Free State fiscal independence, but bound Ulster to the restrictive financial provisions of the 1920 Act.[33] 'The reason of course was obvious', one Whitehall official later explained, 'to offer as much inducement as possible to the North to come in' to a single Irish state.[34] A large part of this study is devoted to exploring these economic and financial inducements, and to their undoing. Within Northern Ireland, the dismantling of these provisions helped to fossilise politics into the sectarianism still practised by both sides. This dismantling enabled Unionist Party leaders to retain the support of working-class Protestants as Roman Catholics were further marginalised in the new state.

Ireland sent ripples through British politics well into the 1920s and beyond. According to Churchill, the Irish Treaty and its aftermath paved the way for the 'Baldwin-MacDonald Regime', nearly a decade and a half during which Baldwin 'in political brotherhood' with MacDonald was 'the ruling

31 See, e.g., M. Laffan, *The Partition of Ireland: 1911–1925* (Dundalk, 1983), pp. 72–125. Lord Longford concludes that successive British governments intentionally misled Free State leaders over the Boundary Commission which was, anyway, a fraud. See F. Pakenham, *Peace by Ordeal* (London, 1935 [1972 edition]), pp. 258, 273, 303–5. Peter Rowland's judgment in *Lloyd George*, p. 555, that Arthur Griffith and Michael Collins 'believed with a touching faith' that the Boundary Commission alone would bring about unity, does not stand up under examination.

32 'The Council of Ireland', Commonwealth Relations Office memorandum, 19 Apr. 1949, HO 45/23466.

33 N. Mansergh, *The Unresolved Question: The Anglo-Irish Settlement and its Undoing, 1912–1972* (New Haven, 1991), pp. 198–9, hints at this aspect of the negotiations.

34 Waterfield to Upcott, 6 Apr. 1923, T 160/163/F.6282. Also, see 'Unemployment Insurance in Northern Ireland', Hawtrey memorandum, 12 Nov. 1923, T 160/187/F.7136/1.

political figure in Britain'.[35] At the same time, settling the Irish Question vindicated the doctrine of appeasement to a generation of politicians who came of age during the inter-war years.[36]

Opposition to Lloyd George's earlier efforts to wage war in Ireland brought into working partnership Sir Samuel Hoare and Edward Wood. With other Tory MPs, they formed the 'Group', a collection of backbenchers who were to figure prominently in inter-war British politics.[37] For different reasons and at different times, two other MPs were to be plucked from obscurity because of their attacks on Lloyd George's Irish legacy. One, Anthony Eden, would become prime minister.[38] The other, Oswald Mosley, would lead Britain's Union of Fascists.[39]

Beginning with a brief background, this book outlines the genesis of Ireland's partition as an issue in post-war British politics. Next, it considers the impact of the Irish Question on the Lloyd George Coalition, the first unravellings of the Treaty settlement, and the role these events played in bringing about the downfall of the twentieth century's last Liberal prime minister. This is followed by an examination of how the Treaty's clauses were further nullified under a succession of governments led by Bonar Law, Baldwin, and MacDonald. Finally, the suppression of the Boundary Commission's report is considered, a move that helped plant the seeds for later conflict which eventually exploded in 1969.[40]

This study does not claim that the Irish boundary dispute was alone responsible for shaping British politics in the twentieth century. But it will show that the Irish Question continued to resonate in the nation's public affairs long after most historians inexplicably shelve it away. Until recently few studies have attempted any detailed examination of the boundary dispute after

---

35   W. S. Churchill, *The Gathering Storm* (Boston, 1948), p. 21.

36   Paul Canning calls the Treaty appeasement's 'first visible manifestation'. See *British Policy*, p. 177. In fact, the term was applied even earlier to the Government of Ireland Bill. See 'The Irish Impasse', *Westminster Gazette*, 30 Mar. 1920.

37   'The Coalition Parliament', unpublished memoir, Templewood Papers, xx: (A) 5, p. 3–4. Also, see J. A. Cross, *Sir Samuel Hoare, A Political Biography* (London, 1977), pp. 61–2.

38   See R. Rhodes James, *Anthony Eden* (London, 1986), p. 82. 'Irish Boundary Bill. Unionists and the Commission', *The Times*, 3 Oct. 1924.

39   O. Mosley, *My Life* (London, 1968), pp. 150–63. R. Skidelsky, *Oswald Mosley* (London, 1975), pp. 96–107.

40   In 'It all Began with a Line on a Map', *Independent on Sunday Magazine*, 22 May 1994, Brian Cathcart points out that had the Commission's award been implemented, most of what security forces later called 'bandit country' – areas loyal to Irish Republican guerrillas – would have been transferred to the South.

the fall of Lloyd George's government.[41] The Irish conflict seems to bore British historians of the inter-war period, many of whom apparently believe that its importance lies in the earlier 1912–1914 Home Rule Crisis.[42]

Irish historians seem to be equally indifferent. In separate works, Ronan Fanning and Joseph Lee have used identical words to claim that the 'story of the Boundary Commission is well known' and, one of them adds, 'soon told'.[43] This aversion masks a general reluctance to delve into an embarrassing episode.[44] It is a chapter in Ireland's history when no one, North or South, Free Stater or Republican, Nationalist or Unionist, covered themselves in honour, never mind glory.

A year after Baldwin was returned to power in 1924, the press magnate Lord Beaverbrook described for an American friend 'three difficulties which might have developed fatally' for the new government. Of the three, the 'far more dangerous risk for the Conservative Ministry was the Report of the Irish Boundary Commission'. Had that report turned out as it should have, Beaverbrook explained, 'the Ministry would have fallen'. Instead, he wrote, 'a miracle happened'.[45]

This is the story of that miracle.

41 An exception is E. Phoenix, *Northern Nationalism: Nationalist Politics, Partition and the Catholic Majority in Northern Ireland, 1890–1940* (Belfast, 1994), though it does not explore the dispute's ramifications in British politics.

42 See, e.g., R. Rhodes James, *The British Revolution: 1880–1939* (New York, 1977). David Marquand's otherwise comprehensive biography of Labour's first prime minister overlooks the threat Ireland posed to MacDonald's government in 1924. See *Ramsay MacDonald* (London, 1977).

43 R. Fanning, *Independent Ireland* (Dublin, 1983), p. 90. J. J. Lee, *Ireland 1912–1985: Politics and Society* (Cambridge, 1989), p. 145.

44 Laffan's *Partition* is much richer in detail though it, too, fails to consider how Britain's political revolution affected the outcome of the partition question. For an Ulster Unionist perspective, see B. Follis, *A State Under Siege: The Establishment of Northern Ireland, 1920–1925* (Oxford, 1995).

45 Beaverbrook to Brisbane, 30 Nov. 1925, BBK C/64.

ONE

PRIME MINISTER FOR LIFE

*[Ireland]... is a most unfortunate country. Something awkward
always occurs at critical moments in her history.*

DAVID LLOYD GEORGE[1]

—

'A story', Graham Greene wrote at the beginning of his novel *The End of the
Affair*, 'has no beginning or end: arbitrarily one chooses that moment of
experience from which to look back or from which to look ahead.' What
Greene said of fiction is no less true of fact, especially when the facts happen
to be Irish ones. Although the story told here covers only a few years after the
end of the First World War, the controversies that give it substance were born
in earlier struggles, just as in this period the seeds were sown for later conflict
in Northern Ireland.

Here, the moment of experience begins with a remarkable statement,
made by one remarkable man about another. The statement itself was the
result of a remarkable event: the general election of 1918.

To anyone who had lived through the previous eight years, the fact that a
coalition of Conservatives and Liberals had remained united to achieve
victory in that election was itself something a miracle. Since 1910, British
politics had been in a state of constant crisis, when a Liberal government led
by Herbert Asquith had sought to curb the power of the Conservative-
dominated House of Lords. The catalyst for this crisis was David Lloyd
George's famous 'People's Budget', with its increased taxation of the wealthy.
But the root of the crisis was Ireland.

In 1885 William Gladstone had wed Liberals to the promise of Irish self-
government, a measure bitterly opposed by Conservatives and their Unionist
allies in Ireland. Gladstone's very modest proposal – Home Rule – began the
weaving of the Irish Question into the fabric of British politics. The defeat of
his Second Home Rule Bill by the House of Lords in 1893 completed the job.

1   Riddell diary, 21 Dec. 1919, in G. Riddell, *Lord Riddell's Intimate Diary of the Peace Conference and
After: 1918–1923* (London, 1933), p. 153.

From that moment, Ireland was tied to the larger question of whether unelected peers should have the right to veto legislation passed by the House of Commons. Asquith's government faced down the Conservatives and the Lords, but only after the country endured two bitterly divisive general elections in 1910, followed by passage of the Parliament Act a year later. To calm matters in the wake of these elections, Churchill advised that the government pursue *'une politique d'apaisement'* (a policy of appeasement); but Ireland blocked the way. The 'shadow of the Home Rule controversy hung over us all', Austen Chamberlain recalled, making compromise impossible.[2]

The tactics employed by Tory MPs to oppose reform of the House of Lords were but a dress rehearsal for the fight ahead over Ireland. These opponents – or, 'Die-hards', as they became known – feared that just as their party's leader, Arthur James Balfour, had acquiesced to parliamentary reform, so he might prove to be 'equally capable of surrendering home rule'. At one time or another, these irreconcilables included Austen Chamberlain, Lords Salisbury and Selborne, F. E. Smith and, from Ireland, Sir Edward Carson and Sir James Craig. Though relatively small in number, the Die-hards exercised an influence out of all proportion to their size and would remain a major factor in the nation's politics for the next 15 years.[3]

The crisis in British politics then took an ominous turn with the introduction of the Third Home Rule Bill in 1912. For the next two years, the United Kingdom teetered on the brink of civil war. Rather than submit to a parliament in Dublin, Irish Unionists threatened to rebel. The overwhelming majority of Unionists were concentrated in Ireland's northernmost province, Ulster. Led by Carson and Craig, these Unionists formed their own army, the Ulster Volunteer Force (UVF). Nationalists responded by forming the Irish Volunteers, forerunner of the Irish Republican Army (IRA). Thus was the gun introduced into modern Irish politics.[4]

---

2   Churchill to Asquith, 3 Jan. 1911, Asquith Papers, MSS 13, ff. 1–4, Reel 6. A. Chamberlain, *Politics from Inside* (London, 1936), p. 190. Asquith later said that the Parliament Act was passed 'very largely with the object of bringing that [Home Rule] Bill upon the Statute Book'. See *HC Deb*, vol. 127, col. 1108, 30 Mar. 1920.

3   R. Fanning, '"Rats" versus "Ditchers": The Die-Hard Revolt and the Parliament Bill of 1911', *Irish Historical Studies*, vol. XI, 1983, pp. 191–210. The name itself was first given to a British regiment for its stubborn resistance during the 1811 Battle of Albuera. See 'The End of the Coalition', *Quarterly Review*, 474, Jan. 1923, p. 199.

4   J. P. Duggan, *A History of the Irish Army* (Dublin, 1991), pp. 1–2. Carson was later denounced for inspiring the IRA. According to one former admirer, the UVF was 'the uncle of Sinn Fein and the stepmother of trouble all over our Empire from Egypt to India'. See *HC Deb*, vol. 118, col. 494, 16 July 1919. Also, see *HC Deb*, vol. 115, cols 1698–700, 14 May 1919; and 'Irish Peace', *Daily Mail*, 4 Sept. 1919.

As genuine as was Ulster Unionist opposition to Home Rule, it never could have threatened British stability had it not been for the support of the Conservatives – above all the support of their new leader, Bonar Law. A Canadian by birth, Bonar Law's Presbyterian kinsmen were from the north of Ireland. Cool and rational in other matters, his mind, one confidant later wrote, was entirely controlled by 'ancient prejudice' when it came to Ulster.[5] Even before the UVF was formed, Bonar Law declared himself in favour of rebellion if it should come to that. '[T]here are things stronger than parliamentary majorities', he famously told one audience. 'I can imagine no length of resistance to which Ulster can go in which I should not be prepared to support them'.[6]

It was to avert such a catastrophe that an obscure Liberal backbencher proposed excluding four Ulster counties from the Home Rule Bill. 'There are some things which will not mingle together', T. Agar-Robartes told the House of Commons. 'I have never heard that orange bitters will mix with Irish whisky'. A few moments later, another member rose to call for the creation of a 'Boundary Commission' to differentiate those parts of Ulster that wished to be governed by a Dublin Parliament from those that did not.[7]

Initially, at least, Conservatives and Irish Unionists were no more interested in Agar-Robartes's compromise than were Liberals and their Nationalist allies in the Irish Parliamentary Party (IPP) . Carson eventually consented to the idea – but only if all nine Ulster counties were excluded from a Dublin Parliament. Both he and the Conservatives believed that Irish Nationalists would force Asquith to reject the offer, and the Tories could then press for their real objective: another general election.[8] When, finally, it became clear that Asquith's government would push ahead with Home Rule no matter what, the two sides found themselves at loggerheads over how much of Ulster should be excluded and for how long. Of the province's nine counties, four – Antrim, Armagh, Down and Londonderry – were considered predominantly Protestant and Unionist. The populations of three other counties – Cavan, Donegal, and Monaghan – were, by contrast, overwhelmingly Roman Catholic and Nationalist. That left Fermanagh and Tyrone.

In the end, Britain was spared a civil war over these two counties only because of conflict in Europe. Shortly after declaring war on Germany in August 1914, Parliament passed the Third Home Rule Bill but immediately

5   'Bonar Law. His Chief Service to the Empire', *Western Mail*, 22 May 1923. Tom Jones is credited with the article in E. L. Ellis, *T. J.: A Life of Dr Thomas Jones, CH* (Cardiff, 1992), p. 251.

6   R. Blake, *The Unknown Prime Minister: The Life and Times of Andrew Bonar Law, 1858–1923* (London, 1955), p. 130.

7   *HC Deb*, vol. 39, cols 771–3, 809–10, 11 June 1912.

8   *HC Deb*, vol. 46, cols 377–91, 1 Jan. 1913. Lansdowne to Bonar Law, 10 Oct. 1913, BL 30/3/16. Strachey to Carson, 27 July 1914, Strachey Papers, S/4/2/1.

suspended it until the end of hostilities. Within a year, Asquith's Liberals were forced to ask their Conservative opponents to join a wartime coalition government. However, the party most endangered by these events was the Irish Parliamentary Party. While its leaders might be willing to allow Ireland's self-government to be held in a state of suspended animation, a new breed of nationalists would not.

The 1916 Easter Rebellion, sparked by a rump of the Irish Volunteers, may have been doomed before it began. Nonetheless, the Rising's long-term impact went far beyond anything that its planners could have envisioned. Ultimately, it spelled the end of the IPP as more and more voters turned to Sinn Féin. The party dropped its initial programme calling for a dual monarchy for both Britain and Ireland and, instead, committed itself to fulfilling the Rebellion's promise of a republic for all Ireland and complete separation from Britain.

More immediately, this latest Irish crisis forced Asquith to turn to his chief rival for help. Unlike many politicians, Lloyd George was ambivalent about Ireland and its problems. Although he liked to call himself a 'Gladstonian Home Ruler', there was less to this claim than his words implied. Ireland, for Lloyd George, was a means to an end; in 1916, that meant taking him one step closer to the premiership. His attempt at brokering a settlement ultimately foundered on the same issues that had kept the two sides apart during the latter stages of the Home Rule Crisis – as well as on the exposure of contradictory pledges that he had made to Carson and to the leader of the IPP, John Redmond.[9]

Despite this failure, by the end of the year Lloyd George had replaced Asquith as Britain's prime minister. If he thought that he had escaped the Irish Question, however, he was wrong. Something had to be done about Ireland, if only to placate American public opinion now that the United States had joined in the war against Germany. In April 1917, the War Cabinet found itself so seriously divided over Ireland that it briefly considered calling a general election.[10] Every proposal caused a rift between government Liberals and Conservatives when they faced the problem of what they should do about Nationalist areas in Ulster; specifically, what should they do about Fermanagh and Tyrone?

9　C 59 (20), Appendix III, 13 Oct. 1920, CAB 23/23. Even those who knew him best disagreed about the extent of Lloyd George's commitment to Home Rule. Frances Stevenson called it 'one of the chief planks' of his political philosophy. See F. Lloyd George, *The Years That Are Past* (London, 1967), p. 189. According to his Welsh alter ego, on the other hand, Lloyd George never was 'a crusader for Home Rule'. See T. Jones, *Lloyd George* (Cambridge, Massachusetts, 1951), p. 186–7. His proposals to Carson and Redmond were formally outlined in Cd. 8310: *Headings of a Settlement as to the Government of Ireland*; 1916, xxii, 415.

10　War Cabinet 120, 16 Apr. 1917, CAB 23/2.

To get round this stumbling block, Lloyd George and his colleagues briefly flirted with the idea of 'weighted' majorities. Any Ulster county would be allowed to vote itself into a Home Rule Parliament – but only if 55 per cent of the county's voters agreed to do so. The plan ultimately was rejected as 'so obviously artificial a departure' from the idea of majority rule that it was impossible to defend.[11]

The committee was less concerned about notions of majority rule when it considered Lloyd George's next alternative to immediate Irish unity: a 'Council of Ireland'. The Council seems to have been inspired by Carson, who proposed joint meetings of Ulster's Westminster MPs with representatives from a Dublin Parliament. To allay fears that Nationalists from North and South might combine to outvote Unionists on the Council, the Cabinet committee suggested that the two groups should 'vote in panel'. Each of the representative groups would be given 'one collective vote, to be exercised according to the wishes of the majority in the group'. In other words, Nationalist MPs from Ulster could not combine with southern Irish members of the Council to outvote their Unionist colleagues. 'The reason for the proposal', the committee noted off-handedly, 'is manifest' – it ensured that Ulster Unionists could veto any Council action.[12]

Eventually, Lloyd George sought to escape the Irish Question by handing it over to the Irish themselves. By convening a convention of Ireland's political parties to sort out their differences, Lloyd George hoped to remove the Home Rule dispute from Westminster, so he could get on with the war against Germany. For both wings of the wartime coalition, however, Ireland remained an obstacle to full co-operation. Even when the Germans' 1918 offensive threatened the Allies with defeat, Lloyd George was warned that catastrophe on the Western Front might be coupled with a Conservative withdrawal from the coalition. The Tories, he was told, would 'break the Government rather than split their Party over Home Rule'.[13]

Nor could Lloyd George put the issue to one side once he and Bonar Law agreed that the coalition should remain united to fight the next general election. This would be the first time that voters would go to the polls since the elections of 1910 had left Liberals and Conservatives evenly divided in the House of Commons. Despite their leader's willingness to side with him, local Tories so mistrusted Lloyd George on Ireland that safeguards for Ulster had to be included in any election manifesto before they would consent to an alliance

---

11 'Draft Bill for the Government of Ireland', GT 8238, 8 May 1917, CAB 24/89.

12 Ibid. Carson memorandum, 20 Mar. 1917, Lothian Papers, GD 40/17/566.

13 Lloyd George to Redmond, 16 May 1917, Redmond MSS 15,189. Guest to Lloyd George, 5 Apr. 1918, LG F/21/2/16.

with the prime minister and his Liberal friends.[14] In November Lloyd George did just that, when outlining the programme for a new coalition government. Only two issues were dealt with in detail: economic policy and Home Rule. After summarising his efforts to solve the Irish Question, Lloyd George claimed 'the right to bring a settlement into effect' based on the exclusion of Ulster's six northeastern counties. Whether partition was to be temporary or permanent was left unsaid; his only bow to Irish unity was a promise to include a Council of Ireland in any final settlement.[15]

Thus agreed, coalition Conservatives and Liberals united to wage the 1918 campaign. The result was one of the greatest electoral victories in twentieth-century British politics. While a coalition win was expected, the scope of its success was staggering. The new government held in its hands a majority of 249 MPs against all other parties combined.[16] By common consent, the victory belonged to one man – Lloyd George, and to him, alone. These were the new realities that prompted Bonar Law to make his remarkable observation about a man who, in the past, had been his opponent but who was now his partner. Surveying this radically changed, this ironically changed, political landscape, Bonar Law said of Lloyd George: 'He can be Prime Minister for life if he likes'.[17]

'WE ARE ALL HOME RULERS TODAY'

Bonar Law was not the only Conservative who believed that their party owed its future to the former Welsh radical. Even before the final results were announced, F. E. Smith informed Lloyd George that successful Tory candidates in the north of England owed their seats to the prime minister's 'personal prestige' – and 'they know it'. These MPs, Smith assured Lloyd George 'will follow *you* anywhere'. In theory, at least, these Conservative MPs were now prepared to follow their prime minister's lead on Ireland. As *The Times* boldly declared a few months after the election: '[W]e are all Home Rulers today'.[18] The problem was that while Britain's politicians finally had come to an agreement on this issue, the Irish themselves had moved onto a different subject.

The earthquake in British politics brought about by the 1918 election was mirrored by an equally dramatic altering of Ireland's political landscape. Prior

---

14   Bayford diary, 5 May 1918, in Lord Bayford, *Real Old Tory Politics: The Political Diaries of Lord Bayford, 1910–35*, J. Ramsden, ed. (London, 1984), p. 102.

15   Lloyd George to Bonar Law, 2 Nov. 1918, LG F/68/1.

16   D. Butler and J. Freeman, *British Political Facts: 1900–1967* (London, 1968), p. 141.

17   Lord Beaverbrook, *Men and Power: 1917–1918* (New York, 1956), p. 325.

18   Smith to Lloyd George, 19 Dec. 1918, LG F/4/7/6. 'Local Government in Ireland', *The Times*, 26 Mar. 1919.

to that election, Ireland's parliamentary constituencies were held by 68 members of the IPP, 18 Unionists, and seven Sinn Féiners. In its wake, Sinn Féin took 73 seats and the Unionists 26, while the IPP held on to only six constituencies. Equally significant, after 1918 all of the Unionist MPs, except for three, and all of the IPP members, save one, represented seats in Ulster.[19]

With their grip on the South secure, Sinn Féin's MPs refused to take their seats in the House of Commons. British leaders affected to be not the least bit concerned by this development. Once the Sinn Féiners discovered that they could not draw their salaries, predicted the Irish viceroy, they would 'soon go bag and baggage to Westminster'.[20] Instead, the Sinn Féin MPs reaffirmed the republic declared during the Easter Rebellion and established their own parliament, Dáil Éireann, on 21 January 1919. The IRA's guerrilla war began that same day.

Instead of confronting this new reality, British politicians were more concerned about the pre-war Home Rule Act. Conservatives were well aware that once the last of the peace treaties ending the First World War was ratified, they would become responsible for enforcing a statute against which they had once threatened civil war. 'Something has to be done', Bonar Law told Balfour. The government could postpone the 1914 Act or repeal it altogether. Alternatively, the Coalition could introduce a new Home Rule measure of its own. This was Lloyd George's preference, as Liberals of all shades were dead set against postponement or repeal. The problem, Bonar Law, pointed out, was in devising a bill that would not lead to 'a complete break up of the present Government'.[21]

Lloyd George saw the problem the other way round. Viewed from his end of the Coalition spectrum, the acute challenge was not Ireland; the problem was how to keep his government together and himself in office. Far from making Lloyd George the unchallenged leader of the country, the 1918 election had made him more dependent than ever on the Conservatives. This was increasingly clear to Coalition Liberals, one of whom compared Lloyd George to Richard the Lionheart. 'Like Coeur-de-Lion', Harry Barnes wrote of the prime minister, 'he has been captured coming home from a Crusade.' With their overwhelming numbers, the Tories set the government's agenda. 'In Ireland, in Egypt, at home and abroad', Barnes observed, 'every indication exists that they control policy.'[22]

---

19 C. O'Leary, *Irish Elections, 1918–1917: Parties, Voters and Proportional Representation* (Dublin, 1979), p. 7.
20 French to Long, 14 Jan. 1919, JDPF 8/3.
21 Bonar Law to Balfour, 9 Oct. 1919, BL 101/3/159.
22 Barnes to Guest, 21 Nov. 1919, LG F/21/4/23(c).

To escape his imprisonment, Lloyd George set himself the task of nothing less than a wholesale restructuring of British politics. By combining or 'fusing' the Coalition's two wings, he planned to create a 'Centre Party' with, of course, himself as its leader.[23] Fusion was the long-term goal of Lloyd George's post-war premiership and much of what he did with regard to Ireland is best understood when this aim is kept in mind.

This was the background for what became Britain's fourth Home Rule Bill, or the 1920 Government of Ireland Act. To allay Unionist suspicions, Lloyd George put Walter Long in charge of drafting the legislation, an idea he had earlier resorted to during the war.[24] The bill eventually drafted by Long's committee called for the creation of two separate parliaments for Ireland. A federal assembly, or 'Council of Ireland', made up of an equal number of members from both North and South, would enable the two parliaments to deal with matters of common concern and, eventually, would serve as the springboard to a single government.[25] Despite objections from some Conservative members of the Cabinet, it was agreed

> that the ultimate aim of the Government's policy in Ireland was a united Ireland with a separate Parliament of its own, bound by the closest ties to Great Britain, but that this must be achieved with the largest possible support, and without offending the Protestants of Ulster . . . .[26]

Yet, deciding to partition Ireland was not the end of the government's troubles. One issue stood out above all others: namely, should the whole of Ulster be separated from the rest of Ireland, or just one part? And if the answer to this question was just one part, which part?

23 The idea had been germinating in Lloyd George's mind for quite some time. See, e.g., Chamberlain to Strachey, 19 Mar. 1918, Strachey Papers, S/4/5/8.

24 The paradox of asking a lifelong opponent of Irish self-government to prepare Home Rule legislation was not lost on Long. 'This Committee on H.R. is very odd!' he wrote. See Long to Balfour, 14 Apr. 1918, AJB-B, Add. MSS 49777, ff. 197.

25 For the genesis of this legislation, see N. Mansergh, 'The Government of Ireland Act, 1920: Its Origins and Purposes; The Working of the "Official" Mind', *Irish Historical Studies*, vol. IX, 1974, pp. 19–48.

26 C 10(19), 3 Dec. 1919, CAB 23/18.

SIX VERSUS NINE COUNTIES

Although Unionists could count on solid and overwhelming majorities in only four Ulster counties, the idea of a four-county partition was never seriously entertained by Long's committee. But neither could they reach a consensus over the only other two available options: a six- or a nine-county split. James Craig, then a junior minister in the Coalition government, made it plain that the idea of governing three overwhelmingly Nationalist counties 'was not relished' by his fellow Ulster Unionists. Other ministers, however, were just as adamant that the Northern assembly's jurisdiction 'should extend over the whole of Ulster' as this 'included both Roman Catholics and Protestants, both urban and rural districts, and by its size was more suited to possess a separate Parliament'. The underlying point was that a more evenly balanced Ulster assembly would likely lead to eventual Irish reunification.[27]

To make a six-county partition more palatable, the idea of creating of a Boundary Commission was discussed by the Cabinet for the first time. After taking a vote of residents 'in those districts on either side of and immediately adjoining the boundary', the commission would be empowered to place Catholic areas in the South and Protestant ones in the North. No mention was made of taking economic or geographic conditions into account; the wishes of the inhabitants would be the sole criterion for any boundary change. Any adjustments, however, would be minor and would not entail the transfer of whole counties. Given future events, it is ironic that the commission was suggested by none other than Craig, himself.[28]

Ultimately, the 'attitude of Ulster' would be the 'deciding factor' in settling the question of how to partition Ireland. For members of the Ulster Unionist Council, though, the answer was far from simple. A six-county partition meant repudiation of the pre-war Ulster Covenant in which Unionists throughout the province pledged 'to stand by one another' in the fight against Home Rule.[29] But any appeals to honour were more than balanced out by fears that the Unionist Party might be outvoted in a nine-county parliament. As well as Nationalist opposition, there was an alarming perception that 'the Unionist working men of Belfast could not be depended on' as had once been the case. This was especially true of 'younger members of the working classes' who, feeling that their needs were ignored by the Unionist hierarchy, were turning

---

27 C 12 (19), 16 (19), 10, 19 Dec. 1919, CAB 23/18. CP 681, 10 Feb. 1920, CAB 24/98.

28 C 15(19), 15 Dec. 1919, CAB 23/18.

29 Dawson memorandum, 8 March 1920, IUA, D/989/A/9/21. 'Why I Voted for the Six Counties' [pamphlet], spring 1920, reprinted the 1912 Covenant, Crawford Papers, D/1700/5/16/4. Also, see Montgomery to Strong, 6 Apr. 1920, Montgomery Papers, D/627/435/21.

instead to Labour politicians.[30] Following a trip to Ireland, Long reported that 'people in the inner circles' adamantly opposed the 'inclusion of Donegal, Cavan, and Monaghan' precisely for this reason. In a nine-county assembly, 'the supremacy of the Unionists would be seriously threatened' and there was 'a real danger that on certain questions the Unionist Labour Party in Ulster might vote with the Roman Catholics'.[31] This threat would be blunted in a smaller parliament, where rural Unionists could be counted on to offset increasing discontent among Protestant working-class voters.

In short, the desire to hold on to power at any cost proved to be irresistible. At a meeting of the Ulster Unionist Council chaired by Carson on 10 March, the decision was taken and the three-county Unionists were thrown over-board. A ruthless choice had been made, illustrated by an equally ruthless analogy. On a sinking ship with lifeboats for only two-thirds of the ship's company why, asked one Belfast MP, should everyone on board 'condemn themselves to death because all could not be saved?'[32]

So it was that the Ulster Unionists, those safely in the lifeboat of the six counties at any rate, rowed away from their drowning brethren as fast as they could. Perhaps to strengthen the hand of those advocating a smaller Northern Ireland, the Cabinet gave its backing to a six-county partition before the Council meeting was actually held. The Cabinet's minutes, though typically vague, indicate that Bonar Law was responsible for this decision.[33]

The arguments rehearsed within the confines of the Council were later aired before the wider world when it fell to James Craig's brother, Charles, to explain the Ulster Unionist position in the House of Commons. 'We quite frankly admit that we cannot hold the nine counties', Charles Craig said. In a parliament for the entire province, Unionists could be sure of a majority of only three or four. 'A couple of Members sick, or two or three Members absent for some accidental reason, might in one evening hand over the entire Ulster Parliament and the entire Ulster position ... a dreadful thing to contemplate.' These 'remarkable admissions', as one Labour MP put it, undercut subsequent Unionist claims that the three outlying counties 'were generously given up' in return for a government promise that this would be the last demand made

---

30 'Ulster and Home Rule. No Partition of Ulster', Apr. 1920, in P. Buckland, *Irish Unionism, 1885–1923: A Documentary History* (Belfast, 1973), p. 221. Dawson Bates to Carson, 30 June 1919, Carson Papers, D/1507/A/30/12. Also, see A. Morgan, *Labour and Partition: The Belfast Working Class, 1905–23* (London, 1991), passim.

31 CI 58, 4 Feb. 1920, CAB 27/69.

32 Ulster Unionist Council minutes, 10 Mar. 1920, UUC, D/1327/18/27. I. Colvin, *The Life of Lord Carson*: vol. III (London, 1936), pp. 383–4.

33 C 12(20), 24 Feb. 1920, CAB 23/20.

upon them. On the contrary, Craig's speech dramatically testified to the fact that such assertions were 'disingenuous in the extreme'.[34]

A PROTESTANT STATE

The determination of Unionists to ensure their ascendant position in a future Northern Ireland went beyond the controversy over the number of counties to be included in the new state. Two additional factors came into play in 1920. The first of these was a Unionist decision to get rid of proportional representation in their elections; the second was the creation of a paramilitary police force, the Special Constabulary.

A year before its introduction of the Government of Ireland Bill, the Coalition instituted proportional representation (PR) for all Irish elections. In place of the traditional winner-take-all system, in which candidates were elected by a simple majority, Irish voters were given the 'single transferable vote' allowing them to cast ballots for several candidates in order of preference. This method was first applied in municipal elections held in Sligo where, to the delight of Southern Unionists, it prevented a Sinn Féin victory less than a month after the party had won both of the county's parliamentary seats. These results increased support within the government to apply PR to local elections throughout the entire United Kingdom to stem support for other 'extremists'.[35]

Such arguments made no impression whatsoever on Ulster Unionists. They openly reviled PR, correctly believing that it was bound to cause them 'difficulties'. Why Conservative members of the Cabinet had ever allowed it to be introduced, Carson scornfully wrote, 'I don't know.' Their abhorrence was confirmed by the results of urban council elections held in January 1920. In Ireland as a whole, Unionists were out-polled by both Sinn Féin and Labour candidates.[36]

Even in Ulster, Unionists had little to cheer about. Although they edged out an alliance of Sinn Féin and the Nationalists, retaining control of 24 townships as against 21, these victories were offset by some spectacular losses.

34 *HC Deb*, vol. 127, cols 990–3, 29 Mar. 1920. 'Irish Boundary', Cope memorandum, 3 Sept. 1924, LG G/20/2/6.

35 'A Message of Hope', *The Irish Times*, 18 Jan. 1919. Also, see 'Sligo: Municipal Elections, 1919', Proportional Representation Society, Pamphlet No. 41, Oct. 1919. HAC, 35th Minutes, 18 July 1919, CAB 26/1.

36 'An Ulster Night', *Belfast Telegraph*, 25 Mar. 1919. Carson to Bonar Law, 26 Jan. 1920, BL 98/6/4. Inspector General's report, 14 Feb. 1920, CO 904/111.

Sinn Féin–Nationalist coalitions took control of Omagh, Newry and, what was the greatest blow to Unionist pride, Londonderry. The results in Belfast were just as unsettling. The city remained in Unionist hands – indeed, it was the only city or borough in all of Ireland which still had a Unionist mayor. But whereas under the old system the party regularly took 52 of the council's 60 seats, under PR its total dropped to 37. Ten seats now went to the Sinn Féin–Nationalist alliance. But what was most disturbing to Carson and his followers was the 12 seats that were won by Labour.[37]

Afterwards, the Proportional Representation Society of Ireland suggested that Unionist anger would subside once they recognised that while their majority in Belfast was smaller than before, it was now based on an 'accurate picture' of voters' intentions. This new, 'secure' majority, the PR Society confidently predicted, would cause Unionists to realise that 'fair play all round' was far better than 'the old plan of stifling every view but one's own'.[38]

But Ulster Unionists realised nothing of the kind. On the contrary, their leaders were more determined than ever to get rid of PR. A provision of the 1920 Bill prevented either Irish parliament from abolishing PR for at least three years. When an attempt was made to extend this moratorium, Carson and his followers thwarted the effort. This action bore out an earlier observation that any Unionist government in Ulster would have little interest in giving 'reasonable representation' to the minority within its own borders.[39]

ARMING THE PROTESTANTS

In June 1920 a wave of deadly sectarian riots swept across the six counties. The first disturbances in Londonderry were followed a month later by the expulsion of 7,500 workers from the Belfast shipyards. Though the declared intent of the expulsions was to rid the yards of Roman Catholics in general and Sinn Féiners in particular, labour activists were ousted as well and even included the ex-master of an Orange Lodge. As the expulsions spread to other businesses, a number of Catholics and Protestants were killed over the next three days.[40] Sporadic rioting continued into September.

---

37   *Irish Bulletin*, vol. 2, no. 11, 17 May 1920, DE 2/81. Morgan, *Labour and Partition*, p. 257.

38   'Report and Analysis of the P.R. Urban Elections in Ulster', PRI Pamphlet No. 43, undated [1920?], Stephens MSS 4240/8/2.

39   *HC Deb*, vol. 134, cols 1240–4, 10 Nov. 1920. 'Local Government in Ireland', *The Times*, 26 Mar. 1919.

40   Morgan, *Labour and Partition*, pp. 265–84. M. Farrell, *Northern Ireland: The Orange State* (London, 1976), pp. 28–30.

According to later analyses, the shipyard expulsions were provoked by IRA action in the six counties.[41] Others traced the immediate cause of the disturbances to the fatal shooting of an Ulster-born police officer in Cork.[42] While IRA activity in the North had increased, the Royal Irish Constabulary's monthly reports show that as late as June its presence in the six counties was negligible when compared with the rest of the country.[43] A likelier explanation for the sudden explosion of Unionist anger can be found in the election returns for county councils and rural district councils held in June.

Announced only days before the Derry riots, these results confirmed the spectacular inroads that Sinn Féin was making throughout Ireland thanks to proportional representation. Unionists were reduced to control of only four county councils, while a Sinn Féin–Nationalist alliance retained control of Fermanagh and, for the first time, took control of Tyrone County Council. The results from the rural district council elections were just as disconcerting for the Unionists. Of Ulster's 55 such councils, 36 were now controlled by Sinn Féin or by the Sinn Féin–Nationalist alliance.[44]

In the face of this latest electoral setback, Carson decided that it was time to rally his supporters. At the annual 12th of July celebrations, he furiously denounced county councils that swore allegiance to the Irish Republic and vowed that Ulster 'would tolerate no Sinn Fein organisation or methods' within its borders. Yet, his toughest words were reserved for the leaders of the independent Labour movement, whose 'real object', he declared, was 'to bring about disunity amongst our people'. Like an Old Testament prophet, Carson exhorted his wayward followers to return to the true religion lest they find themselves 'in the same bondage and slavery as is the rest of Ireland'.[45]

In such a tinderbox atmosphere, Carson's rhetoric all but invited the shipyard expulsions that took place a few days later. There was scant evidence that Protestant labour leaders were in league with Sinn Féin. There was, however, a good deal of evidence, supplied by that year's local elections, to demonstrate

41   See, e.g., C. Townshend, *Political Violence in Ireland: Government and Resistance Since 1848* (Oxford, 1983), pp. 341–2. Laffan, *Partition*, pp. 75–6, claims that the riots were the result of Unionist 'unease' over violence in the South.

42   Belfast RIC Commissioner's report, 1 Aug. 1920, CO 904/112. T. H. Burns to Tallents, 7 July 1922, CO 906/23.

43   See Inspector General's reports, 14 Feb., 18 Mar., 14 July 1920, CO 904/111 and 112. According to the chief secretary's office, between 1 Jan. 1919 and 29 Mar. 1920, there were 95 outrages in Ulster, none of them fatal. The total number of outrages in the other three provinces was: Connaught – 137; Leinster – 269; Munster – 588. See Cmd 63: *Outrages (Ireland)*; 1920, XL, 799.

44   SFM, 22 Jan. 1920, MSS Film, P3269, ff. 93. Phoenix, *Northern Nationalism*, pp. 84–6. D. Macardle, *The Irish Republic* (New York, 1937 [1965 edn]), p. 352.

45   'Record Twelfth in Ulster', *Belfast News-Letter*, 13 July 1920.

that independent Labour posed a serious challenge to the Unionist Party. That could not be allowed to continue. As Richard Dawson Bates pointed out, it was imperative 'for all Unionists to work as one Party' if they were to retain their dominant position.[46]

One way to glue the old Unionist alliance back together would be to resurrect the pre-war Ulster Volunteer Force. Carson had, in fact, mooted this idea at the 12th of July celebrations in 1919. Then, his proposal was roundly denounced by English supporters; Bonar Law even considered condemning the speech.[47] But by the time Carson raised the issue a year later, a change of attitude had taken place.

During those intervening twelve months, the notion of forming the UVF into officially sanctioned units was floated about in government circles.[48] At a Cabinet conference on 23 July, both Lloyd George and Churchill were attracted to the idea as a way of relieving troops for duty not only in the south of Ireland but elsewhere in the empire.[49] Craig, not surprisingly, jumped at the idea and came up with a plan that went well beyond establishing the UVF as a paramilitary police force. In addition, he called for the appointment of an RIC commissioner with sole authority in the six counties and, more importantly, proposed that an under-secretary of state should be appointed to represent the British government in the North. To gain support for his proposal, which would effectively partition Ireland even before the 1920 Bill was passed, Craig made a thinly veiled reference to Sinn Féin's recent electoral victories. The party had already established its dominance 'over a considerable portion' of Ulster, he pointed out, and 'rebel influences are spreading'.[50]

Bonar Law promptly backed Craig's proposals. 'We cannot afford to have everyone in Ireland against us', the Tory leader reasoned. Unless the government acted promptly, there was 'a danger of the Orangemen getting completely out of hand and something like a general massacre happening in Belfast'.[51]

This logic was perverse, as was underscored by the response of both civil and military authorities. Sir John Anderson was horrified. 'I sincerely trust there is no foundation for [this] rumour', he wrote to the Conservative leader. 'You cannot in the middle of a faction fight recognise one of the contending parties and expect it to deal with disorder in the spirit of impartiality and fairness'. General Sir Nevil Macready, the commander of British military

---

46 Morgan, *Labour and Partition*, p. 224.
47 'Statesmanship in Ulster', *The Times*, 14 July 1919. Bayford diary, 19 July 1919, pp. 127–8.
48 See, e.g., French to Long, 1 July 1920, JDPF 8/3.
49 CP 1693, 23 July 1920, CAB 24/109.
50 Craig to Bonar Law, 1 Sept. 1920, BL 102/10/3. C 53 (20), Appendix IV, 2 Sept. 1920, CAB 23/22.
51 Bonar Law to Lloyd George, 2 Sept. 1920, LG F/31/1/43.

forces in Ireland, was equally appalled and wanted to have no part in 'raising Carson's army from the grave'. The chief of the imperial general staff agreed. The government's plan, Sir Henry Wilson wrote, was 'simply inviting trouble'.[52]

According to Wilson, Bonar Law realised that 'arming the Ulstermen means civil war'.[53] Nevertheless, at a conference on 8 September, the Cabinet gave Craig everything he asked for. By creating a Unionist paramilitary force, observed the *Daily News*, Lloyd George and his colleagues had abandoned any pretence of impartiality and in the process raised serious questions about 'the sanity of the government'. Wrote one army officer in Dublin: 'Where, oh where, are Gilbert and Sullivan!' Macready saw less a comic opera than a tragedy in the making. Once the Specials began operating in the six counties, he predicted, they 'would most assuredly paint the place red'.[54]

Appeals for a government investigation into the continuing violence in Ulster were, meanwhile, brushed to one side.[55] Irish Chief Secretary Sir Hamar Greenwood showed a callous indifference to the plight of the expelled workers, telling the House of Commons that it was quite beyond his power 'to compel employers to employ or workmen to work'.[56] While the government sat on its hands, the problem was allowed to fester so that, as Craig later put it, the expulsions became 'one of the most delicate and difficult stumbling blocks to peace'.[57]

PAYING FOR PARTITION

After the Government of Ireland Bill went onto the Statute Book, one Presbyterian minister lamented that his fellow Ulster Protestants had accepted 'a form of Home Rule that the Devil himself could never have imagined'.[58] But most of his co-religionists were more than happy with the bargain they had struck. By any measure, it was a victory for the Ulster Unionists and their Conservative allies. Summing up their achievement, Charles Craig told

---

52   Anderson to Bonar Law, 2 Sept. 1920; Macready to Anderson, 18 June 1920, CO 904/188(1) and (4). Wilson to Macready, 14 Sept. 1920, HHW 2/2B/2.

53   Wilson to Macready, 2 Sept. 1920, HHW 2/2A/50.

54   C 53(20), Appendix V, 8 Sept. 1920, CAB 23/22. '"Order" in Belfast', *Daily News*, 15 Sept. 1920. Greer[?] to Anderson, 1 Sept. 1920, BL 102/7/1. Macready to Wilson, 1 Sept. 1920, HHW 2/2A/49. For a history of the force, see M. Farrell, *Arming the Protestants: The Formation of the Ulster Special Constabulary, 1920–27* (London, 1983).

55   See, e.g., *HC Deb*, vol. 134, col. 1379, 11 Nov. 1920.

56   *HC Deb*, vol. 132, col. 1977, 2 Aug. 1920.

57   Craig to Churchill, 30 Jan. 1922, WSC 22/11/52–3.

58   J. Bardon, *A History of Ulster* (Belfast, 1992), pp. 440, 514.

Belfast shipyard workers that once the Unionists had their own Parliament 'no power on earth would ever be able to touch them'.[59]

If that achievement can be marked down to one man, his name was Bonar Law. Without his 'uncompromising support' there would have been no Northern Ireland.[60] That said, he himself realised that the 1920 Act was not the end of the Irish contest. On the contrary, Bonar Law was playing a long game which, at this stage, meant passing the 1920 Bill 'with as little alteration as possible'. This would then place the Unionists in a strong position for the real battle over Ireland's future which still lay ahead. 'I feel certain', he told Walter Long,

> that at the moment it is not possible to have any sort of an understanding with the Sinn Feiners; that such an understanding may be possible later but, if so, the fewer concessions we make now the better for whatever we give at present would not be looked upon as final but would be regarded as a jumping off ground for further concessions.[61]

On one issue, however, Bonar Law and the Ulster Unionists had failed to secure their six-county state.

Except for the provisions partitioning Ireland, nothing in the 1920 Act aroused as much criticism as its financial clauses. Opponents attacked the provisions as so complicated and so restrictive that it would be nearly impossible for the two Irish parliaments to govern.[62] Fourteen of the Act's 76 articles and nine schedules dealt solely with tax and finance.[63] Roughly speaking, revenue for the Dublin and Belfast Parliaments was to come from two sources. 'Transferred taxes', such as death and motor vehicle duties, were to be collected directly by the Irish governments within their respective areas. 'Reserved taxes', such as customs and excise duties, and income and corporation taxes, were to be collected by the imperial government so that they would be maintained at the same level throughout the United Kingdom. Estimates vary as to the percentage of total revenue that the two parliaments were expected to take in from transferred taxes. In any case, it was known from the outset that the main source of revenue for both Irish governments – reserved taxes – would be beyond their control.[64]

---

59 'Despair in Ireland', *The Times*, 7 Oct. 1920.

60 Blake, *Unknown Prime Minister*, p. 531.

61 Bonar Law to Long, 30 Sept. 1920, BL 103/5/9.

62 Stephen Gwynn called the provisions 'wanton'. See 'The Better Government of Ireland Act', *Contemporary Review*, vol. CXVII, Apr. 1920, p. 483.

63 Follis, *State Under Siege*, p. 117. For the government's defence of the bill's taxation scheme, see *HC Deb*, vol. 127, col. 1032–6, 29 Mar. 1920. Also, see Cmd 645: *Outline of Financial Provisions;* 1920, XL, 771.

64 R. J. Lawrence, *The Government of Northern Ireland: Public Finance and Public Services, 1921–1964* (Oxford, 1965), pp. 40–1. P. Buckland, *The Factory of Grievances: Devolved Government in Northern Ireland, 1921–39* (Dublin, 1979), pp. 81–3.

Moreover, London held prior claim to revenue collected from reserved taxes for what was called the 'imperial contribution'. This sum went towards defence, foreign affairs, and payment of the United Kingdom's debts. Once the imperial contribution was paid for, a separate deduction would then be taken from the reserved taxes to pay for 'reserved services', i.e. those governmental duties to be administered in Ireland by London. Both the contribution and the reserved services bill would be determined annually by a Joint Exchequer Board made up of British and Irish officials.

Only after the imperial contribution and reserved services had been paid for would the two Irish governments receive most of their funding. This amount, known as 'reserved revenue', would then be added to whatever was received from transferred taxes. From this combined total the two governments were expected to fund 'transferred services', i.e. those governmental duties for which they were now responsible – notably law and order, and social services such as unemployment insurance.

While the 1920 Bill was still winding its way through Parliament, the Ulster Unionist Council sought to alter the financial provisions, arguing that they were based on unrealistic estimates of Ireland's wealth. The Treasury, then and later, just as vigorously denied this assertion.[65] In any case, because the long-term implications of these clauses were not adequately thought through they were bound to cause problems down the road.

'THE TROUBLES'

The problem with the 1920 Act, F. S. L. Lyons once wrote, was that it was '[t]otally divorced . . . from the realities of political life in Ireland'. This same verdict could as easily be applied to the government's Irish policy in general. Confronted by an insurrection unlike anything previously experienced, the government's reaction was contradictory and, ultimately, self-defeating. Publicly, ministers vowed to use every available force and every available resource to defeat Sinn Féin's campaign of secession. But, despite this tough rhetoric, they refused to admit that they were fighting a war; this, the Cabinet agreed, 'would be a confession of failure'. Rather than increase the number of regular army units stationed in Ireland, the Cabinet decided to recruit ex-soldiers who would then be deployed as members of the RIC. The soon-to-be-nicknamed 'Black and Tans' were joined a few months later by a separate contingent of ex-officers, or Auxiliaries. A policy of unofficial, followed by

---

65   See Finance Committee reports, Apr.–Oct. 1920, UUC, D/1327/15/4. Cmd 786: *Government of Ireland Bill – Basis of Financial Estimates; 1920*, XL, 787. Niemeyer to Colwyn, 19 May 1922, T 163/6/8/G.256/042.

officially sanctioned reprisals soon turned the conflict into a struggle between alien mercenaries and the native population.[66]

Politically, this course was ruinous. In Britain, no one was pleased; nearly everyone was alienated. While the government's policy did not go far enough to satisfy those who wished to wage all out war on Sinn Féin, it drove away those who believed that there should be a compromise settlement. 'Collective punishment', Robert Cecil told his brother, Lord Salisbury, was 'sometimes a necessary evil'. He could live with that. 'Casual felony' was quite another matter.[67]

In spite of such criticism, senior Conservatives in the government were determined that there should be no reversal of policy.[68] Their stubbornness, though, was costing Lloyd George politically, and that was something he could not ignore. Being saddled with a Government of Ireland Act which his own supporters admitted fell 'far short of the Liberal standard', left him especially vulnerable to the denunciations of former colleagues led by Herbert Asquith.[69] These anti-Coalition, or 'Wee Free' Liberals exploited every opportunity to assail the government's Irish policy. These attacks hit home and helped defeat Lloyd George's initial bid to launch his Centre Party early in 1920.[70]

At the same time, the Irish War was having a corrosive effect on Lloyd George's relations with a group of young, first-time MPs who formed the nucleus of the New Members Coalition Group. Though hardly sympathetic to Sinn Féin, many of these MPs were disgusted by British conduct in Ireland.[71] The Group included 'one of the most interesting of the newcomers', Oswald Mosley. Although a disreputable future lay ahead, Mosley at this time established himself as a courageous figure in Parliament, where his attacks on the government won him praise for breaking up 'the Black and Tan savagery'.[72]

66   F. S. L. Lyons, *Ireland Since the Famine* (London, 1971), p. 412. *HL Deb*, vol. 40, col. 430, 19 May 1920. C 23(A), 30 Apr. 1920, CAB 23/21. For a vivid eyewitness account of life in Ireland at this time, see Celia Shaw's diary, MSS 23,409. For a comprehensive, and up to date, analysis of the conflict, see M. Hopkinson, *The Irish War of Independence* (Dublin and Montreal, 2002).

67   Cecil to Salisbury, 11 Oct. 1920, S(4) 93/122–3.

68   Long memorandum, 25 July 1920, LG F/180/5/6/272.

69   Scott diary, 16 Mar. 1920, in C. P. Scott, *The Political Diaries of C. P. Scott: 1911–1928*, T. Wilson, ed. (London, 1970), p. 382.

70   'Ireland a Dominion', *Daily Telegraph*, 21 May 1920. K. O. Morgan, *Consensus and Disunity: The Lloyd George Coalition Government, 1918–1922* (Oxford, 1979), p. 186.

71   D. Close, 'Conservatives and Coalition After the First World War', *Journal of Modern History*, vol. 45, no. 2, June 1973, p. 244. Colin Coote, e.g., in *A Companion of Honour: The Story of Walter Elliot* (London, 1965), p. 63, recalled that his former colleague was 'more distressed' by the government's conduct in Ireland 'than by any of the other post-war disappointments'.

72   C. Coote, *Editorial: The Memoirs of Colin R. Coote* (London, 1965), p. 103. O'Connor to Cynthia Mosley, 10 Dec. 1923, in Mosley, *My Life*, p. 157. Also, see O'Connor to Dillon, 8 Mar. 1921, Dillon MSS 6744, ff. 820.

As the months passed, it seemed to some that the government's only real objective in Ireland was a desire to avoid 'traversing the old difficulty' lest it cause a break-up of the Coalition. Even worse, it was all too apparent that plans to implement the 1920 Act had no chance of success, at least in the 26 counties. The threatened alternative, crown colony government, made no impression on the Irish people. This point was brought home to the Cabinet when, in December, Macready warned its members to prepare for an IRA-led boycott of elections for the Southern Parliament. As Lloyd George pointed out, if Sinn Féin leader Michael Collins 'could stop three million people using their vote it did not say much for the policy His Majesty's Government were now pursuing.'[73]

BONAR LAW RESIGNS

From about the middle of 1920, nothing seemed to go right for the Coalition. A post-war economic boom, for which the government had claimed credit, burst towards the end of the year and, Lloyd George told his colleagues, the country was 'in for a bad time'.[74] Between December 1920 and March 1921, unemployment more than doubled. By the following June, over two million would be out of work. Although this figure then began to fall, the jobless rate would never drop below one million for the next 20 years.[75] More immediately, these conditions led to the threat of a general strike which, it was feared, might easily turn into a full-scale revolution. Within the United Kingdom, the army had enough units to fight the Irish rebellion or to contain industrial unrest. It could not do both at the same time. 'Denuded of troops', Edwin Montagu wrote early in 1921, the Cabinet faced the unknown 'with a certain grim determination; but with no undue optimism'.[76]

In the middle of this crisis, Bonar Law unexpectedly resigned from the government. Despite emphatic statements that his departure was brought on by ill-health, 'a genuine case of "doctor's orders"', as Lady Spender put it, it was soon being rumoured that a split had erupted between the Tory leader and Lloyd George over the Irish Question.[77] Bonar Law's own physician helped feed this speculation, telling one newspaper editor that his patient's sudden departure was 'due to one thing only – cold feet about Ireland'.[78]

---

73   *HC Deb*, vol. 127, col. 977, 29 Mar. 1920. 'Memorandum on the present political situation in Southern Ireland', 12 Feb. 1921, LG F/181/1/1. C 79A(20), 29 Dec. 1920, CAB 23/23.

74   C 61 (20), 17 Nov. 1920, CAB 23/23.

75   Taylor, *English History*, p. 145.

76   Montagu to Reading, 7 Apr. 1921, IO, MSS Eur. E. 238/3, no. 1.

77   Spender diary, 19 Mar. 1921, D/1633/2/24. Also, see Sturgis diary, 20 Mar. 1921, PRO 30/59/4.

78   Stevenson diary, 11 Nov. 1921, in F. Lloyd George, *Lloyd George: A Diary by Frances Stevenson*, A. J. P. Taylor, ed. (New York, 1971), pp. 236–7.

According to Maurice Hankey, Bonar Law was indeed ill – 'his heart weak & his blood pressure too high'.[79] It is altogether possible that both sides were correct, that Bonar Law's symptoms were real but were brought on because he knew that talks with Sinn Féin could no longer be avoided. By January 1921 Lloyd George was clearly toying with the idea and at one meeting persistently raised the issue even though Bonar Law 'tried to put the subject off'.[80] At an earlier meeting, the Cabinet was told that any negotiations must include Michael Collins, as he was the only Irish leader 'with whom effective business could be done'. Perhaps shaking hands with 'the organiser of murder' was something that Bonar Law could not bring himself to do.[81]

For Conservatives, the shock of Bonar Law's sudden exit was compounded by Walter Long's retirement a month earlier. Although Long's departure was not unexpected, his resignation meant that yet another member of the government who regarded negotiations with Sinn Féin as 'unthinkable' had departed the scene. Isolated, only Arthur Balfour remained.[82]

Almost by default, the Conservative leadership fell to Austen Chamberlain. This proved to be a momentous decision both for the party and for the course of Anglo-Irish relations. Although Chamberlain's promotion was supported by the Conservative hierarchy, most Tory MPs found him to be an aloof, even distant figure – a problem that he himself recognised. Nor was Chamberlain popular in the country. As chancellor of the exchequer, it had fallen to him to put through a series of measures that had proved to be particularly odious to Tory voters.[83]

His greatest problem, though, was summed up by one of his successors. 'He was respected', Harold Macmillan wrote of Chamberlain, 'but never feared'.[84] This fact, more than any other, did not augur well for a government about to face its toughest challenge since the war. To grasp the nettle of the Irish Question, Chamberlain would have to take his party where it did not want to go. For that, he would need to be both feared and trusted by his followers and he was neither.

---

79   Hankey diary, 17 Mar. 1921, HNKY 1/5/198.

80   Thomas Jones, *Whitehall Diary*, 3 vols, Keith Middlemas, ed. (London, 1969–71), 30 Jan. 1921, vol. III, pp. 49–50.

81   C 77 (20), 24 Dec. 1920, CAB 23/23.

82   J. Ramsden, *A History of the Conservative Party: The Age of Balfour and Baldwin, 1902–1940* (London, 1978), p. 150. Long to Midleton, 26 July 1920, PRO 30/67/43. Jones diary, 6 July 1921, vol. III, p. 85.

83   Davidson to Bonar Law, 24 Mar. 1921, BL 107/1/4. Austen to Hilda Chamberlain, 20 Mar. 1921, AC 5/1/194. George Younger[?] to Long, 18 Mar. 1921, Long Papers, Add. MSS 62,426, ff. 33–8.

84   H. Macmillan, *The Past Masters: Politics and Politicians, 1906–1939* (London, 1975), p. 128.

NEGOTIATIONS VERSUS WAR

In late April and again in mid-May, the Cabinet engaged in a wide-ranging debate over whether or not it should make a public offer to negotiate with Sinn Féin. At both meetings, Lloyd George stubbornly opposed concessions or any let-up in the war against the IRA. 'These people will come round sooner or later', he assured his colleagues.[85] Yet, within a mere six weeks he was preparing for talks with Sinn Féin's president. 'No British Government', Winston Churchill later wrote, 'has ever appeared to make so complete and sudden a reversal of policy'.[86]

The reasons for this turnaround are extraordinarily tangled, but roughly three factors added up to make for Lloyd George's decision to negotiate: the results of the Irish elections, the military situation and, an issue that is seldom explored – his own political survival.

THE IRISH ELECTIONS

At the end of May, voters went to the polls to elect representatives to the two Irish parliaments created by the 1920 Act. In the South, Sinn Féin candidates stood virtually unopposed in 124 of 128 seats, putting paid to any lingering hopes that the party might be sidelined. Their victory was then used to constitute the Second Dáil Éireann.[87]

The results for the Northern Parliament told a different story. Despite a sustained effort, Sinn Féin won only six seats and the Nationalists an identical number, while Unionists swept the polls electing 40 MPs.[88] This was true even in the depressed, working-class areas of Belfast. Independent Labour candidates, who had declared that partition was 'an unworkable stupidity', were soundly rejected.[89]

In any event, these elections were important from Lloyd George's perspective, because they demonstrated that he was fulfilling his pledges to the Ulster Unionists. This then gave him some leeway to explore an alternative arrangement with the South.

---

85   Jones diary, 27 Apr., 12 May 1921, vol. III, pp. 55–63, 66–70.
86   Churchill, *World Crisis:* V, p. 303.
87   O'Leary, *Irish Elections*, p. 9.
88   Ibid. SFM, 19 Feb., 19 Mar., 13 Apr., 4 May 1921, MSS Film P3269, 148–53.
89   'To the Electors of South, East, and West Belfast', *Irish News*, 21 May 1921. Follis, *State Under Siege*, Appendix I, pp. 195–7.

THE MILITARY DEADLOCK

In the early months of 1921, it looked as if British military efforts in Ireland were at last bearing fruit. 'The Forces of the Crown are gradually wearing down the Irish Republican Army', Greenwood confidently told Lord Curzon, 'and bringing this Irish business to a head.'[90] All too soon, however, it was clear that these estimates had been wildly optimistic. In late spring, the Cabinet's Irish Situation Committee began to discuss imposing martial law throughout the 26 counties. Given that the government still refused to admit that a war was even taking place in Ireland, it was going to be hard to justify so drastic a step. In any event, Macready warned that there must be no more 'half-hearted coercion'. It had to be 'a case of "all out" or "nothing"', he told the committee. 'Could the Government go "all out"?'[91]

Both politicians and generals faced a conundrum. Sir Henry Wilson advocated 'flattening out the rebels' with a summer-long, win-the-war offensive. Yet he was well aware that success was not possible 'unless England was on our side'. In other words, such a strategy was bound to fail unless the army could count on widespread public support for the war. And that was something the government could not give. England, Sir Laming Worthington-Evans had to admit, 'was not on our side and could not be got on it'. At that, even Wilson had to concede 'that it would be madness' to carry on with the war any further.[92]

THE COUP AGAINST LLOYD GEORGE

A couple of weeks before the Irish elections, Frances Stevenson confided to Mark Sturgis that 'in his inmost heart' Lloyd George still hoped to impose the 1920 Act on southern Ireland 'without any additions whatsoever'.[93] Despite Sinn Féin's victory at the polls, he held on to this conviction and pressed ahead with plans for all-out war against the IRA until the end of June.

Then, the turnaround. This points to another factor behind the decision to negotiate with Sinn Féin: namely, Lloyd George's own political survival.

Throughout his four and a half years as prime minister, Lloyd George was beset by heirs apparent, none more so than Birkenhead and Churchill. His relations with both men, and with Churchill in particular, reached a breaking

90 Greenwood to Curzon, 8 May 1921, IO, MSS Eur. F. 112/220(a), ff. 68.
91 SIC 9th Conclusions, 15 June 1921, CAB 27/107.
92 CP 2965, 24 May 1921, CAB 24/123. Wilson diary, 22 June 1921, HHW 1/30/1.
93 Sturgis diary, 11 May 1921, PRO 30/59/4.

point in the spring of 1921 when he thwarted his junior partner's ambition to become chancellor of the exchequer. According to Lord Beaverbrook, Churchill was now 'the bitter enemy of [Lloyd] George', while Birkenhead intended to 'challenge Chamberlain's leadership of the Tory Party'.[94]

Initially, it seems that the two men attempted to concoct a plot centring on Lloyd George's removal of Dr Christopher Addison from the Ministry of Health and his subsequent appointment as a minister without portfolio. When this scheme failed to attract support, it was decided that a far larger collection of opponents might be assembled against the prime minister based on the charge that he had lost his way in Ireland.[95]

Within both wings of the Coalition, discontent with the government's Irish policy was by now boiling over. Even in Lloyd George's own backyard, Asquith's Liberals were making inroads by focusing on the government's handling of the Sinn Féin rebellion. 'Ireland, Ireland, Ireland', reported one of the prime minister's Welsh supporters, 'they keep harping on that one string and people listen, – to our loss!'[96]

From the other side of the Coalition, members of the 'Group', a collection of influential Tory backbenchers, had also emerged as leading opponents of government policy. After a trip to Ireland in March, one of the Group's main figures, Sir Samuel Hoare, confronted Lloyd George at a private meeting, telling him that 'his show in Ireland was rotten from top to bottom'.[97]

With the premiership seemingly ready to drop like a piece of overripe fruit, Lloyd George's opponents proceeded to shake the tree for all they were worth. Throughout the spring and summer, Lord Beaverbrook attempted to broker an alliance between discontented leaders such as Birkenhead and Churchill and backbench Tories.[98] In the hothouse atmosphere of Westminster it was impossible to keep such a plot secret for long. For the better part of a month, Lloyd George bided his time pretending that nothing but the usual problems troubled him. 'Crises', he airily wrote to Bonar Law, continued to chase 'each other like shadows of clouds across the landscape. Miners, unemployment, reparations, Siberia and always Ireland'.[99]

---

94   See, e.g., Neville to Hilda Chamberlain, 18 Jan. 1920, NC 18/1/240. Churchill had set his eyes on the chancellorship as early as 1919. See Wilson diary, 25 Oct. 1919, HHW 1/28/1. Beaverbrook to Borden, 12 May 1921, BBK C/51.

95   Morgan, *Consensus and Disunity*, pp. 98–103. Cowling, *Impact of Labour*, p. 120.

96   C. Price White to Winifred Coombe Tennant, 24 Mar. 1921, LG F/96/1/15.

97   Hoare to Beaverbrook, 13 June 1921, Templewood Papers, I: 12 (36).

98   See, e.g., Birkenhead to Bonar Law, 5 May 1921, BL 107/1/22; and Beaverbrook to Hoare, 9 July 1921, Templewood Papers, I: 12 (37).

99   Lloyd George to Bonar Law, 7 June 1921, BL 107/1/35.

On 21 June, Birkenhead implicitly attacked the government's Irish policy while ostensibly defending it in the House of Lords. Contrary to the government's previous claims, he now admitted that 'a small war' was going on in Ireland. Worse, he conceded that British efforts to defeat the IRA were failing. Under the current leadership, however, there would be no change of policy, no concessions, nothing to leaven the terms of the 1920 Act.[100]

At this moment, Lloyd George chose to strike back.[101] Word of a plot to oust the prime minister because of his Irish policy was leaked to two newspapers: first to the *Daily Mirror*, and a day later to the *Manchester Guardian*.[102] No one who might be a challenger escaped censure in one or other of the reports, including Bonar Law. Immediately, the articles punctured any schemes to remove Lloyd George from the premiership. A 'Coup D'Etat' now, Lord Winterton admitted, 'would be . . . fatal'. The best that could be hoped for was 'a gradual stampede' in the autumn, and that would depend on Birkenhead and Churchill leaving office to lead the dissidents.[103] In the circumstances, however, neither man was willing to take such a risky move.

With his position secure, at least for the time being, Lloyd George could at last change course on Ireland. The issue had proved to be a potential Achilles Heel. But, as he had earlier told his colleagues, it was important to wait for the '*best* opportunity', not the 'first opportunity', to negotiate with Sinn Féin.[104] The end of June afforded Lloyd George the best opportunity to make his move. It might not come again.

THE OFFER TO TALK

While the plot against Lloyd George was spinning out in London, George V was in Belfast for the formal opening of Northern Ireland's Parliament. The occasion allowed the king to appeal for reconciliation between North and South, and to call on Irish men and women to 'forgive and forget'.[105] What was said was less important than the fact that the speech gave the government the excuse it needed for a dramatic break in policy.[106]

---

100 *HL Deb*, vol. 45, cols 679–96, 21 June 1921.

101 Lord Beaverbrook, *The Decline and Fall of Lloyd George* (London, 1963), pp. 72–4.

102 'Queer Plot to Oust Mr. Lloyd George', *Daily Mirror*, 22 June 1921. 'The Scheme that Failed', *Manchester Guardian*, 23 June 1921.

103 Winterton to Hoare, 11 July 1921, Templewood Papers, I: 12 (38).

104 Jones diary, 12 May 1921, vol. III, p. 67.

105 'King's call for a new Spirit in Ireland', *Manchester Guardian*, 23 June 1921.

106 But see Lyons, *Ireland*, p. 425.

Two days later, at an emergency Cabinet meeting, Lloyd George suggested that the time was right to invite both Craig and Sinn Féin President Eamon de Valera to come to London for talks. Disregarding his own previous advice, he now said that such an offer would not be a sign of weakness. On the contrary, if de Valera refused, the government would be in a much stronger position to wage all-out war against the IRA. At any rate, a 'last attempt at peace' had to be made, Chamberlain told his sister, Hilda, 'before we go the full lengths of martial law'.[107]

As it happened, de Valera was willing to talk – but he refused to have anything to do with a conference where he and Craig would be treated as equals. On reflection, this also suited the British, as separate discussions might enable them to put the Ulster Question to one side. On 8 July Macready and de Valera met at the Mansion House in Dublin where they signed a formal truce ending the Anglo-Irish War. Fighting lasted another three days, before hostilities finally ended at noon, on Monday, 11 July. 'The last revolver shot' of the Anglo-Irish War was fired at five minutes before the hour. In Ulster.[108]

THE LLOYD GEORGE–DE VALERA TALKS

According to those who knew him best, Lloyd George's encounter with de Valera was not one of his happier experiences. After their first meeting, an assistant later wrote, Britain's prime minister emerged 'white and exhausted' having made no impression whatsoever.[109]

Nor did Lloyd George find the going any easier in separate talks with Craig and his colleagues. At a meeting with the Unionists on 18 July, Lloyd George made it plain that a settlement with Sinn Féin was impossible unless the six-county state accepted some sort of arrangement for an all-Ireland government. He then outlined five suggestions for an accommodation, only to be told that 'none of them were acceptable'. Instead of putting forward counter-proposals, Craig abruptly announced that further discussions 'would serve no useful purpose' and that he and his colleagues were returning to Belfast. So far as Craig was concerned, the negotiations with Sinn Féin turned solely on relations between southern Ireland and Great Britain. If, and when, the interests of Ulster became involved 'in a practicable manner', the Northern Ireland Cabinet would return to London for further consultations.[110]

---

107 Jones diary, 24 June 1921, vol. III, pp. 79–81. Austen to Hilda Chamberlain, 26 June 1921, AC 5/1/202.

108 CP 3130, 13 July 1921, CAB 24/126.

109 G. Shakespeare, *Let Candles be Brought In* (London, 1949), p. 76.

110 'Rough Notes' of a meeting, 18 July [misdated June] 1921, PRONI, CAB/4/3/1.

News of Craig's departure nearly brought the entire negotiations crashing down. Lloyd George managed to hold the situation together just long enough to put forward his government's initiative for a comprehensive settlement with Sinn Féin. Compared to the 1920 Act, these proposals were an extraordinary step forward. In a carefully worded letter to Bonar Law, Tom Jones explained that the Irish were being offered "'Dominion Status" with all sorts of important powers, but no Navy, no hostile tariffs, and no coercion of Ulster'. As usual, Jones wrote, the 'crux of the problem' was 'this question of unity'.[111]

De Valera's immediate response was, in Lloyd George's own words, 'not very hopeful'. The Sinn Féin president was unwilling to accept Dominion status unless it included Ulster. His 'only other alternative', Lloyd George told Craig, was 'complete independence for Southern Ireland'. Lloyd George hoped that Craig would meet with de Valera to demonstrate that Ulster was a 'fact' not a 'figment' created by the British. Otherwise, he feared, 'a settlement will always be unattainable'.[112]

Craig was not about to do anything of the kind. On the contrary, he refused to have any such meeting until de Valera first acknowledged Northern Ireland's separate existence. Ulster had already made its 'sacrifice' for peace by agreeing to have its own government. 'Much against our wish', Craig disingenuously wrote, 'we accepted this as a *final settlement*' and, he emphatically concluded, 'we have nothing left to give away'.[113]

THE POLITICAL FALLOUT

The dramatic turn of events in Ireland had an immediate impact on British politics. On his left, Lloyd George's move suddenly cut the ground out from underneath anti-Coalition Liberals. Though they wanted a settlement ('God grant it', wrote Lord Crewe), peace in Ireland would remove one of the Wee Frees' main grievances against the government. Furthermore, if Lloyd George could pull a deal out of his hat, he would almost certainly call a general election for which the Asquith Liberals were totally unprepared.[114]

On Lloyd George's right, a number of Conservative MPs were 'a good deal perturbed' that de Valera had been invited to London in the first place. A

---

111   De Valera to Collins, 19 July 1921, FLK, de Valera Papers, File No. 151. 'Proposals of the British Government for an Irish Settlement', 20 July 1921, *Dáil Éireann: Official Correspondence Relating to the Peace Negotiations, June–September 1921* (Dublin, 1921), pp. 6–8. Jones to Bonar Law, 22 July 1921, BL 107/1/46.

112   Lloyd George to Craig, 21 July 1921, Grigg MSS Film 1010.

113   Craig to Lloyd George, 29 July 1921, LG F/11/3/15(a).

114   Crewe to Asquith, 11 July 1921, Crewe Papers, C/40.

party resolution 'condemning such dealing altogether' was resisted but only in return for another which expressed 'anxiety' about the talks – hardly a ringing endorsement of the government or its leaders.[115] As time dragged on, these misgivings increased. 'I think that we shall have a split over the Irish question', Austen Chamberlain confided to his stepmother, with as many as 30 or 40 MPs defecting from the party. 'Ireland will be the reason for some and the excuse for others.'[116]

The 20 July proposals were not officially rejected by the Irish Cabinet until 10 August. Among other objections, de Valera denied that Britain had any right to solve 'our local problem' by partitioning the six counties. 'If your Government stands aside', he asserted, 'we can effect a complete reconciliation'. Quite how this was to be accomplished was unclear, though international arbitration was suggested as one possibility. But the most obvious method was specifically ruled out. Sinn Féin, de Valera announced, would not 'contemplate the use of force'.[117]

Although Lloyd George welcomed de Valera's pledge, he was not about to refer the Irish Question to foreign mediators.[118] Throughout August and September, newspaper accounts continued to stress that Ulster was 'the crux of the Irish problem'.[119] In fact, the real bone of contention was de Valera's demand for the recognition of Irish national sovereignty and Lloyd George's refusal to concede it. The knot was finally cut by the prime minister's proposal to ascertain 'how the association of Ireland with the community of nations known as the British Empire may best be reconciled with Irish national aspirations'. In his reply, de Valera simply agreed to disagree.[120] Formal talks were set to begin on the 11th day of October.

The two sides had taken 'a big step', Mark Sturgis wrote in his diary.[121] Even so, he and others recognised that the Ulster Question might still block a final settlement. 'To ask the Irish people to leave Ulster out', one Cabinet official observed, 'would be like asking the English Parliament to leave Yorkshire outside their jurisdiction.'[122]

---

115 Bayford diary, 16 July 1921, p. 158.

116 Austen to Mary Chamberlain, 25 Aug. 1921, AC 4/1/1207.

117 De Valera to Lloyd George, 10 Aug. 1921, LG F/14/6/14.

118 Lloyd George to de Valera, 13 Aug. 1921, LG F/14/6/15.

119 See, e.g., 'The Crux of the Irish Problem', *The Observer*, 28 Aug. 1921; and 'A Signal for Peace', *Manchester Guardian*, 7 Sept. 1921.

120 See Lloyd George–de Valera correspondence, 24 Aug.–30 Sept. 1921, LG F/14/6/16–28.

121 Sturgis diary, 30 Sept. 1921, PRO 30/59/5.

122 'Rough notes on views of Irish delegates', 21 July 1921, LG F/29/4/61(b).

THE POINT OF NO RETURN

By opening negotiations with Sinn Féin, Lloyd George crossed his Rubicon, setting in motion a chain of events that would lead to his downfall a year and a half later. In direct response to his Irish initiative, 18 Die-hards formed the nucleus of the group that was to be instrumental in overthrowing the Coalition.[123] Equally important, this was the issue which might draw out of retirement the one man capable of rallying the Conservative Party against Lloyd George. The question was not if, but rather how long Bonar Law could ignore appeals to lead the opposition to the 'Surrender policy in Ireland'.[124]

In that sense, Lloyd George was taking an enormous gamble; but did he have any choice? The Coalition's initial response to the Irish Question – its 1920 Government of Ireland Act, coupled with suppression of Sinn Féin – had clearly failed. Moreover, while these actions may have satisfied Ulster Unionists and a section of the Tory Party they had eroded support for the Coalition in general.

However much members of the Cabinet, including Lloyd George, might have despised the Irish rebels and what they stood for, they could not be wished away. This point was driven home by the government's chief civil servant, the permanent secretary to the Treasury, Sir Warren Fisher. It was no good 'withholding recognition of Sinn Fein as a political party', Fisher wrote. 'It *is* a political party, however much people may dislike it'.[125] Lloyd George, no less than his Tory allies, was reluctant to accept this advice. But once the political damage being inflicted on the Coalition and on his plans for a future Centre Party began to tell, he had no hesitation about altering course.

Although this sudden change of direction opened Lloyd George to the charge that his Irish policy was unprincipled and capricious, this was not the case. Quite the contrary, by his lights it was the sort of action that made the difference between 'ordinary and extraordinary men'. As he explained to Lord Riddell, 'when the extraordinary man is faced by a novel and difficult situation, he extricates himself by adopting a plan which is at once daring and unexpected'.[126] No other words better sum up Lloyd George's own approach to Ireland.

Even so, by the summer of 1921 Lloyd George had still not escaped his dilemma. If anything, the 1920 Act and the related concessions made to the Ulster Unionists had created new difficulties from which he would find it hard

123 Kinnear, *Lloyd George*, pp. 96–7.

124 Menzies to Bonar Law, 13 Aug. 1921, BL 107/1/51.

125 Fisher memorandum to Lloyd George, Bonar Law and Chamberlain, 15 May 1920, HO 317/50.

126 Riddell diary, 3 Apr. 1919, *Intimate Diary*, p. 45.

to extricate himself. Bargaining with Sinn Féin saw off the immediate threat
to his premiership but only at the cost of giving his opponents a possible issue,
and a possible alternative leader, around whom to rally.

A fortnight after the failed coup to oust Lloyd George, Harold Laski
penned a letter to American Supreme Court Justice Oliver Wendell Holmes.
'I think Lloyd George will be in for another ten years', Laski unhappily
predicted, 'so that one might as well cultivate one's private garden and be
screened from the public view'.[127]

Lloyd George would have been amused by that thought. If only he could
be so sure.

127   Laski to Holmes, 6 July 1921, in M. DeWolfe Howe, ed., *Holmes–Laski Letters: The
Correspondence of Mr Justice Holmes and Harold J. Laski, 1916–1935*, vol. 1 (Cambridge, 1953), p. 348.

TWO

A TREATY FOR IRELAND

Not much rest for the wicked in this life.

LORD BIRKENHEAD[1]

—

On the evening of 10 October 1921, the Meteorological Office reported that weather conditions over the British Isles were about to assume 'a somewhat complex character'. Through the night a low-pressure system rolled in from Ireland, breaking a spell of unseasonably warm temperatures. On the 11th rain fell over London, accompanied by thunder and lightning.[2]

In this unpromising atmosphere, the Irish Treaty negotiations finally got under way. Five delegates representing Dáil Éireann – Arthur Griffith, Michael Collins, Eamon Duggan, Robert Barton, and George Gavan Duffy – were to press the claim for an independent, united Ireland. Eamon de Valera, his status recently elevated to that of president of the Irish republic, refused to attend. Facing the Sinn Féin delegates across a conveniently wide table, sat Lloyd George, Birkenhead, Churchill, Greenwood, Worthington-Evans, and Sir Gordon Hewart. Austen Chamberlain joined the negotiations the next day.[3]

Little was accomplished at these early sessions. Incredibly, the Irish delegates were sent to London without a detailed alternative to Lloyd George's 20 July proposals. While de Valera continued to spin out his theory of 'External Association', a halfway house between his cherished republic and Dominion status, the Irish delegates were sent packing with a bare-bones proposal called 'Draft Treaty A' which, revealingly, did not address the Ulster Question. According to Griffith, the British were equally ill-prepared. His opponents, he reported, were 'remarkably ignorant' about the north of Ireland.[4]

Such were the uncertain beginnings of the negotiations that were to end with Ireland's independence. Five issues stood in the way of agreement: free

1   'Notes, Irish meeting', 5 Dec. 1921, LG F/101/139(e).

2   See weather reports, *The Times*, 11, 12 Oct. 1921.

3   'Difficult Problems for the Irish Conference', *Daily Telegraph*, 14 Oct. 1921.

4   'Draft Treaty A' is reprinted in Macardle, *Irish Republic*, pp. 937–9. Griffith to de Valera, 14 Oct. 1921, DE 2/304/8.

trade within the British Isles versus protection for Irish industry; Ireland's liability for a proportion of the United Kingdom's debt versus Irish claims of over-taxation; defence; Dominion status versus a republic; and partition. Neither of the first two issues was likely to disrupt the talks; nor was defence, although the problems there were trickier. The break, if it were to come, would be over Ireland's continued allegiance to the crown, or over the partition of Ulster.[5]

In his day-by-day, sometimes hourly, chronicle of the Treaty talks, Lord Longford maintained that 'Ulster was not the main issue' dividing British and Irish negotiators, but instead became 'a strange abstract factor in tactics'.[6] This conclusion has proved to be surprisingly resilient, the evidence for it based on the fact that the Ulster Question hardly figured in the Dáil's subsequent Treaty debates. It is indeed astonishing that in a public debate which took some 338 pages to record, only nine of those pages are devoted to partition. The private sessions are even less revealing, 'as fewer than five of 182 pages deal with Ulster'.[7]

Undeniably, some Irish nationalists viewed the province as a foreign land and 'secretly saw the South as well rid of the North'. This was true of the republic's president, however much he might protest that he 'felt as strongly on the subject of unity as on the subject of Self-determination'. Throughout the Treaty negotiations, it is clear that 'the big question' for de Valera was allegiance to the crown. Ulster was, for him, a purely secondary consideration.[8] But that was not the way the matter was viewed by those who directly participated in the Treaty negotiations.

Nothing better illustrates their differences on Ulster than to compare the way in which de Valera and Collins had earlier approached the question of Sinn Féin involvement in Northern Ireland's first parliamentary elections. De Valera's main concern was how the party's abstention or participation would affect its popularity in the South. Collins, on the other hand, argued for a policy of '*active* non recognition of Partition'. His aim, beyond safeguarding Sinn Féin's interests, was to give 'hope of salvation for the North'.[9]

5   Pakenham, *Peace by Ordeal*, pp. 89–97.

6   Ibid, p. 93.

7   See, e.g., M. Laffan, *The Resurrection of Ireland: The Sinn Féin Party, 1916–1923* (Cambridge, 1999), p. 351; and E. Phoenix, 'Michael Collins – The Northern Question, 1916–1922', in G. Doherty and D. Keogh, ed., *Michael Collins and the Making of the Irish State* (Dublin, 1998), pp. 96–7. M. Wall, 'The Ulster Question', in D. Williams, ed., *The Irish Struggle: 1916–1926* (London, 1966), p. 87. J. M. Curran, *The Birth of the Irish Free State: 1921–1923* (University, Alabama, 1980), p. 314, n. 7.

8   T. Garvin, *1922: The Birth of Irish Democracy* (Dublin, 1996), p. 156. 'Partition's Perils', *Irish News*, 29 Sept. 1921. De Valera to Griffith, 25 Oct. 1921, DE 2/304/8.

9   See de Valera–Collins correspondence, 13, 15 Jan. 1921, DE 2/266. Collins's attitude about the North is discussed in further detail in chapter 3.

In his own quieter way Griffith was equally determined to uproot partition. So far as he was concerned, Lloyd George was personally to blame for tearing Ireland in two. Griffith aimed to overturn that policy. At the same time, he was under no illusion that he could 'bring back the Republic' from London. '[N]obody in his senses would have gone there', he later told the Dáil, believing that they could accomplish any such thing. What Griffith did believe was attainable was what he began to call Ireland's 'essential unity'. Put another way, Griffith decided to pursue a strategy in which the British could be made to guarantee a reunited Ireland in exchange for the nation's allegiance to the crown.[10]

Not least important, Ulster was a question that Lloyd George and his colleagues would not, and could not, ignore unless they wished to jeopardise their own political careers. At no point did Britain's leaders seriously entertain the idea of an Irish republic or anything like it. The 'fly in the ointment', wrote Alfred Cope, was 'the "Ulster Question" and not the "Republic"'.[11]

In fact, so far as British politicians were concerned, partition continued to be the fly in the ointment throughout the Treaty negotiations and after. Once it became clear that the Ulster Unionists would not agree to a single government for Ireland, and that this refusal would be supported by the Conservative Party, Lloyd George devised a complex arrangement to turn this refusal inside out. This arrangement became the Treaty's Ulster clauses, of which the Boundary Commission was just one part. Hidden beneath the other clauses was a trap designed to ensnare the Ulster Unionists in the complicated restrictions of the 1920 Act. Compared with the freedoms offered to those inside an Irish Dominion, these restrictions would be so onerous as to make the lure of a single parliament irresistible. In this way, Lloyd George could say that he had kept his pledge not to fiddle with the 1920 Act while, at the same time, he could sell the Treaty to Griffith and his colleagues as a contract that made reunification inevitable.

What is important to remember is that Lloyd George's goal in the autumn of 1921 was to remove the Irish Question from his agenda once and for all. An agreement would take a political liability and, with a bit of skilful handling, turn it into a pretext for calling the next general election. This in turn could provide the springboard from which to launch his long-desired Centre Party. Viewed from this angle, the details of an Irish agreement were secondary. As Lloyd George reminded his colleagues: 'We are after a settlement – that [is] our objective.'[12] Coming to grips with the consequences of that settlement would be for a later time.

10   SFM, 12 Aug. 1921, MSS Film P3269, ff. 165–7. *Dáil Deb II: Private Sess.*, 14 Dec. 1921, p. 106. Griffith to de Valera, 24 Oct. 1921, DE 2/304/8.

11   Cope to Jones, 15 Aug. 1921, TJ G/2/11.

12   Jones diary, 14 Nov. 1921, vol. III, p. 164.

For now, Lloyd George's concern was that he not become bogged down in a war fought over Ireland's partition. 'Men will die for the Throne and Empire', he pointed out to his Cabinet. 'I do not know who will die for Tyrone and Fermanagh.'[13] If the war had to be renewed, the government would need the widest measure of public support. Should a breakdown occur, it had to be over allegiance to the crown, not over two distant Irish counties.

A few days into the negotiations, the twin rocks of Fermanagh and Tyrone emerged, just as they had in 1914 and in 1916, to block Lloyd George's way. In no uncertain terms, the Irish delegates made it clear that they could not agree to a partition including those two counties. 'This', Lloyd George scribbled on a note to Jones, 'is going to wreck [the] settlement'.[14]

THE EARLY ULSTER DISCUSSIONS

Because no instructions concerning Ulster were received from Dublin until nearly a week after the Treaty talks began, Griffith managed to forestall discussion of the topic until, finally, he could avoid it no longer. Hammering home Sinn Féin's contention that the six-county partition was 'unnatural', Griffith argued that the dispute in Ireland was not between Protestant and Catholic. Sectarianism, he held, was being used to divert the average Ulsterman 'from industrial questions', from the bread and butter issues that dominated politics elsewhere. Absent this artificial religious divide, Ireland would develop along the same lines as any other modern, European state.[15] If the British stood aside, Sinn Féin would make 'a fair proposal' to persuade Unionists to join a single Irish government. If the Ulstermen refused, they could retain their separate Parliament; but its reach would cover only those constituencies voting for exclusion and which formed a 'territorially continuous group'. Moreover, any such government must be subordinate to the national Parliament in Dublin, not to Westminster.[16]

Lloyd George dismissed this proposal out of hand, telling the Sinn Féiners that they 'must face facts'. No British government could coerce the Ulster Unionists into an all-Ireland Parliament; it 'would only lead to civil war'. Yes, the six county partition was not 'logically defensible'. But would the Sinn Féiners prefer putting all nine Ulster counties under a Belfast Parliament?[17]

13   Ibid., 7 Sept. 1921, pp. 110–11.
14   'Notes at Cabinet meetings', 17 Oct. 1921, TJ G/2/32.
15   Chamberlain's Notes, 14 Oct. 1921, CAB 21/253/1.
16   SF (C) 7, 17 Oct. 1921, CAB 21/208. 'North East Ulster Draft Clause', 17 Oct. 1921, DE 2/304/8.
17   Ibid., SF (C) 7. Chamberlain's Notes and Jones's Notes, 14 Oct. 1921, CAB 21/253/1 and 3.

The first breakthrough came a few days later, when Griffith dangled the possibility of Sinn Féin accepting Dominion status – but only if the British ended partition. This link was more explicitly drawn the following day. 'In the end', Griffith wrote, 'I told them that no Irishman could even discuss with his countrymen any association with the British Crown unless the essential unity of Ireland was agreed to' by both sides. This position was formally confirmed a few days later by the Irish delegation as a whole.[18]

If the offer was sincere, the British negotiators were on dangerous ground. 'We can't give way on the six counties', Churchill pointed out, 'we are not free agents.' As it was, Lloyd George and his colleagues were about to face a censure vote in Parliament because of the Irish negotiations. It would be politically suicidal for them to propose an all-Ireland Parliament, at least for the time being. In any case, Lloyd George was not willing to play Griffith's game. Before he would take any risks on Ulster, the Irish first had to give up their republic.[19]

LLOYD GEORGE 'SMITES THE DIE-HARDS'

At the end of October roughly three dozen Tory MPs tabled a motion demanding that the government abandon its talks with Sinn Féin and work the 1920 Act. The number of Conservatives supporting the motion was not unexpected, Chamberlain told his wife, though 'one or two of the names are a surprise to me'. Faced with what amounted to a vote of no confidence, Lloyd George decided it was time that he 'threw down the glove'. If the motion succeeded, he announced, he would resign.[20] At the same time, he decided to use the parliamentary drama to focus minds in the Irish delegation.

On the 27th, Griffith and his colleagues received a memorandum from their British counterparts insisting that they declare once and for all whether or not they were prepared to accept Dominion status, as well as the government's other demands concerning defence, trade, and finance. Ulster was carefully sidestepped. Griffith's response was to turn these questions back on the British, making any agreement conditional on the 'unimpaired unity of Ireland'.[21]

This sparring match set the stage for a private meeting between Lloyd George and Griffith on the eve of the Commons censure debate. Here, according to Collins, the two sides reached 'absolute dead level'. In return for a

18 Griffith to de Valera, 24, 25 Oct. 1921, DE 2/304/8. SF (C) 21A, 29 Oct. 1921, CAB 43/3.

19 Grigg's Notes, 25 Oct. 1921, CAB 21/253/2.

20 *HC Deb*, vol. 147, col. 1367, 31 Oct. 1921. Austen to Ivy Chamberlain, 26 Oct. 1921, AC 6/1/433. Sturgis diary, 28 Oct. 1921, PRO 30/59/5.

21 SF (C) 21 and 21A, 27, 29 Oct. 1921, CAB 43/3.

united Ireland, the Dáil would have to accept membership within the British Commonwealth, along with safeguards for the Ulster Unionists and guarantees for British security. Otherwise, Collins told the IRA's adjutant-general, there would be war and 'no fooling about it either'. According to Griffith, the British wanted to be 'certain of real good-will on our side' before they would risk their careers in a fight with the Die-hards. 'If I would give him [Lloyd George] personal assurances on this matter', Griffith wrote, 'he would go out to smite the Diehards, and would fight on the Ulster matter to secure essential unity.'[22]

It is difficult to see how Lloyd George could have kept such a bargain, unless he were prepared to sacrifice his Coalition partners. As Chamberlain explained to his wife: 'F. E. and I are so pledged that we could not honourably alter the Ulster boundaries (by subtraction, I mean) or powers without Craig's consent'. If an attempt was made to 'force Ulster into a sacrifice', both men would be compelled to resign from the Cabinet.[23] Whether Lloyd George was willing to carry matters that far is unclear, though he did put out feelers to the Wee Frees suggesting that together they might form an alternative government. At the same time, Lloyd George bandied about the idea that he might call a general election, though this threat was never really serious. 'It would be foolish to do so', he admitted to Donald Maclean, 'unemployment being as rampant as it was.'[24]

In the end, no such measures were needed to survive the censure vote. Lloyd George did indeed smite the Die-hards, crushing his opponents by 439 votes to 43. It was a brilliant performance, though Tom Jones had to admit that more than once his master 'was on very thin ice'.[25]

On 2 November, the personal assurance that Griffith had given to Lloyd George in the run-up to the Commons debate was put into writing. Again, everything was 'conditional on the recognition of the essential unity of Ireland'.[26] The British, he reported to de Valera, were now 'satisfied to face the "Ulster" question on it, and assure me that if "Ulster" proves unreasonable they

22   Collins to 'A/G' [Gearóid O'Sullivan], 31 Oct. 1921, RM, P7/A/72. Griffith to de Valera, same date, DE 2/304/8.

23   Austen to Ivy Chamberlain, 30–31 Oct. 1921, AC 6/1/441.

24   Maclean memorandum, ? Oct. 1921, Maclean Papers, Dep. c. 466, ff. 103. At least 1.75 million were one the dole. See Austen to Ida Chamberlain, 17 Oct. 1921, AC 5/1/219. Also, see T. P. O'Connor to Dillon, same date, Dillon MSS 6744, ff. 859.

25   *HC Deb*, vol. 147, cols 1412–27, 1479–84, 31 Oct. 1921. Jones diary, same date, vol. III, p. 152.

26   SF (B) 45, 2 Nov. 1921, CAB 43/2. In an earlier draft, Griffith explicitly stated that he could not recommend Dominion status if 'the unity of Ireland were denied in form or in fact' [*sic*]. See Griffith to Lloyd George, same date, LG F/21/1/1.

are prepared to resign rather than use force against us'. Even if they failed, Griffith was certain that no one could form an alternative government which committed itself to 'a war-policy against Ireland'. Britain's military commander in Ireland agreed. It would be insane, Macready wrote, to go to war 'merely if Ulster objects to a plebiscite in Tyrone and Fermanagh.'[27]

BONAR LAW INTERVENES

On 5 November Craig was summoned to London for urgent consultations. The gist of the British proposal to be presented to him was that Ulster's government would retain its powers within the six counties but that its representatives would sit in Dáil Éireann rather than the British Parliament. Austen Chamberlain thought that the British might persuade Ulster's premier to see the advantages of this new arrangement. As matters stood, it would be difficult if not impossible for Craig to govern Tyrone and Fermanagh 'with their Sinn Fein majorities'.[28]

Though warned by his colleagues in Belfast that they considered any such proposals to be 'unthinkable', Craig seems to have been unprepared for what awaited him in the British capital. The government's plan, he said afterwards, gave him 'the biggest shock' he had ever had in his life. Worse still, he discovered 'many "backsliders" amongst old friends and colleagues'.[29] His reaction was to seek help from any quarter but, above all, from Bonar Law. As early as September Lloyd George had foreseen just such a scenario if the Irish negotiations became sticky. His solution had been to dispatch Bonar Law, along with Balfour, to represent Britain at the Washington Naval Conference. Balfour accepted, as did Bonar Law – until he learned that Lloyd George was to remain in London to orchestrate the discussions on Ireland.[30]

Just as Lloyd George feared, Bonar Law quickly emerged as the chief obstacle to the government's peace plan. 'B.L. is rampaging', Chamberlain told his wife, and 'seeing red on the subject of Ulster'. It was only a matter of time before the former Tory leader's attitude began to infect the Cabinet. Chamberlain knew that he could depend on Birkenhead. Robert Horne was also reliable, though he seemed at times 'puzzled and troubled' by the government's Irish policy. Lord Curzon, Chamberlain suspected, 'does not

27 Griffith to de Valera, 3 Nov. 1921, DE 2/304/8. Macready to Wilson, same date, HHW 2/2F/46.
28 Austen to Ivy Chamberlain, 2 Nov. 1921, AC 6/1/447.
29 Conclusions, 4 Nov. 1921, PRONI, CAB/4/26/19. Lady Craig's diary, 5 Nov. 1921, D/1415/B/38.
30 Grigg to Curzon, 14 Sept. 1921, IO, MSS Eur. F. 112/220(a), ff. 78–81.

know where he is. Worthy puzzles me a little and, if trouble arises, Baldwin would be much under Bonar's influence.'[31]

Despite their pledges of loyalty, Lloyd George also suspected that his Coalition partners would desert him if the Irish issue became too hot. Five years earlier, many of these same men had pledged their loyalty to Asquith – just before Lloyd George forced his resignation. Within days, he reminded Tom Jones, 'I was putting the nose bags of office round their necks. Curzon, L. W.-E. and Baldwin, they will all go over to Bonar if the opportunity comes.'[32]

THE BOUNDARY COMMISSION

With support ebbing away, it seems that Lloyd George actually considered resignation in early November. 'There is just one other possible way out', he told Jones. Namely, Southern Ireland would be granted Dominion status, while Craig's government would retain the powers granted to it by the 1920 Act, as well as representation in the imperial Parliament. But, the Ulstermen could do so only at the cost of bearing a higher proportion of taxation than the South. Under no conditions would Northern Ireland be granted Dominion status. Furthermore, the Unionists would have to accept a Boundary Commission which would be charged with redrawing the Irish frontier.[33]

What prompted Lloyd George to resurrect the Boundary Commission is unclear. When he had mooted the proposal during an earlier round of the Treaty negotiations, the Irish were decidedly cool to the idea.[34] It is plausible that Lloyd George returned to the concept because a similar commission, then at work redrawing the border between Germany and Poland, was much in the news.[35] An additional attraction was that Craig himself had proposed just such a commission the year before.[36] In that case, it would be hard for him to object to it now.

Whatever its origins, Collins instinctively disliked the idea when it was put to him and Griffith. Jones raised the offer again the following day, this time with Griffith and Duggan. Lloyd George, he said, 'was prepared to play the

---

31 Austen to Ivy Chamberlain, 7, 8, 9 Nov. 1921, AC 6/1/455, 458, and 459.

32 Jones diary, 8 Nov.1921, vol. III, p. 156.

33 Ibid., 7 Nov. 1921, p. 155.

34 Jones's Notes, 14 Oct. 1921, CAB 21/253/3.

35 The Upper Silesia commission, like others created by the Treaty of Versailles, would figure in the Free State's case to the Irish Boundary Commission. See North-Eastern Boundary Bureau, *Handbook of the Ulster Question* (Dublin, 1923), pp. 149–52.

36 See chapter 1.

Boundary Commission as an absolutely last card', but he would do so only 'if he could feel sure that Sinn Fein would take it, if Ulster accepted'. Jones's choice of words was crucial, and so was Griffith's. 'It is not our proposal', the Irish leader replied, and he refused to guarantee that his colleagues would accept the scheme. 'We would prefer a plebiscite', he told Jones, 'but in essentials a Boundary Commission is very much the same.'[37]

The idea for a Boundary Commission was initially put to Griffith with only the six counties in mind. Jones was told to make it plain that the Commission's writ must apply to all nine Ulster counties. In that case, the Commission actually might add territory to Northern Ireland, given that there were Unionist majorities south of the border. Jones claimed that he passed this information along to the Irish leader.[38] Yet, this qualification appears nowhere in Griffith's reports to de Valera, and it is hard to believe that he would have withheld so vital a fact from the Irish president. On the contrary, throughout his correspondence Griffith makes it clear that the Commission's sole function would be to 'delimit' Northern Ireland's territory.[39] There was no question that the tribunal might add as well as subtract people and land from the six-county state.

THE TRAP OF THE 1920 ACT

The exact goal of the Boundary Commission was even more important when set within the context of the Treaty's other Ulster clauses. As both Jones and Lloyd George explained to Griffith, after the Commission had finished 'delimiting' the six-county state, what remained of Northern Ireland would find itself handcuffed by the terms of the 1920 Act. Specifically, the truncated Ulster state 'would have to bear itself its proportion of British taxation' and would be 'subject to equal financial burdens with England'.[40]

In order to win Cabinet approval to negotiate with Sinn Féin in the first place, Lloyd George's 20 July offer had to stipulate that any settlement 'must allow for full recognition of the existing powers and privileges of the Parliament of Northern Ireland, which cannot be abrogated except by their own consent'.[41] Craig and his supporters in the Conservative Party assumed

---

37 Jones diary, 8–9 Nov. 1921, vol. III, pp. 155–7. Griffith to de Valera [two letters], same dates, DE 2/304/8.

38 Ibid, Jones diary, 9–10 Nov. 1921, pp. 157–8.

39 Griffith to de Valera, 8, 9, 11, 12 Nov. 1921, DE 2/304/8. Austen Chamberlain also spoke of a 'new delimitation' of the six-county state. See Chamberlain to Lloyd George, 11 Nov. 1921, LG F/7/4/31.

40 Ibid., Griffith to de Valera, 9, 12 Nov. 1921.

41 See British proposals, 20 July 1921, DE: *Official Correspondence*, p. 7.

that this statement would make it impossible for Lloyd George to do a deal with the Irish rebels behind their backs.

The genius of Lloyd George's latest proposal was that it turned this pledge on its head. If, he pointed out to his colleagues, 'Belfast wanted to remain with Gt. Britain then she must carry the same burdens as Glasgow, Liverpool and Birmingham'. The choice before Craig and his followers was both simple and fair: either join the Irish Dominion or remain within the United Kingdom. The Unionists, he said, 'can't expect to get all the benefits of both systems'. According to Jones, 'the atmosphere was at once electric' when the 'great and sudden revelation' of Lloyd George's offer to Griffith dawned on the Conservatives. Chamberlain, in particular, was 'disturbed' by its implications, but no one could refute the prime minister's logic.[42]

Lloyd George's arguments carried the day in Cabinet, setting the stage for a series of letters exchanged between the British and Ulster prime ministers during mid-November.[43] The first of these placed two alternatives before Northern Ireland's Cabinet: participation in an all-Ireland Parliament with Belfast's government retaining the powers conferred on it by the 1920 Act, the advantages of lower taxation, a voluntary imperial contribution, and the assurance that trade and commerce between the North and the rest of Ireland would not be hindered. Alternatively, Northern Ireland could maintain its separation from the rest of Ireland, but only at the price of bearing higher taxation, a 'proportionate share' of the imperial debt, and the certain erection of a customs barrier on the Irish frontier. As for the boundary, this question was in either case 'reserved' for further discussion; but it was made clear that 'an amicable settlement' of the issue would be much more likely if the Unionists were willing to participate in a single Irish government.[44]

The response of Craig's Cabinet was unyielding. So far as they were concerned, Unionists had already made the 'supreme sacrifice' by accepting the 1920 Act. Furthermore, negotiations were out of the question so long as the possibility of an all-Ireland Parliament was 'open to discussion'. But Craig and colleagues then tried having it both ways. Although Northern Ireland's territory was deemed to be an 'essential' component of the 1920 Act, the legislation itself was far from sacrosanct. On the contrary, Craig and his colleagues now proposed that Northern Ireland should be granted Dominion status as well. Such a move meant, of course, the end of the United Kingdom. But this was a price

---

42   Jones diary, 10 Nov. 1921, vol. III, p. 159, 161.

43   Cmd 1561: *Correspondence Between His Majesty's Government and the Prime Minister of Northern Ireland Relating to the Proposals for an Irish Settlement*, 1921, Sess. II., i, 83.

44   Ibid., Lloyd George to Craig, 10 Nov. 1921.

Unionists were willing to pay, as they regarded 'the loss of representation at Westminster as a less evil than inclusion in an All-Ireland Parliament'.[45]

Griffith was elated by Craig's reply. Here was proof of 'Ulster's sordidness', all 'for the sake of a lower income tax'. Jones encouraged this thinking, telling the Irish leader that if Lloyd George could rely on the Sinn Féiners' continued support, 'we might have Ulster in before many months had passed'.[46]

Although Craig's arguments found some support within the Coalition, they were soon given short shrift. Lloyd George even enlisted the help of an unlikely ally to support his cause. At a Cabinet meeting on 12 November, he informed his colleagues that Bonar Law was willing to accept a Boundary Commission and, further, that he agreed that the Ulster Unionists must pay the same taxes as those levied in Britain. 'That is coercion of Ulster', Lloyd George observed. 'It is fair but it is fiscal pressure.'[47]

As was so often the case with Lloyd George, this was only half the story. Far from backing Lloyd George's strategy, Bonar Law's point was that if the Unionists could not be won over by the promise of lower taxation, then Irish unity could be achieved only by force or some other form of coercion. That, he would never support.[48] Nevertheless, he made it clear to Craig that he was no more inclined to give the Unionists the 'benefits of both systems' than was Lloyd George. 'As regards the question of the taxation of Ulster', Bonar Law wrote:

> I will repeat the exact conversation between Craig and myself on that subject the first day I saw him. I said to him 'you will be told that the alternative to going into an All-Ireland Parl. is remaining in the U.K. and paying our taxes – what do you say to that?' His reply was 'We would jump at it.' I told him that his reply was very gratifying to me as I could not have undertaken to share in fighting their battle here on any other terms. He said to me that any other position was quite indefensible. They could not say when it is a question of the form of Govt. 'We are part of the U.K. and our right to remain part of it is not diminished because we live in the island of Ireland' and then say when it is a question of taxation 'We are a part of Ireland and must be treated not in the same way as the rest of the U.K. but in the same way as the rest of Ireland.' In other words they cannot claim the privileges (such as they are) of remaining with us and refuse to bear our burdens.[49]

45 Ibid., Craig to Lloyd George, 11 Nov. 1921.
46 Jones diary, 12 Nov. 1921, vol. III, p. 163.
47 Ibid. Worthington-Evans memorandum, SF (B) 25, 12 Nov. 1921, CAB 43/2. Also, see Amery to Worthington-Evans, 22 Nov. 1921, W-E, MSS Eng. hist., c. 910, ff. 209–10.
48 Bonar Law to Croal, 12 Nov. 1921, BL 107/1/83.
49 Bonar Law to Salisbury, 2 Dec. 1921, BL 107/4/17.

Craig and his friends appeared to be trapped. 'I do not know of any explicit pledge that the North should have economic equality with the South', admitted Ronald McNeill. '[W]e have to face the fact that our demand has always been for a "clean cut" out of Home Rule and it may be said against us that if we demand the privileges of remaining in communion – if not union – with England, we must bear our share of the burdens.'[50]

Be that as it may, the Coalitionists themselves were in an equally vulnerable position. At this most delicate moment of the Irish negotiations, the Conservatives were due to hold the annual meeting of their National Unionist Association. For Chamberlain, the circumstances could not have been worse. This occasion would mark his first speech to the party's rank and file as their leader, a speech that would be delivered in of all places, Liverpool – 'the stronghold of Orange Toryism'. Taking full advantage of their good luck, the Die-hards proposed a series of resolutions condemning the government's negotiations with 'the Irish rebel Junta' and vowing opposition to any settlement that did not 'absolutely respect' Ulster's partition from the rest of Ireland. Added to Chamberlain's 'catalogue of troubles' was Bonar Law, 'itching to be back in politics where he is disposed to think that the first place might & ought to be his'. Chamberlain believed that he was fighting for his political life.[51] And not just his alone. Watching from the sidelines, Edwin Montagu wrote: 'I can't say whether the Government will survive or not'.[52]

THE LIVERPOOL CONFERENCE

In the run-up to the Liverpool Conference, the Coalition's opponents believed that their hour, and their man, had finally come. Bonar Law's letter bag was filled with correspondence urging him to rejoin the battle to save Ulster from 'the tender mercies' of the IRA. Initially, this was exactly what he intended to do. 'If L.G. goes on with his present proposals I will oppose them', he told one confidant. More than that, 'I shall try to get the Conservative party to follow me.'[53]

50　McNeill to Hugh Cecil, 19 Nov. 1921, Quickswood Papers, 29/231–2.

51　Austen to Hilda Chamberlain, 13 Nov. 1921, AC 5/1/220. Austen to Neville Chamberlain, same date, NC 1/27/57. NUA Council Report, 16–18 Nov. 1921, NUA 2/2/6.

52　Montagu to Reading, 17 Nov. 1921, IO, MSS Eur. E. 238/3, no. 24.

53　See, e.g., Ormsby-Gore to Bonar Law, 15 Nov. 1921, BL 107/1/68. Bonar Law to Croal, 12 Nov. 1921, BL 107/1/83.

It was all but certain that if the former Tory leader appeared at the Liverpool Conference there would be a stampede of support in his direction. Prior to the conference, Sam Hoare warned Churchill that deep resentments were welling up among Tory MPs. 'Give them a big issue and they will move off in a solid formation. Ulster will give them the issue they want, it may also give them the leader they need.'[54]

But Bonar Law did not lead a revolt at Liverpool; in fact, he did not even attend the conference.

Instead, on 10 November the former Tory leader met with Lloyd George and told him that he could not coerce Ulster and preserve the Coalition at the same time. Bonar Law had another suggestion. 'Don't confine your bullying to Ulster. Try it on the Sinn Feiners too.' Warming to his idea, Bonar Law proposed telling Griffith that, despite their best efforts, the British had found it impossible to win any concessions from Northern Ireland's Cabinet. That being the case, the Southern Irish would be invited to form their own Dominion government with the knowledge that it would be in Ulster's material interest eventually to join with the South.[55]

Two days later, Lloyd George held another private meeting with Griffith. Closeted together at the home of Lloyd George's friend, Philip Sassoon, Griffith was given another, 'hurried' glance at the correspondence between Craig and the British government. Clearly, the Ulster Unionists were refusing all attempts at compromise. Bonar Law, Griffith had been told, was acting behind the scenes to create a crisis that would enable him to 'snatch a majority' from Chamberlain at Liverpool and bring down the Coalition. Lloyd George then solemnly declared that, despite these dangers, his government would refuse Craig's demand for Dominion status and would press ahead with its offer of an all-Ireland Parliament. Craig and his colleagues could vote out of this assembly – but at the price of having a Boundary Commission 'delimit the area' that they governed and with the knowledge that they would then be 'subject to equal financial burdens with England'.[56]

As happened in the run-up to the censure vote, Griffith agreed to Lloyd George's proposal, but only as a tactical manoeuvre designed to show that the Ulster Unionists would refuse any sort of compromise. According to Griffith, both he and Lloyd George believed that the Unionists would turn down either British offer. Once that occurred, Lloyd George vowed to 'fight, summon Parliament, appeal to it against Ulster, dissolve, or pass an Act establishing an All-Ireland Parliament'.[57]

54 Hoare memorandum to Churchill [copy], 12 Nov. 1921, BBK C/307.
55 Bonar Law to Croal, 12 Nov. 1921, BL 107/1/83.
56 Stevenson diary, 14 Nov. 1921, p. 237. Griffith to de Valera, 11, 12 Nov. 1921, DE 2/304/8.
57 Ibid., Griffith to de Valera, 12 Nov. 1921.

A day after his meeting with Lloyd George, the Irish leader was shown a memorandum prepared by Jones summarising this latest discussion. Griffith, it seems, quickly skimmed the document, agreed to its contents, and thought no more of the matter. It was a fatal mistake. Although the document confirmed that Northern Ireland would be subject to British taxation if it opted out of a single Irish state, the Boundary Commission outlined in this memorandum was altogether different from the one he had now discussed with the British on several occasions. As described here, the tribunal would 'revise' the Irish boundary and would 'adjust the line both by inclusion and exclusion'. In other words, Craig and his colleagues could expect to gain as well as lose territory in this process. That was a far cry from a commission set up to 'delimit' the six-county state.[58]

For a man who had made his livelihood with words (he was a journalist), it is hard to fathom how Griffith could have overlooked so radical a change. In his haste – Griffith did not sign or even initial the document – he may have believed that Jones's memorandum merely clarified his promise not to repudiate the Boundary Commission proposal while Coalition Tories faced their opponents at the Liverpool Conference. Alternatively, he may have decided that the Commission's frame of reference really did not matter. It was, after all, a bargaining ploy, one which both he and Lloyd George agreed the Unionists were certain to reject. In that case, as Lloyd George himself put it, the Coalition government would push through a bill creating a single Irish state or dissolve Parliament and bring on a general election.[59]

Whatever the explanation, Griffith had foolishly given hostages to fortune. With the Jones memorandum in hand, Lloyd George began to move towards the position advocated by Bonar Law. This soon would be evident in the draft Treaty sent to the Irish delegates a day before the Liverpool Conference was due to vote on the Die-hard resolutions. Meanwhile, Jones's memorandum was shown to Coalition Conservatives in a light very different from what Griffith thought it to mean. According to Chamberlain, it signified that the Irish would not break off negotiations over partition. Bonar Law was also reassured that his Ulster kinsmen would not be sacrificed for an Irish settlement. Without their former chief, the Die-hard threat at Liverpool began to disintegrate.[60]

However, the overwhelming defeat of the Die-hard motion condemning the Irish talks 'was far from being a vote of confidence in the P.M.' The situation, Lord Derby warned Lloyd George, looked good only 'on the

58 Memorandum, 13 Nov. 1921, LG F/181/4/1/218.
59 Griffith to de Valera, 12 Nov. 1921, DE 2/304/8.
60 Austen to Ivy Chamberlain, 13, 19, 23 Nov. 1921, AC 6/1/463, 466, and 470.

surface'. Underneath, there was 'a good bit of disquiet' among the party faithful, and this disquiet would erupt at the mere hint of a 'breach of faith' regarding Ulster.[61]

TREATY TALKS: THE FINAL PHASE

The outcome of the Liverpool Conference confirmed Lloyd George in his determination to follow Bonar Law's advice that he 'bully' the Irish delegates into an agreement. On 16 November Griffith and his colleagues were handed a proposed draft treaty. Ireland would be firmly situated within the British empire as a Dominion and would allow the Royal Navy to maintain bases on its soil to guarantee British security. Craig's government would have up to one year to opt out of the new Irish state. If it did so, 'the provisions of the Government of Ireland Act, 1920, . . . shall continue to be of full force and effect' – code words meaning that the six counties would pay British rates of taxation and a proportion of the imperial debt. At the same time, a Boundary Commission would determine a new Irish frontier. The sole criterion for any border change would be 'the wishes of the inhabitants'.[62]

This draft serves to confirm the later testimony of one of the Irish delegation's principal secretaries. According to John Chartres, Griffith's willingness to accept Dominion status was 'expressly contingent' on the agreement also ending the 'exclusion of large bodies of Nationalist Irishmen' from the Irish state. 'No one ever mentioned "minor rectifications" of the existing boundary', Chartres wrote, and he rejected claims that Griffith would have made even a tentative offer to recognise the crown in return for so minor a commitment.[63]

To support his assertion, Chartres pointed to the 16 November proposal. 'In that draft', he pointed out, 'the wishes of the inhabitants are made subject in the proviso to *NO LIMITATION WHATEVER*. There is not a word about economic or geographical considerations.' Chartres continued:

> The limiting words were introduced afterwards in case the Boundary Commission should feel itself obliged to transfer small, distant, non-contiguous districts, such as the Glens of Antrim. The Glens of Antrim were mentioned by Lloyd George (pointing to a map) to illustrate possible exceptions to the general rule. On Mr

61 Jones to Hankey, 25 Nov. 1921, CAB 63/34. Derby to Lloyd George, 18 Nov. 1921, LG F/14/5/33.
62 SF (B) 46, 16 Nov. 1921, CAB 43/2. Liddell's Notes, 18 Nov. 1921, CAB 21/253/6.
63 Chartres to Mulcahy, 5 Feb. 1924, D/T, S 1801/E. 'Note on the Boundary Negotiations', 19 Oct. 1924, F.L.K., de Valera Papers, File No. 354.

Collins acquiescing in this, Mr Lloyd George said, 'Then there will be no difficulty about the wording.' The limiting words were inserted simply and solely to provide for such a case as the Glens of Antrim, Mr Lloyd George himself raising and stating the point in the presence of all the British none of whom made any demur, correction, exception or addition.[64]

Nearly a week elapsed before the Irish responded to the 16 November offer with a proposal for External Association; a complete breakdown of the talks was only narrowly averted by a meeting of the principal players.[65] This episode set the tempo for a series of nerve-wracking back and forth encounters that lasted until the Treaty was finally signed. The nadir occurred during a disastrous confrontation on 4 December when Griffith, along with Barton and Gavan Duffy, once again proposed External Association as the basis for a settlement. No new proposals were put forward concerning the Ulster question, justifying a British belief that partition was no longer an issue.[66] Instead, the impasse was reached on the crown and allegiance. 'Our difficulty', Duffy admitted, 'is to come inside the Empire'.[67]

'In that case it is war', declared one of the British negotiators, bringing the discussion to an abrupt end.[68]

It is commonly acknowledged that at this juncture Tom Jones's intervention was decisive. The result was a personal meeting between Lloyd George and Collins on the morning of the 5th. With characteristic bluntness, Collins said that he was 'perfectly dissatisfied' with the British proposals and especially 'with the position as regards the North East'. Shortly afterwards, Collins wrote:

> He [Lloyd George] remarked that I myself pointed out on a previous occasion that the North would be forced economically to come in. I assented but I said the position was so serious . . . that for my part I was anxious to secure a definite reply from Craig and his Colleagues, and that I was as agreeable to a reply rejecting as accepting. In view of the former we would save Tyrone and Fermanagh, parts of Derry, Armagh and Down by the Boundary Commission . . . .[69]

64   Ibid., 'Note'.
65   SF (B) 47, 22 Nov. 1921, CAB 43/2. File No. 22/N/1, 23 Nov. 1921, CAB 21/208.
66   C 89(21), 5 Dec. 1921, CAB 23/27.
67   File No. 22/N/1, 4 Dec. 1921, CAB 21/208.
68   Ibid.
69   Collins memorandum, 5 Dec. 1921, F.L.K., de Valera Papers, File No. 1327.

This encounter was just enough to keep the negotiations going. Collins walked away from the meeting under the impression that Britain's prime minister agreed with his assessment of what would result from the proposed Ulster clauses. A couple of hours later, however, Lloyd George was saying something quite different. In this instance, he assured his Cabinet colleagues that the Boundary Commission would provide for nothing more than 'a readjustment of the boundaries'. Nor was anything said about Ulster being 'forced economically to come in' to an all-Ireland Parliament.[70]

Later that same day, the two sides met again. This time Collins was joined by Griffith and Barton; Lloyd George had assembled Chamberlain, Birkenhead, and Churchill. Griffith again tried to make Sinn Féin's acceptance of Dominion status conditional on Craig's government accepting Irish unity. Lloyd George refused and accused the Irish delegates of breaking faith, producing as proof the 13 November memorandum.

In the most widely disseminated account of this meeting, Griffith then replied: 'I said I would not let you down on that, and I won't.'[71]

However, Austen Chamberlain's notes show that there was much more to this exchange than is implied by Lord Longford's account. When challenged about his earlier acceptance, Griffith said to Lloyd George: 'Then in that case, if you stand by the Boundary Commission' – and, by implication, their other agreements regarding Ulster – 'I stand by you.' Britain's prime minister agreed.[72]

Then followed Griffith's more celebrated remark, after which Lloyd George's colleagues said that they too 'stood by the proposal for a Boundary Commission'. Before leaving the issue altogether, the Irish delegates insisted on one last concession. Instead of allowing Northern Ireland six months to a year to decide whether or not to join the new Irish state, they asked that Craig's government 'should give its answer at once', i.e. within a month of Parliament's approval of the Treaty. Griffith and his colleagues had good reason to insist on this final demand, believing, as they did, that it was likely that Bonar Law might be prime minister within the year. In that case, the Treaty's Ulster clauses might 'be put into the waste paper basket with all other promises'.[73]

Having satisfied himself on these points, Griffith announced that he was ready to sign the Treaty. But he was speaking for himself only, not for his colleagues. This final snag prompted Lloyd George's controversial threat to declare war – 'and war within 3 days' – unless the agreement was signed by all of the Irish delegates.[74]

---

70 Ibid. C 89(21), 5 Dec. 1921, CAB 23/27.   71 Pakenham, *Peace by Ordeal*, p. 237.
72 Chamberlain's Notes, 5 Dec. 1921, CAB 21/253/1.
73 Ibid. Sturgis diary, 6 Dec. 1921, PRO 30/59/5.   74 Ibid., Chamberlain's Notes.

Others have recorded the emotional, sometimes bitter struggle that ensued between the Irish delegates and the final dramatic moments before the agreement was finally signed in the early hours of 6 December.[75] The 'Articles of Agreement for a Treaty', or the 'Treaty' as most were soon calling it, was a richly complex document, intricate in its simplicity. The first 10 of its 18 articles spoke of Ireland as a whole, granting to it 'the same constitutional status' as the other Dominions of the British Empire.[76] Not least, the Irish Free State, as it was to be called, was granted full fiscal autonomy. Article 5 pledged the Irish to assume a share of the United Kingdom's debt up to the granting of independence. The exact figure would be settled by arbitration.

These measures alone signalled a fundamental change. Where the two Irish states were treated as equals under the 1920 Act, these clauses placed the Ulster Unionists at a decided disadvantage should they insist on remaining outside the Irish Dominion.

This set the stage for Articles 11 through 15, what became known as the Treaty's 'Ulster clauses'. Both of the first two of these articles declared that the 'provisions of the Government of Ireland Act of 1920 . . . shall, so far as they relate to Northern Ireland, continue to be of full force and effect'. Later arguments over these clauses have focused almost exclusively on the second half of Article 12, which established the Boundary Commission. Article 11 and the first half of Article 12 have been overlooked.[77] But in the view of British civil servants familiar with the negotiations, the financial obligations confirmed in these two articles posed at least as big a threat to Craig's government as the Boundary Commission.

According to a later Treasury memorandum, the two articles made formal 'a pledge [that] was given by H.M.G. to the Southern Ireland representatives' not to extend the Ulster government's powers in any way, shape, or form. 'The reason of course was obvious':

> namely to offer as much inducement as possible to the North to come in. If she could hope for a gradual extension of her autonomy . . . naturally she would be less disposed to abandon her independence.[78]

75   Pakenham, *Peace by Ordeal*, pp. 243–9. T. P. Coogan, *Michael Collins: A Biography* (London, 1990), pp. 274–6. Churchill, *World Crisis*: v, pp. 321–2.

76   It has been suggested that in these articles 'the prospect of reunification was more imaginary than real'. See Fanning, *Independent Ireland*, p. 23. Ulster Unionists felt rather differently. See Craig to Lloyd George, SF (B) 42, 14 Dec. 1921, CAB 43/2; and Hugh de F. Montgomery to Ross, 17 Dec. 1921, Montgomery Papers, D/627/439/26.

77   See, e.g., Lee, *Ireland*, pp. 148–9.

78   Waterfield to Upcott, 6 Apr. 1923, T 160/163/F.6282.

Explained another Treasury official, it was because of the 1920 Act's restrictive financial provisions 'that the Free State representatives secured the insertion of Article 11', and any 'concession which makes separate existence more attractive to Northern Ireland is really a breach of this condition of the Treaty'.[79]

These interpretations, along with a memorandum written by Lionel Curtis, explain the wording of Lloyd George's letter to Craig which accompanied a copy of the Treaty. The letter, in confirming Northern Ireland's right to opt out of an all-Ireland Parliament, explicitly told Craig that the price of such a decision would be to 'share the rights and obligations of Great Britain'.[80]

If these inducements were not enough to bring about unity, Article 13 ensured that Dublin nevertheless would have a voice in the North's affairs through the Council of Ireland. No such reciprocal right for Belfast remained. The last two articles provided for the North's entry into the Free State, guaranteeing to its government a range of safeguards concerning patronage, taxation, trade and, even, the right to establish and control its own military force.

Almost without exception, the British press greeted news of the settlement as an unrivalled triumph.[81] Beyond Ireland itself, the Treaty vindicated a much broader policy of appeasement. 'Nothing henceforth can be as it was before', the *Manchester Guardian* confidently predicted. In the Treaty's wake, not only would appeasement 'make itself felt far more widely' across the British empire; it had 'lessons also for [British] policy in Europe'.[82] For a man already casting an eye in that direction, this was music to Lloyd George's ears.

An ocean away, one absent member of the Cabinet was rather more restrained in his appraisal of the Irish agreement. Arthur Balfour conceded that there was much to be said for the Treaty, not least that it would 'make an immense difference' to Anglo-American relations. But, he told his sister, 'I cannot help feeling a little uneasy about Ulster, – I trust without good reason.'[83]

79 Upcott to Snowden, 30 Jan. 1924, T 160/131/F.4855/02/1.

80 Curtis to Devonshire, 17 Nov. 1922, CO 739/8/56786. Lloyd George to Craig, 5 Dec. 1921, LG F/11/3/25.

81 'Downing St. Drama of the Negotiations', *Daily Chronicle*; and 'A Free State', *Pall Mall and Globe*, both dated 7 Dec. 1921. 'Towards Irish Peace', *The Times*; and, for a restrained appraisal, 'The Settlement', *Daily Telegraph*, both dated 8 Dec. 1921.

82 'The New Peace', *Manchester Guardian*, 8 Dec. 1921. Just days after the Treaty was signed, one leading journal advocated an appeasement policy in all but name in an article foreshadowing many of the crises that were to plague Europe for the next 20 years. See 'From the Old Policy to the New', *The Nation*, 10 Dec. 1921.

83 A. J. to Alice Balfour, 9 Dec. 1921, AJB-S, GD 433/2/76, Reel 8.

Balfour's misgivings did not begin to compare with the unease felt by his friends in Northern Ireland. The predominant reaction of the Unionist press to news of the Treaty was 'one of profound astonishment', which soon turned to anger. 'Ulster has been betrayed', declared the voice of Unionism in County Tyrone, by that 'Judas Iscariot' – Lloyd George. This same newspaper was even more scathing, if that is possible, when it came to Chamberlain and Birkenhead, the last of whom was 'the most despicable of all'.[84] This sense of betrayal carried right the way across the Unionist community. A friend told Lady Spender that

> it was the saddest day of her life. 'England *doesn't want* us,' she said, with a depth of bitterness I cannot convey. . . . And now we know that worse is to come, and further pledges are to be broken, for two of the six counties may be taken from us – Tyrone and Fermanagh.[85]

Craig, 'very suspicious of [the] Boundary clauses and financial arrangements', rushed to London where he conferred with Lloyd George and Chamberlain on the 9th. Accounts of what took place vary wildly. Lloyd George emerged from the discussions telling friends that Craig was ready to consider Sinn Féin's proposals for an all-Ireland settlement. According to Lady Craig, her husband said nothing of the kind; far from it, he insisted that 'on no account' would he give up portions of the six counties. Craig further demanded that the Treaty's financial arrangements should 'be drastically amended'. She also wrote that Lloyd George assured Craig that 'mere rectifications of the Boundary' were all that was envisaged in Article 12, and that any territorial changes would involve 'give and take on both sides'.[86]

It is clear, however, that Craig toyed with the idea of appointing a Boundary Commissioner – provided that the British government would guarantee 'full compensation' to any Unionist who was transferred to the Free State.[87] Two peers (Lords Dunedin and Clyde) were approached about chairing the Commission, either of whom, Bonar Law hinted, 'would be good'.[88]

84 'Belfast Uneasiness', *Irish Independent*, 8 Dec. 1921. 'The Agreement with Sinn Fein'; and 'Ulster Betrayed', *Tyrone Constitution*, 9, 16 Dec. 1921.

85 Lady Spender's diary, 16 Dec. 1921, D/1633/2/25.

86 Lady Craig's diary, 7, 9 Dec. 1921, D/1415/B/38. Jones diary, 9 Dec. 1921, vol. III, p. 186. Also, see Craig to Lloyd George, SF (B) 42, 14 Dec. 1921, CAB 43/2.

87 Craig to Chamberlain [not sent], 14–15[?] Dec. 1921, PRONI, CAB/9Z/3/1.

88 Bonar Law to Lloyd George, 19 Dec. 1921, LG F/31/1/60.

Meanwhile, an unnamed person was approached to represent Northern Ireland on the tribunal. With either Dunedin or Clyde as chairman, Charles Craig told his brother, 'and with our friend as our Commissioner, nothing very serious could happen to us'.[89] But Craig was not convinced. 'There is nothing in the terms of the treaty', he pointed out to Bonar Law, 'to show that the Boundary Commission must necessarily limit its functioning' to 'little re-adjustments'.[90]

Any last thoughts that Craig had about going along with the Ulster clauses were erased by Lloyd George's performance during the Treaty debates in the House of Commons. His address, especially on the 'vexed question of Ulster', was vintage Lloyd George, giving with one hand what he took away with the other.

'[N]ever for a moment' had the government sought to coerce Ulster – but, that 'did not preclude us from endeavouring to persuade Ulster to come into an All-Ireland Parliament.'

A 're-adjustment of boundaries' was all that was envisaged when the Treaty's negotiators drafted Article 12. On the other hand, there was 'no doubt – certainly since the Act of 1920 – that the majority of the people of two counties prefer being with their Southern neighbours to being in the Northern Parliament.'

Just as it would be wrong to coerce Ulster, the government did not 'believe in Ulster coercing other units.'

Before sitting down, Lloyd George also confirmed John Chartres's later assertion that the economic and geographical qualification in the boundary clause was inserted solely to prevent the transfer of isolated areas such as the Glens of Antrim.[91]

The speech immediately set off alarm bells. Craig sent a threatening letter to Chamberlain insisting on the right of Unionists to arm themselves 'forthwith'. As matters stood, he warned, many of his followers now believed that 'violence is the only language understood by Mr. Lloyd George and his Ministers'.[92] Chamberlain flatly rejected Craig's allegations that the Unionists had been betrayed. They had only themselves to blame if they were presented with a *fait accompli*, he reminded Ulster's premier, because Craig and his colleagues had refused to join the Treaty negotiations unless an all-Ireland Parliament was ruled out of the discussions. If the British 'had accepted your condition for attending the Conference', Chamberlain pointed out, 'there would have been no Conference for you to attend'.[93]

89 Charles to James Craig, 21 Dec. 1921, PRONI, CAB/9Z/3/1.

90 Craig to Bonar Law, 13 Dec. 1921, BL 107/1/93.

91 *HC Deb*, vol. 149, cols 38–42, 14 Dec. 1921.

92 Craig to Chamberlain, 15 Dec. 1921, AC 31/2/48.

93 Chamberlain to Craig, 16 Dec. 1921, PRONI, CAB/9Z/3/1.

In any event, the Tory leader assured Craig, the British had not 'over-looked your interest'. It was obvious that any boundary revision could not 'be carried out by Counties as a whole'. To back up his argument, Chamberlain cited Bonar Law's speech in the Commons only the day before, which 'quite correctly interpreted the spirit and the method' in which the Boundary Commission would work.[94] Indeed, to the surprise of many, certainly to the chagrin of quite a few, Bonar Law endorsed the Treaty when he spoke in the House of Commons. Notwithstanding his 'serious objection' to Article 12, he was convinced that the Ulster Unionists had nothing to fear from the agreement.[95]

Lloyd George, meanwhile, quickly back-peddled from the controversial statements made during the first day of the Treaty debates. Faced with accusations that he had promised Tyrone and Fermanagh to the Irish negotiators, he declared that no deals had been struck. He also now implied that the economic and geographic qualifications in Article 12 would sufficiently curb the Boundary Commission's reach.[96]

The sharp exchanges displayed in the Commons were more acrimonious still when debate on the Treaty switched to the House of Lords. 'What a fool I was', Lord Carson bitterly declared. 'I was only a puppet, and so was Ulster, and so was Ireland, in the political game that was to get the Conservative Party into power.' Interestingly, in his catalogue of charges against the Treaty, Carson did not address himself to the Boundary Commission. Instead, he zeroed in on the agreement's financial clauses which he believed to be the greater threat to his Ulster followers.[97]

Birkenhead's response, in which he likened Carson's speech to the ravings of an 'hysterical school-girl', was withering. Turning on his old friend, he rebutted Carson's accusation that the government was attempting to coerce Northern Ireland. Was it coercion, he asked, to insist that Ulstermen pay the same rate of income tax as other British subjects if they remained in the United Kingdom? Surely not. '[W]ith the single exception of the Boundaries Commission', Birkenhead declared, the Ulster Unionists retained all the powers granted to them by the 1920 Act.[98]

Both houses of Parliament voted for the Treaty by lopsided majorities on 16 December. In the Commons, 401 MPs supported the agreement; 58 were opposed. In the Lords, 166 peers voted for the Treaty; 47 members voted against. Three days later, Parliament was prorogued until the end of January.[99]

94   Ibid.

95   Salisbury to Bonar Law, 13 Dec. 1921, BL 107/1/92. Sturgis diary, 17 Dec. 1921, PRO 30/59/5. *HC Deb*, vol. 149, cols 196–209, 15 Dec. 1921.

96   Ibid., *HC Deb*, cols 314–15, 16 Dec. 1921.   97   *HL Deb*, vol. 48, cols 36–53, 14 Dec. 1921.

98   Ibid., cols 196–213, 16 Dec. 1921.   99   *Annual Register: 1921*, p. 146.

While these debates were taking place in London, a longer drama was being played out in Dublin. Others have explored Dáil Éireann's Treaty debates in such detail that it would be superfluous to cover them here.[100] And, as has already been pointed out, the agreement's Ulster clauses played but a minor role in these debates. Irish unity hardly rated as a concern to the Treaty's critics, so consumed were they by hatred of the oath of fidelity. 'The difficulty', de Valera admitted during one private session, 'is not the Ulster question'.[101]

Nevertheless, the Dáil's dilatory handling of the agreement dashed Griffith's hopes of settling the Ulster Question in the near term. His willingness to sign the Treaty was based in part on Lloyd George's pledge to submit the agreement to Parliament 'as early as possible'. Griffith, in turn, planned to call the Dáil 'within a week' to have the Treaty ratified.[102] Instead, nearly three weeks elapsed between the Dáil's opening debate on the agreement and its acceptance of the Treaty by the slender margin of 64 votes to 57. The result, Austen Chamberlain ruefully admitted, 'does not promise any too well for the future'.[103]

Lloyd George was 'furious' when the Dáil failed to come to a quick decision on the Treaty. With his Irish triumph in hand, he wanted to call a snap general election to lay the foundation for his long-delayed Centre Party. But those plans could not be advanced while the decision in Dublin was in doubt. 'It has only lately dawned on him', said one observer, 'that the signing in London hasn't disposed of the matter.'[104]

'GROPING IN THE DARK'

The Irish Treaty was the crowning achievement of Lloyd George's post-war administration. 'Nothing has happened since the Armistice', *The Nation* told its readers, 'that is comparable to this act in importance.' The political ramifications were enormous. Many saw the Treaty not merely as a 'vindication' of coalition government; they also saw it as the 'funeral of Unionism'. In the Commons debate on the Treaty, wrote one reporter, 'the listener could hear the hollow thud of the earth upon the coffin'.[105]

100 See, e.g., M. Hopkinson, *Green Against Green: The Irish Civil War* (Dublin, 1988), pp. 34–40.

101 *Dáil Deb II: Private Sess.*, pp. 153, 15 Dec. 1921.

102 Chamberlain's Notes, 5 Dec. 1921, CAB 21/253/1.

103 *Dáil Treaty Deb*, pp. 345–6, 7 Jan. 1922. Austen to Ivy Chamberlain, 8 Jan. 1922, AC 6/1/474.

104 Sturgis diary, 20 Dec. 1921, PRO 30/59/5.

105 'Events of the Week', *The Nation*, 10 Dec. 1921. 'The Peace', *Evening Standard*, 7 Dec. 1921. 'The Funeral of Unionism', *Westminster Gazette*, 17 Dec. 1921. Carson agreed. See *HL Deb*, vol. 48, col. 36, 14 Dec. 1921.

And that was why so many Tories detested the agreement.

At first glance, the biggest losers to come out of the Treaty negotiations were the Ulster Unionists and their Die-hard allies. Seeing his government placed on an unequal footing with its Southern counterpart, Craig spent the last days of 1921 fending off Northern Irish businessmen who, 'afraid of their pockets', thought 'they would be better under Dublin than Westminster'.[106] Even if Belfast's government could withstand the economic pressure designed to bring it into an all-Ireland Parliament, there was still the Boundary Commission, whose decision would be 'a matter of life and death' to Unionists.[107]

But the reality was that Craig and his colleagues were in a much stronger position than had been true only a month before. To retain the loyalty of Tory backbenchers during the Commons censure debate on 31 October, Lloyd George gave in to a demand made by Ulster Unionist MPs for the transfer of executive power to the Northern Ireland government.[108] On 22 November a range of executive functions were handed over to the Belfast ministries, further entrenching partition. Most importantly, Craig's government was given 'unfettered control' of law and order and the administration of justice within the six counties, including supervision of the Special Constabulary. This decision was taken even though it was well known within government circles that relations between Northern Catholics and the Specials were 'extremely bitter' and likely to cause trouble. As Mark Sturgis predicted, the government's decision now made 'Ulster the danger point' in the Irish conflict.[109]

It is against these concrete gains that the Treaty's transitory promises must be weighed. At the outset, it should be said that Griffith and his colleagues were sent to London to do the impossible: to secure Irish unity and, if not a republic, then a form of government with greater independence than that of a Dominion. This is not the place to renew the debate over External Association. Rather, the question here is did Griffith and Collins really believe that the Treaty's Ulster clauses would bring about Irish unity in the near term?

Most certainly, the answer is yes. At their meeting with the British negotiators on the afternoon of 5 December, both men pressed Lloyd George to ask Craig whether or not he would join an all-Ireland Parliament. 'It might help us even if it was a negative', Collins said, as this would mean that they

---

106 Lady Craig's diary, 20 Dec. 1921, D/1415/B/38. Also, see Fawsitt memorandum, 14 Dec. 1921, DE 2/478.

107 *HC Deb*, vol. 149, cols 56–7, 14 Dec. 1921.

108 CP 3369, 6 Oct. 1921, CAB 24/128. Charles to James Craig, 28 Oct. 1921, PRONI, PM/1/45/2. *HC Deb*, vol. 147, cols 1414–15, 31 Oct. 1921. Birkenhead to Lloyd George, 1 Nov. 1921, LG F/4/7/32.

109 'Ulster Special Constabulary', Cope note to Jones, ? Nov. 1921, CAB 21/243(II). Sturgis diary, 14 Nov. 1921, PRO 30/59/5.

would 'have a Boundary Commission at once'.[110] Because reunification was not achieved, Griffith and Collins have since been accused of too readily assuming that Article 12 meant the same thing to both sides.[111]

But according to Lloyd George, it did. Writing many years later, he argued that in such disputes the 'guiding principle' of peace should be the allocation of national groups 'to their motherlands'. This 'human criterion', he held, 'should have precedence over considerations of strategy or economics or communications, which can usually be adjusted by other means.'[112] If this was true for other parts of Europe, how was the Irish situation any different?

Moreover, in the Irish case, the Boundary Commission did not stand on its own. Both Griffith and Collins were sure that Craig's government would find itself slowly strangled by the financial restrictions of the 1920 Act, and de Valera, by accepting these articles of the Treaty, seems to have agreed. This would explain why so little was said about the Ulster clauses in the Dáil debates. Both British and Irish governments were pledged not to coerce the Ulster Unionists. In fact, these clauses did exactly that. They were 'a form more subtle than coercion by brute force, yet coercion none the less'.[113]

This inescapably leads back to the promises made, or not made, by Lloyd George. It is tempting to write off his handling of the Treaty negotiations as crafty at best and, at worst, 'an offence against the light of nations'.[114] But judgments such as these have been made too easily and, anyway, they fail to take account of the state of British politics at the time. It should be remembered that Lloyd George had decided to negotiate with Sinn Féin for a number of reasons. Beset on all sides by threats to his government, his aim was to use an Irish agreement first to neutralise his opponents, then as a stepping-stone to a new general election, which would itself lead to the creation of his Centre Party. Once he realised that he could not achieve Irish unity, he looked for the next best thing.

This helps to explain his sudden willingness to drop the goal of an all-Ireland Parliament and to switch the pressure he had applied to the Ulster Unionists onto Griffith and his colleagues. As was pointed out earlier, the details of the Irish agreement were not important to Lloyd George. 'We are after a settlement', he reminded his colleagues, 'that [is] our objective'.[115]

On at least one front, Lloyd George scored a clear-cut victory. From his left, Ireland was one topic on which both Labour and Wee Free Liberals could successfully attack the Coalition. But, Lloyd George said triumphantly, 'we've

---

110 Chamberlain's Notes, 5 Dec. 1921, CAB 21/253.   111 See, e.g., Lee, *Ireland*, pp. 52–3.

112 D. Lloyd George, *The Truth About the Peace Treaties*: vol. I (London, 1938), pp. 40–6.

113 *Dáil Deb II: Private Sess.*, p. 153, 15 Dec. 1921. 'The Provisional Agreement', *Morning Post*, 7 Dec. 1921.

114 Pakenham, *Peace by Ordeal*, p. 259.   115 Jones diary, 14 Nov. 1921, vol. III, p. 164.

got rid of it'.[116] Carson was another casualty. His intemperate opposition to the Treaty accelerated his political eclipse, so much so that one former colleague was forced to conclude that Carson was doing 'a lot of harm' to the Unionist cause.[117]

None the less, the British politician who was to pay the highest price for the Irish Treaty turned out to be Lloyd George himself. During the Irish negotiations, he more than once lived up to his own definition of the 'extraordinary man', extricating himself time and again by doing the 'daring and unexpected'.[118] But in the process, Lloyd George justified the worst suspicions about himself. The Irish Treaty was very much his own creation, and thus was a reflection of him at his best and at his absolute worst.

These suspicions were confirmed by Lloyd George's performance during the Treaty debates. The result was 'a strained atmosphere all round', especially on the Conservative backbenches. 'Half are dissatisfied with Austen', Freddie Guest reported, and few believed that the Treaty had any real chance of success. The only thing stopping a full-fledged revolt was the absence of a leader of 'sufficient standing'.[119]

Yet, that was no longer true. Despite repeated denials, Bonar Law had emerged as the unofficial leader of the Die-hard movement. Even if he still sat on the backbenches, his 'designs', as one reporter put it, 'are on the command' of the Conservative Party.[120]

Earlier in the year, Tom Jones had suggested to Lloyd George that 'if he settled Ireland he might be satisfied and "go to Heaven,"'. But retirement was not for Lloyd George. 'There is still Europe', he told Jones. With Ireland at last 'settled', he was now making plans for a 'Conference on the economic world outlook'.[121] The truth, of course, was that he had not settled Ireland, nor had he conjured it out of existence. Bonar Law recognised this, even if Lloyd George did not. 'It is absurd to think we have settled the Irish Question', he told the Commons. On the contrary, Bonar Law saw 'terrible difficulties' ahead.[122]

Mark Sturgis called the Dáil's vote in favour of the Treaty 'another milestone' in settling the Irish conflict. But, he wrote, 'if Ireland – or England – expects that the Golden Age is dawning I hope they won't be too roughly disillusioned. It is a huge gamble and we are groping in the dark.'[123]

116 Ibid., 9 Dec. 1921, p. 187.   117 Long to Bonar Law, 6 Feb. 1922, BL 107/2/9.
118 Riddell diary, 3 April 1919, *Intimate Diary*, p. 45.
119 Guest to Churchill, 14 Dec. 1921, WSC 2/118/66.
120 'Comments', *New Statesman*, 3 Dec. 1921.
121 Jones to Bonar Law, 22 July 1921, BL 107/1/46. Jones to Hankey, 6 Dec. 1921, CAB 63/34.
122 *HC Deb*, vol. 149, col. 208, 15 Dec. 1921.   123 Sturgis diary, 7 Jan. 1922, PRO 30/59/5.

THREE

THE CHURCHILL DISPENSATION

Then came the Great War. Every institution, almost, in the world was strained. Great empires have been overturned. The whole map of Europe has been changed. The position of countries has been violently altered. The modes of thoughts of men, the whole outlook on affairs, the grouping of parties, all have encountered violent and tremendous changes in the deluge of the world. But, as the deluge subsides and the waters fall short we see the dreary steeples of Fermanagh and Tyrone emerging once again. The integrity of their quarrel is one of few institutions that has been unaltered in the cataclysm which has swept the world.

WINSTON CHURCHILL[1]

—

In December 1921 Lloyd George stood at the summit of his post-war premiership. Accolades for his Irish settlement flowed in from every nation. 'Even the French', Maurice Hankey reported from the Washington Naval Conference, 'crowded round with tributes'.[2] Bonar Law's earlier prediction that Lloyd George could be prime minister for life looked as if it might be true, after all. Much as Beatrice Webb detested Lloyd George, she too agreed that he had 'revolutionised the political situation'. With the Irish Treaty in his pocket, he could now call a general election and romp home with 'a secure majority of personal followers' leaving his critics in the dust.[3] Then, at long last, he could build his Centre Party.

But instead of going from strength to strength, the last ten months of the Coalition government were to be punctuated by a succession of crises in which, more often than not, Ireland was the source of trouble. Lloyd George's plans for a snap general election had to be delayed and then finally abandoned in the face of stubborn Conservative opposition. Neville Chamberlain was far from being the only Tory MP who was determined not to be led into the next election by that 'dirty little Welsh attorney'. Nor would Chamberlain fight a

1   *HC Deb*, vol. 150, col. 1270, 16 Feb. 1922.
2   Hankey to Lloyd George, 9 Dec. 1921, CAB 63/34.
3   Webb diary, 7 Dec. 1921, 4 Jan. 1922, vol. 36, 3871–2, 3881.

campaign based on an Irish policy which was 'not yet settled' and which Conservatives supported 'very reluctantly'.[4]

Once the Treaty election was abandoned, Lloyd George turned his back on Ireland to embark on a series of international conferences aimed at restoring Europe's pre-war prosperity. '[A]ll his hopes are concentrated on Genoa', wrote Lord Riddell, about one such conference.[5] Irish affairs were turned over to the Colonial Office and to a Cabinet committee chaired by Churchill, where they could absorb his boundless energy.[6]

Far from proving to be an asset, the Treaty settlement turned out to be something of a liability for the Coalition, not least among Conservatives. The Anglo-Irish War did not end so much as degenerate into a series of violent clashes within Northern Ireland and along the Irish frontier. By June 1922 Irish Nationalists and Ulster Unionists would be in a virtual state of war with one another. Only the advent of civil war in the South between pro- and anti-Treatyites would prevent the resumption of full-scale hostilities between Britain and the IRA.

These events have been explored many times, elsewhere.[7] The purpose here is to examine how the Treaty settlement began to unravel as Lloyd George and his colleagues found themselves in an increasingly untenable situation. Both the Treaty and the Coalition's deteriorating position reflected and, in the process, altered the other. Just as mounting chaos in Ireland accelerated the Coalition's demise, so the government's increasing instability forced its leaders slowly to back away from inducements in the Treaty that were supposed to bring about Irish reunification.

Of all these men, no British politician was more important to the conduct of Irish affairs during the last ten months of the Lloyd George government than was Winston Churchill. This period of time coincided with the beginning of what would be Churchill's long trek from the Liberal Party back to the Conservatives. The decisions he took on Irish policy were bound to be affected by this journey and by his isolated position in British politics.

Churchill's efforts, in any case, would not be enough to save the Coalition government. Looking back many years later, Leo Amery recalled that with each new incident in Ireland Tory MPs felt a mounting 'sense of shame and indignation' that they had ever allowed themselves to be persuaded to support the Treaty.[8] Far from fading away, Ireland was the thunder of a storm gathering

---

4   Neville to Ida Chamberlain, 7 Jan. 1922, NC 18/1/333.

5   Riddell diary, 23 Mar. 1922, in G. Riddell, *The Riddell Diaries: 1908–1923*, J. M. McEwen, ed. (London, 1986), pp. 366–7.

6   PGI 1, 21 Dec. 1921, CAB 27/154.

7   See, e.g., Curran, *Irish Free State*, and Hopkinson, *Green Against Green*.

8   L. S. Amery, *My Political Life*, vol. II: *War and Peace, 1914–1929* (London, 1958), p. 231.

just beyond the horizon. The rumble of discontent over the Irish settlement was a warning of what was to come when the storm finally hit, sweeping Lloyd George from power forever.

AMBIGUITIES IN THE TREATY

A week after Dáil Éireann voted for the Treaty, the Southern Ireland Parliament created by the 1920 Act met to elect a Provisional Government to administer Ireland until the Free State formally came into being. It then dispersed, never to sit again. Two days later, Collins, as head of the Provisional Government, formally took possession of Dublin Castle and the British Army began its withdrawal from the 26 counties. Here was an 'outward and visible sign that British rule was indeed at an end'.[9] Already, though, there were problems with the agreement. It was clear that the British and the Irish interpreted the Treaty differently and that their disagreements centred, not surprisingly, on Ulster.

As Sir James Masterton-Smith, the Colonial Office's chief civil servant, explained it, the matter boiled down to a distinction between two words. The Irish were under the impression that the British Parliament's December vote on the Treaty had 'ratified' the agreement, when in fact it had merely been 'approved'. Ratification of the Treaty would come later with the simultaneous ratification of the Irish Free State Constitution, a process that was going to take several months to complete. Only then would the Treaty's 'Ulster month' commence, the four-week interval during which Craig's government would have to decide if it was going to join the Free State. 'This', Masterton-Smith conceded, 'will be a disappointment to the Irish signatories, who took the view that they ought to be informed, within a month or two of the *approval* of the Treaty by the Dail, whether Northern Ireland intended to stay out or come in'.[10]

That was an understatement. The new Free State leaders were more angry still when they learned that instead of proceeding with the Treaty's ratification, Parliament first had to give the Provisional Government 'a legal existence', allowing it to administer the South, to write a Constitution, and to call an election. Both Griffith and Collins objected. Collins pointed out that the Treaty was signed on the understanding that Ulster would have a month in which to decide whether or not to join the new dominion. If not, the South could expect to gain 'two whole and two half counties' from Craig's state. Now, however, they 'found the Treaty working out on different lines'.[11]

9   Griffith to Duffy, 12. Jan. 1922, Duffy MSS 15,440 (4). *Annual Register: 1922*, pp. 9–10.
10 Masterton-Smith to Churchill, 4 Jan. 1922, WSC 22/11/2.
11 Minutes of Conferences with Irish Ministers, 22/N/60(3) and (5), 5–6 Feb. 1922, CAB 21/249.

Collins's determination to settle the Ulster dispute sooner rather than later had already resulted in the first of what became known as the Craig–Collins Pacts.[12] In short order the Pact set aside the Boundary Commission and proposed that the two leaders would 'mutually agree' to Ireland's 'future boundaries'. Likewise, the Council of Ireland was to be dropped in favour of 'a more suitable system . . . for dealing with problems affecting all Ireland'. Collins further pledged to end the 'Belfast Boycott', a Sinn Féin-led campaign against the city's businesses in response to the shipyard expulsions of 1920. Craig, in turn, pledged to see to it that the expelled workers were allowed to return to their jobs – economic conditions permitting. Collins also pressed for the release of political prisoners being held in Northern jails.[13]

Although the agreement was widely hailed in the British press as a 'step towards Irish unity', it soon ran into trouble.[14] According to Craig, his discussions with Collins were premised on his opening statement that 'an All Ireland Parliament was out of the question' and that one could not be expected for 'years to come – 10, 20, or 50 years'. Craig pointed out to his Cabinet that the new boundary agreement, as well as getting rid of the hated Commission, was significant for two reasons: first, it meant that Collins recognised that Northern Ireland was here to stay and, second, amending Article 12 meant that the entire Treaty 'was now no longer inviolate'. In other words, the Provisional Government could have no room for complaint if the Ulster Unionists and their Conservative allies further revised the Treaty in the House of Commons. Craig said little about the Pact's economic clauses, except about the Boycott. As for the promise of an amnesty, Ulster's premier told his colleagues that he 'looked upon political prisoners as '"trump" cards to be played' in return for Sinn Féin displays of good behaviour.[15]

Collins's reasons for signing the Pact could not have been any more different. His object was to 'exclude English influence' from Irish affairs, especially on the boundary question. It had lately dawned on Collins that the real power to determine Ireland's frontier lay with the Boundary Commission's British-appointed chairman. Taking London out of the equation changed all that. 'It will be for us to insist upon our interpretation', Collins declared, and although his government was committed to a 'peace policy', it was prepared to 'fight for that [interpretation] in the event of the North refusing to come in'. [16]

12   M. Hopkinson, 'The Craig–Collins Pacts of 1922: Two Attempted Reforms of the Northern Ireland Government', *Irish Historical Studies*, vol. XXVII, no. 106, 1990, pp. 145–58.

13   CP 3644, 21 Jan. 1922, CAB 24/132.

14   'The First Step Towards Unity', *Westminster Gazette*; 'A Step Towards Irish Unity', *Yorkshire Post*; 'Towards Irish Unity', *Liverpool Post*; 'Irish Union', *Manchester Guardian*, all dated 23 Jan. 1922.

15   Conclusions, 26 Jan. 1922, PRONI, CAB/4/30/1.

16   Collins to King, 26 Jan. 1922, D/T, S 1801/Q. PG Minutes, 30 Jan. 1922, D/T, G 1/1.

The breakdown of the Craig–Collins Pact on 2 February exploded 'like a bombshell' in Coalition ranks. Parliament was due to begin debate on the Irish Free State (Agreement) Bill to give the Provisional Government legal standing. The bill stood no chance in a Conservative-dominated House of Commons if the Treaty would allow counties or parts of counties to vote themselves out of Northern Ireland.[17] Even Churchill was baffled. 'Everything is in the soup again', he told Curzon, 'and I have no idea at present what ought to be said about it.'[18]

Up to this point, the Provisional Government was in a stronger position than Craig and his lieutenants. This advantage began to shift when the partition issue became entangled in what amounted to a spate of state-sanctioned kidnappings of Unionists along the Irish frontier. From this point until the onset of the Irish Civil War, the boundary region was a scene of ongoing violence. Collins may have felt that he had good reason to back such operations, as they turned the attention of anti-Treaty elements of the IRA against a common enemy.[19] In the long run, however, this decision was self-defeating because it cost the Provisional Government much of its credibility in London. Churchill was right when he told Collins that a 'bloody fight' on the frontier would benefit only those 'who wish to see Ireland partitioned permanently'.[20]

Just as Churchill had predicted, the chain-reaction of events along the border had a 'disturbing effect' on Conservative MPs. Within the government itself, a group of Tory junior ministers decided 'to act together' to thwart any large-scale handover of Ulster's territory to the South. 'The only way out', Lord Bayford wrote, 'seems to be to appoint as Chairman someone who is sure to decide as we want' though, he admitted, 'that seems a poor game'.[21] Poor game or not, Chamberlain could ill afford to ignore this seething rebellion in his own ranks. Unless the Provisional Government took clear steps to release the kidnapped men and end the border disturbances, he warned Griffith, 'I will consider myself absolved from the Treaty'.[22]

It was no idle threat.

17 'Coalition Teetering Over New Irish Abyss', *Sunday Express*, 5 Feb. 1922.
18 Churchill to Curzon, 4 Feb. 1922, IO, MSS Eur. F 112/223, ff. 95–6.
19 Hopkinson, *Green Against Green*, pp. 77–88.
20 Churchill to Collins, 13 Feb. 1922, CO 906/20.
21 'Attack on Irish Treaty', *The Times*, 15 Feb. 1922. Bayford diary, 14 Feb. 1922, p. 173.
22 Conference minutes, 22/N/153, 9 Feb. 1922, CAB 21/254.

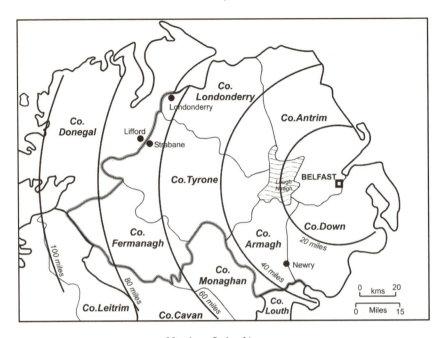

Northern Ireland in 1922.
The circles indicate radius from Belfast at a distance of 20 miles between each circle.
Based on a map in *The Times*, 25 March, 1922

'LEGALISING' THE PROVISIONAL GOVERNMENT

In the spring of 1922, the struggle over Ireland's future was fought on two fronts in the British political arena. Publicly, the government and its opponents battled one another over the Irish Free State (Agreement) Bill. Privately, Craig was engaged in an all-out effort to rewrite the financial provisions of the 1920 Act and, hence, the Treaty.

Aware that they did not have enough votes to kill the Free State Bill outright, Die-hards planned to introduce a series of amendments most of them directed at the Treaty's boundary clauses. If Churchill failed to give definite assurances on Northern Ireland's territorial integrity, as many as 150 Conservatives were ready to bolt from the government. On the other hand, if Parliament narrowly defined the Commission's remit, an open breach would be created with Collins and Griffith.[23] Either way, the aim was to mortally wound the Coalition and bring about its collapse.

---

23 'Attack on Irish Treaty', *The Times*, 15 Feb. 1922. James to Charles Craig, 11 Feb. 1922, PRONI, CAB/9Z/3/1.

Churchill faced the Die-hard challenge head-on. He admitted that the Boundary Commission's award might affect Northern Ireland's existing frontiers; indeed, it might 'affect them prejudicially'. There was no point glossing over this fact. But what was the alternative? Short of 'tearing up the Treaty', Parliament had no power whatsoever to alter Article 12. Later, though, he dismissed the 'absurd supposition' that Northern Ireland would be reduced 'to its preponderatingly Orange areas'. Not only would this create 'a fatal and permanent obstacle' to Irish unity; if Ulster was so 'maltreated and mutilated', Churchill suggested, the government would be bound to protect Northern Ireland as a separate 'economic entity'.[24] By such gestures – now on one side, now on the other – Churchill steered the Irish Bill through the Commons to complete its passage on 8 March. A similar effort by Birkenhead ensured its passage in the House of Lords later that same month.[25]

THE FINANCIAL BALANCE

While the fight over the Treaty's boundary clauses took place in public, Craig was involved in an equally intense struggle to undo the financial arrangements which already were adversely affecting his government. There were three pressing issues: Craig was determined to roll back his government's imperial contribution, to secure financing of the Special Constabulary, and to ensure the solvency of the Northern Ireland Unemployment Insurance Fund. Giving in to these demands, however, meant that Lloyd George and his colleagues would have to break their pledge to the Irish Treaty signatories that Northern Ireland's status would not be altered, for good or ill, if it opted out of the Free State.

Craig's immediate problem sprang from his demand for the transfer of executive power to the Belfast government in the autumn of 1921. Even before the transfer took place, his ministers knew that they did not have enough money to administer the departments they would soon control. Complicating matters was the fact that the British government was nearly two thirds of the way through its 1921–22 fiscal year when the transfer took place. Two civil servants, R. G. Hawtrey, representing the Treasury, and Ernest Clark, representing Northern Ireland's Department of Finance, were told to devise an arrangement which would eliminate the deficit while still remaining 'within the four corners of the Government of Ireland Act'.[26]

---

24 *HC Deb*, vol. 150, cols 1269–71, 1279, 16 Feb. 1922.
25 See, e.g., *HL Deb*, vol. 49, cols 901–12, 27 Mar. 1922.
26 Pollock to Craig, 30 Aug. 1921, PRONI, CAB/6/1. Hawtrey memorandum, 10 Dec. 1921, T 163/4/10/G.256/08.

To square the circle, Craig accepted the Treasury's method for allocating revenue for the last third of the fiscal year; in return, he received an additional grant of £600,000. This arrangement conveniently covered a £530,000 short-fall in Ulster's unemployment fund and provided an additional cushion for last-minute emergencies. Immediate funding for the Specials was taken care of by Lloyd George's suggestion that the Constables should be temporarily classified 'as a military force', so that this shifted the burden of paying for law and order onto imperial shoulders. According to Otto Niemeyer, the Treasury's controller of finance, the deal was also probably illegal. Certainly, it was not 'within the four corners of the 1920 Act' nor of the Treaty.[27]

Both civil servants and politicians were uneasy about continued British sub-sidies for the Specials. A report to Churchill's Irish Committee recommended terminating British support of the force 'at the earliest date that is legal or possible'. Privately, the chancellor of the exchequer assured Niemeyer that the government did not intend 'to let N. E. Ireland have Specials *ad libitum*'.[28]

Even so, in early March the Cabinet granted £850,000 to underwrite the Specials through the first six months of fiscal year 1922–23. Knowing that such a move would likely lead to protests in the House of Commons, the Cabinet approved a plan – conceived by Horne – to hide the assistance in 'a general grant of money to Ulster for unemployment and other services'. Collins was incensed by the deal. In effect, he told Churchill, His Majesty's Government was arming an 'openly partisan force' and 'no matter what they do or how they carry on, your Parliament will foot the bill'. Nor was this the only concession made in Craig's favour. Churchill's committee also agreed that the Joint Exchequer Board should be asked to reconsider the amount of Ulster's imperial contribution for the next two years. The committee also concluded that if it could be shown that the establishment of the Free State resulted in a higher cost of reserved services for Northern Ireland, the difference would be made up by the British Treasury.[29]

Taken together, these measures disguised a fundamental reordering of Northern Ireland's financial relations with Great Britain. The complaint 'could reasonably be made', pointed out one member of Churchill's committee, that

> Ulster was being bribed to remain disassociated from the South, whereas in the negotiations with the Southern Irish the British Government had always stated

27 Niemeyer memorandum; Niemeyer to Cuthbertson, 12, 16 Dec. 1921, T 163/4/10/G.256/08.
28 Ibid., 'Draft Report on the Special Constabulary', 17 Jan. 1922; and Horne to Niemeyer, 15 Dec. 1921.
29 Collins to Churchill, 24 Mar. 1922, PRONI, CAB/6/75. C 15(22), 6 Mar. 1922, CAB 23/29. PGI 56(Revise), 7 Mar. 1922, CAB 27/154. Blackett to Colwyn, 16 Mar. 1922, T 163/6/8/G.256/042.

that if Ulster chose to disassociate herself from the South, she would have to bear her full share of the financial burdens of the United Kingdom.[30]

Put another way, these decisions were a 'breach of faith' with Irish leaders.[31] As both Tom Jones and Lionel Curtis reminded the Cabinet, Arthur Griffith had accepted that Northern Ireland might remain outside the Free State. But, if so, its 'powers, privileges and revenues were to be no greater and no less than they would have been' under the 1920 Act. On top of everything else, a military force, the Specials, was in the making whose ultimate purpose might be to thwart 'the most vital provisions of the Treaty'. Despite the fact that Austen Chamberlain believed that Jones and Curtis were 'substantially right', their objections went unheeded.[32]

NORTHERN IRELAND'S UNEMPLOYMENT INSURANCE FUND

Although these developments went some way towards alleviating Craig's financial worries, they did not solve a potentially longer-term problem. Few other regions of the British Isles suffered from the post-war economic depression as much as Northern Ireland.[33] Under the 1920 Act, however, unemployment relief was a 'transferred' service, for which the Belfast government was solely responsible – a fact that Treasury officials repeatedly reminded Craig and his ministers, not to mention their own political masters.[34]

Again, Ulster's prime minister found himself in a dilemma largely of his own making. In March he publicly declared that where 'unemployment and benefits are concerned', Ulster's workers would receive the same assistance as their British counterparts. Making this guarantee was highly irresponsible, because Craig was again committing his government to spend money it did not have. He admitted as much in this same speech, pointing out that such programmes would be 'difficult to finance at the moment'.[35]

30 PGI 16th Conclusions, 10 Mar. 1922, CAB 27/153.

31 Jones to Lloyd George, 17 Mar. 1922, LG F/26/1/17.

32 CP 3873, 18 Mar. 1922, CO 739/4/15533. Chamberlain to Churchill, 24 Mar. 1922, WSC 22/12/66.

33 According to one historian, by the summer of 1922, 25 per cent of Northern Ireland's workforce was unemployed. In the other regions of the United Kingdom most severely affected by the economic downturn, the unemployment rates were 21 per cent (Scotland) and 18 per cent (the Midlands and North-east England). See Rhodes James, *British Revolution*, p. 438.

34 Niemeyer memorandum, 12 Dec. 1921, T 163/4/10/G.256/08. Niemeyer to Horne; and Blackett to Horne, 5 May, 12 June 1922, T 163/6/11/G.256/049.

35 *NI HC Deb*, vol. 2, cols 18–19, 14 Mar. 1922.

But whereas the imperial government was ready to lend a hand when it came to financing the Specials, this time there was to be no bail out for Craig's government. It soon became obvious that Ulster's premier was getting round this refusal by using funds for the Special Constabulary to employ jobless Protestants. In May, he informed Horne and Churchill that he needed another £5 million for the Specials to carry 'us over the immediate few months'. At the same time, he asked for an additional £160,000 to cover an earlier shortfall in the unemployment budget, arguing that the deficit had occurred before his government took over responsibility for the fund.[36]

Viewed from the Treasury, Craig's incessant demands simply proved that he wanted 'the best of both worlds'.[37] In early June, Horne outlined for his Cabinet colleagues the extent to which the British Exchequer was propping up Craig's government. This support had 'already gone far beyond what was contemplated in the [1920] Act', and it was becoming 'increasingly difficult' to defend such grants in the House of Commons.[38] But, having fed the Belfast government's appetite, Horne and his colleagues were discovering that its needs were insatiable. At the end of May, the Committee of Imperial Defence approved a request allowing active military officers to be temporarily assigned to the Specials. The committee also approved the 'loan' of munitions and other supplies, including 23,000 rifles and nearly 300 machine guns.[39]

On 19 July, Horne agreed to contribute another £2 million to the Specials, doing so 'on the definite understanding that it is *all* that I can grant for the financial year 1922/23'. While Craig readily accepted this condition, the deal provoked a storm of protest in Churchill's Irish Committee. However, its members had little choice but to accept the deal once they were told that 'any Prime Minister of Northern Ireland would resign if he were deprived of the "B" and "C" specials'.[40] Despite the condition imposed by Horne's 'final' offer, within two months Craig was back again. This time, he wanted another £200,000 for fiscal year 1922–23, and a British commitment to grant £1.35 million to the Specials for the following year.[41] It is true that the deteriorating situation in Ireland played its part in persuading Lloyd George and his colleagues that they must come to the aid of Ulster's government.[42] But that does not explain why the Coalition so readily gave in to Craig's demands. To do that, it is necessary to return to the world of British politics.

36 Craig to Churchill; Niemeyer memorandum; and Craig to Horne, 17, 22 May, 5 June 1922, T 163/6/11/G.256/049.

37 Ibid., Blackett to Horne, 12 June 1922.   38 CP 4201, 9 June 1922, CAB 24/137.

39 SS (I.C.) 5th Minutes, 22 May 1922, CAB 16/42/1.

40 Horne to Craig; Craig to Horne; and PGI 24th Conclusions, all dated 19 July 1922, T 160/131/F.4855/1.

41 Ibid., Craig to Churchill, 19 Sept. 1922.   42 See, e.g., C. 27(22), 16 May 1922, CAB 23/30.

CONSERVATIVE REBELLION

In the early months of 1922, Lloyd George and his colleagues were, one of them wrote, 'in a very awkward position'. Simply put, the government was running out of ideas and of support.[43] This dilemma was particularly acute for Tory members of the Coalition. As Leo Amery pointed out to Chamberlain, there was not 'a single item' in government policy that appealed to the 'instincts or traditions' of the Conservative Party. 'What shall we have to offer', Amery asked, 'beyond a vista of Conferences which may, or may not, bring us nearer to European peace?' As for Ireland, Amery felt that most Tories would concede that 'the Irish arrangement was inevitable, possibly even wise'. But, he went on, 'their main feeling is one of despondency and moral unsettlement'. [44]

In mid-January, a group of activists that included Carson, Lord and Lady Londonderry, Lord Salisbury, Ronald McNeill, and Sir Henry Wilson (though he was still chief of the imperial general staff) discussed the formation of 'a real Conservative Party'. As one dissident put it, 'unless Mr Chamberlain's action in surrendering to Sinn Fein be repudiated' there seemed to him no reason for the party's continued existence. 'If it does not matter whether you are a Unionist or a Home Ruler', he asked, 'does anything matter at all?' The trouble for the Die-hards was, as always, finding someone to lead the rebellion.[45]

With Bonar Law still holding back, Die-hard hopes turned to Arthur Balfour. Recently returned from the Washington Naval Conference, both pro- and anti-Coalitionists believed that Balfour still retained a good deal of influence within the party. Carson, who was certain that the former leader could be won over to the Die-hards, openly advocated a 'Conservative election headed by A. J. B.' If nothing else, another Die-hard wrote, Balfour's defection would give their movement the 'push off' needed to 'get rid of L. G.' For this reason alone, Lloyd George was just as determined to keep him in the Coalition.[46] The stumbling block for both sides was Balfour's notable, and disturbing, silence on Ireland.

To head off Balfour's defection, Birkenhead drafted one of the most controversial, not to say oft-quoted, pronouncements ever made on the Treaty by one of its framers. In a personal letter to Balfour, he assured his elder colleague that, whatever anyone else might say, there was no possibility of Northern

43 Montagu to Reading, 23 Feb. 1922, IO MSS Eur. E. 238/4, No. 6. 'Electioneering', *The Times*, 2 Feb. 1922.

44 Amery to Chamberlain, 26 Jan. 1922, AC 24/4/1.

45 Wilson diary, 14 Jan. 1922, HHW 1/31/1. Oliver to Salisbury, 15 Mar. 1922, S (4) 100/89. Lady Carson's diary, 23 Jan. 1922, D/1507/C/7.

46 Wilson diary, 1 Mar. 1922, HHW 1/31/1–2. Riddell diary, 28–29 Jan. 1922, *Intimate Diary*, p. 351.

Ireland losing counties to the Free State. The Boundary Commission, 'not being presided over by a lunatic', would be aware of the limits of its jurisdiction and 'reach a rational conclusion'. [47] As will be shown in a later chapter, Birkenhead's justification was not nearly as conclusive as he led Balfour to believe. For the moment, though, he succeeded in his primary aim. 'If a "lead" from me is what people want', Balfour told Sir Edward Grigg the next day, 'they shall certainly have it'. [48]

In a major address delivered on 7 March, Balfour gave a ringing endorsement not only to the Coalition but also to its handling of Ireland. [49] Instead of boosting support for Lloyd George, however, Balfour's speech only served to undermine his own credibility with many Tories who now saw him as hopelessly out of touch. After his glorious 'resurrection' at the Naval Conference, there were hopes that Balfour might again become a major political figure. But, wrote one disappointed admirer, these hopes were dashed by his 'shocking relapse in the city last week!' [50]

Despite murmurings of discontent among Conservatives of all shades, Chamberlain, like Balfour, was also out of touch with the mood of his party. Convinced of a 'growing movement of opinion' against the Die-hards, he called a meeting of Conservative MPs in mid-March, to ask that they endorse his 'determination to stand by the Prime Minister'. Instead, the backbenchers rebelled. In particular, they made it plain that they would do nothing to cause a split with those who opposed the government 'on the ground of its Irish policy'. For Lloyd George, the resulting situation was 'worse than if the meeting had never been held'. [51]

Emboldened by their success, the Die-hards went over to the attack. On 5 April, William Joynson-Hicks and Ronald McNeill laid down a parliamentary motion demanding to know 'whether in principle the Coalition is Liberal or Conservative'. Much of the ensuing debate provided a foretaste of the charges that were to swirl round the government later in the year. Months before the storm burst over Lloyd George's sale of honours, his opponents rained down abuse on the government for promising to pursue 'one policy and one set of principles in regard to Ireland' only to lead Parliament in the opposite direction. This, said Viscount Wolmer, explained why the public had 'lost faith in the sincerity of the Coalition' and in politicians in general. [52]

47   The letter is reprinted in Appendix III.
48   Balfour to Grigg, 4 Mar. 1922, AJB-S, GD 433/2/1, Reel 1.
49   '"Coalition Best." Sir A. Balfour on Unity', *The Times*, 8 Mar. 1922.
50   Tyrrell to Strachey, 17 Mar. 1922, Strachey Papers, S/19/4/11.
51   Austen to Ida Chamberlain, 11 Mar. 1922, AC 5/1/229. 'The Expiring Coalition', *The Times*, 15 Mar. 1922.
52   *HC Deb*, vol. 152, cols 2344–57, 2375–6, 5 Apr. 1922.

Chamberlain, in his own words, turned on these tormentors 'like a nasty, vicious beast' and gave what some regarded as the best fighting speech of his career. The gamble worked, and the Die-hards' motion was soundly defeated by a vote of 288 to 95. Although justifiably proud of his victory, Chamberlain drew the wrong conclusions from this episode. Combined with a vote of support for Lloyd George's Genoa policy, held two days earlier, this turn of events led the Tory leader into a false sense of security. It would prove to be a costly mistake.[53]

CHURCHILL'S DILEMMA

The rumblings of Conservative discontent over Ireland were not solely a problem for Tory members of the government. By the spring of 1922, Churchill found himself increasingly out of step with his Coalition Liberal colleagues in general and, more seriously, with Lloyd George in particular. Depending on the issue, one of them complained, 'Winston jumps from the diehard to the Liberal camp as he works from Egypt or India to Ireland.'[54]

There was every indication that Churchill would not follow Lloyd George out of office if he could help it.[55] But where was he to turn? The Conservatives – many of whom saw him as 'the friend of our enemies, and the enemy of our friends' – did not want him.[56] Having left the party in 1904, it was difficult to see how he could work his way back into its ranks. Nevertheless, Churchill at this time began to re-establish himself as a 'Tory Democrat'.[57] Such a transformation was bound to affect his outlook on any number of issues, none more so than Ireland.

Churchill's change of direction was evident during debate on the Irish Free State (Agreement) Bill. He was careful to maintain that 'fair play' must be the watchwords in Britain's dealings with both Irish governments. But he then went on to say that 'though we are impartial we cannot be indifferent. Naturally, our hearts warm towards those in the North who are helping, and have helped so long, to keep the old flag flying.'[58]

---

53 Ibid., cols 2365–74, 2387–90. Austen to Hilda Chamberlain, 18 Apr. 1922, AC 5/1/233. Dutton, *Chamberlain*, p. 178. *Annual Register: 1922*, p. 44.

54 H. A. L. Fisher diary, 17 Jan., 21, 28 Feb. 1922, Fisher MSS 18. Montagu to Reading, 23 Feb. 1922, IO, MSS Eur. E. 238/4, No. 6.

55 Sassoon to Lloyd George, 13 Feb. 1922, LG F/45/1/8. Beaverbrook to Lloyd George, 13 Mar. 1922, LG F/4/6/6.

56 'Duke's Angry Shriek', *Irish Independent*, 12 June 1922.

57 'I am what I have always been – a Tory Democrat', he later said. Riddell diary, 30 May 1923, [McEwen] p. 388.

58 *HC Deb*, vol. 150, col. 1281, 16 Feb. 1922.

In unguarded moments, he went much further, as occurred at a dinner party in early March. 'My chat with Winston was most interesting', Lady Craig wrote in her diary. His assurance that no one in Lloyd George's Cabinet 'would stand more than rectification of boundaries' and that 'Ulster would come out top' was then repeated to Craig himself – so boisterously that Ulster's premier turned to Clementine Churchill for help. 'Take him home', Craig implored, 'before he incriminates himself further!' It would be easy to dismiss one such incident. However, Churchill then repeated these same assurances to Craig when the two met the following day. As he later told Tom Jones, it was important to him that he 'retain the confidence of the Ulster people'.[59] Such thoughts and deeds cast a shadow over Churchill's own later claims that he was impartial in his dealings with the two Irish governments.

THE ROAD TO CIVIL WAR

In the early months of 1922, Churchill's immediate objective in Ireland was to restore peace in the six counties, where killings had become a daily occurrence. At the end of March, he convinced both Craig and Collins to meet again at the Colonial Office. The result was an 11-point agreement which became known as the second Craig–Collins Pact.[60] Much of the accord dealt with the restoration of law and order in the six counties; but it also included a British promise of up to £500,000 to employ the jobless. Craig again pledged to 'use every effort to secure the reparation of the expelled workers' of 1920, economic conditions permitting. Clause 7 pledged the three governments to meet again after Parliament's ratification of the Free State Constitution, but before the end of the Ulster month, to ascertain '[w]hether means can be devised to secure the unity of Ireland' or, barring that, whether it was possible to settle this issue other 'than by recourse to the Boundary Commission'.[61]

Although the Pact opened with a Churchillian flourish – 'PEACE is today declared' – the immediate result was more, not less, killing in the six counties. This violence reached an even higher pitch after Collins agreed to a highly risky 'invasion' of the North by both pro- and anti-Treaty factions of the IRA. A series of attacks, mounted along the border between mid-May and early June, climaxed when pro-Treaty forces clashed with British troops in the towns of Belleek and Pettigo on the Fermanagh–Donegal border. Despite efforts to hide Provisional Government involvement, Craig soon had enough

59 Lady Craig's diary, 9, 10 Mar. 1922, D/1415/B/38. Jones diary, 7 June 1922, vol. III, p. 210.
60 Summary of negotiations, 29–30 Mar. 1922, D/T, S 1801/A.
61 Ibid.

evidence linking Dublin to the border violence.[62] The result of the invasion, aside from its abject failure, was to blight Collins's credibility with the British. Worse, perhaps, it enabled Craig's government to impose a series of repressive measures, including the wholesale internment of Nationalist and Sinn Féin leaders in the North.

The fracturing between London and Dublin was further complicated by the fact that southern Ireland was well on the road to civil war. Challenges to the Provisional Government's authority were rampant, the most spectacular being the occupation of Ireland's legal centre, the Four Courts, by members of the anti-Treaty IRA. In an effort to avoid disaster, Collins startled everyone when, on 20 May, he signed an electoral pact with de Valera. Both pro- and anti-Treaty wings of Sinn Féin were guaranteed a proportion of seats in the new Dáil Éireann to be elected in June, based on their equivalent strength in the previous assembly. While this gave the pro-Treatyites a slight advantage, it made the coming election something of a farce.[63]

Even before the pact was announced, Churchill feared that he was witnessing Ireland's 'social disintegration'. Chamberlain was equally apprehensive. On the eve of the Sinn Féin pact, he still believed that Collins and Griffith were 'playing straight'. Afterwards, he spoke for most of his Cabinet colleagues when he said that while he continued to trust Griffith, he no longer believed that Collins was 'keeping faith with us'.[64]

Collins was not the only member of the Provisional Government who would have found that accusation hard to stomach. Richard Mulcahy was so disturbed over British financing of 'the sectarian murder campaign' in the North that he even reconsidered his support of the Treaty. With each new pronouncement, it seemed, London was reinterpreting the agreement's Ulster clauses to favour Craig's government. The British 'would do nothing to put Belfast right', Collins complained to Tom Jones; 'even the P.M. was incredibly callous about the murder of Ulster Catholics'. [65]

In Belfast, Craig used the Collins–de Valera agreement to justify repudiating his own second pact with the Provisional Government chairman. Nor would he hear any more foolishness about altering Northern Ireland's frontiers. 'What we have now we hold, and we hold against all combinations.' Churchill privately scolded Ulster's premier for publicly challenging a treaty negotiated by His Majesty's ministers. 'You ought not to send us a telegram asking

62 Spender to Tallents, 29 June 1922, CO 906/23.

63 Hopkinson, *Green Against Green*, pp. 72–3, 97–101.

64 C 27(22), 16 May 1922, CAB 23/30. Chamberlain to Long, 19 May 1922, AC 33/1/63. Conference minutes, 23 May 1922, CAB 21/208.

65 See, e.g., Mulcahy to Griffith, 24 Mar. 1922, RM, P7/B/152. Jones diary, 30 May 1922, vol. III, p. 203.

for help on the largest possible scale', the colonial secretary pointed out, 'and announce an intention to defy the Imperial Parliament on the same day.' A chastened Craig accepted the rebuke, though he excused his transgression by blaming the Treaty itself. The Boundary Commission, Craig told Churchill a few days later, 'has been at the root of all evil'. [66]

Amid this turmoil, Collins and Griffith presented the Free State's proposed Constitution to the British Cabinet. In an effort to win over anti-Treatyites, they proposed a document which, in the words of one historian, 'would be short, simple, and easy to change as Ireland moved to complete freedom'. [67] Put another way, it was a document that was bound to be wholly unacceptable to any British government that depended on the Conservative Party to stay in office. This was not a Dominion constitution, Lloyd George told the Irish, 'it was a Republic in disguise'. [68]

In fact, the two sides were still grappling with the same issues that had divided them during the Treaty negotiations, with partition on the one hand and allegiance to the crown on the other. On partition, Lloyd George pointed out, 'our case was weak', and even more so given the fact that most of those who had been killed in the six counties were Catholics. 'No one had been punished, we had made no enquiry, we had armed 48,000 Protestants.' Craig's Specials, Lloyd George argued, were no different from Mussolini's Black Shirts – and just as ill-disciplined. It was therefore imperative, he told his Cabinet, that they 'eliminate the Ulster issue and leave a clean issue of "Republic versus the British Empire"'. [69]

In the end, a complete breakdown over the proposed Constitution was averted by Griffith's answers to a series of questions which securely anchored the Free State within the British Commonwealth.[70] Collins, meanwhile, repudiated his pact with de Valera two days before the Irish went to the polls on 16 June. When the votes were tallied, only 36 anti-Treaty candidates were victorious. The new Dáil Éireann would be composed of 58 pro-government TDs, along with 34 members representing Labour and several other smaller parties all of whom also supported the Treaty.[71]

Despite this encouraging result, Ireland's troubles further eroded support for Lloyd George and his colleagues within the House of Commons.

66 *NI HC Deb*, vol. 2, col. 598, 23 May 1922. See Churchill–Craig correspondence, 25–26 May 1922, PRONI, CAB/6/75.

67 Curran, *Irish Free State*, p. 200.

68 According to Churchill, the document had a 'Bolshevik character'! See 'Irish Conference', and chronology of negotiations, both dated 27 May 1922, CAB 21/257.

69 C 30(22), 30 May 1922, CAB 23/30.

70 Lloyd George to Griffith, SF (B) 62, 1 June 1922, CAB 21/256(II).

71 *Annual Register: 1922*, p. 63.

Opposition from the Die-hards was taken for granted. What was worrying was the evident restlessness of more moderate Tory MPs such as Sam Hoare. Though he still counted himself a 'friend' of the Treaty, Hoare and others like him were manifestly dissatisfied with the course of events. Leo Amery felt that in some ways the government was in a 'far worse mess' than if the Treaty had never been negotiated in the first place.[72]

If these tribulations were not enough, the government was also being battered from other directions. By mid-May it was clear that Lloyd George's plans for restoring Europe's pre-war prosperity at the Genoa conference had failed. With it went the last hopes for his political survival. In June a wholly unexpected crisis erupted over the Coalition's sale of honours for the creation of a Lloyd George political fund, giving the Die-hards yet another front from which to attack the Coalition.[73] On the 21st, Henry Wilson spent the afternoon in the Commons watching fellow Die-hard John Gretton assail the government front bench. 'Austen was rather heckled about L.G.'s Honours List', Wilson wrote in his diary, 'and Gretton told me he was going to have a go at it again tomorrow. . . . A lovely day.'[74]

But Wilson never saw the speech delivered. The next afternoon the former chief of the imperial general staff was shot to death on the front-step of his home in London by two members of the IRA.

IRELAND'S CIVIL WAR

Henry Wilson's assassination echoed round Westminster and produced a profound shock which soon turned to profound anger. In Britain, his murder drew a veil over his activities in Northern Ireland, where he had acted as Craig's military adviser. Churchill soon forgot that only a few weeks earlier he had held the field marshal and de Valera to be equally culpable for the violence then raging in the six counties. Meanwhile, the assassination exposed Lloyd George and his colleagues, and Austen Chamberlain in particular, to scorching abuse. Even Chamberlain's brother began to have doubts about the Treaty. The assassination, Neville Chamberlain wrote, was 'enough to make anyone despair of Ireland and curse the Irish as a hopeless and impossible race'.[75]

72   Wilson diary, 31 May 1922, HHW 1/31/1. *HC Deb*, vol. 154, col. 2158–62, 31 May 1922. Amery diary, 31 May 1922, in L. S. Amery, *The Leo Amery Diaries*, vol. 1: *1896–1929*, J. Barnes and D. Nicholson, ed. (London, 1980), p. 286.

73   Morgan, *Consensus and Disunity*, pp. 339–40.   74   Wilson diary, 21 June 1922, HHW 1/31/2.

75   Bayford diary, 25 June 1922, p. 176–7. Memorandum of meeting with Belfast businessmen, 2 June 1922, CO 906/25. McNeill to Chamberlain [two letters], 23 June 1922, AC 24/4/19–20. Neville to Ida Chamberlain, 24 June 1922, NC 18/1/354.

On the same day that Wilson's body was laid to rest in St Paul's Cathedral, the House of Commons assembled to discuss the Irish situation. MPs were so ill tempered that Lloyd George was not at all sure if the Coalition would survive the debate. By most accounts, Churchill's speech saved the day. Having linked Wilson's assassins to the Irregular IRA contingent which occupied the Four Courts, Churchill demanded that the Provisional Government clear out this 'nest of anarchy and treason'; otherwise, His Majesty's Government would do the job for it.[76]

However, the mood of the House was captured by Bonar Law. In effect, Amery wrote, the former Tory leader told Lloyd George and his colleagues 'that this was their last chance'. Though he had supported the Treaty in December, Bonar Law now declared that he would not have voted for it had he known then 'what the position would have been today'. This warning shot, made 'amid loud cheers', was the clearest sign yet that he was ready to lead a revolt against his former colleagues.[77]

The Coalition's ultimatum to the Provisional Government very nearly backfired. Another 'crack of the English whip', Alfred Cope warned the Colonial Office, would do more harm than good. In any case, the Provisional Government had decided to attack the Four Courts before news of Churchill's speech was received. More important than the dire warnings issuing from London was a change in Collins's own mind. 'I think we'll have to fight these fellows', he is said to have told Richard Mulcahy. From that moment, there was no turning back.[78]

For Churchill, the attack on the Four Courts erased his suspicions about the Provisional Government and his doubts about the Treaty settlement. 'Now', he wrote to Collins on 7 July, 'all is changed'. Once the National Army established order in the South, 'as I do not doubt you will in a short time',

a new phase will begin far more hopeful than any we have hitherto experienced. In this phase the objective must be the unity of Ireland. How and when this can be achieved I cannot tell, but it is surely the goal towards which we must all look steadfastly.[79]

---

76 Stevenson diary, 26 June 1922, p. 243. H. A. L. Fisher diary, same date, Fisher MSS 18. Amery diary, same date, pp. 287–8. *Annual Register: 1922*, p. 64.

77 Ibid., Amery and Fisher diaries. *HC Deb*, vol. 155, col. 1744, 26 June 1922.

78 Curran, *Free State*, pp. 229–32. Hopkinson, *Green Against Green*, pp. 116–18. Cope to Curtis, 27 June 1922, LG F/10/3/8. Churchill to Cope, 1 July 1922, LG F/10/3/13(b).

79 Churchill to Collins, 7 July 1922, CO 739/6/36749.

In this same letter, it was necessary for Churchill to address himself to yet another dispute between North and South: Craig's proposal to abolish proportional representation in Northern Ireland's local elections. 'Minor irritations' such as these should not be allowed to 'lead us off track', Churchill counselled.[80] However, the abolition of PR was anything but a minor irritation to Collins. His fight against it would be his last major battle on behalf of Northern Nationalists and the last major Irish dispute for the Lloyd George Coalition.

ABOLISHING PROPORTIONAL REPRESENTATION

On 31 May Craig's government introduced a bill to repeal proportional representation for elections to all local government bodies in the six counties.[81] Alfred Cope suspected that Craig wanted to abolish PR before the next round of local elections, scheduled for January, because he feared the loss of Belfast city council to an alliance of Nationalist and Labour councillors. It is, indeed, revealing that the only member of the Ulster House of Commons to speak against abolition argued that the bill was aimed as much against Labour as it was against Nationalists or Republicans.[82]

In addition, it is likely that Craig and his colleagues were looking for an opportune moment to rush the legislation through their Parliament before anyone in Dublin or London took notice. With the Provisional Government seeming to be on the verge of collapse, the early summer of 1922 afforded as good a chance as any. The 'South is so busy with its own affairs', Craig pointed out, 'that little attention will be paid to what happens in the North'.[83]

If that was Craig's plan, he miscalculated. Even as the attack on the Four Courts was still in progress, Collins found time to send Churchill a stinging denunciation of the proposed statute. Its repercussions, Collins protested, would effectively eliminate the 'representation of Catholic and Nationalist interests' especially in counties Fermanagh and Tyrone and Derry City. He also pointedly reminded Churchill that while safeguards for Southern Unionists 'have been frequently demanded and readily granted by us', the rights of Northern Nationalists 'under the Craig regime are not protected in the slightest degree'. [84]

---

80 Ibid.

81 *NI HC Deb*, vol. 2, col. 748, 31 May 1922.

82 Cope to Curtis, 9 Sept. 1922, HO 45/13371/15. *NI HC Deb*, vol. 2, cols 845–51, 917, 26 June and 5 July 1922.

83 Craig to Masterton-Smith, 22 July 1922, HO 45/13371/1.

84 Collins to Churchill, ITC 53, 28 June 1922, CAB 27/160.

Using Craig's own words, Collins maintained that abolishing PR was part of a wider strategy to 'wipe out the Boundary Commission'. A glance at the bill's provisions shows what he meant. Besides restoring the winner-take-all system of elections, the proposed legislation required all local officials to swear an oath of allegiance both to the king and to the Northern Ireland government. To increase Ulster Unionist representation on these councils, members of the Special Constabulary and their wives were to be allowed to vote in local elections even if they were not permanent residents.[85] These measures struck at the heart of the case that Nationalists planned to make to the Boundary Commission. What better evidence of the 'wishes of the inhabitants' could there be than local councils which refused to recognise the Belfast Parliament?

Beyond the bill itself, Alfred Cope reminded the Colonial Office, Irish acceptance of the Treaty 'was based on an understanding' that both London and Dublin would work for 'an early United Ireland'.[86] This assurance was repeated by Churchill himself in his 7 July letter to Collins and, yet again the following month. 'With Mr. Churchill's authority', Cope reported, 'I gave them hope of the North coming in on terms provided the P[rovisional]. G[overnment]. won through their present troubles and did not compromise' with the Republicans.[87]

Churchill was in an extremely awkward position. While he himself was 'no lover' of PR, Collins nevertheless had a strong case. To get round the problem, at least for the moment, the imperial government withheld the royal assent, an official explaining that it was necessary to examine the bill's ramifications.[88]

At a meeting on 28 July Craig did not contradict Churchill when the latter pointed out that London had every right to prevent the repeal of PR. Instead, he merely fell back on his favoured weapon of last resort, making it clear that if the bill were not allowed onto the Statute Book he would resign and take his whole government with him. The meeting ended with Churchill promising that the royal assent would be granted after all, an assurance that Craig then passed on to his Cabinet.[89]

Churchill's decision infuriated Collins. 'Do you not see, or have His Majesty's advisers not disclosed the true meaning of all this?' The abolition of PR was intended to accomplish one end – 'to paint the Counties of Tyrone

85   Ibid. Richard Best memorandum, 6 July 1922, HO 45/13371/1(a).

86   Cope to Curtis, 21 Aug. 1922, HO 45/13371/4.

87   Cope to Masterton-Smith, 10 Aug. 1922, CO 906/31.

88   Churchill to Craig [not sent], 6[?] July 1922, CO 739/14/31545. See Spender–Tallents correspondence, 13, 15 July 1922, HO 45/13371/1.

89   Masterton-Smith memorandum, 28 July 1922, HO 45/13371/2. Cabinet minutes, 9 Aug. 1922, PRONI, CAB/4/51/15.

and Fermanagh with a deep Orange tint in anticipation of the . . . Boundary Commission'. So far as Collins was concerned, this was nothing less than 'an attempt to defeat the obligations of His Majesty's Government contained in the Treaty', and on that score alone Churchill could expect trouble not only from Collins, but from Griffith as well.[90]

In a matter of days, however, both men were dead. On 12 August Griffith died suddenly from a cerebral haemorrhage, the result of years of overwork and the stresses and strains brought on by the Civil War. Ten days later Collins was killed during an ambush near his home in County Cork. The loss of these two men to the Nationalist cause was incalculable. Having played no part in the Treaty negotiations, William Cosgrave, the Provisional Government's new chairman, was less likely to retaliate if the British acquiesced in Craig's wishes.

The fate of the PR Bill was finally decided at a meeting of British Treaty signatories on 7 September. Although Lloyd George conceded that the legislation was 'a breach of the spirit of the Treaty', the government was unwilling to force a showdown with Ulster's Cabinet. In a conciliatory gesture, Craig said that he would postpone county and rural district council elections; but on the main issue he stood firm. He would hear of no further delays on the bill itself. Nor would he hold up local urban elections scheduled for January.[91]

The return of winner-take-all elections signalled the resurrection of Unionist hegemony in Ulster local government. As Craig promised, county council and rural district council elections were postponed until 1924, the excuse being that time was needed to redraw electoral districts. The following January, Nationalist disunity combined with the abolition of PR to return Londonderry to Unionist control, while the party reasserted its dominance of Belfast city council.[92]

The battle over PR was a turning point in relations between London and Belfast. As Curtis pointed out in the middle of the dispute, if the British refused to allow the PR Bill onto the Statute Book, Craig and his fellow ministers 'would have no option but to resign'. The ensuing general election in the six counties almost certainly would endorse their action, and the imperial government then would be at an impasse.[93] Practically speaking, there were only two courses of action: allow the Ulster Unionists to abolish PR, or return the six counties to direct rule from London. Fifty years later those were still the only alternatives when a Conservative government reimposed direct rule.

---

90 Collins to Churchill, 9 Aug. 1922, LG F/183/1/402.
91 SF (B) 32nd Conclusions, 7 Sept. 1922, CAB 43/1.
92 Phoenix, *Northern Nationalism*, pp. 269–71.
93 Buckland, *Factory of Grievances*, pp. 267–8. Curtis to Churchill, 1 Sept. 1922, HO 45/13371/9.

THE FALL OF THE COALITION

It has been written that the collapse of the Lloyd George Coalition 'occurred quite suddenly and spectacularly'. In retrospect, so it would seem. But as Kenneth Morgan has also pointed out, the government's demise had little to do with the honours scandal. Nor, in the end, was the Chanak crisis by itself a decisive blow.[94]

Quite the contrary, the Coalition's handling of the crisis in Turkey won it a measure of grudging respect from some of its most inveterate foes. 'The last thing the Goat did – the thing wh[ich] finally undid him – is in my opinion the most virtuous act of his recent years', wrote F. S. Oliver.[95] Viscount Cave was like-minded. It was precisely because 'I could not agree with you about Ireland', Cave told Chamberlain, that he felt all the more bound to disassociate himself from other attacks which 'appear to me to be wholly unjustified'.[96]

The government's demise occurred when it did because of the decision to call a snap general election in the middle of the Chanak crisis. This in turn brought about the famous Carlton Club meeting of 19 October. Much has been written elsewhere about these proceedings – about which speakers were influential, and which were not; about which issues were uppermost in the minds of Tory MPs when it became time to vote for or against the Coalition.[97] It is fair to say that Bonar Law's speech at the meeting was decisive, if only because he at last put himself forward as an alternative leader. This made it safe for middle-of-the-road MPs to turn against Chamberlain, who had 'revealed himself as an unrepentant and convinced Coalitionist'.[98]

Stanley Baldwin's speech was also influential. Lloyd George, he famously declared, was 'a dynamic force', and it was because of him that the Conservatives now found themselves in such turmoil. This same dynamic force had destroyed the once great Liberal Party, and, if the Coalition continued, the Conservative

---

94   Morgan, *Consensus and Disunity*, p. 346. Following the First World War, Allied forces remained in and around Constantinople to contain Turkish nationalists led by Mustapha Kemal. In the summer of 1922, Kemal's army swept through the region, threatening a British garrison at Chanak. Although Lloyd George, along with Churchill and Birkenhead, was willing to go to war, many of their Conservative colleagues were not. The crisis was peacefully resolved and all Allied forces were withdrawn from the region in 1923.

95   Oliver to Selborne, 21 Nov. 1922, Selborne MSS 87, ff. 83–4.

96   Cave to Chamberlain, 15 Oct. 1922, Cave Papers, Add. MSS 62,464, ff. 68.

97   See, e.g., Cowling, *Impact of Labour*, p. 209–12. Kinnear, *Fall of Lloyd George*, pp. 87, 120–34. Morgan, *Consensus and Disunity*, pp. 348–50. Ramsden, *Balfour and Baldwin*, pp. 164–7. Cross, *Hoare*, p. 364, n. 61, disputes Kinnear's conclusions.

98   Amery diary, 19 Oct. 1922, p. 300. 'A Chamberlain Apologia', *The Times*, 14 Oct. 1922.

Party too would be 'smashed to atoms'.[99] These words crystallised what those at the meeting most feared: by continuing to associate with Lloyd George and his methods, their leaders were forsaking Conservative principles and, in the end, would destroy the unity of their own party.

But, when it came to pinning specific allegations to this general charge, no one mentioned the honours scandal. Only Chamberlain dwelt at length on the Chanak crisis. Only Bonar Law devoted much time to the threat posed by Labour. As Balfour pointed out, and as one Die-hard had earlier admitted, when it came to the charge that Conservative principles had been abandoned, one issue stood out above all others, and that was Ireland.

The seething discontent about this issue was at the bottom of the Conservative revolt.[100] 'The extraordinary thing', Lord Derby observed some months before, was that the Coalition's critics could not 'point to any one thing, except perhaps the Irish matter, which the Government have done wrong'.[101] Edward Wood echoed this sentiment when he later drew a connection between 'distrust of the Prime Minister' and disaffection over Ireland. While most Conservatives had no desire to go to war again with the IRA, they none the less thought that their party 'existed to fight for a particular Irish policy'. Instead, they were forced to watch the 'apparently complete reversal of this policy' by their 'accredited spokesmen'. Was it any wonder, then, that the party was in 'a state of irritation and bewilderment'?[102]

The onset of Ireland's Civil War only served to reinforce the impression that the government's Irish policy had failed. In the South, Unionists became a favoured target of the Irregular IRA. Although Northern Ireland experienced a lull in violence following the attack on the Four Courts, by September 'the situation in Ulster was unsatisfactory and becoming worse'. It is revealing that even when troops were desperately needed for service in Turkey at the height of the Chanak crisis, Churchill refused to transfer any military units from Ireland. Forces in Ulster, he said, 'could in no case be weakened'. [103]

This is where Irish matters stood when the Carlton Club meeting took place. The Treaty had not answered the Irish Question. Instead,

99 'Unionist M.P.s' Decision. Mr Chamberlain Defeated', *The Times*, 20 Oct. 1922.

100 David Close maintains that the Treaty was the Die-hards' 'main grievance' against the Lloyd George Coalition. See 'Conservatives and Coalition', p. 254.

101 Derby to Chamberlain, 22 Mar. 1922, AC 33/1/51.

102 'Thoughts on Some of the Present Discontents of the Conservative Party', Summer 1922, Halifax Papers, A4.410/9.

103 Spender to Tallents, 2 Aug. 1922, CO 906/21. SF (B) 32nd Conclusions, 7 Sept. 1922, CAB 43/1. Lady Spender's diary, 27 Sept. 1922, D/1633/2/26. Conference No. 147, 26 Sept. 1922, CAB 23/39.

the endless continuance of civil strife in Ireland – where peace had been promised with such vain assurance – and the outbreak of a new crisis in Asia Minor – for which the Prime Minister appeared to be in some degree personally responsible – combined to vex the faithful supporters of the Cabinet'.[104]

It was enough. When the votes at the Carlton Club meeting were counted, only 87 MPs stood by Chamberlain. The overwhelming number, 187, were ready to back Bonar Law.

'THE IRONY OF FATE'

Lloyd George was nonchalant when news of the Carlton Club vote reached Downing Street. 'That's the end', were his only words, and he walked out to tender his resignation to the king.[105] As it happened, he was to remain prime minister for another four days until Bonar Law secured the leadership of the Conservative Party. In the interim, one of Lloyd George's first acts was to assure Cosgrave that no action would be taken to 'compromise the Treaty' and that Britain was still pledged to ratifying the Free State Constitution by the 6 December deadline. His telegram was later given to the press, lest any of Bonar Law's Die-hard friends had other ideas.[106]

By most accounts, Lloyd George was almost jocular about this twist of fate.[107] When, finally, it came time to leave Downing Street, there were no sad partings. True, he had sustained a reversal. But this was only temporary. He would be back.

Instead, he never crossed the threshold of power again.

In less than a year, Lloyd George descended from what seemed to be an unassailable position to the abyss of defeat. As for his colleagues, Churchill, as he himself famously put it, was without an appendix, without an office and, soon, without a Parliamentary seat.[108] Chamberlain, Birkenhead, Balfour, Horne, and Worthington-Evans also found themselves cast into the wilderness. Of the lot, Conservatives were especially unforgiving towards Birkenhead. He, 'far more than Lloyd George', was held responsible for the attempts to force the party into a general election after the Irish Treaty was signed and,

---

104 'The End of the Coalition', *Quarterly Review*, no. 474, Jan. 1923, p. 202.

105 A. J. Sylvester, *The Real Lloyd George* (London, 1946), p. 99.

106 Lloyd George to Cosgrave, 19 Oct. 1922, LG F/10/3/56. Jones diary, 21 Oct. 1922, vol. III, p. 217.

107 See, e.g., Hankey diary, 21, 23 Oct. 1922, HNKY 1/5/208–17.

108 Churchill had to undergo an emergency appendectomy in the middle of the crisis. R. Rhodes James, *Churchill: A Study in Failure, 1900–1939* (London, 1970), p. 147.

again, that autumn. Birkenhead, according to George Younger, 'has been the evil genius of the piece all through'.[109]

In the end, a number of factors combined to bring about the Coalition's downfall. As Chamberlain wrote some weeks after the event, no government could have held office 'for four such critical and difficult years' without inciting 'discontent and disappointment' among its followers. Nor was it surprising that these same adherents had grown uneasy with Lloyd George's leadership and his unsettling habit 'to startle and surprise the country'.

> Here you have matter enough for widespread discontent and grumbling. Then comes the Irish settlement accepted by the great majority of the Party, but bitterly resented as a betrayal by a small section of it. Gradually around this section all the discontents crystallised and . . . the feeling against a continuation of the Lloyd George premiership grew into a formidable force.[110]

Churchill agreed. 'Much of the bitterness which suddenly exploded at the Carlton Club was due to the fury of the Die-Hards at the Irish Treaty', he wrote from his sick-bed. 'This was the deed they could not forgive and for which they were determined to exact vengeance.' [111]

Yet, by this time the Irish Treaty was not the same agreement that had been signed less than a year before, and for that Churchill was largely responsible. Under his guardianship, the Boundary Commission was postponed and the financial restrictions that were meant to serve as an inducement to unity made far less onerous. Consequently, the prospects for reuniting the island were not what they had been before he took charge of Irish affairs.

But where, exactly, did Churchill stand on the question of Irish unity? Alfred Cope believed that Churchill's personal view was that 'the practical working of the Treaty would inevitably lead to a reunited Ireland'.[112] Indeed, during the Treaty negotiations, Churchill advocated a policy that 'might well include the creation & recognition of an all-Ireland Parliament'. His only condition was that 'no *physical* force' should be employed against Ulster.[113]

Even before the Coalition's downfall, however, Churchill had moved far away from this position. Craig privately told one of his secretaries that, of all

109 Younger to Strachey, 20 Nov. 1922, Strachey Papers, S/19/4/26. 'If Lord Birkenhead were to play cards the way he plays the game of politics', one foe scornfully wrote, 'he would be kicked out of decent society for cheating'. See de Montmorency to Carson, 16 Jan. 1922, Carson Papers, D/1507/A/42/1.

110 Chamberlain to Lloyd, 7 Dec. 1922, AC 18/1/35.

111 Churchill to Robertson, 27 Oct. 1922, WSC 5/28(a)/20–30.

112 Cope to Masterton-Smith, 13 Oct. 1922, CO 739/2/51232.

113 Churchill to Lloyd George, 9 Nov. 1921, LG F/10/1/40 [emphasis added].

the government's ministers, Churchill was 'the one man who is helping us'. During the 1922 general election campaign, this shift was made public when Churchill announced that he would 'oppose *all* attempts to coerce Ulster' into joining the Irish Free State.[114] He would oppose efforts to bring economic pressure to bear on Craig's government, and he was now committed to resisting any Boundary Commission award which might endanger Northern Ireland's separate existence. These were Churchill's new touchstones, and their consequences would be far reaching if he ever again become involved in Irish affairs.

For the moment, however, those affairs were in other hands. Churchill took a certain pleasure in knowing that the Treaty settlement would now be carried out by the very men who for 'so long fomented the quarrel' between Britain and Ireland and who had spent the past year 'abusing in the harshest terms the men who had made the peace'. It was, as he called it, 'the irony of fate'.[115]

114 Craig to Blackmore, 29 Aug. 1922, PRONI, PM/9/4. Oakley to Churchill; Churchill to Oakley, 1, 2 Nov. 1922, WSC 5/28(a)/79-80 [emphasis added].
115 Churchill to Robertson, 27 Oct. 1922, WSC 5/28(a)/20–30.

FOUR

THE LEGACY OF BONAR LAW

*Before the war there were only two things which I really cared for as matters
of conviction, – the rest was mainly a game. One was tariff reform; the other
was fair play to Ulster, and I feel as strongly about it [now] as I did then.*
ANDREW BONAR LAW[1]

—

If it had not been for Ireland it is likely that Andrew Bonar Law never would
have become prime minister. In virtual retirement less than twelve months
before taking office, he re-emerged only to intervene in the Treaty negotiations,
smashing Lloyd George's plans to force Ulster Unionists into a single Irish
state. Now he was in Lloyd George's place, having acquired from the
Coalition what one contemporary journal called 'a heritage of mismanaged
problems . . . the most disquieting' of which was Ireland.[2]

Bonar Law was the first modern British prime minister not to appoint an
Irish chief secretary to his government. And, as John Ramsden has written, he
did not 'intend to have an Irish policy either'.[3] But even by doing nothing,
Bonar Law in effect would have been doing something. That 'something'
would be to change the whole dynamic of the Treaty settlement. The centre-
piece of Lloyd George's Irish policy was to hold out to Nationalists the hope
of eventual North–South reunification. With the Tories in power, 'a definite
change in political facts' took place.[4] 'Henceforth', Paul Canning has noted,
'British policy was directed almost solely towards preserving the *status quo* in
Ireland.' This change was well concealed, so that it seemed as if Britain's Irish
policy was allowed to drift throughout Bonar Law's ministry.[5]

1   Bonar Law to Croal, 12 Nov. 1921, BL 107/1/83.
2   'The End of the Coalition', *Quarterly Review*, no. 474, Jan. 1923, pp. 211–12.
3   Ramsden, *Balfour and Baldwin*, p. 169.
4   Curtis to Cope, 20 Oct. 1922, CO 739/7/52403.
5   Canning, *British Policy*, pp. 73, 74–85.

For evidence of this drift critics needed to look no further than the Colonial Office and its new secretary, Victor Cavendish, 9th Duke of Devonshire.[6] Of all the legacies left by the Lloyd George Coalition, the most 'complicated' was 'Winston Churchill's policy in Ireland'.[7] But where Churchill was conspicuous in directing Colonial Office policy, nothing of the sort could be said of his successor. Craig was among those who noted the difference. Devonshire's activities, the Ulster premier later said, were for the most part 'confined to nodding and receiving notes on slips from officials.'[8]

Of these officials, none was more important than Lionel Curtis. Active though he had been in shaping the Coalition's Irish policy, Curtis now assumed a crucial role in constructing a framework for Anglo-Irish relations. His importance was such that colleagues considered him 'the repository of tradition concerning the Treaty'.[9] An unblushing imperialist, Curtis's primary objective was to anchor the Free State firmly within the British Commonwealth. Irish unity – and, it must be said, the rights of Northern Nationalists – were secondary concerns. Curtis argued that these issues could be resolved only after Dublin had shown Ulster Unionists that it could be trusted.[10]

These judgments are true, but only so far as they go. Even if Devonshire abdicated responsibility for Irish policy, it would be wrong to assume that the rest of the Cabinet, not least the prime minister, followed suit. Upon reflection, it is hardly likely that a man as committed to the Ulster Unionists as was Bonar Law would have passed up any opportunity to further their cause. The advent of Bonar Law marked a decided shift in British policy on two matters that were essential for ending Ireland's partition. The first of these was the Council of Ireland; the more important issue was Northern Ireland's financial relations with Great Britain.

The evidence that Bonar Law played such a decisive role is, admittedly, fragmentary, his interventions in Irish affairs not nearly as obvious as those of his flamboyant predecessor. Britain's new prime minister took the role of one who remains discreetly in the background. Nevertheless, Bonar Law marked off new parameters in Irish policy beyond which his successors could not, or would not, go.

---

6   Although Ulster affairs were transferred to the Home Office, Craig and his colleagues were outraged that the Colonial Office continued to view the North as part of its 'All Ireland' responsibilities. See C 70(22), 11 Dec. 1922, CAB 23/32, and Cabinet Conclusions, 15 Jan. 1923, PRONI, CAB/4/68/8.

7   'The End of the Coalition', pp. 211–12.

8   Tallents to Anderson, 8 May 1924, HO 144/3915/7.

9   Upcott to Piercy, 25 Apr. 1923, Piercy Papers, 10/15.

10   D. Lavin, *From Empire to International Commonwealth: A Biography of Lionel Curtis* (Oxford, 1995), pp. 197, 204–26. Canning, *British Policy*, pp. 73–85.

TOWARDS A NEW 'STATUS QUO'

The day after the Carlton Club vote brought an end to the Lloyd George Coalition, a group of leading Conservatives met to discuss policy now that the party was again on its own. According to Leo Amery, Bonar Law was 'anxious' to have their views on only two subjects: 'Ireland and fiscal policy'.[11] Because of the events that had brought him to power, Bonar Law decided that his new government must call a general election. But his desire to go to the country for a mandate immediately ran into a complication. Hemmed in by Lloyd George's public declaration that Britain would honour its commitment to ratify the Irish Constitution by the Treaty's December deadline, any election would have to be held immediately. Although at least one member of Bonar Law's government saw no reason for going to the polls, a general election it was decided there would be, and because of the Irish commitment it would have to be held by mid-November at the latest.[12]

This decision caused no small amount of anxiety on both sides of the Irish frontier. 'Naturally', Kevin O'Higgins confided to Lady Lavery, 'our hearts are with the men who forged the settlement'.[13] Like many others, the Provisional Government's leaders fully expected that Lloyd George soon would be back to lead the British nation. North of the border, Bonar Law's decision was viewed as being 'of the very gravest moment for Ulster, no matter how the fight goes'. In the six counties, partition was bound to be the main issue, the only issue, and one that was 'full of deadly peril'.[14]

Unionists were right to be anxious. Their Nationalist opponents meant to use the campaign 'to register another emphatic protest against Partition'. In outlining this strategy, Kevin O'Shiel, a legal adviser to the Provisional Government, pointed out that the Nationalists' only realistic chance of winning any seats was in the twin constituency of Fermanagh and Tyrone. By concentrating their energies on a constituency where voters elected two MPs, a win there would be 'an important victory in view of the Boundary Commission'.[15]

Although Eamon de Valera called for a boycott of the election, his appeal was largely ignored. The 1922 campaign proved to be one of those instances in which Northern Nationalists buried their differences and profited as a result.

---

11   Amery diary, 20 Oct. 1922, p. 307.

12   Ibid, 19 Oct. 1922, p. 300. Jones diary, 23 Oct. 1922, vol. I, p. 216.

13   O'Higgins to Lavery, 27 Oct. 1922, BL 114/1/20. How such a potentially embarrassing letter found its way into Conservative hands is unclear. A note accompanying the letter says that Devonshire 'has seen it with satisfaction'.

14   'Gravest Moment for Ulster', *Belfast Telegraph*, 23 Oct. 1922.

15   O'Shiel to Collins, 26 Oct. 1922, JHC, D/921/2/3/1.

Two candidates were nominated to stand for the Fermanagh–Tyrone seats: the Irish Parliamentary Party MP T. J. S. Harbison, and the pro-Treaty Sinn Féin journalist Cahir Healy who, at the time, was one of several hundred Nationalists interned on the prison ship *Argenta*. When the votes were counted, both men decisively beat their Unionist opponents, registering majorities of over 6,000 apiece. Beyond rejecting the Unionist candidates, border Nationalists believed their votes had sent a warning shot across the bow of the new Conservative ship of state. 'The inhabitants had declared their wishes', said the chairman of Omagh Urban Council, 'and if Bonar Law did not accept them, then he must tear up the Treaty.' In that case, his new government would face a 'fight for the liberty of all Ireland'.[16]

Although he had no intention of reigniting the Anglo-Irish War, the notion of tearing up the Treaty must have appealed greatly to Bonar Law. Fate had played a wicked trick on the man who had taken his country to the brink of civil war over Home Rule. Now, he found himself responsible for shepherding through Parliament a Constitution giving the Irish greater independence than anyone had dreamed of in 1914 – and the sort of freedom that only two years earlier he himself had declared could not be given unless Britain was prepared to commit 'national suicide'.[17]

Bonar Law was deeply ambivalent about the Irish settlement. Only a few months after supporting the Treaty, he renounced his vote, making this 'vital' point:

> I thought that those who signed the Treaty . . . accepted the position that Ulster could never be brought in [to an all-Ireland government] until they were willing to be brought in. Everything that has happened since has shown that I was wrong.[18]

In other words, Bonar Law had come to realise that the Treaty was an instrument designed to bring about the eventual unity of Ireland that he had fought against for most of his political life.

The new prime minister's suspicions of Ireland outside Ulster were deep-rooted. 'When I was young', he told one confidant, 'I used to travel frequently to Ireland.' Belfast was, to him, 'less different from Glasgow probably than Edinburgh is'. Not so, Dublin. There, a young Bonar Law found himself in 'a

---

16 'Tyrone–Fermanagh Election Result', *Ulster Herald*, 25 Nov. 1922. Phoenix, *Northern Nationalism*, pp. 262–3.

17 'Mr Bonar Law on Ireland', *The Times*, 1 Dec. 1920. Also, see *HC Deb*, vol. 127, col. 1120–33, 30 Mar. 1920.

18 *HC Deb*, vol. 155, col. 1744, 26 June 1922.

foreign atmosphere', a conviction he held for the rest of his life. Among those who worked with him, Bonar Law's reputation for a 'granite-like resistance to any tampering with the rights of Ulster' was well known.[19] Most of his supporters shared these prejudices, and this further explains why he was anxious to create a new Irish *status quo* – which he would define.

On top of these worries, Bonar Law inherited a Conservative Party whose confidence had been badly shaken. Having consorted with Lloyd George for so long, many Tories were uncertain about the party's future. Even those who applauded the Carlton Club vote doubted that there was support in the country for a 'pure Conservative Government' and that 'another form of Coalition' would be the most likely outcome of the next election.[20]

The split between former Coalitionists and their opponents also marked a divide between those Conservatives who were proud of the role that they had played in ending the Irish conflict from those who 'felt a sort of hurt that so old a sore could be healed'.[21] Although they conceded that the time was 'not yet ripe', Bonar Law's Die-hard supporters fully expected that it soon would be necessary to reimpose British rule in Ireland.[22] In this divisive atmosphere, it was hardly surprising that one Cabinet minister gloomily predicted that the new government might 'be only an affair of weeks', while Bonar Law himself 'talked of being out of office in a fortnight'.[23]

Instead, the Tories won a clear-cut victory in the 1922 election, surprising even themselves. Bonar Law now commanded a comfortable majority in the House of Commons and needed the support of no other party to maintain his position.[24] Yet Ireland remained a potential source of friction within his government. From the Die-hard wing of the party, Lords Cave and Salisbury were particularly 'obstinate' about the Treaty and were 'unwilling to realise that it had to be swallowed without change and the Constitution ditto'.[25] Others counselled that the 'Free State Government must be given a fair

19 Bonar Law to Croal, 12 Nov. 1921, BL 107/1/83. 'Bonar Law: His Chief Service to the Empire', *Western Mail*, 22 May 1923.

20 Peel to Reading, 27 July 1922, IO, Eur. E. 238/5, No. 16. Wood to Chamberlain, 'draft', ? Oct. 1922, Halifax Papers, A.4.410/26/2.

21 Coote, *Elliot*, p. 75. According to Lord Winterton, the Treaty 'caused heart-burnings in the Conservative Party'. See *Orders of the Day* (London, 1953), p. 105.

22 Gretton memorandum, 16 Oct. 1922, S (4) 103/27–39.

23 Salisbury to Selborne, 25 Oct. 1922, Selborne Papers, MSS 7, ff. 146–7. Hankey diary, 31 Oct. 1922, HNKY 1/5/223.

24 The Conservatives and their Ulster Unionist allies took 344 of the 615 seats in the Commons. See *Annual Register: 1922*, p. 120.

25 Jones diary, 16 Nov. 1922, vol. I, p. 223.

chance', and even some Die-hards recognised that their room for manoeuvre might be limited. Salisbury, for one, was consoled by the fact that 'the men *principally* responsible [for the Treaty] are out of office, and we all want to forget and make friends'.[26]

It was time to move on. Independence for the South was a done deal. The Treaty had been accepted by the British people in the 1922 election, and Conservatives had campaigned on a promise to restore 'tranquillity' to the country. Once in office they could not very well turn round and create a situation that might bring on a new Anglo-Irish war.[27] In the end, Bonar Law's ministers resigned themselves to the fact that they 'had no alternative' but to carry on with the Treaty. As Amery later wrote, 'there could only be loyal acceptance of the existing position'.[28] At this same meeting, the Cabinet also agreed that they would adhere to the Treaty 'not only in the letter but in the spirit'. As Bonar Law explained to Tom Jones, 'if the Treaty and Constitution must be put through it was better to do it handsomely than in any niggardly spirit'.[29]

Yet this decision, however magnanimous Bonar Law may have thought it to be, was storing up trouble for the Conservatives. It was all very well to promise to adhere to both the letter and the spirit of the Irish agreement. But what would the party's attitude be when, as had happened already and was bound to happen again, interpretations of the 'letter' and the 'spirit' differed in London and Dublin? Though willing to give Cosgrave's government its 'fair chance', Sir Arthur Griffith-Boscawen warned Bonar Law that the party would allow 'no interference with the rights and position of Ulster'.[30]

26   Griffith-Boscawen to Bonar Law, 25 Oct. 1922, BL 110/1/1. Salisbury to Bonar Law, 22 Oct. 1922, BL 111/29/37.

27   Austen to Ida Chamberlain, 21 Nov. 1922, AC 5/1/252.

28   C 68(22), Appendix II, 22 Nov. 1922, CAB 23/32. Amery, *My Political Life*, p. 241.

29   Ibid, CAB 23/32. Jones diary, 16 Nov. 1922, vol. I, p. 223. Also, see 'Extract from Mr Bonar Law's Election Address to his Constituents at Glasgow, October 27th, 1922', in Cmd 2264: *Irish Boundary Extracts from Parliamentary Debates, Command Papers, etc., Relevant to Questions Arising out of Article XII of the Articles of Agreement for a Treaty Between Great Britain and Ireland, Dated 6th December 1921*, 1924, xviii, 113. That said, implementing the Treaty was a task which gave Bonar Law 'neither enthusiasm nor satisfaction'. See J. C. C. Davidson *Memoirs of a Conservative: J. C. C. Davidson's Memoirs and Papers, 1910–37*, R. Rhodes James, ed. (London, 1969), p. 138.

30   Griffith-Boscawen to Bonar Law, 25 Oct. 1922, BL 110/1/1.

'A STIFFER ATTITUDE'

Whatever worries Bonar Law's supporters had about the direction of his Irish policy were nothing compared to the nightmare a Tory government posed for Irish Nationalists.[31] Within days of the Carlton Club meeting, Provisional Government Chairman William Cosgrave travelled to London for a hastily arranged meeting with the new prime minister. Warned to 'anticipate a stiffer attitude', Cosgrave was worried that the Conservatives might engineer fundamental changes in the Treaty or delay Parliament's ratification of the Irish Constitution. For this reason, he chose to discuss the Irish settlement only in general terms. Cosgrave let it be known that his government's policy was 'the Treaty'. Upon it and it alone the new Free State 'meant to stand in the spirit and the letter' – and he 'looked to the British Government to do the same'. Despite press speculation that the Treaty's Ulster clauses must have been a main topic of discussion, the subject never crossed anyone's lips. No one thought it politic to mention the Boundary Commission.[32]

Bonar Law never had to face the boundary issue directly, and for that he had Irish Republicans to thank. So long as civil war raged in the South, it was impossible for Dublin to raise the boundary issue. The disastrous impact of the Civil War was put nowhere more forcefully than by the *Irish News*. 'Every life that is taken', the paper pointed out:

> every train that is wrecked, every home that is burned, every outrage committed in the name of an Irish Republic in the Irish Free State confirms the convinced Partitionist in his faith and drives the citizen who dislikes Partition further and further away from the Idea of National Re-union.[33]

Kevin O'Shiel, the newly appointed director of the North-Eastern Boundary Bureau, agreed. 'What a ridiculous position we would cut', he wrote, 'both nationally and universally – were we to argue our claim at the Commission for population and territory when at our backs in our own jurisdiction is the perpetual racket of war'.[34]

31   See, e.g., 'Our Dublin Letter', *Ulster Herald*, 4 Nov. 1922.

32   Curtis to Cope, 20 Oct. 1922, CO 739/7/52403. 'Meeting between Mr Bonar Law and the Irish Ministers', 24 Oct. 1922, CO 739/7/54174. 'Free State Leader Mr Cosgrave Received by Mr Bonar Law', *Morning Post*, 25 Oct. 1922.

33   'Partition Arguments', *Irish News*, 16 Jan. 1923.

34   O'Shiel to Cosgrave, 17-page memorandum, undated, RM, P7/B/101.

THE COUNCIL OF IRELAND

With the Provisional Government caught up in the struggle to establish its authority in the 26 counties, it was evident that it would have little time for problems north of the border. This fact, particularly after Collins's death, did not go unnoticed in either London or Belfast, and the supporters of Ulster Unionism quickly took advantage of it. As well as ratifying the Irish Constitution, Bonar Law's government was committed to enacting additional legislation to resolve several disputes created by the Treaty. Chief among the issues to be addressed in the Consequential Provisions Bill was the 'anomaly' of the Free State's role in the Council of Ireland.[35]

The 1920 Act gave both Irish governments an equal say in matters handled by the Council on both sides of the border. But whereas the Treaty gagged Belfast on southern Irish affairs, Dublin retained its say in matters related to Northern Ireland. Craig wanted the Council abolished altogether, to be replaced by joint meetings of the Belfast and Dublin Cabinets. While Collins was alive, this demand was rejected unless Craig would concede moves aimed at reunification.[36]

As a gesture of goodwill Cosgrave's government offered to set aside the Council for up five years. During that time, the British would exercise the Council's powers in Northern Ireland, while the two Irish governments considered possible alternatives. If no agreement was reached at the end of five years, the Council could then be called into being. This gesture was spurned by Craig, who wanted no time limit. Hugh Kennedy, the Provisional Government's legal adviser, rejected his demand, arguing that it would 'in effect wipe out the Council of Ireland altogether'.[37]

At a Cabinet committee meeting called to discuss the dispute, Sir John Anderson pointed out that, strictly speaking, 'the Northern Government had no say in the matter'. That kind of advice, Lord Salisbury pointedly answered, failed to take account of the new political reality. The Conservatives were not about to override Craig's objections and 'put Ulster under the South', even when Curtis and other senior civil servants pointed out that they had no other choice short of repudiating the Treaty. In this instance, 'the bargaining power' entirely lay in the hands of the southern Irish. 'It was a mistake to think that these provisions were put into the Treaty by inadvertence', Anderson explained;

---

35   CIL 3rd Meeting, 22 Nov. 1922, CAB 27/157. *HC Deb*, vol. 151, col. 800, 3 Mar. 1922.

36   Ibid., CIL 3rd Meeting. Appendix II, Articles 12 and 13. Craig to Devonshire and Craig memorandum, 6 Nov. 1922, CO 739/1/55311. Conference minutes, 29 Mar. 1922, CAB 43/5.

37   'Irish Free State (Consequential Provisions Bill)', 25 Nov. 1922, BL 117/7/7. *HC Deb*, vol. 159, cols 388–9, 423–33, 27 Nov. 1922. CIL 3rd Meeting, 22 Nov. 1922, CAB 27/157.

'on the contrary, Mr. Griffith and Mr. Collins had attached great importance to them'. Sir James Masterton-Smith agreed. If 'Collins were now alive', he told the Conservatives, the Provisional Government's offer never would have been made without 'some substantial concession' from the Ulster Unionists. So far as Masterton-Smith was concerned, 'the Northern Government were getting something for nothing and would be ill-advised to refuse'.[38]

So it was that the Council of Ireland was put into cold storage by the Consequential Provisions Act. Bonar Law and his colleagues were 'anxious' to avoid the issue and were happy to leave Dublin and Belfast to 'thresh the matter out' themselves over the next five years.[39] What is extraordinary is that a full eighteen months would elapse before this concession was raised in Dáil Éireann, and only then by accident. During debate on a railways bill, Kennedy, by then Free State attorney-general, flabbergasted opposition TDs when he off-handedly mentioned the moratorium. Kennedy defended the agreement, claiming that to do otherwise would have given Northern Ireland a voice in Southern affairs.[40] It is unclear whether he actually believed this explanation or whether he was attempting to avoid an embarrassing situation. Whatever the case, as the government's chief legal expert, he ought to have known that this was untrue.

Opposition leader Tom Johnson returned to the issue in mid-June, attacking the moratorium and pointing out that, in British eyes at least, this was a change or 'variation of the Treaty'.[41] But more importantly, Johnson argued that the chances of ending partition were far greater through the Council than anything that might be achieved with the Boundary Commission. Once 'you have secured unification of control', Johnson told the Dáil, 'you have ensured ultimate unity'.[42]

Yet Johnson and other government critics were hardly innocent in this matter. Their failure to take notice of the moratorium when it was made public in November 1922 was staggeringly incompetent, and was surpassed only by the arrogance of Cosgrave's later rebuke. Opposition TDs, the Irish president said, could not take 'the ostrich line' and claim they had been kept in the dark about the Consequential Provisions Act. Its terms were fully reported in Irish newspapers during its passage through the British Parliament. This was true.

38 Ibid, CIL 3rd Meeting. CIL 4, 12 Nov. 1922, CAB 27/157. Curtis to Devonshire, 17 Nov. 1922, CO 739/8/56786.

39 *HC Deb*, vol. 159, col. 389, 27 Nov. 1922.

40 *Dáil Deb*, vol. 7, cols 1498–503, 28 May 1924.

41 *HC Deb*, vol. 159, col. 388, 27 Nov. 1922. The phrase was used by William Ormsby-Gore, under-secretary of state for the colonies.

42 *Dáil Deb*, vol. 7, cols 2355, 2379, 13 June 1924.

Still, it begged the question of his own government's failure to inform the Dáil of legislation which, even he admitted, 'greatly concerned us'.[43]

Cosgrave backed away from Kennedy's assertion that the Council would have given the Ulster Unionists a say in Free State affairs. Instead, he argued that the North–South body was 'defective' and this necessitated the agreement. In fact, this explanation masked a larger concern. As one government supporter told the Dáil, a Council devised for two 'subordinate Parliaments could not possibly . . . suit a Sovereign Parliament'.[44] This, rather than any 'defects', explains Cosgrave's decision to forgo the Council. Not for the last time, a Dublin government felt that staking out the Free State's separate identity was more important than Irish unity.

THE FINANCIAL TRAP

On 6 November Craig penned a letter to Devonshire, outlining the changes he expected his Conservative friends to make to the Irish settlement while they were in power. With the outcome of the 1922 general election still uncertain, Craig was determined to seize the moment. Abolition of the Council of Ireland was only one item on his agenda. Equally important, he wished to renegotiate certain '[o]utstanding Financial questions'.[45]

Northern Ireland, as one historian has pointed out, was created as a political unit 'not an economic one'. In financial or economic terms, the six-county state was a 'near disaster'. As Churchill later pointed out, although it was based on the British model, the six-county state was neither large enough nor diverse enough to sustain the same level of services as were found elsewhere in the United Kingdom.[46]

Throughout the remaining months of the Lloyd George Coalition, the consequences of this situation had been held at bay by a series of emergency grants from the British Treasury. These 'temporary expedients', as Craig called them, were 'calculated to stave off the most pressing difficulties of the moment'. But they were in no sense a long-term solution. Moreover, officials in Belfast chafed at the knowledge that under the restrictive conditions of the 1920 Act they 'must always appear in the character of a suppliant'.[47]

43 Ibid., cols 2606–8, 18 June 1924.

44 Ibid., col. 2608, 18 June 1924; col. 2829–31, 20 June 1924.

45 Craig to Devonshire, 6 Nov. 1922, T 160/150/F.5814/1.

46 Mansergh, *Unresolved Question*, p. 245. Churchill to Steel-Maitland, 13 Mar. 1925, T 160/187/F.7136/4.

47 Craig to Devonshire, 6 Nov. 1922, T 160/150/F.5814/1. Clark to Piercy, 8 Sept. 1923, Piercy Papers, 10/12.

Craig intended to rectify this situation, using as his pretext southern Ireland's establishment as a dominion. Ultimately, he aimed at nothing less than a complete reappraisal of Ulster's financial relationship with London, focusing on three issues: Northern Ireland's imperial contribution; the funding of its social services, particularly its unemployment insurance programme; and payment for its security force, the Ulster Special Constabulary.

Craig's letter to Devonshire also marked the beginning of Stanley Baldwin's role in Irish affairs, a central role that he took up as Bonar Law's chancellor of the exchequer. On receiving a copy of Craig's letter, Baldwin's subordinates at the Treasury reacted to its demands with undisguised irritation. His 'proposals would be incredible', Otto Niemeyer told Baldwin, 'if they were not in black and white'. In an accompanying memorandum, Niemeyer argued that the basis of Craig's demands was 'wholly false'. Ratifying the Irish Constitution would in no way affect the operation of the 1920 Act in Northern Ireland. And, he added for good measure, Craig was proposing a fundamental change in the Act which 'is regarded by Ulster in other connections as inviolable'.[48]

THE COLWYN COMMITTEE

The day after Niemeyer submitted his memorandum, Craig met privately with Baldwin and Bonar Law. By the time the three men left the room, they had agreed that 'all outstanding financial questions between the British Treasury and that of Northern Ireland . . . should be submitted for arbitration'. Why Bonar Law agreed to this arrangement is unclear. It is likely that Craig persuaded him that unless there were changes in the financial relationship between Northern Ireland and the rest of the United Kingdom, the Ulster government soon would be bankrupt. Whatever the reasons, Baldwin told Craig that, 'as far as possible', he wanted a 'clean cut'. Put another way, he wanted a settlement that would 'clear up the existing uncertainties and reduce to an absolute minimum' any possible future controversy between London and Belfast.[49]

This was the genesis of what was officially called the Northern Ireland Special Arbitration Committee, but what was better known as the Colwyn Committee, named after its chairman, Frederick Henry, 1st Baron Colwyn. The committee was to determine if, in light of the establishment of the Irish Free State, 'any alteration is needed in the present scale of the contributions of Northern Ireland to the cost of Imperial Services'. Before its work was

48 Niemeyer to Baldwin and Niemeyer memorandum, both dated 20 Nov. 1922, T 160/150/F.5814/1.
49 Baldwin to Craig, 22 Nov. 1922, T 160/150/F.5814/1.

finished, the committee issued two reports. First, it recommended a series of changes to the imperial contribution required of Northern Ireland for fiscal years 1922–23 and 1923–24. A second report prescribed a method for determining Belfast's future imperial contribution.[50]

Along with Lord Colwyn, who also chaired the Joint Exchequer Board, the committee was made up of Sir Laming Worthington-Evans and Sir Josiah Stamp. Both Colwyn and Worthington-Evans had been proposed by Craig, the latter because he 'was mainly responsible' for the 1920 Act's financial provisions. Stamp's appointment turned out to be equally advantageous for the Ulster Unionists. In a 1921 article written for the journal of the Royal Economic Society, Stamp anticipated many of the arguments that the Northern Ireland government would make to the committee. As one historian has noted, that Stamp should hold these same views proved to be 'most fortunate' for Craig's government.[51]

Early in their deliberations, the Colwyn Committee was cautioned to do nothing that Dublin might interpret as adversely affecting the 'ultimate fusion' of Southern and Northern Ireland. In a letter to William Piercy, the committee's secretary, G. C. Upcott explained that since the Treaty negotiations of 1921 Northern Ireland 'has often tried in one way or another to get herself put on an equality of status with the Free State'. The demands now being put before the committee by Craig's government were merely another attempt to achieve this same end and should be rejected.[52] Not surprisingly, Belfast officials took the opposite view, arguing that 'should they consider it necessary' it was within the committee's power to suggest 'drastic alterations' to the 1920 Act.[53]

According to a later Treasury memorandum, the first Colwyn Committee report 'gave substantial advantages to Ulster', reducing its contribution to the Imperial Exchequer from £6.74 million to £5.85 million for 1922–23, and from £5.8 million to £5 million for 1923–24. In addition, the committee awarded Craig's government £500,000 to supplement a previous British grant of £1.5 million to cover claims for malicious damages inflicted since January 1922; another £400,000 was awarded for the construction and maintenance of colleges and other public buildings. However, the committee went against the

50   Cmd 2072: *First Report of the Northern Ireland Special Arbitration Committee*, 1924, xi, 341. Cmd 2389: *Final Report of the Northern Ireland Special Arbitration Committee*, 1924–25, xiv, 125.

51   See Craig–Baldwin correspondence, 23, 27 Nov., 4 Dec. 1922, T 160/150/F.5814/1. Follis, *State Under Siege*, p. 137.

52   'Note of a conversation with Mr. Upcott', 13 Apr. 1923; Upcott to Piercy, 25 Apr. and 12 Oct. 1923, Piercy Papers, 10/15.

53   'Future Contribution', ? Jan. 1923, PRONI, FIN/11/2.

Unionists on two other claims. First, the unemployment relief grant embodied in the second Craig–Collins Pact was reduced from £500,000 to £300,000, although Belfast authorities were given an unlimited amount of time to dispense the money. Nor would the committee back Craig's claim for a larger share of funds from a housing grant for Irish ex-servicemen. Based on population, Northern Ireland had been awarded 28 per cent of £1.5 million allocated to house Irish war veterans; the remaining amount was awarded to the Free State for the same purpose. Craig wanted 40 per cent of the total, or the equivalent in the form of a separate grant to his government.[54]

The Colwyn Committee's second report, presented in December 1924, accepted the substance of Northern Ireland's case. Niemeyer was vindicated in his earlier prediction that the imperial contribution would become 'a last charge' on Ulster's government, allowing it to 'deduct all that they are likely to spend locally from their revenue and give us only what is left'. Niemeyer was no less scathing after the report was issued, calling it 'an unsatisfactory document in every way'. In a note to Churchill, who was by then chancellor of the exchequer, he concluded that, 'instead of getting at any rate peace with penury in the future, I fear we shall have incessant disputes'.[55]

Although some writers have blamed the final Colwyn award for snuffing out Northern Ireland's long-term economic and financial development, they admit that the report gave Ulster Unionists nearly everything they wanted and was, indeed, heartily welcomed in Belfast. Craig was sanguine about the payments, predicting that in time the contribution would 'melt away altogether.' Which is exactly what happened. Between 1924 and 1931, Ulster's annual payments to the British Treasury tumbled from £4.5 million to £500,000. This latter contribution was virtually wiped out when, also in 1931, an identical sum of £500,000 was given to Stormont by the British government. With it, the imperial contribution disappeared.[56]

Even more than the decisions taken by the Coalition in its waning months, the Colwyn awards substantially altered Northern Ireland's financial relationship with the British government. Committee members may have felt there were good reasons for doing so; but their decisions violated the Treaty and further entrenched partition. Given this fact, an obvious question arises: why did the Free State not object to what was a breach of, if not the letter, at least

54 Snowden memorandum to MacDonald, 26 Sept. 1924, JRM, PRO 30/69/61. Cmd 2072. Upcott memorandum to Snowden, 30 Jan. 1924, T 160/131/F.4855/02/1.

55 Niemeyer memorandum, 20 Nov. 1922, T 160/150/F.5814/1. Niemeyer to Churchill, 25 Mar. 1925, T 160/150/F.5814/2. Also, see Hawtrey memorandum, 27 May 1924, T 208/83.

56 Follis, *State Under Siege*, pp. 146–7, 152. Lawrence, *Northern Ireland*, pp. 46–9, 53. But see Pollock and Craig speeches, *NI HC Deb*, vol. 6, cols 451–2, 468, 7 May 1925.

the spirit of the Treaty settlement? The answer was supplied by the Boundary Bureau's economics adviser, Joseph Johnston. If national re-unification was the main objective, it should have been Dublin's aim to see to it that Ulster's imperial contribution was 'fixed at as high a level as possible'. But, there was a conflicting interest at work. The Free Staters had to bear in mind that they, too, faced a similar adjudication of financial claims mandated by Article V of the Treaty. If Northern Ireland's contribution was 'fixed as low as possible', this would establish 'precedents and definitions' that Cosgrave and his colleagues could later use to their advantage.[57] Given the near bankruptcy faced by the Free State government, it is not surprising that the Colwyn awards went unchallenged.

NO 'CLEAN CUT'

Not long after the Colwyn Committee began its work, Baldwin discovered he was not going to get the 'clean cut' that he thought he had agreed to with Craig. Far from it, Ulster's leader wished to see the committee become a 'standing tribunal to which fresh claims may be referred'. Baldwin, in a letter written only days after he succeeded Bonar Law as prime minister, told Craig he 'could not possibly agree' to any such thing.[58]

But Craig was not so easily deterred. As the Colwyn Committee was on the verge of submitting its first report, Piercy received a letter from Sir Ernest Clark, secretary to Northern Ireland's Department of Finance. Although the issue was not mentioned in Craig's 6 November letter to Devonshire, nor was it 'part of the case originally put forward' by the Belfast government, Clark's superiors now wanted the Colwyn panel to consider a claim of assistance for Northern Ireland's unemployment insurance fund.[59]

Throughout the early 1920s, Northern Ireland's economy continued to stagnate leaving large numbers of men and women out of work. So far as Clark was concerned, obtaining imperial support for Ulster's unemployment insurance fund was 'of greater importance to us than the Special Constabulary'. Yet, even with the active support of Worthington-Evans, the Ulster Unionists were unable to budge the rest of the Colwyn Committee on this issue. Any

---

57 'Preliminary memorandum on the First Report of the Colwyn Committee', 28 Mar. 1924, NEBB, Box 28.

58 Upcott memorandum Neville Chamberlain, 15 Sept. 1923, T 160/131/F.4855/02/1. Baldwin to Craig, 28 May 1923, T 160/163/F.6282.

59 Clark to Piercy, 5 Sept. 1923, Piercy Papers, 10/12.

request for assistance for the unemployment fund, Clark was informed, could be referred to the committee only by the chancellor of the exchequer.[60]

Craig did not act on this advice for the better part of three months. After the 1923 general election, however, when a Liberal or even a Labour government seemed likely to replace the Conservatives, he suddenly deemed it urgent that the Colwyn Committee should issue its report on the future of Northern Ireland's imperial contribution. He also wanted the committee to reconsider imperial backing for his government's unemployment insurance fund.

'Your proposal', Neville Chamberlain told Craig, 'in the present political circumstances is, I fear, quite impossible.' Time would not allow the committee to issue its final report before a new government came into office. Nor, as chancellor of the exchequer, was Chamberlain willing to refer 'an entirely new claim' to the Colwyn Committee. Such a move would bind the next government to the panel's decision – which is precisely what Craig was after.

Even if the Conservatives' fall from power had not been in the offing, Chamberlain doubted that he could back the Unionists' claims for support of their unemployment fund. Doing so, he reminded Craig, would involve 'a fundamental amendment' to the 1920 Act.[61] That should have been the end of the matter. But as officials at the Treasury were learning, the Unionists were more adept at saying 'no', than they were at taking it for an answer.

PAYING FOR THE SPECIALS

In his letter establishing the Colwyn Committee, Baldwin determined that there should be a 'sole exception' to the range of issues in which it could intervene. This one matter, 'to be reserved for separate consideration', was also the most contentious dispute between the two governments: Britain's continued funding of the Ulster Special Constabulary.[62]

Though conceived as a temporary force during the Anglo-Irish War, the 'A', 'B', and 'C-1' Special Constabulary still numbered roughly 42,000 at the end of 1922.[63] During the remaining months of the Coalition government, Craig was able to ensure continued imperial backing for the force by claiming that various Cabinet members had promised to 'see him through'. His ploy

---

60 Clark to Pollock, 21 Aug. 1924, PRONI, FIN/11/12. See Worthington–Evans–Piercy correspondence, 26 Sept., 3 Oct. 1923, Piercy Papers, 10/14. Piercy to Clark, 8 Oct. 1923, Piercy Papers, 10/12.

61 Chamberlain to Craig, 3 Jan. 1924, T 160/187/F.7136/1.

62 Baldwin to Craig, 22 Nov. 1922, T 160/150/F.5814/1.

63 A. Hezlet, *The 'B' Specials: A History of the Ulster Special Constabulary* (London, 1972), p. 93.

confounded Treasury officials – not least because it was seldom challenged and, even then, the Ulster leader still got his way.[64]

Craig seems to have thought that his claim on Treasury funds for the Specials would be immune from Bonar Law's 1922 election promise to reduce the government's budget. This time, however, he was in for a shock. On 23 November, Craig urgently wrote to Baldwin concerning a matter that had to be taken care of 'as speedily as possible': namely, funding for the Specials for the next financial year, as well as an additional request for £200,000 needed for 'the *current* financial year, promised by Winston Churchill' while he was still colonial secretary. Citing the 'present burdens of the British taxpayer', Baldwin did not see how he could possibly promise any future aid for the Specials. As for the £200,000 request, he was 'informed that Winston Churchill made no [such] promise'.[65]

This rebuke forced Craig to fall back to his position of last resort: he implicitly threatened to resign. 'I doubt if anyone could be found to carry on here unless they were assured that the present magnificent system of Special Constabulary was maintained at a sufficient strength', Craig told Baldwin. And the price tag for that 'sufficient strength' had just gone up. As Craig explained it, his home minister and inspector-general had 'underestimated' the number of 'A' Specials needed to maintain order. Therefore, his government was now asking for £1.5 million for financial year 1923–24, instead of the £1.35 million initially requested.[66]

Once again, the Ulster Unionist position was saved by Bonar Law. On 4 December Baldwin informed Craig that, after consulting with the British prime minister, Belfast's demand for an additional £200,000 would be granted after all. Even so, Baldwin felt bound to insist that Churchill had no authority to commit the British Treasury to such a promise. Nor, he pointedly added, 'do I think that he did in fact do so'. The matter of future budget requests was, for the moment, put to one side.[67]

Officials at the Treasury warned that underwriting the Specials marked a serious departure not only from the spirit but also the letter of the 1920 Act. It also breached Article 11 of the Treaty. G. C. Upcott pointed out to Baldwin that with the South absorbed in a civil war, the Specials no longer could be

---

64 Niemeyer to Horne, 5 May 1922, T 163/6/11/G.256/049.

65 See Craig–Baldwin correspondence, 23, 27 Nov. 1922, T 160/150/F.5814/1.

66 Ibid., Craig to Baldwin, 28 Nov. 1922.

67 Ibid., Baldwin to Craig, 4 Dec. 1922. Baldwin agreed to the £1.5 million grant in February. See Niemeyer memorandum, 22 Feb. 1923, WO 32/5330. In total, the Specials received £2.7 million from the British Treasury for financial year 1922–23. See Snowden memorandum to MacDonald, 26 Sept. 1924, JRM, PRO 30/69/61.

regarded as an adjunct to the British Army. Their main function now consisted of maintaining internal order in the six counties and as 'a means of providing for unemployment [*sic*] in Ulster'. If previous experience was anything to go by, Upcott continued, 'only direct financial pressure on Northern Ireland will secure substantial reductions in this expenditure'.[68]

Lord Derby, Bonar Law's secretary of state for war, was also critical of Craig's spendthrift habits when it came to the Specials. Nor was he confident about the relationship between the Specials and army units stationed in the North. In case of trouble, Derby confided to the home secretary, 'we might be badly let down by the Constabulary.' But, far from disbanding the Specials, Derby's solution was to absorb the force into the British military as a division in the Territorial Army.[69]

Derby's proposal came about because the War Office was under intense pressure to reduce the number of army units throughout the empire. As many as 16 battalions were stationed in Northern Ireland, a number Derby wanted reduced to five. As an incentive, he pointed out that if the money Belfast wanted for the Specials was used to raise a Territorial division, 'Craig could have something like 65,000 men for the same cost as he now has some 25,000 Constabulary.'[70] There was also a political motive behind Derby's proposal – a motive baldly laid out by the War Office in its 'Report on the Organization of the Constabulary Forces in Northern Ireland'. The two officers who wrote the report argued that the formation of such a unit was necessary because:

> There exists in Northern Ireland amongst all classes a grave mistrust of the British Government. We do not mean particularly the present one, but rather of any Government which may be in power in Great Britain in the future. This mistrust will take years to remove, and . . . can only be eradicated by bringing Northern Ireland more and more into the United Kingdom, and particularly as regards military matters.

Having said all that, the report's authors then laid down a series of exceptions for use of the Ulster Division, exceptions which would apply to no other Territorial unit. First, the division could not be removed from the province without the consent of Northern Ireland's government. Conversely, this same government would be empowered to mobilise the division for service in the province, 'irrespective of whether the remainder of the Territorial Army has been called out or not'.[71]

68 Upcott memorandum to Baldwin, 6 Feb. 1923, T 160/131/F.4855/02/1.

69 Derby to Bridgeman, 11 Dec. 1922, WO 137/4/11–12.

70 Ibid. Derby to Bonar Law, 9 Dec. 1922, BL 111/13/71.

71 Memorandum by Major General Sir Archibald A. Montgomery and Colonel H. H. S. Knox, 12 Feb. 1923, WO 32/5330.

While the War Office might have fancied the idea of clothing the Specials with the authority of the British Army, others were appalled. Sir Charles Wickham, the RUC's inspector-general, warned that the 'C-1' constables were 'a highly political body'. Even if they were converted into a Territorial division, he was certain that in any dispute between Belfast and London, the 'C-1s' would 'refuse orders from their Imperial officers' creating, as he put it, a 'difficult situation'.[72]

The idea that he would be provided free of charge with a fully equipped army division was beyond Craig's wildest dreams and, in the end, any possible realisation. Despite War Office support, the plan was allowed to hang fire through the summer and autumn of 1923. In early November, Craig attempted to resurrect the proposal, telling Derby that his government was now prepared to 'acquiesce' in the conversion of the 'C-1' Specials into a Territorial division. But Craig had been overtaken by events. Derby explained that the plan faced 'considerable legislative and financial difficulties' and, despite his own personal support, he could not promise 'anything definite in the present fluid state of politics'.[73]

Even after the Conservatives left office, Craig could not let go of the idea of his own army division. In late January 1924, the new war secretary, Stephen Walsh, received the first of a series of letters from Craig claiming that 'in accordance with the wishes' of his predecessor, the 'C-1' Specials had been retained to prepare for their formation as a Territorial division. Craig was employing the same tactic that had worked so well in his dealings with the Treasury. But this time his bluff was called. Pleading that Walsh's refusal to honour Derby's 'request' would cause the Ulster government acute 'embarrassment', Craig then tried to salvage the situation by using the denial to win yet further grants for the Specials. When even this ploy failed, he became aggressive. 'You are doubtless aware', Craig sternly reminded Walsh on 11 March,

> that Northern Ireland, in contributing her quota to the Imperial Exchequer, is paying for her share of the National Debt and the Imperial expenditure on the Forces of the Crown. We have a claim, therefore, that Northern Ireland should be put on the same footing as other parts of the United Kingdom when it comes to the expenditure of these sums. . . .

72 Tallents to Anderson, 27 Aug. 1923, HO 144/3915/8.
73 See Craig–Derby correspondence, 9 Nov., 19 Dec. 1923, WO 32/5309.

Craig wrote these words all the while he was doing everything he could to reduce his government's imperial contribution.

Derby's suggestion finally was put to rest by the former war secretary himself. After receiving copies of Walsh's correspondence with Craig, he denied committing the War Office to any plans for an Ulster Territorial Division. Derby's letter was a useful warning to anyone dealing with Ulster's premier. 'It just goes to show how careful one ought to be not to make any casual remark which can be construed into a definite statement of policy', he ruefully admitted.[74]

'A VERY DANGEROUS TOPIC'

By the time Derby penned those words, Bonar Law was dead. A victim of throat cancer, he resigned as prime minister on 20 May 1923 and did not live to see the end of the year. Shortly before Bonar Law's resignation, Cosgrave wrote to inform him of the 'collapse of armed resistance' and the end of the Irish Civil War. Unaware of Bonar Law's condition, the Free State president suggested that it would soon be time for their governments to make ready for the Boundary Commission.[75] Four days later Bonar Law stepped down as prime minister.

One last time the poisoned chalice had passed from his lips. Bonar Law could go to his grave as the uncompromising champion of Ulster. According to his biographer, Northern Ireland's existence was his legacy as much as, if not more than, Edward Carson's or James Craig's.[76]

What Bonar Law would have done about the boundary issue had his health not given way can be no more than a matter for speculation. One possible answer was given nearly a year after his death by the former Canadian Prime Minister Sir Robert Borden. According to Borden, Bonar Law was 'prepared to let Ireland go', meaning that he would have accepted the declaration of a republic in the South.[77] If this is true, it is likely that Bonar Law would have gone along with such a declaration not so much as an acceptance of the will of the Irish people, but as a way of scuppering once and for all any chance of reconciliation and reunion between North and South.

---

74   Ibid, Craig–Walsh correspondence, 23 Jan., 25, 28 Feb., 6, 11 Mar. 1924; Derby to Kenneth Lyon, 17 Mar. 1924.

75   Cosgrave to Bonar Law, 16 May 1923, D/T, S 1801/C.

76   Blake, *Unknown Prime Minister*, p. 531.

77   Borden to Beaverbrook, 9 Oct. 1924, BBK C/51.

Moreover, by the time of his death, support for this trade-off was gaining ground in both Conservative and Unionist ranks.[78] Yet such a solution would have required a good deal of explanation. Under Bonar Law, it was a Tory article of faith that an Irish republic would be a direct threat to the future of the British Empire.

Bonar Law held his country's highest elected office for only 210 days. In that short time, Britain's Irish policy veered further away from the course that had been charted in December 1921. The Boundary Commission was indefinitely postponed; the Council of Ireland, too, was put on hold. Equally important, under Bonar Law the process of altering the Treaty's financial clauses was advanced so that these, too, would no longer pose a threat to Northern Ireland's existence. His feat has gone largely unrecognised, then or since, an unknown triumph for the 'Unknown Prime Minister'.

Ever the pessimist, he himself seems not to have realised his accomplishment. A few weeks after leaving Downing Street, Bonar Law was paid a visit by the Cabinet's assistant secretary, Tom Jones. The dying man thought his successor was making a good start as prime minister. Nevertheless, he confided to Jones, 'the real trouble' for Stanley Baldwin 'would be over the Boundary Commission – it was a very dangerous topic.'[79]

So it was. But the rest of the Treaty's Ulster clauses, especially those designed to bring about economic pressure on Northern Ireland, had largely been rendered impotent. This change marked a serious blow for the prospects of Irish unity, a change that might never have taken place but for the return of Bonar Law to politics.

---

78 See e.g., 'Ireland, Rome, and the Republicans', *Quarterly Review*, No. 477, Oct. 1923, p. 415. Churchill to Curtis, 8 Sept. 1924, Curtis Papers, MSS 89, ff. 89–90.

79 Jones diary, 10 June 1923, vol. III, p. 221.

FIVE

MR BALDWIN TAKES CHARGE

*The fact is that a big fight is coming on in Great Britain over the
Protection issue and they are unable to think of any thing else.*

EOIN MACNEILL[1]

—

As the Irish negotiations edged to their climax on the evening of 5 December
1921, at least one member of the British Cabinet was unmoved by the history
being made round about him. 'It's rather a depressed SB this afternoon',
Stanley Baldwin confided to a friend, 'for I have been done out of my dinner
at Trinity (and a stay at the Lodge, if you please!)'.[2]

Unlike the man he was destined to succeed as prime minister, Baldwin had
never shown much interest in Irish affairs. Those who knew him would not
have been surprised that he found a reunion at his old college far more con-
genial than awaiting the outcome of the Irish negotiations, however dramatic
that might be. By his own reckoning, Baldwin's feelings about Ireland were
those of 'an ordinary rank-and-file member of the Unionist [i.e. Conservative]
Party'.[3] The description was apt. Like most of his fellow Tories, Baldwin had
little sympathy for the Nationalist cause and, also like most other Tories, what
views he did have were coloured by a degree of anti-Catholic prejudice.[4]

As president of the Board of Trade in the Coalition government,
Baldwin was bound to support the Irish Treaty.[5] This support, however, was
conditional. In return, the Free State must remain a faithful member of the
Commonwealth and, more importantly, Ulster's 'equal rights' within the
United Kingdom must not be disturbed. 'Whether in years to come she thinks
fit to enter a United Irish Parliament', he wrote in the *Popular View*, 'is her
business and her business alone.' Baldwin was among those who saw the Treaty

---

1   MacNeill to O'Higgins, 2 Nov. 1923, D/T, S 1801/C.

2   Baldwin to J. C. C. Davidson, 5 Dec. 1921, Davidson Papers.

3   S. Baldwin, 'Why I Support the Irish Agreement', *Popular View*, vol. 1, no. 9, Jan. 1922, p. 3.

4   K. Middlemas and J. Barnes, *Baldwin: A Biography* (London, 1969), p. 67.

5   See, e.g., *HC Deb*, vol. 149, cols 119–24, 14 Dec. 1921.

as a final settlement, a new status quo, and like many other 'rank-and-file' Conservatives he was more than ready to see the Irish problem disappear from Britain's political agenda.[6]

Yet, however much they may have desired to put the Irish question behind them, post-war Conservatives could not walk away from Ireland, and this proved to be truer for Baldwin than for most. The history of the Conservative Party in the first years after the fall of Lloyd George is above all the story of men seeking first to reunite former Coalitionists with their Tory opponents, before going on to re-establish the party as the dominant player in British politics. In their hearts, most Conservatives were glad that the Coalition had produced the Irish Treaty, that it was 'impossible to put the clock back to 1920'.[7] But because Ireland's most contentious issue – the relationship between North and South – had not been settled, this conflict was bound to re-emerge, thus threatening to upset the party's drive towards unity and electoral dominance.

For Baldwin in particular, the events that took place on the night of 5–6 December 1921 continued to shadow his career. As chancellor of the exchequer, he had already played an important role in altering the contours of that settlement, making it less likely that financial considerations would spur the two Irish governments towards unity. Now, as the leader of his country, it was left to him to face what his predecessor had called that 'very dangerous topic'.

'INDEFINITE POSTPONEMENT'

When Conservative MPs met to confirm Baldwin as their leader in May 1923, the most 'striking feature' of the gathering was the 'appeal for unity within the party'. Baldwin picked up on this theme in his acceptance speech, appealing to his followers to 'avoid any discussions that may prevent or delay a final and a complete reunion' which, he hinted, might be brought about 'at no very distant date'.[8]

Despite these warm words and a 'now or never' appeal from his followers, Austen Chamberlain refused to have anything to do with the party he once led. From Paris, he issued a letter freeing his colleagues from 'any obligations arising out of our joint action in the Irish Treaty and last October' (i.e. the Carlton Club meeting) so that they could accept office in the new government.

6   Baldwin 'went out of his way to identify with the rank and file' of the Tory Party. See Ramsden, *Balfour and Baldwin*, pp. 207–15. For an alternative view, see P. Williamson, *Stanley Baldwin: Conservative Leadership and National Values* (Cambridge, 1999).

7   'The End of the Coalition', *Quarterly Review*, no. 474, Jan. 1923, p. 212. Also, see Cowling, *Impact of Labour*, pp. 127–8.

8   'Prime Minister as Leader', *The Times*, 29 May 1923.

As for his own position, however, Chamberlain was under no illusions 'as to my unpopularity with the Die-hards', who now dominated the Tory inner circle.[9] Much as Baldwin might wish to restore party unity, many in the Cabinet opposed Chamberlain's inclusion in the leadership, and they were even more hostile towards Birkenhead.[10]

Chamberlain's foes had not forgotten the part that he and Birkenhead had played in the Treaty negotiations. Above all, the two stood condemned for the settlement's Ulster clauses, which the *Belfast News-Letter* called 'as gross a betrayal as it is possible to imagine'.[11] In November 1922, Chamberlain attempted to refute these allegations, telling delegates from the Ulster Unionist Council that he believed the Boundary Commission would make only minor readjustments to the Irish frontier. But he then went on to say that the current border was neither a 'logical or good boundary'. Worse, he admitted that the Coalition 'never affected to believe that the Act of 1920 could be permanent.'[12]

Chamberlain compounded his woes the following spring, when he involved himself in a very public exchange over allegations that a 'Ministerial under-taking' was given to Irish leaders guaranteeing that the Treaty would end partition.[13] Although Chamberlain was absolved of any responsibility for the pledge, the timing of this incident could not have been worse. When, finally, he and Baldwin met, Chamberlain had little choice but to accept Baldwin's explanation that he had simply 'never thought of' including Austen in his new government.[14]

Baldwin was dissembling. In fact, he had given the idea a good deal of thought.

As a formality, on Baldwin's assumption of the premiership all members of the Cabinet tendered their resignations. As told to Neville Chamberlain, the Duke of Devonshire offered to step down from the Colonial Office to make way for another appointee if that would help to restore party unity. 'Accordingly', Neville wrote in his diary, 'Baldwin had thought of offering the C.O. to

9   See Worthington-Evans and Chamberlain letters, 22, 24 May 1923; and Chamberlain to Birkenhead, 31 May 1923, AC 35/2/2, 6, and 18.

10 Peel to Reading, 30 May 1923, IO, MSS Eur. E. 238/6, No. 17.

11 'Mr. Chamberlain and Ulster', *Belfast News-Letter*, 2 Nov. 1922.

12 Ibid. Also, see 'Mr. Chamberlain and Ulster', *The Times*, 2 Nov. 1922.

13 'The Irish Revolution', 12 May 1923; 'Irish Settlement. Mr. A. Chamberlain on Partition', 18 May 1923; 'Irish Partition. The Alleged Promise', 25 May 1923; and 'Irish Boundary. The Alleged Secret Understanding', 12 Sept. 1923, all in *The Times*. In *The Irish Revolution and How It Came About* (Dublin, 1923), pp. 441–5, William O'Brien claimed that the assurance was given by Churchill and Lloyd George.

14 Chamberlain memorandum, 27 May 1923, AC 35/2/11(b).

Austen but had reflected that he would be prejudiced by his Irish record (!)'.[15] Neville Chamberlain's story was confirmed a few days later by Lord Peel. Two issues stood in the way of Austen's return to the party's inner circle, Peel told India's viceroy. The lesser of the charges was that 'he had shown little friendliness' towards Bonar Law's government. The graver charge, the one that his colleagues still could not forgive, was that 'he had been one of the signatories of the Treaty with Ireland'.[16]

Much as Chamberlain wished to put Ireland behind him, the Die-hards were unwilling to forgive or to forget.[17] In late June, Ronald McNeill, now a junior minister in Baldwin's government, used the first anniversary of Sir Henry Wilson's assassination to mount a savage attack on Coalition leaders. Lloyd George, 'jointly with Mr Austen Chamberlain, was the author' of the policy that led directly to Wilson's killing, McNeill told his audience. As well as attacking Chamberlain, McNeill also took aim at the Free State. His speech provoked a stinging rebuke from Dublin which Baldwin, in turn, feared might cause a 'serious reaction' within his own party.[18]

Even without these distractions, it was going to be impossible for Baldwin to ignore the Irish Question for long. Less than three weeks after he took over as prime minister, Cosgrave informed Britain's new leader that the Irish government would soon be ready to present its case to the Boundary Commission. The day after Cosgrave wrote, Tom Jones discussed the problem with Bonar Law, and the two agreed that it could cause Baldwin 'real trouble'. In that case, it might be best to play for an 'indefinite postponement' of the entire issue.[19]

15   Chamberlain diary, 1 June 1923, NC 2/21. The source for this story was Bonar Law. If Devonshire's offer was made in writing, Baldwin seems not to have kept it. But see the cryptic postscript in Devonshire to Baldwin, 23 May 1923, SB vol. 42, ff. 46. According to Worthington-Evans, Baldwin told Robert Horne that he had intended to offer the Colonial Office to Chamberlain but changed his mind after learning 'that Conservative feeling was strongly against Austen' in both Cabinet and party circles. See memorandum, undated, W-E, MSS Eng. his., c. 894, ff. 32–42.

16   Peel to Reading, 12 June 1923, IO, MSS Eur. E. 238/6, no. 20.

17   Lord Crawford found it amusing, 'in a grim fashion', that while the Die-hards would not forgive Chamberlain for his role in the Irish Treaty, they were willing to accept the former Liberal Reginald McKenna as chancellor of the exchequer, even though he had been 'the bitterest opponent of Ulster'. See Crawford diary, 26 May 1923, in Earl of Crawford, *The Crawford Papers: The Journals of David Lindsay, 27th Earl of Crawford and 10th Earl of Balcarres, 1871–1940, During the Years, 1892 to 1940,* J. Vincent, ed. (Manchester, 1984), pp. 483–4.

18   'Irish Chaos. Mr. R. McNeill's Reply to Mr. Lloyd George', *Morning Post,* 25 June 1923. EC Min., 25 June 1923, D/T, G2/2, C.1/128. Curtis to Masterton-Smith, 26 June 1923; and Cosgrave to Baldwin, 27 June 1923, CO 739/18/34181. Baldwin to Cosgrave, 2 July 1923; and ? to Curtis, 3 July 1923, SB vol. 99, ff. 8–10. Incidents like this occurred throughout Baldwin's first government. See, e.g., Curtis to Jones [letter excerpt], 3 Oct. 1923, vol. III, p. 225.

19   Cosgrave to Baldwin, 9 June 1923, CO 739/18/30127. Jones diary, 10 June 1923, vol. III, p. 221.

Whether or not Jones passed on the advice, these two words became the alpha and omega of Baldwin's Irish policy for the next six months. Like Bonar Law, he avoided public discussion of the issue whenever he could – and was evasive when he could not.[20] The issue was quarantined in the Colonial Office by Devonshire and his subordinates. Never, during Baldwin's first government, was the boundary question discussed in Cabinet.[21]

THE RIGHT 'PSYCHOLOGICAL MOMENT'

While avoiding the boundary question may have been an option for Baldwin, it was not for Cosgrave. No longer fettered by the diversion of civil war, Free State leaders faced increasing pressure to direct the same energy towards ending partition as they had devoted in their fight against the Irregulars of the IRA.[22] Such criticism was particularly galling when it came from Northern Nationalists who were themselves divided over how to achieve reunification. In fact, Nationalists in the six counties were bitterly split into several factions. These divisions included not only pro- and anti-Treatyites. There was also the older rift between Sinn Féin and the Irish Parliamentary Party led by Joseph Devlin. This second division, in part, mirrored yet another split. On one side were those in the border counties who expected to be transferred to the Free State by the Boundary Commission. On the other were those Nationalists living in eastern Ulster, especially Belfast, who could expect no such 'rescue'. If anything, their position would be made that much worse if the boundary award did not end partition entirely but, instead, left them in an even more homogeneous Protestant state.[23]

This latter group, overwhelmingly Devlinite in its political allegiance, was highly critical of Cosgrave's Northern policy throughout the Civil War. The corrosive effect of such criticism soon told on Free State supporters. One of these supporters was John Henry Collins, a Newry solicitor recently employed by the Free State's North-Eastern Boundary Bureau. Collins's primary job for the bureau was to gather evidence to present to the Boundary Commission; his other duty was to 'keep in touch' with Nationalist sentiment in his area.[24]

20 See, e.g., Baldwin's exchange with Oswald Mosley in *HC Deb*, vol. 167, cols 1699–1700, 2 Aug. 1923.

21 Although the Cabinet held several discussions on disputes with Dublin over compensation payments and land purchases, there was no discussion of the boundary issue between 30 May 1923 and 22 Jan. 1924. See CAB 23/46.

22 'Boundary Commission – Memorandum', 11 July 1923, D/T, S 1801/C.

23 See Phoenix, *Northern Nationalism*, for a detailed history of these divisions.

24 Ibid., pp. 173, 259–60.

As early as January 1923, Collins warned bureau director Kevin O'Shiel of growing scepticism 'about the honesty and bona-fides of your Government'. Although the Civil War had not yet been won, Collins pressed for the Boundary Commission's immediate establishment, to 'have the thing brought to a head'. As long as the panel worked 'honestly and quickly', he told O'Shiel, 'I cannot conceive of anything that will be of greater assistance to the Irish government'.[25]

O'Shiel's response was one Collins may have reflected on bitterly in later years. The Northern Nationalists had to be 'patient', O'Shiel told Collins, and judge the Free State '*not* by their fears of what they *think* it *may* do, but by the ultimate results of the issue'.[26] By early May, however, the situation was, if anything, worse. 'One thing I can tell you', Collins wrote to another bureau official,

> and I cannot emphasise it enough – that the longer you leave these Counties in the position they are in without enforcing the Boundary Commission, the worse it is for the Irish Supporters here . . . it is hard to convince them that the South has not abandoned them entirely. It is time . . . that something definite was stated from Dublin regarding the Commission.[27]

Such advice was not taken kindly in the Irish capital. When a delegation of Northern Nationalists requested a meeting to press their demands, the Executive Council's minutes described their accompanying resolution as one 'breathing' a 'spirit of hostility to the Free State Government'. Eoin MacNeill, the minister of education, and O'Shiel were instructed to tell the delegates that the government was 'making active and unceasing preparations for the Commission' but that it would not act until the right 'psychological moment.' At the same time, the Nationalists were warned that their Southern allies would not 'allow themselves to be stampeded into any hasty action'.[28]

The charge often levelled against the Free State's founding fathers is that the deaths of Griffith and Collins 'sanctified' the Treaty so that it became for them not a means to an end but an end in itself.[29] While true in one sense, this accusation paints an incomplete picture. Although the Civil War was over, the country was just beginning to reckon with its cost, and the Ulster Question

25 Collins to O'Shiel, 27 Jan. 1923, JHC, D/921/2/4/1.
26 O'Shiel to Collins, 30 Jan. 1923, JHC, D/921/2/4/2.
27 Collins to E. M. Stephens, 8 May 1923, JHC, D/921/2/4/90.
28 EC Min., 14 May 1923, D/T, G 2/2, C.1/106.
29 Fanning, *Independent Ireland*, p. 42. According to Roy Foster, 'the dominant pre-occupation of the regime was self-definition against Britain'. See *Modern Ireland: 1600–1972* (London, 1988), p. 516.

was not the only concern bearing down on Cosgrave and his colleagues. The Free State was shattered physically, emotionally and, on a more immediate if prosaic level, financially. Detractors were quick to contrast conditions in the 'stable' North with those in the 'unstable' South. While Craig's government could boast a small budget surplus of £32,042, the Free State was saddled with a staggering deficit of £26 million. The greater part of this sum, the *Annual Register* reported, 'was directly due to the losses entailed by the Republican campaign of destruction'. In 1923–24 alone, fully 37 per cent of the new country's revenue was spent on defence or compensation for personal injury or property damage resulting from the Civil War.[30]

This burden of debt would not begin to ease until the end of the decade. Until then it would be a continual source of weakness which the southern Irish could not ignore in their dealings with Britain. 'When the Free State was founded', Kevin O'Higgins's biographer noted, 'it was probably the only country in the world without a National Debt'. A year later, 'it was on the verge of bankruptcy'.[31]

Given this situation, Cosgrave and his lieutenants can hardly be blamed for concentrating on the necessary, if mundane, duties of building a new state. Nor is it logical to claim that because the Free State's leaders focused their attention on implementing the Treaty settlement, they were willing to forsake their Northern brethren. One did not preclude the other, and there is no reason to doubt Cosgrave's sincerity when he said that Article 12 was 'just as vital as any other clause of the Treaty'.[32]

The dilemma facing Ireland's new leaders was more complicated than that. Much as they desired to end partition, the Free Staters also had to show that de Valera and the Republicans were wrong, that the Treaty gave Ireland real independence. The problem was that whenever these two goals collided the Dublin government found that asserting Irish independence was far more likely to produce results than was making sacrifices for Irish unity.[33]

Further complicating the Free State's Ulster policy was Bonar Law's victory in the 1922 general election. In a December memorandum, O'Shiel reminded the Executive Council that the 'object' of the Free State's Ulster policy was '*not the setting up of a Boundary Commission*' but the larger goal of '*National*

---

30 *Annual Register: 1923*, p. 151, 155. Fanning, *Independent Ireland*, p. 39.

31 T. de Vere White, *Kevin O'Higgins* (Tralee, 1966), p. 151.

32 'President Cosgrave in Tirconaill', *Ulster Herald*, 18 Aug. 1923.

33 At this time, e.g., Dublin became involved in a prolonged wrangle with London over its decision to issue Irish passports and to establish an embassy in the United States. See G. MacMillan, 'British Subjects and Irish Citizens: The Passport Controversy, 1923–24', *Eire-Ireland*, vol. XXVI, no. 3 (Fall, 1991), pp. 25–50.

Union'. With 'a strong Conservative government in power in Great Britain', he pointed out, the Commission might further entrench partition, not end it.[34]

Despite this concern, the Free State government continued to work on the assumption that the Boundary Commission would make substantial changes to the border, and the Executive Council was asked to consider the 'maximum' and 'minimum' territorial claims that it might demand. Were the Commission to base its findings solely on the wishes of the inhabitants and to the exclusion of 'every conceivable geographic and economic principle', Northern Ireland would be reduced to a rump consisting of nothing more than 'Co. Antrim, the extreme north east corner of Co. Derry, [a] portion of north and mid Armagh (excluding Armagh City) and north and mid Co. Down.'

A more realistic claim, and the one O'Shiel felt was 'the best possible line' to take before the Commission, would still give the Free State all of Ireland 'except Co. Antrim, the extreme east portion of Co. Tyrone bordering Lough Neagh, the eastern half of Co. Derry, the northern portion of Co. Armagh and the northern portion of Co. Down.' This latter claim, O'Shiel told the Executive Council, 'should be regarded as the minimum claim of the Free State beyond which they could not recede'.[35]

'GRAVE POLITICAL DISADVANTAGES': THE IRISH TARIFF

The Boundary Commission was not the only vehicle by which the Dublin government hoped to convince Ulster Unionists of the folly of partition. In late February 1923, Cosgrave surprised the British by announcing the erection of a customs barrier to begin operations on 1 April.[36] The Free Staters seem to have thought that they could achieve two goals with this one act. Besides generating income for the struggling government, taxing British-made goods would be an obvious demonstration of Irish independence. Second, imposing a tariff was in keeping with the strategy outlined by Michael Collins if the Ulster Unionists refused to come into an all-Ireland government. The resulting economic war, Collins had promised one County Derry ally, would be 'in the nature of Tariffs far far more effective than the Boycott ever was'.[37]

But of these two goals, it was clear that unity took second place. According to N. G. Loughnane, the Colonial Office's representative in Dublin, the Free

34 'The Boundary Commission', ? Dec. 1922, EB, P24/171/1–19.

35 EC Min., 5 June 1923, D/T, G 2/2, C.1/116. 'Our Territorial Demand at the Boundary Commission', 17 May 1923, D/T, S 2027.

36 Loughnane to Curtis, 23 Feb. 1923, CO 739/20/11976.

37 Collins to Walsh, 7 Feb. 1922, D/T, S 9241.

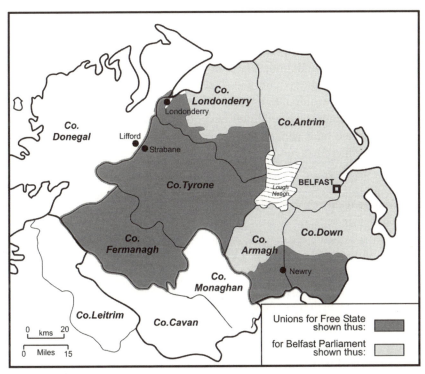

Free State claims to Northern Ireland territory, based on Poor Law Unions.
Based on North-Eastern Boundary Bureau, *Handbook of the Ulster Question*
(Dublin, 1923), p. 52.

Staters settled on their tariff policy 'without, apparently, having given the matter serious – or at least adequate – consideration'. Evidently, they believed that the British government was itself about to establish tariff barriers. The Irish set theirs up first, Hugh Kennedy told Loughnane, 'in order to demonstrate the Free State's independence of British control'. Timothy Healy, Ireland's governor general, dismissed this sort of thinking as 'madness'. By making Northern goods more expensive in the South, he predicted, even 'the Catholic population of Tyrone and Fermanagh will be given a financial interest in partition'. Cosgrave soon admitted that establishing the customs barrier was going to cause 'grave political disadvantages' in North–South relations; but, by then, it was too late to go back.[38]

Dublin's leaders had demonstrated that the Irish Free State was indeed sovereign – though at a cost. Less than a year after the decision to erect a customs barrier was announced, one Free State officer reported that the line separating North from South had become one of the most 'jealously defined

38   See Loughnane–Curtis correspondence, 27, 24, 28 Feb. 1923, CO 739/20/11976.

and guarded' boundaries in Europe. Echoing Healy's earlier warning, the Boundary Bureau's secretary noted that as the fiscal systems of Ireland's two parts diverged, 'new vested interests' were being created, making re-unification 'daily more difficult'.[39]

ELECTIONS, 1923: THE IRISH FREE STATE

The need to demonstrate Ireland's independence was made urgent by the fact that the Free State Constitution required the government to call elections before the end of 1923. Unpopular in some quarters for their ruthless suppression of the Irregulars, and in others because the Irish economy was in a slump, Cosgrave and his colleagues felt that they had to play the national card to ward off de Valera and Sinn Féin. They could ill afford to be vulnerable on the Ulster Question, and this explains why Cosgrave began to press first Bonar Law and then Baldwin to call the Boundary Commission into being.[40]

Even so, opinion in the Executive Council was sharply divided over how the boundary would develop as an election issue. Although they agreed that 'progress must have been made in the matter of the Boundary Commission before the coming General Election', Free State leaders realised that they could not predict with any certainty how events would play out once set in motion. Provided that the British government did not respond too quickly to the Irish request, Cosgrave and his associates could go to the electorate without having to explain what they would do if, as expected, Craig's government formally refused to name its Commissioner. Others in the Dublin ministry feared just the opposite, that the British would generate 'extended delays at every stage', exposing the Free Staters to a charge of impotence. Still another faction believed that Craig's refusal could itself be turned to their advantage, if the government called on Irish voters to rally behind their 'efforts to compel the terms of the Treaty to be carried out'.[41]

On 19 July Healy formally notified Devonshire that Eoin MacNeill had been chosen as the Free State's Boundary Commissioner. The next day Cosgrave made the appointment public, telling Dáil Éireann that 'the opportune moment' had at last arrived to put Article 12 into operation. That did not mean, however, that he was looking for an immediate British response. As

39   J. J. O'Connell memorandum, 4 Jan. 1924, O'Connell, MSS 22,133. Stephens to McGann, 18 Jan. 1924, NEBB, Box 27.

40   Lee, *Ireland*, p. 94.

41   'Boundary Commission – Memorandum', 11 July 1923, D/T, S 1801/C.

Devonshire explained to Baldwin, 'We know that Mr Cosgrave does not want or expect that anything further should be done while the elections are in progress'.[42] In this, Baldwin and his colonial secretary were only too willing to co-operate.

As a matter of fact, officials in the Colonial Office hoped that the Boundary Commission might be sidelined altogether. In this same letter to Baldwin, Devonshire proposed that after the Irish election Cosgrave and Craig should be invited to London to see if they could reach a mutual agreement on the boundary. Despite the willingness of both Irish leaders to meet with one another, the portents for a such a conference were not good. Cosgrave and Craig met at least twice during the Civil War and failed to see eye to eye on any significant matters.[43] When Cosgrave raised the boundary question at one such meeting, Craig was stubbornly 'unreceptive' and would not even discuss the issue. The meeting fizzled out with the two men reduced to a pointless conversation about 'cricket and the weather'.[44]

Although he realised that his friends in London would find themselves in 'a great difficulty' unless Baldwin 'stuck to the Treaty', Craig was increasingly confident that the boundary dispute would 'very likely die down' once the Free State elections were out of the way. On the face of it, such optimism was ill founded. The Ulster Unionist press was quick to label MacNeill's Boundary Commission appointment an election 'stunt'. Craig, very publicly, then slammed the door on any accommodation with Dublin and again refused to appoint a Commissioner.[45]

Predictably, Cosgrave and his colleagues felt that they had to show themselves to be equally determined. To audiences throughout the South they made expansive claims for what could be expected from a Boundary Commission award, claims that could not be justified even in the heat of an electoral campaign. The Free State's case 'was a good one', Ernest Blythe said in one speech, and the South was 'bound to be awarded a very considerable tract of territory'. Cosgrave was even less reticent. 'If there are any people who think we are going to allow any clause of the Treaty to be inoperative, they are making a very grave mistake', he declared. What many voters failed to notice was that these

42 Healy to Devonshire, 19 July 1923, Cmd 2155: *Correspondence Between His Majesty's Government and the Irish Free State and Northern Ireland Relating to Article 12 of the Articles of Agreement for a Treaty Between Great Britain and Ireland*; 1924, xviii, 69, no. 1. *Dáil Deb*, vol. 4, cols 1223–5, 20 July 1923. Devonshire to Baldwin, 20 July 1923, CO 739/18/36328.

43 Hopkinson, *Green Against Green*, p. 252.

44 Curtis to Devonshire, 30 July 1923, CO 739/20/42192.

45 Cabinet Conclusions, 30 July 1923, PRONI, CAB/4/84/12. 'Irish Boundary "Crisis." Ulster Premier's Declaration', *Manchester Guardian*, 23 July 1923.

pledges were conditional. As Blythe admitted to an audience at Clones, Free Staters could redeem their lost territories in the North only if the Commission was led by 'a fair chairman' – and that was something the Dublin government could in no way guarantee.[46]

Moreover, by this time Cosgrave had secretly committed himself to Devonshire's conference proposal even though this might effectively scrap the Boundary Commission. 'It will cost me a good deal of support among my followers', he told Curtis when the idea was put to him informally. But he believed that this 'is the way in which it ought to be settled'.[47]

Publicly, however, the government's new political party, Cumann na nGaedheal, was still committed to the Boundary Commission when the country went to the polls on 27 August. The results, according to one contemporary source, were a 'smashing defeat for the Republicans', given that Independent, Labour, and Farmer representatives, as well as Cumann na nGaedheal, all backed the Treaty settlement. But as a later analysis pointed out, the 'overall result' of the election was that Cosgrave now headed a minority government. Had it not been for de Valera's refusal to lead Sinn Féin's 44 TDs into the Dáil, the Free State's founders would have been forced to form a coalition. Instead, they found themselves in a situation where they could take decisions 'characterised by a boldness rarely associated with minority governments'.[48] This boldness would be nowhere more on display than when the boundary crisis reached its climax in 1925.

'SAVING ENGLAND'S FACE'

In late September Devonshire formally invited Cosgrave to the proposed boundary conference with Baldwin and Craig.[49] Among Cosgrave's advisers, the invitation aroused deep misgivings. The North-Eastern Boundary Bureau's secretary, E. M. Stephens, pointed out that the Free State had little to gain and much to lose from such a meeting. The 'rights of the Free State on the Boundary question are secured', he observed, whereas 'the very fact of entering a conference suggests that they are going to be reduced'. Worse still, the conference might be used to 'let England slip out of her liabilities in the matter' and allow the British to 'escape the odium' of breaching the Treaty

46 'The Boundary Commission. After the Free State Election'; and 'President Cosgrave in Tirconaill', 4, 18 Aug. 1923, *Ulster Herald*.

47 Curtis to Jones [letter excerpt], 28 June 1923, vol. III, p. 222.

48 *Annual Register: 1923*, p. 156. O'Leary, *Irish Elections*, pp. 21–2. Lee, *Ireland*, pp. 94–5.

49 Devonshire to Healy, 22 Sept. 1923, Cmd 2155, no. 4.

should Northern Ireland refuse to name its Boundary Commissioner. Stephens saw no reason for 'saving England's face'.[50]

O'Shiel was equally dubious. If the Free State accepted Devonshire's invitation, he felt that conditions must be attached. Like Stephens, O'Shiel believed that any conference concerned solely with Article 12 was not in the Free State's interest. Both men urged the government to have nothing to do with the conference unless its goal was Irish unity. Barring that, the Free State should attend only if the British guaranteed that in the event of a breakdown they would 'enforce the Boundary clause by delivering to us the areas where our supporters are in a majority, whether the North consents or not'. Otherwise, O'Shiel warned, the cry would go up among Northern Nationalists that they had been 'betrayed again'.

O'Shiel also suggested that Cosgrave could use the recent Irish election results to his advantage. The 44 Sinn Féin TDs were a 'blessing in disguise, as they will enable us to . . . drive a harder bargain than we could have done, say before the last Election'. Their mere presence, hovering at the entrance of Dáil Éireann, ready to turn the Free State into a republic, would allow Cosgrave to be uncompromising in the talks. 'We can blame everything on them and the British cannot say anything in reply', he wrote.[51]

Nor were these the only advantages now at hand. In another show of independence that autumn, the Free State was admitted to the League of Nations. By making specific reference to the Boundary Commission when defining the state's frontiers in their League application, Irish representatives shifted the Ulster Question from the realm of British politics and potentially made it a cause for international concern.[52] 'We can no longer say, as we could formerly about the whole Irish question, that it is an internal matter', one Colonial Office official reported from Geneva. This same official, M. E. Antrobus, further warned that the Irish could now take their 'complaint against us' to the League because delays in appointing the Commission violated an international agreement, the 1921 Treaty.[53]

50 Stephens to O'Higgins, 25 September 1923, D/T, S 1801/C.

51 Ibid. O'Shiel to Cosgrave, 5 October 1923, D/T, S 1801/C.

52 The link between the Free State's League application and the boundary issue was drawn by O'Shiel in 'Memo. Some Possible Dangers in the N.E. Situation', undated, D/T, S 1801/C. Also, see D. Harkness, *The Restless Dominion: The Irish Free State and the British Commonwealth of Nations, 1921–31* (London, 1969), pp. 35–7. Lavin, *Curtis*, pp. 213–15.

53 Antrobus to Curtis, 19 Sept. 1923, CO 739/25/45749. As early as April, O'Shiel had proposed just such a strategy, arguing that continued British inaction would allow the Free State to take the boundary dispute either to the League or to the Imperial Conference. See 'The Boundary Issue and North-Eastern Policy', 21 Apr. 1923, EM-UCD, LA1/H/92(1-6).

Lionel Curtis also saw the danger. If, as expected, Northern Ireland refused to appoint its Boundary Commissioner, a declaration by Baldwin's government that it could not enforce Article 12 might then provoke an Irish appeal for League intervention. Having said that, the alternatives were just as unappealing. Baldwin could appoint Ulster's representative, or London itself could act on Belfast's behalf on the Commission. Either of these options, though, required additional legislation. And that spelled political trouble for the Conservatives. Taking this issue to Parliament, Curtis predicted, 'might seriously divide the Govt. supporters and even the Cabinet'.[54]

Nevertheless, Cosgrave failed to resort to any of these tactics to strengthen his hand. Without any conditions whatsoever, the Free State government accepted Devonshire's invitation.[55] Cosgrave made no attempt to use the Sinn Féin threat against his government, nor did he even hint at a possible appeal to the League of Nations.

Why?

Given political conditions in Britain, the Irish president may have felt that a hardline stance would be counterproductive and that it was anyway better to play for time. As O'Shiel himself pointed out, the present Conservative government was hardly likely to nominate a Boundary Commission chairman who would be sympathetic to Dublin's case. This view was also shared by Tim Healy. The Free State's governor general informed Cosgrave and his colleagues that, according to a 'leading personage in political and journalistic circles in England', Bonar Law continued to back the Ulster cause even in retirement. '[A]s long as he wields his present influence', Healy warned, 'quarters that might otherwise be friendly will not be inclined to assist us openly.'[56] Cosgrave possibly felt that it was better to co-operate with the British initiative when delay was, anyway, the best option.

A simpler explanation may be that Cosgrave said what he meant: that the boundary question ought to be settled between the two Irish governments with as little outside interference as possible. This would account for the fact that the Executive Council seems never to have seriously considered taking the issue to the League of Nations. Yet either of these possibilities fails to account

---

54 Curtis to Devonshire, 10 Sept. 1923, CO 739/20/49361. Edward Wood, one of Britain's League delegates, later claimed that the Free State's application implied a 'narrower interpretation of the Boundary Commission's functions'. Even so, his 'devout hope' was that the issue should never be raised in the international forum. See Wood to Curtis, 9 Sept. 1924, JRM, PRO 30/69/61.

55 Healy to Devonshire, 8 Oct. 1923, No. 7; for Craig's acceptance, see Abercorn to Bridgeman, 13 Oct. 1923, no. 8, both in Cmd 2155.

56 'Boundary Commission – Memorandum', 11 July 1923, D/T, S 1801/C. Healy's likely source was Beaverbrook.

for a third factor. By the end of 1923 Cosgrave knew better than anyone that Craig was impervious to negotiation on this issue. In that case, a conference was going to be a waste of time. Perhaps Cosgrave hoped that by being reasonable he would garner British support at Craig's expense. But there is no direct evidence that he ever took this into consideration, leaving a question mark over his failure to heed the Boundary Bureau's advice.

'A SEDATIVE TO IRISH NERVES'

When the boundary conference was initially proposed, Curtis had hoped that it might be coupled with the Imperial Conference scheduled for October. The presence of other Dominion leaders in London, he thought, 'might help to produce an atmosphere more favourable to settlement'.[57] In fact, these meetings further delayed work on the boundary question. This was beginning to cause trouble for Cosgrave, for which he and his colleagues had only themselves to blame. Having promised swift action during the general election campaign, the Free State government fell silent on the issue as summer faded into autumn.[58] Finally, on 2 November Cosgrave announced that he had accepted Devonshire's invitation to a boundary conference but only after news of the proposal had been leaked to the press either in London or Belfast. Despite an assurance from Dublin that they had nothing to fear, the announcement sparked outraged protests among Northern Nationalists. 'One thing is certain', a priest warned Ernest Blythe about the Free State pledge, 'your government will live or die on it.'[59]

Events were about to take nearly as dramatic a turn.

On 25 October, Baldwin surprised nearly everyone by linking his party's fortunes to tariff reform. As it was, Devonshire had already informed Eoin MacNeill (who was in London to attend the Imperial Conference) that a meeting on the boundary question could not be held before January at the earliest. In the wake of Baldwin's startling announcement, further postponement was unavoidable. 'The fact is that a big political fight is coming on in Great Britain over the Protection issue', MacNeill told O'Higgins, 'and they are unable to think of anything else.'[60]

57 Curtis to Loughnane, 22 Oct. 1923, CO 739/17/50990.
58 Anderson to Tallents, 31 Oct. 1923, CO 739/20/52770.
59 Executive Council secretary to MacNeill, 3 Nov. 1923, D/T, S 1801/C. 'Boundary Commission: Index to Dates and Conferences', 1–19 Nov. 1923, D/T, S 1801/P. Coyle to Blythe, 6 Nov. 1923, EB, P24/204/30–4.
60 MacNeill to O'Higgins, 2 Nov. 1923, D/T, S 1801/C.

Amid this increasingly fevered political atmosphere, Curtis told Loughnane that there was 'considerable likelihood of a general election within the next three months, if not the next three weeks'. But that was not necessarily a bad thing. Curtis and Sir James Masterton-Smith felt that the intervening lull would give civil servants time to review the boundary problem, 'to see what cards the British government will have in its hands', and 'in what manner they can best be played'.[61]

A meeting of those civil servants most intimately involved in Irish affairs was scheduled for 15 November and seems to have led to a 27-page memorandum written after the 1923 election.[62] This document is crucial, because it foreshadowed subsequent British policy in the boundary dispute, and also because it laid the foundation of Whitehall's view of the Treaty settlement for years to come.

According to this rendering of events, partition was, indeed, the 'real crux' of the 1921 Treaty negotiations. A settlement based on a single Irish government was reached early on, only to be scuppered by Craig. In return for allowing Northern Ireland to opt out of an all-Irish Parliament, Lloyd George told the Sinn Féin delegates that they would be 'entitled to a revision' of the boundary. The Irish accepted solely because of Lloyd George's threat to 're-open hostilities within 72 hours'. Subsequent claims of a British guarantee that the Free State could expect the transfer of whole counties from Northern Ireland were dismissed as a figment of Michael Collins's imagination. Equally important, Article 12's wording was now turned on its head. When determining the boundary, economic and geographic conditions were no longer to be read as a qualification to the wishes of the inhabitants. On the contrary, they were now granted a status equal to – perhaps greater than – the desires of the border population.[63]

At the same time, the memorandum's writer refused to countenance any assertion that Ulster Unionists could scrap the Boundary Commission simply by refusing to appoint a representative. Were that to happen, 'the face of England would be blackened for ever not only in Ireland but throughout the civilized world'. Only one thing could be worse, and that would be to allow the Commission to do its job. 'It is difficult to picture an award', the writer

61 Curtis to Loughnane; and Curtis to Anderson, both dated 9 Nov. 1923, CO 739/20/54021.

62 Curtis to Jones [letter excerpt], 10 Nov. 1923, TJ Z/132. Those invited to the meeting were: Masterton-Smith, Curtis, Anderson, Jones, Mark Sturgis, G. G. Whiskard, Loughnane, and Tallents. Another, smaller meeting may also have taken place. According to CO 783/4, the records of these meetings were destroyed. See, instead, 'Memorandum on the Boundary question', dated '?late 1923', TJ GG/2/2. All subsequent quotations in this section are from this memorandum unless otherwise indicated.

63 This interpretation is rebutted in chapter 2 above.

maintained, 'which would not precipitate war between the North and South' – especially as there now existed a 'large force of Specials equipped and armed by the British taxpayer', a force that almost certainly would 'resist the findings of the Boundary Commission'.

Delay, yet again, seemed to be the only answer, though this time with a purpose. To allay fears in both parts of Ireland, it was suggested that a Boundary Commission chairman should be appointed immediately. This would show that while the British had 'no intention of being rushed over the boundary question neither have they any intention of playing fast and loose with the provisions of the Treaty'. Most importantly, a chairman was needed so that he could 'act as a sedative to Irish nerves in North and South'.

Once appointed, it was suggested that the chairman should then visit the Irish border, where he 'would have time to study the whole subject until he had fully grasped the issues at stake'. As soon as he realised that the 'peace of Ireland' depended on his actions, he could then put forward recommendations accept-able to both governments, obviating the need to appoint the Commission's other two members. The list of these possible proposals was simply incredible. Loughnane actually seems to have believed that the Free Staters would accept a plan *expanding* Northern Ireland's territory to include County Donegal, as this would be attractive 'from the point of view of administrative convenience'. In return, Craig's government would be asked to provide 'certain safeguards to the Catholic minority'. These included restoring proportional representation and redrawing constituency boundaries for Parliamentary seats. It was also suggested that additional powers might be given to the Council of Ireland.[64]

Whatever its shortcomings, this document set the pace for Britain's Irish policy over the next year. The Boundary Commission was a threat, not least because of that large force of Specials armed and paid for by the British taxpayer. It would be better to bury the Boundary Commission which, according to this new official version of the past, was never meant to make any great changes anyway. As had occurred with the advent of Bonar Law in political circles, so now among British civil servants, the goal was no longer Irish unity nor, even, an equitable settlement. The goal now was to find a 'sedative to Irish nerves in North and South'.[65]

---

64 According to Wilfrid Spender, Cosgrave later proposed just such an expansion of the Ulster state. However, the offer, made through an intermediary, was probably part of an overall plan to bring about reunification. Even if Cosgrave would have agreed to this expansion, it is unlikely that his government could have withstood opposition to the move. See Spender to Londonderry, 22 Aug. 1924, PRONI, CAB/9Z/8/1.

65 Curtis almost certainly penned the memorandum. Its content and style bear striking similarities to contemporary documents written by him. See, e.g., Curtis to Loughnane, 25 Dec. 1923, CO 739/26/433; 'Appreciation of the Present Political Position in Ireland', 9 May 1924, CAB 21/281; and Curtis to Churchill, 19 Aug. 1924, Curtis Papers, MSS 89, ff. 76–83.

ELECTIONS, 1923: THE UNITED KINGDOM

Unlike the hotly contested campaigns between Conservative, Liberal and Labour candidates in Great Britain, the election brought on by Baldwin's embrace of tariff reform was very much a one-party affair in most of Northern Ireland. Official Unionist candidates were challenged in only three constituencies. Of that number, they were opposed by Nationalist candidates in only one of them: again, the two-seat constituency of Fermanagh–Tyrone. And, as happened the year before, border Nationalists used the election as a referendum on partition, giving both T. J. S. Harbison and Cahir Healy convincing victories over their Unionist opponents. Viewed from London, the result inconveniently 'complicated' matters, showing once again that 'in Fermanagh and Tyrone there exists a substantial majority' favouring inclusion in the Free State.[66] Unionists were no less annoyed by the Nationalist victory which, the *Northern Whig* acidly predicted, would be 'hailed as fresh proof that a large majority of the two counties are eager to break away from Ulster'.[67]

In Britain, by contrast, no party won a clear-cut victory. Instead, the election held in early December resulted in a disaster which, Tom Jones recorded in his diary, 'S.B. never foresaw or imagined.' The number of Conservative MPs dropped from 345 to 258, a net loss of 87 seats. Although still the single largest party in the House of Commons, Conservatives faced a combined Liberal–Labour opposition of 159 and 191 members respectively. Baldwin's gamble, far from winning a mandate for tariff reform, reunited the Liberal Party, a feat, Austen Chamberlain bitterly told one of his sisters, 'no Liberal could do'. The Liberals, in turn, were ready to place Labour 'in office, but not in power', and Baldwin suddenly faced the very real prospect of losing not only the leadership of his nation but that of his party as well.[68]

WESTMINSTER INTERLUDE

Much ink has been spilled trying to explain why Baldwin decided to call the 1923 election barely 11 months after Bonar Law had won a convincing mandate for the Conservative Party. This is not the place to carry on that debate.

66 *Annual Register: 1923*, p. 153. An Independent Unionist in North Belfast and a Labour candidate in West Belfast offered the only other opposition to the official Unionists. Both were defeated. 'Memorandum on the Boundary question', dated '? late 1923', TJ GG/2/2.

67 Quoted in D. Kennedy, *The Widening Gulf: Northern Attitudes to the Independent Irish State, 1919–1949* (Belfast, 1988), p. 136.

68 Jones diary, 22 Dec. 1923, vol. I, p. 261. Butler and Freeman, *British Political Facts*, p. 142. Austen to Ida Chamberlain, 17 Nov. 1923, AC 5/1/298. Taylor, *English History*, p. 210.

Nonetheless, as one Conservative historian has written, the election's 'consequences were to be of weighty significance' for years to come, a judgment that
is as true for Ireland as it is for Britain.[69] For this reason, it is necessary to
explore those consequences in order to see how, by changing Britain's political
landscape, they affected the settling of Ireland's boundary question.

When anti-Coalition Tories cast Lloyd George into the political wilderness in 1922, they were motivated by more than a simple desire to get rid of an
unpopular leader. At the Carlton Club meeting, Kenneth Morgan has written,
the Conservative Party turned its back on 'high policy' for the 'more parochial
but more reassuring world' of two-party politics. This was Labour's desire, as
well, and all the more so after the 1923 election. According to Maurice Cowling,
both Conservative and Labour strategies 'were based on the assumption that
the two-party system was natural and desirable'. The problem was that 'the
Liberal Party refused to die'.[70]

And, therein, for both Conservatives and Labour, lay the danger.

There is a tendency among some historians to judge the outcome of the
1923 election through the prism of the election that followed it less than a year
later. Thus, it is said that the 'principal casualty was the Liberal Party', while
Baldwin and the Conservatives actually came out of the 1923 debacle 'in a
strong position'.[71] That was not the way matters looked at the time. Only after
the dust had cleared did Baldwin realise that he had an opportunity to destroy
the Liberals from the right, while MacDonald saw that Labour now had the
chance to stake its claim as the party of the left. Even then, it would not have
been safe to wager that the doom of the Liberals was a foregone conclusion.[72]

That outcome was not possible so long as the three parties remained on
roughly equal terms. This unstable situation also increased the chances for
another coalition government, and in fact many at the time thought that this
would be the outcome of the 1923 election. Both Labour and the Conservatives
had to bear in mind that a new coalition could be hatched from either side of
the political spectrum – and that either of those outcomes could be achieved
by one man: Lloyd George.

There is much evidence that at this time not only Lloyd George but other
members of the old Coalition contemplated a regrouping of their forces.
Although these plans came to nothing, Birkenhead's attempt to put together
an anti-Labour (some would say, anti-Baldwin) coalition in the wake of the

69 Rhodes James, *British Revolution*, p. 467.

70 Morgan, *Consensus and Disunity*, p. 356. Cowling, *Impact of Labour*, p. 362. Taylor, *English
History*, p. 195.

71 Rhodes James, *British Revolution*, p. 467. Ramsden, *Balfour and Baldwin*, p. 183.

72 Cowling, *Impact of Labour*, pp. 361, 419–20. Marquand, *MacDonald*, p. 312.

1923 election meant that Lloyd George's resurrection could not be written off as pure fantasy.[73]

Baldwin later asserted that by staking his claim to protectionism he 'dished the Goat', thus thwarting any plans Lloyd George had to form a new coalition centred on this issue. While such an explanation may have been 'devised after the event', what is not open to dispute is that Baldwin had to put an end to any hopes of a revived Coalition once and for all if he was to reunite the Conservative Party.[74]

Asquith's decision to allow Labour to take office did much of Baldwin's job for him, for it left 'a painful impression on those members who still hankered after some form of coalition' between Conservatives and Liberals. Austen Chamberlain 'upbraided' Asquith for this decision when the House of Commons met in mid-January 1924, doing so, one contemporary noted, 'more in sorrow than in anger'. Baldwin, on the other hand, 'prophesied that the future would lie between Conservatism and Labour, to the exclusion of Liberalism'.[75] Over the next ten months, the Tories would use every opportunity to remind voters that the Liberals were responsible for 'handing over power to a Socialist Government'.[76] The task of destroying the Liberal Party was one for Baldwin to relish, fuelled, as it was, by his hatred of Lloyd George – a hatred one backbench MP remembered as 'quite pathological'.[77]

MacDonald's antipathy toward Lloyd George was not nearly as obsessive, never mind pathological. That said, the two intensely disliked each other. On the one hand, 'Lloyd George was a threat to MacDonald's personal ambition, his only rival as a charismatic popular leader'. On the other, MacDonald was the one man who could prevent Lloyd George from regaining his former glory as the 'national leader of the Left'. Nor was MacDonald, any more than Baldwin, in favour of coalition government. MacDonald's primary goal was to

---

73   See, e.g., Churchill to Lloyd George, 8 Nov. 1923, LG G/4/4/6. Horne to Lloyd George, 2 Jan. 1924 [misdated 1923], LG G/10/6/1. Campbell, *Lloyd George*, pp. 49–52. Also, see A. J. P. Taylor, *Beaverbrook* (London, 1972), pp. 217–20.

74   Taylor, *English History*, p. 207. But see Jones diary, 22 Dec. 1923, vol. I, p. 261. J. C. C. Davidson was equally certain that Baldwin's fear of Lloyd George precipitated the 1923 election. See Davidson, *Memoirs of a Conservative*, pp. 184–5.

75   *Annual Register: 1924*, p. 7.

76   Peel to Reading, 3, 21 Jan. 1924, IO, MSS Eur. E. 238/7, nos 1 and 4.

77   Coote, *Editorial*, p. 100. According to Tom Jones, Baldwin's malice for Lloyd George amounted to an 'obsession'. See his diary entries, 30 Sept., 25 Nov. 1923, vol. I, pp. 243, 255. Also, see Campbell, *Lloyd George*, p. 3, 7, 41, 46-47. This ill will was returned in full measure. Urged to back Baldwin's tariff plan, Lloyd George replied that if Baldwin 'had been one of the men who stood by me' in 1922 he would do so. 'But Baldwin knifed me and I shall knife Baldwin.' See Amery, *My Political Life*, p. 281.

show that his party was fit to govern and that it could do so without a formal alliance with the Liberals. 'Coalitions are detestable', he was to tell the House of Commons. And, he added for good measure, 'dishonest'.[78]

Like Baldwin and his colleagues, MacDonald and his fellow Labour leaders believed that their party's position would not be secure until the Liberals were destroyed once and for all. 'The real and significant issue before the country is Liberalism v. Labour', Beatrice Webb wrote at the beginning of the 1923 election. Webb held Lloyd George personally responsible for 'reviving the old glamour of the great Liberal Party' which 'has suddenly blazed out again into a possible, some would say probable, *Alternative Govt.*' Were that to happen, 'Labour would be set back for a decade or more'.[79]

On the morrow of the 1923 election, Webb's anxieties had, if anything, increased. Although she felt that Labour '*must accept* rather than refuse office', she knew that it would do so without a mandate, for which it would later pay a price. 'The honest way out of the *impasse*', she wrote,

> the course which would be approved by the majority of the British people, would be a Liberal–Conservative Coalition – [an] Asquith, Baldwin, Chamberlain, Lloyd George Cabinet, Free Trade and anti-socialist in home affairs and pacific in foreign policy. It is only the struggle for power between the leaders and parties that prevents this carrying out of the clearly expressed will of the people.[80]

The manoeuvrings of Britain's party leaders in the wake of the election were watched with keen interest in Dublin. An analysis prepared by the North-Eastern Boundary Bureau in mid-December considered four possible outcomes: a reconstructed Conservative government; a Labour government; a Liberal 'caretaker' government, allowed to take office with the support of one or both of the other parties; or the Conservative–Liberal coalition which Beatrice Webb thought most voters wanted but which the bureau regarded as 'unlikely'.

The bureau felt that either a Labour or Liberal government 'would probably give the strongest support to our claims' made to the Boundary Commission. That said, if either such government attempted to force a settlement on Craig the likely effect would be to 'consolidate the Conservatives in opposition'. In fact, the bureau fancifully suggested that 'pressure on the North from a Conservative government is best' as that would mean 'there can be no opposition in England' to a settlement of the boundary question. However true

78 Campbell, *Lloyd George*, p. 86. Cowling, *Impact of Labour*, p. 354. Taylor, *English History*, p. 210. Marquand, *MacDonald*, pp. 297–300, 311, 339.

79 Webb diary, 19 Nov. 1923, vol. 37, 3987–8.

80 Ibid., 12 Dec. 1923, 3997–4002.

that may have been, it was unrealistic to hope that Conservatives would ever force Craig to accept a settlement that he did not like. Even after MacDonald accepted the seals of office, the Free Staters would have to bear in mind the unstable condition of British politics. A minority Labour government, the bureau warned, meant the 'possibility of another strong Conservative government after the next election, which may come at any time'.[81]

MacDonald intended to put off that day for as long as possible. But because the Liberals were at best an unreliable ally, he realised that 'it was essential to be on good terms with the Conservative leaders'.[82] Among other things, this meant that MacDonald dare not take any initiative on issues likely to provoke the Tory rank and file. Ireland, he need not have been told, was one such issue.

Time, also, figured in Baldwin's calculations. Once the soon-to-be-ex-prime minister rode out the storm following the 1923 defeat, John Ramsden writes that 'the next eight months saw very little discord' in Conservative ranks. In fact, Baldwin's hold on the party was not really secure until after the 1924 election. 'S. B. will remain leader', Neville Chamberlain told one his sisters, 'but whether he is the next P. M. of our party will depend on how he shapes in opposition.'[83] For his part, well into May Baldwin still feared 'the cynical combination of the chief three forces of the Coalition' – Lloyd George, Churchill, and Birkenhead – a fear he publicly expressed in a controversial newspaper interview with *The People*.[84] Although Baldwin disavowed much of what was said in the article, he had once again shown 'his habit of bursting out with some inconceivable folly'. For months to come the question continued to be asked in the Tory heartland: 'What is the Conservative Party going to do about Mr Baldwin?'[85]

Only as 1924 wore on would it truly become fashionable to renounce Lloyd George and all his works, to view the idea of coalition government as, somehow, ignoble, and for the 'survivors of 1922' to look back with 'embarrassment' on their former associations.[86] Austen Chamberlain, ironically, seems to have realised this earlier than most. No more in sorrow, nor in anger, but as a cold-blooded politician, he told Sam Hoare that 'our business now is to smash the

---

81   North-Eastern Boundary Bureau memorandum, 13 Dec. 1923, D/T, S 1801/C.

82   Cowling, *Impact of Labour*, p. 380.

83   Ramsden, *Balfour and Baldwin*, p. 190. Cowling, *Impact of Labour*, pp. 382–7, 392. Neville to Hilda Chamberlain, 9 Feb. 1924, NC 18/1/425. Also see Beaverbrook to Brisbane, 13 Mar. 1924, BBK C/64; and Cecil to Salisbury, 10 Apr. 1924, Cecil Papers, MSS 51085, ff. 126.

84   'Baldwin Turns and Rends His Critics', *The People*, 18 May 1924. 'Memorandum: Stanley Baldwin's Interview with "The People" reporter, May 18, 1924', AC 24/6/3.

85   Austen to Ida Chamberlain, 29 June 1924, AC 5/1/322. 'Life and Politics', *The Nation*, 24 May 1924.

86   Morgan, *Consensus and Disunity*, pp. 7, 357, 365.

Liberal Party'. Past associations, past loyalties, past commitments, none of these things mattered any more. For Austen Chamberlain, 'the world of party was now the only loyalty that counted'.[87]

Chamberlain's days as the prodigal son of Conservative politics were drawing to a close. Defeat finally gave Baldwin the opportunity to bring the Coalitionists 'back into the true fold'. Nevertheless, Chamberlain told one of his sisters, 'the old difficulties' had not gone away. While most party leaders were now willing to receive him in 'full communion', others continued to hold Chamberlain 'responsible for two of the worst acts of the Coalition – the Irish Treaty and the Indian policy'.[88] Like an albatross, the Irish settlement hung round Austen Chamberlain's neck and would do so for years to come.

Tory Die-hards were not alone in finding it hard to let go of the past. Others were equally reluctant to accept that they now stood on the threshold of a new political landscape, and this was true of Lloyd George most of all. Frustrated as Asquith's second-in-command in a reunited Liberal Party, he hankered for a revived Coalition. As Herbert Gladstone wrote of him in the summer of 1924:

> Ll.G., himself, appeared to live in [a] constant ferment of activity as a Statesman, Politician, Orator, Newspaper Proprietor, and the holder of large financial resources. Disturbing rumours were prevalent of close interviews with Beaverbrook, Robert Horne, Churchill, and others. He seemed to be manoeuvring for position, but not with the Liberal Party alone. . . .[89]

Unlike Baldwin and MacDonald, Lloyd George was not interested in a period of calm. 'Still dynamic, creative, and ambitious', he 'was eager for combat and did not much care how things worked out so long as there was turmoil.'[90]

With so much at stake, an issue as delicate as Ireland could create just the sort of 'ferment' that Lloyd George thrived on, and which both Labour and the Conservatives were determined to avoid at all costs. Before he left office, Baldwin tried making this clear to Craig when the latter defied appeals for the release of the imprisoned Cahir Healy, one of the two Nationalist MPs

87 Chamberlain to Hoare, 28 Jan. 1924, Templewood Papers, V: 1 (51). Morgan, *Consensus and Disunity*, p. 363.

88 Salisbury to Baldwin, 26 Jan. 1924, SB vol. 159, ff. 258–61. Austen to Hilda Chamberlain, 24 Jan. 1924, AC 5/1/304. Salisbury to Robert Cecil, 28 Jan. 1924, Cecil Papers, MSS 51085, ff. 116–17. Baldwin to Salisbury, 25 Jan. 1924, S (4) 108/83–4.

89 'Narrative of the General Election 1924', undated, Gladstone Papers, MSS 46,460/309.

90 Taylor, *English History*, p. 218. See Churchill to Balfour, 3 Apr. 1924, AJB-S, GD 433/2/19, Reel 4, for Lloyd George's proposal for a 'future "Conservative and Liberal Union" Administration'.

representing Fermanagh and Tyrone. 'I think I see your difficulties', Baldwin told the Northern Ireland premier in mid-January,

> but I want you also to see some of mine. If we go into Opposition, as is now most probable, and I am still Leader of the Party, my hands will be full with our own problems over here. I do not want the Irish conflict revived in the House of Commons in any shape or form if it can justly be avoided.[91]

The man about to succeed Baldwin in Downing Street could not have agreed more.

91 See Baldwin–Craig correspondence, 19, 27 Dec. 1923, 14[?] Jan. 1924, SB vol. 101, ff. 178–9, 183–6, 197–8. Healy was released in late January, only to find himself banned from a quarter of his constituency, including his home town, Enniskillen. This order was finally lifted at MacDonald's insistence in mid-February. See Craig to MacDonald, 16 Feb. 1924, JRM, PRO 30/69/191. Phoenix, *Northern Nationalism*, pp. 300–1.

SIX

LABOUR'S 'TROUBLESOME SUBJECT'

*... We all ought to work to close a chapter in English
and Irish history that is best forgotten.*

J.H. THOMAS[1]

—

James Ramsay MacDonald stepped into No. 10 Downing Street on a day 'for which English history afforded no precedent'. Great Britain would have a minority government – one not formed by the largest party in the House of Commons but, and here was the unprecedented part, by a party which most of the establishment viewed with disdain at best, or 'boundless alarm' at worst. No less than a revolution had taken place, 'a revolution in English politics as profound as that associated with the Reform Act of 1832'.[2]

Ireland has largely been written out of the history of this, Britain's first Labour government.[3] It is a strange omission. Just because Ireland's quarrels did not conform to the party's ideas about class politics, this did not mean that the problem would disappear, a lesson that MacDonald and his colleagues learned many times over while in office. Still, this oversight among historians is itself revealing, because in a very real sense it mirrors the ambivalent attitude that the party's early leaders felt about the Irish Question.

However much Labour opposed imperialism and colonialism, its support for Irish self-government in the years leading up to the First World War was not to be taken as a given, a point which MacDonald himself made abundantly clear in 1905. As secretary of the Labour Representation Committee, MacDonald did not hide his distaste for the Irish cause, as was demonstrated

1   'No Coercion of Ulster', *The Times*, 5 May 1924.
2   *Annual Register: 1924*, pp. 1–2, 8.
3   See, e.g., R.W. Lyman, *The First Labour Government, 1924* (London, 1957), pp. 193, 238; and T. Cradden, 'Labour in Britain and the Northern Ireland Labour Party, 1900–70', in P. Catterall and S. McDougall, ed., *The Northern Ireland Question in British Politics* (London, 1996), pp. 71–87. Possibly the only attempt to explore Labour's mixed emotions about Ireland is G. Bell's *Troublesome Business: The Labour Party and the Irish Question* (London, 1982). Bell, however, does not claim that his study is definitive and, on the contrary, hopes that 'others will correct and expand this work'.

to a group of supporters who had assumed that the LRC was a pro-Home Rule organisation.

'On what grounds?' he tartly replied.[4]

Whatever he had imbibed from socialism, Labour's first prime minister could never quite shake his Scottish Protestant's hostility towards the Church of Rome. MacDonald 'disliked Catholics', the historian of the Clydesiders has written, 'particularly Irish Catholics', a verdict given added weight by the Labour MP, Emanuel Shinwell. Anti-Catholicism, Shinwell remembered, was 'a factor in Ramsay MacDonald's attitude to the Irish question, and coloured his policy towards Bonar Law'.[5]

Nor were others in the Labour movement any more keen to support Irish self-determination. While the Fabians were, at best, 'unenthusiastic supporters' of Home Rule, the Independent Labour Party viewed Ireland as a diversion from the 'bread and butter issues' which were its main concern. It is notable that the Irish question was not even debated at the party's annual conferences until 1918.

This ambivalence continued through the Anglo-Irish War. At the party's 1920 conference, one observer noted, speaker after speaker 'reveal[ed] considerable impatience with the Sinn Fein platitudes'. While Labour officially opposed partition, J. H. Thomas warned conference delegates that it was 'idle to deny there was an Ulster problem'. What party leaders really thought about the Irish Question was best summed up by J. R. Clynes in 1919. Ireland, Clynes told the House of Commons, was a 'troublesome subject' – a fact that Labour's first government would learn several times over.[6]

LABOUR'S IRISH TRIUMVIRATE

Labour's 'inarticulate' attitude towards Irish affairs made it difficult for officials in Dublin to gauge how Britain's new government would handle the boundary dispute. While MacDonald was reputed to be 'an honest politician', Kevin O'Shiel warned that he was in many ways 'a dark horse'. Not so the new colonial secretary, J. H. Thomas, who had 'never shown himself to be conspicuously friendly' to the Free State cause. According to O'Shiel, although he

---

4   Bell, *Troublesome Business*, pp. 16–17.

5   R. K. Middlemas, *The Clydesiders: A Left Wing Struggle for Parliamentary Power* (New York, 1968 [London, 1965]), p. 110. E. Shinwell, *I've Lived Through It All* (London, 1973), p. 53.

6   Bell, *Troublesome Business*, pp. 7, 10, 38, 42–3, 56–7. 'Report on Irish Question in England', 17 July 1920, IUA, D/989/A/9/21. *HC Deb*, vol. 114, col. 1505, 3 Apr. 1919.

had voted for the Treaty Thomas made it plain that he supported 'special treatment' for Ulster.[7]

Given his analysis, O'Shiel would have been dismayed to learn that Ireland, in fact, was the reason for Thomas's appointment. During an audience with George V, MacDonald pointed out to the king: 'Perhaps your Majesty forgets that Ireland now comes within the domain of the Colonial Office.' As the new prime minister explained it to C. P. Scott, he needed someone with Thomas's negotiating skills to handle the Irish and that 'had been the ground for his selection'.[8]

Thomas provoked strong reactions. Birkenhead called him 'the cleverest politician' yet to emerge from Labour's ranks. He was at the same time, Hazel Lavery observed, *'very vain'*. In any event, his importance to Anglo-Irish relations over the next nine months would be second only to MacDonald's.[9]

The third member of Labour's government who would have to confront the boundary question was Arthur Henderson, the new home secretary. Henderson's biographer has described his performance in the 1924 government as 'undistinguished', and he seems to have played, at most, a supporting role to Thomas's lead in handling the boundary question. A vocal critic of the Coalition's early Irish policy, Henderson, like others in the Labour movement, was deeply ambivalent when the question turned to Ulster. Perhaps his most revealing remark on this subject was made during the Treaty debates. If any members of Parliament were Ulster's natural allies, Henderson told the House of Commons, it was 'those of us who are and have been so long officially connected with trade unions . . . [which] have large numbers of members in the North of Ireland.'[10]

7   'RE. North-Eastern Position', ? Jan. 1924, D/T, S 1801/D. Thomas, however, denied that the 1920 Act 'meant that the six counties were to be left intact and free from all further consideration'. See *HC Deb*, vol. 150, col. 1445, 17 Feb. 1922.

8   Scott diary, 2–3 Feb. 1924, MSS 50907, vii, pp. 89–92.

9   Lord Birkenhead, *Contemporary Personalities* (London, 1924), p. 185. S. McCoole, *Hazel: A Life of Lady Lavery, 1880–1935* (Dublin, 1996), p. 114.

10   C. Wrigley, *Arthur Henderson* (Cardiff, 1990), p. 144. Bell, *Troublesome Business*, pp. 53, 65–8. *HC Deb*, vol. 149, col. 309, 16 Dec. 1921. John Wheatley, the one Cabinet member who might have been sympathetic to the Free State was excluded by MacDonald from discussions of the boundary question whenever possible. See Canning, *British Policy*, pp. 88–9.

'A LOSS OF PRESTIGE'

In his analysis of MacDonald's incoming government, Kevin O'Shiel predicted that the Free State could expect fair treatment from Labour if only because the party depended on Irish votes in a large number of British constituencies. While this may have been true, it missed the point. MacDonald and his lieutenants had not accepted the seals of office to solve the Irish Question. Rather, they meant to use this time to disprove once and for all Churchill's allegation that Labour was 'unfit to govern'.[11] Whatever the merits of this strategy, it most certainly meant that there would no bold initiatives on Ireland. Quite the contrary.

Inexperienced in government, Labour's ministers relied heavily on civil servants, and this was as true in Irish affairs as in other matters. According to one North-Eastern Boundary Bureau report, Labour was 'weary of the Irish question' and had come to office with 'no concrete plan' of its own to solve the problem. Mindful, too, of the need to remain on good terms with the Conservatives, it is not surprising that Thomas and Henderson fell back on Devonshire's proposed conference, which was scheduled for early February.[12]

But while there was no new thinking on this issue in London, a fundamental reassessment of the boundary question was under way in Dublin. In mid-January, Cosgrave privately admitted to the Executive Council that while reunification continued to be the government's ultimate goal, it was 'not a likely probability and appears so far off as to be out of the arena of practical politics for the present'. Instead, he believed that Craig, with British backing, would propose that the two Irish parliaments remain separate 'with a link of the two cabinets'; their joint meetings would act as a substitute for the Council of Ireland. Cosgrave was willing to consider this idea – if Dublin was seen to be the dominant partner. As he bluntly put it, when explaining how the joint Cabinets should function: 'We preside.'[13]

Cosgrave's prediction proved to be largely accurate. After only two days of meetings, the boundary conference adjourned so that the Irish governments could consider a seven-point plan put forward by Thomas. As Cosgrave

11 'RE. North-Eastern Position', ? Jan. 1924, D/T, S 1801/D. Taylor, *English History*, p. 210. Marquand, *MacDonald*, pp. 310–12. For Churchill's allegation, see 'Mr. Churchill on Russia', *The Times*, 16 Feb. 1920.

12 MacDonald diary, 3 Feb. 1924, JRM, PRO 30/69/1753/1. Cowling, *Impact of Labour*, p. 380. Marquand, *MacDonald*, p. 307. See Thomas-Healy and Henderson-Abercorn correspondence, 24, 29 Jan. 1924 in *Cmd. 2155*, Nos. 9–12. MacCartan to Stephens, 23 Feb. 1924, NEBB, Box 27.

13 See Cosgrave memorandum, 17 Jan. 1924; and 'Conference on Boundary Commission', 28 Jan. 1924, D/T, S 1801/D.

thought, the British proposal revolved around the Council of Ireland with the two Irish Cabinets acting in its place for a provisional period of one year. Meanwhile, the Dáil and the Northern Ireland House of Commons would also hold joint sittings to enact legislation enabling the two Cabinets to function as one. Crucially, no measure would become law unless it received a 'double majority', i.e. separate majorities would be required in both parliaments to enact legislation. During the provisional period, the Free State would stay its demand for the Boundary Commission. In return, Craig's government would delay its plans to abolish proportional representation for county council and rural district council elections.[14]

Thomas's scheme pleased no one. 'The most fatal criticism of the proposals', O'Higgins wrote, 'is that the country would not touch them.' In Irish eyes, Thomas's proposal struck at the heart of the Free State's newly won sovereignty, whose importance the Colonial Office never seemed to understand. This failure was summed up by Lionel Curtis following the Free State's admission to the League of Nations the previous September. 'Our friends' heads are, of course, pretty full at the moment', Curtis observed. That would soon change once they realised that their position in the rest of the world counted for little 'apart from their position in the British Commonwealth of Nations.'[15]

But the Irish were discovering no such thing. Far from it. Having won international recognition, they were not about to allow the British to engage in a 'whittling down' of their status even if that was the price to be paid for ending partition. Gaining 'the political semblance of national union' was, one Free Stater wrote, 'a very big thing indeed but we shall have come down at least 50 degrees in our world status'. Thomas's proposal looked like an attempt to do exactly that. Accepting the plan, Cosgrave argued, meant 'a loss of prestige' while Craig's government was 'called upon to sacrifice nothing' so long as Northern Ireland continued to send MPs to Westminster. 'Is there not a great danger', Cosgrave asked, 'of such a plan tending in time to pull the whole of Ireland, through the North, more and more towards London?'[16]

From his perch in the Cabinet secretariat, Tom Jones had few illusions that the proposal would get the British out of their Boundary Commission pledge. The 'snag', Jones wrote, was Ulster's demand for 'fifty-fifty' representation in the joint Cabinet meetings, in effect giving the Unionists a veto over its deliberations.[17]

14 Ibid., 'Outline of Proposals for Consideration', 2 Feb. 1924.

15 O'Higgins memorandum, ? Feb. 1924, D/T, S 1801/E. Curtis to Antrobus, 25 Sept. 1923, CO 739/25/45749.

16 'Some Possible Dangers in the N.E. Situation', undated, D/T, S 1801/C. 'Notes of the President on the Proposals Made at the London Conference, February 2, 1924', undated, D/T, S 1801/E.

17 Jones diary, 2 Feb. 1924, vol. III, pp. 225–6.

Although Craig and Lord Londonderry reportedly favoured the proposal, it was given a stormy reception by their colleagues in the Northern Ireland Cabinet. Hugh Pollock heatedly denounced the scheme, calling it 'unthinkable'. In this instance, Pollock, not Craig, reflected the feelings of their grassroots supporters. While Craig was spending less and less time in Northern Ireland, his ministers were daily exposed to public opinion on the streets of Belfast and they were unwilling to antagonise rank and file Unionist opinion.[18]

Unwanted and unloved, Thomas's scheme became an orphan like so many other British attempts, before and after, to reconcile the Irish. Despite Pollock's opposition, Tallents believed that Craig might have been able to convince his Cabinet to give the plan a chance, were it not for the fact that his health broke down. Due to reassemble at the end of February, the Irish Conference had to be postponed when Craig fell ill with a debilitating attack of influenza. His doctor informed Wilfrid Spender that under no circumstances could Craig attend any more sittings of the conference before the end of March, and then only after an extended sea voyage to regain his health. While Craig's symptoms were real enough, the illness itself may have been psychosomatic or, at least, was made worse by his worries over the boundary dispute. In any case, the conference was now indefinitely put on hold.[19]

'SPOILED CHILDREN OF POLITICS'

This unexpected suspension left Cosgrave dangerously exposed to attack at home. Free State supporters could not understand why their government was not pressing for the Boundary Commission now that the Conservative Party had 'lost control' in London. Postponing the conference gave added credence to charges made in the pro-Republican journal *Eire* that Article 12 had been a 'fraud' and a 'delusion' all along. 'It matters not whether it is a Labour, Liberal or Conservative government', *Eire* told its readers. The British had no intention of enforcing the boundary clause, and another round of meetings in London would be a 'farce'.[20]

Cosgrave, albeit reluctantly, had come to the same conclusion. Although he realised that setting up the Commission would be 'the real beginning not

18   Tallents to Anderson, 18 Feb. 1924, HO 45/12296/1(b). Buckland, *Factory of Grievances*, p. 200.

19   Ibid., Tallents to Anderson. Thomas to Cosgrave, 18 Feb. 1924, CO 739/26/8213. Bryan Follis disputes the notion that Craig consciously used his illness to delay the boundary negotiations. See *State Under Siege*, p. 160.

20   County Monaghan Constituency Committee to Blythe, 25 Jan. 1924, EB, P24/204/52. 'Mr. Thomas Breaks the Treaty', *Eire*, 8 Mar. 1924.

the end of his boundary worries', he too saw no point in another round of meetings. In an interview with N. G. Loughnane, he 'described the Ulster Protestants as the spoiled children of politics' who were 'quite incapable of making concessions'. Faced with high unemployment and the 'disquieting symptom' of demobilised Free State soldiers being won over by Sinn Féin, the government could ill afford to alienate their supporters any further by not pressing the boundary issue. If there was one piece of good news in this interview for British officials, it was Cosgrave's assurance that the army, at least, had shown 'no manifestations of disloyalty'.[21]

Just days later the Free State Army mutinied.[22]

Although the mutiny had nothing to do with the boundary question, its repercussions were soon felt north of the border. Acting in Craig's absence, Lord Londonderry postponed planned reductions of the Special Constabulary, telling Henderson that the Free State Army was now led by men 'who are notorious for their hostility to Northern Ireland'.[23] Jones unfairly concluded that because Cosgrave and his colleagues had 'shown themselves weak in handling the mutiny', they had to demonstrate a new toughness in their negotiations with the British and Ulster Unionists.[24] In fact, the sudden hardening of attitudes in Dublin had little to do with troubles in the army, but reflected growing frustration in government circles over the continued postponement of the boundary conference.

This situation became critical when the Irish learned that Belfast now wanted to rule out another meeting of the conference before the end of April. Resumption had been delayed several times owing to Craig's illness, despite the fact that the 2 February meeting had adjourned on the understanding that discussions would resume within 28 days. Although the Free State had requested a resumption as early as mid-February, the Home Office did not formally contact Northern Ireland's governor general about the matter until 4 March. Four days later, Tallents learned that Craig intended to go on a Mediterranean cruise from the middle of March to the middle of April. After his return the Unionists would not be ready to meet their British and Free State counterparts until the end of the month, as Craig would need 'a day or two in Northern Ireland after his voyage so as to sense the position before entering into Conference'.[25]

21   Loughnane to Curtis, 4 Mar. 1924, CO 739/26/10823.

22   The mutiny was sparked by the army's plans for large-scale demobilisation and by conflict between secret societies within its ranks. See Duggan, *Irish Army*, pp. 129–37.

23   Londonderry to Henderson, 11, 26 Mar. 1924, PREM 1/34.

24   Jones diary, 19 Mar. 1924, vol. III, p. 226.

25   Healy to Thomas; Henderson to Abercorn, 16 Feb., 4 Mar. 1924, Cmd 2155, nos 13 and 14. Tallents to Anderson; Abercorn to Henderson, 8, 10 Mar. 1924, in HO 45/12296/1(b).

For the Irish, this was one delay too many. On 15 March a strongly worded letter from Healy asked that the British take whatever steps were necessary to set up the Boundary Commission. An accompanying memorandum rejected Thomas's February proposals as 'unworkable'.[26]

In an attempt to hold the conference together, a reluctant Tom Jones was dispatched to Dublin, where he was to persuade the Free Staters 'to resume negotiations on Craig's return and make one more desperate effort at a solution which would further postpone [the] boundary issue'. Jones's choice of words is revealing. While the Dublin government's aim was to settle the boundary problem, the object of their British counterparts still was to put off the final reckoning.[27]

Jones succeeded, but only after narrowly averting Cosgrave's demand that the Boundary Commission should be established on 1 May if the conference failed to achieve a breakthrough. '[W]e must not think of failure', Jones urged, 'but rather of every means of making your next meeting a real step forward towards unity.' Thomas took this same line several days later. If they were to achieve the Treaty's 'real object' – an Ireland 'as united as Great Britain herself' – there had to be one more attempt at negotiations. Any steps taken to set up the Commission, he persuaded Cosgrave, were bound to leak to the press. The Unionists would then stage a walkout and 'almost certainly bring the Conference to an immediate end'.[28]

FINANCIAL PRESSURE

If the boundary conference was to have any hope of success, it was essential that the British wrestle concessions from the Ulster Unionists in Belfast. To win those concessions, the new Labour ministers believed that they had an effective weapon at hand: i.e., financial pressure. With the imperial government continually short of funds, there was every incentive to cut expenditure wherever possible. Civil servants in London did not hesitate to point to the steady flow of sterling across the Irish Sea, and Treasury officials in particular were determined to put an end to the 'perpetual demands from Northern Ireland'.[29]

---

26   Thomas to Healy, 11 Mar. 1924, Cmd 2155, no. 17. Healy to Thomas, 15 Mar. 1924, with undated Free State memorandum, CO 739/26/12703.

27   Jones diary, 27 Mar. 1924, vol. III, p. 227. Jones to Curtis, 30 Mar. 1924, TJ GG/2/9.

28   See Jones-Cosgrave and Thomas–Cosgrave correspondence, 1, 5, 10, and 15 Apr. 1924, D/T, S 1801/F.

29   Upcott memorandum to Snowden, 30 Jan. 1924, T 160/131/F.4855/02/1. Also, see Snowden memorandum to MacDonald, 26 Sept. 1924, JRM, PRO 30/69/61.

While the Conservatives had hesitated to make use of this weapon, MacDonald came to office intending to wield it for all it was worth. The link between the boundary negotiations and Northern Ireland's dependence on the imperial exchequer was explicitly drawn by G. C. Upcott in a memorandum to the new chancellor of the exchequer, Philip Snowden. The British, Upcott pointed out, were in 'a position to put considerable pressure on Sir James Craig should they desire to do so'. This would explain Snowden's refusal to allocate £1 million for the Special Constabulary that Neville Chamberlain had reluctantly promised to recommend in the 1924/25 budget. Clearly, it was on MacDonald's mind when he discussed the Irish situation with C. P. Scott. The grant 'could be discontinued at any time', MacDonald intimated, if the Unionists 'showed an intractable spirit' in the boundary negotiations.[30]

This is what Labour leaders had in mind when they met with Pollock on 11 April. At Thomas's instigation, Snowden played 'bad cop' to the colonial secretary's 'good cop' in order to win concessions on the boundary question.[31] Unfortunately for Thomas, Ulster's finance minister was singularly unimpressed with their performance, and the financial weapon broke in his hands.

In fact, Labour's colonial secretary was proving to be not at all successful when it came to Ireland. Yet Thomas never lost faith in his own negotiating skills. Behind the scenes, he was willing to 'bring every possible pressure' to bear on Craig to solve the boundary question, blurting out at one point: 'He can have a b[lood]y Dukedom if it will do the trick'. What Thomas never seemed to realise was that such temptations had no effect on Northern Ireland's prime minister. Nor, in the end, did the weapon of financial pressure have the effect it might have had if it had been wielded by more determined hands. That might have been different had Labour stayed in office; Snowden later claimed that he would have opposed 'any grant whatever' for the Specials.[32] As it happened, though, Labour was never put to the test.

'UNDER CRAIG'S THUMB': THE CONFERENCE COLLAPSES

Any hopes that the boundary conference would finally achieve a breakthrough were dashed almost as soon as discussions resumed on 24 April.

The talks began well enough. Cosgrave was willing to accept Craig's idea for a 'voluntary' body of experts representing both Irish governments to examine

30   Ibid., Upcott memorandum. Chamberlain to Craig, 4 Oct. 1923, T 160/131/F.4855/02/1. Snowden to Craig; Craig to Snowden and to MacDonald; and MacDonald to Craig, 18, 20, 22 Feb. 1924, CJ 1/2. Scott diary, 2–3 Feb. 1924, MSS 50907, vii, pp. 89–92.
31   Jones diary, 24 Apr. 1924, vol. III, pp. 229–30. Follis, *State Under Siege*, p. 130.
32   Ibid., Jones diary. *HC Deb*, vol. 180, col. 1681, 23 Feb. 1925.

their claims. That was until he learned that the price of such a deal was Dublin's surrender of its right to the Boundary Commission if this group failed to reach an agreement. Even Curtis and Jones saw that Cosgrave could not possibly accept these terms and, on the 26th, the Free State formally asked the British government to bring the Boundary Commission into operation.[33]

Curtis blamed Thomas for the breakdown. When it was clear that the talks were foundering after only one day, Jones suggested that MacDonald should be brought in to add the weight of the prime minister's office to the negotiations. But Thomas 'would not hear of it'.[34] The colonial secretary was 'under Craig's thumb', Curtis believed, and 'as usual, it is Craig's word which carries most weight in Whitehall'. Curtis told Jones that he was willing to stay on at the Colonial Office as long as he believed the 'Government here were making an honest effort to put the Treaty through.' Instead, it was clear that both Thomas and Craig were playing a 'game of delay' which, in the latter's case, was carried on in hopes that 'this Government may be succeeded by a Tory Government ere many months are past'.[35]

Indeed, this was Craig's strategy from the beginning. The longer the Boundary Commission could be delayed, the less likely that it would ever be formed at all. Craig's official biographer admitted as much when he described the outcome of the April meeting. 'The Conference ended without a decision', St John Ervine later wrote, 'which was, in effect, a decision in favour of Craig.'[36]

Faced with the Ulster leader's intransigence, Jones believed that the Labour government ought to involve Baldwin, along with Asquith and Lloyd George, in the negotiations. 'Once Craig can be made to realise that he could not split the parties', Jones wrote, 'it would make an immense difference.' Yet again, Thomas blocked the way. Henderson warned that his colleague would oppose any such step 'which took away from his own importance' in the discussions.[37]

MacDonald became a major player in the boundary negotiations only when illness temporarily removed Thomas from the scene. Preoccupied with foreign affairs, MacDonald had been happy to leave the Irish problem to the Colonial Office. His initial contact with Cosgrave in February had, in any event, done nothing to dispel his prejudices about Ireland or its leaders. In his

---

33 Jones diary, 24 Apr. 1924, vol. III, pp. 229–30. Lavin, *Curtis*, p. 221. *Dáil Deb*, vol. 7, cols 178–80, 25 Apr. 1924. Healy to Thomas, 26 Apr. 1924, Cmd 2155, no. 27.

34 Ibid., Jones diary.

35 Ibid., 15 May 1924, pp. 231–2.

36 St John Ervine, *Craigavon: Ulsterman* (London, 1949), p. 490.

37 Jones diary, 8 May 1924, vol. III, pp. 230–1.

estimation, the Free State president was 'a weak man, but one who wd. fight hard if driven into a corner'.[38]

Proposing one last-ditch round of negotiations, MacDonald invited Cosgrave and Craig to meet with him at the prime minister's country residence at Chequers. Already, his government had informed Dublin and Belfast that Northern Ireland's refusal to appoint its Commissioner took the problem beyond the realm of party politics. Constitutional issues were now involved: namely, was the province bound by a Treaty ratified by the Imperial Parliament? Unless the three men could reach an agreement, Belfast's refusal would have to be settled by the Judicial Committee of the Privy Council.[39]

By this time, British officials were well aware that it was no longer certain that Cosgrave could attend any further meetings even if he wanted to. 'Open conferences', O'Higgins complained, 'have repeatedly failed and hold no promise of future success.' Cosgrave appears to have decided to defy his Cabinet after receiving what he believed was an assurance from Thomas. Should a further round of meetings fail, Free State High Commissioner James MacNeill was told that Craig had agreed to do all that was 'needful to facilitate the operation of Article XII'.[40]

MacNeill's source for this extraordinary claim was, of all men, Alfred Cope. Although he had left the Irish Office in 1922, Cope seems to have acted as an unofficial go-between for the Colonial Office, sounding out the Irish on possible alternatives to the Boundary Commission such as 'joint administration' of Northern Ireland. It is certain that both Thomas and Jones were behind his 13 May discussion with MacNeill. What is not clear is who, if anyone, authorised Cope to commit Ulster's leader to the pledge mentioned by MacNeill.[41]

The Chequers conference of 31 May began as a two-way discussion because, wrote an annoyed Sir John Anderson, Cosgrave arrived 'about three hours late'.[42] In his absence, Craig confided to MacDonald that, 'notwithstanding all his previous utterances', he was prepared to appoint Northern Ireland's

38 Scott diary, 2–3 February 1924, MSS 50907, vii, pp. 89–92.

39 MacDonald to Cosgrave and to Craig, 27 May 1924; and Cosgrave to MacDonald, 28 May 1924, Cmd 2166: *Further Correspondence Relating to Article 12 of the Articles of Agreement Between Great Britain and Ireland* ; 1924, xviii, 97, nos 1–3. Thomas to Healy, 23 May 1924; and Henderson to Abercorn, 24 May 1924, Cmd 2155, nos 32 and 33.

40 Jones diary, 13 May, vol. III, p. 231. O'Higgins to Cosgrave, 10 June 1924; and James MacNeill to Cosgrave, 13 May 1924, both in D/T, S 1801/H.

41 Ibid., Jones diary. See Fitzgerald–James MacNeill correspondence, 14, 16, 17 Apr. 1924, DFA, G 10/1923.

42 'Notes of a Conference Between the Prime Minister and Mr Cosgrave and Sir James Craig at Chequers on 31st May, 1924', HO 246/2. All subsequent quotations from the meeting are taken from this source.

Boundary Commissioner – but at a price. Just as Thomas had sought to bring financial pressure to bear on Ulster, Craig now turned the tables. A deal on the boundary could be had, he intimated, if Labour was willing to meet his demands.

In exchange for accepting the Boundary Commission and its award – which must be unanimous – Craig also wanted assurances that a series of issues dividing the two governments would be 'satisfactorily disposed of'. Top of his list was amalgamation of Britain's and Northern Ireland's unemployment insurance funds. Returning to the Boundary Commission later in the discussions, Craig promised to support the handover of any area 'provided the inhabitants clearly expressed their wish to go'. He would do so, however, only if 'provision' was made to resettle anyone who did not wish to be transferred into a new jurisdiction. The financial implications of this demand were staggering. MacDonald chose to side-step them, concentrating instead on Craig's insistence that any Commission award must have the backing of all three members. Such a concession, MacDonald pointed out, 'would be to give Northern Ireland a veto on any changes she did not like.'

The meeting's atmosphere did not improve with Cosgrave's arrival. The Irish leader, whose demeanor was 'polite but cold', rejected MacDonald's suggestion that the soon-to-be-appointed Boundary Commission chairman might be asked to mediate a settlement. On this matter, at least, the two Irish leaders were as one. Pointing to the 'complicated pattern of the carpet' on the floor, Craig told MacDonald that he was underestimating just how tangled this problem really was.

MacDonald's next proposal seems to have been designed to shake his guests out of their complacency. Why not follow the precedent used after the First World War to resolve the Polish–German dispute in Upper Silesia, he suggested. Such a plan could begin with a determination of the areas to be considered for transfer, followed by a plebiscite. If MacDonald meant to stir up the meeting, he succeeded. The idea left Craig 'obviously alarmed', Anderson wrote, especially 'at the prospect of large areas such as whole counties being even brought under examination in a preliminary way'.[43]

MacDonald's suggestion prompted Craig's appeal to Cosgrave to 'give the go-by to Article 12' and settle the issue between them. That was impossible, the Free State president responded. No one in Dublin had the power to bypass Article 12, his supporters would not stand for it – an odd thing to say in the circumstances. Cosgrave claimed that Nationalists were not laying claim to specific territory, explicitly mentioning Fermanagh and Tyrone. Rather, theirs was a 'demand for the "discovery" of the facts', in other words, whether

---

43 In fact, the Silesian precedent figured prominently in the Boundary Commission's origins. See chapter 2 above.

the people of the border wished to be in the Free State or under Belfast's jurisdiction. It was soon clear that Craig and Cosgrave disagreed on just about everything when it came to the boundary question. Where Cosgrave believed that Article 12 put the wishes of the local inhabitants above all other consider-ations, Craig was adamant that geographical and, even more, economic, factors should be given equal weight. The three sides were again at an impasse, and Cosgrave informed his counterparts that it was impossible for him to be involved in any further discussions. Bitter recriminations 'that the Treaty was not "fool-proof" or that the Imperial Parliament could not make its recalcitrant province toe the line' already were being heard throughout the South. Once these accusations took hold, his government would be overthrown in favour of de Valera's Republic. The stakes, he told MacDonald and Craig, were that high.

'A PROBABLE ENEMY'

Cosgrave's demand that London make the Ulster Unionists 'toe the line' was delivered at just that moment when British officials were questioning their power to do so. As one of his last acts before resigning from the Colonial Office, Lionel Curtis drafted an unofficial memorandum outlining the trouble that British forces would likely encounter once the Boundary Commission set to work. If the Commission decided that a plebiscite was necessary, 'the situation will become very difficult' as it was 'almost certain to meet with the armed resistance of the Protestant majority throughout Northern Ireland', especially from the British-funded Special Constabulary.

If, on the other hand, the Commission restricted itself to minor border revisions, or if the North's refusal to appoint a representative prevented it from functioning, Curtis agreed with Cosgrave that a republic would likely be declared in Dublin. In that case, the British would find themselves right back where they were before the Treaty was signed in 1921. 'The most merciful course' to follow should this happen, Curtis advised, would be a blockade of the 26 counties, until power could 'gravitate into the hands of the more reasonable propertied classes'.[44]

Curtis's analysis raised disturbing implications for British security far beyond Ireland. Simply put, the nation no longer had the resources needed to meet its far-flung imperial commitments. Whichever way the Boundary Commission ruled, the War Office explained, at least three divisions would be needed to implement its award. 'The Empire will thus be deprived for an indefinite period of its only mobile reserve', a situation that would have dire

44 'Appreciation of the Present Political Position in Ireland', 9 May 1924, CAB 21/281.

consequences should a crisis erupt in Iraq or Egypt. Nor was the army as sanguine as Curtis about containing trouble in the South by means of a blockade. If it failed, 'no other course beyond the re-conquest of S. Ireland seems possible'. Plainly, the War Office wanted to have nothing to do with the Boundary Commission. Such a commitment would be 'unlimited, indefinite and fraught with serious dangers both for the army itself and for Imperial defence'.[45]

In fact, there was reason to question the army's willingness to implement a Commission award that went against Northern Ireland's wishes. Only a decade had elapsed since the Curragh mutiny, and among officers there remained a wellspring of sympathy for the Ulster cause. This included the commander of British forces in the six counties, A. R. Cameron.

In a memorandum written as part of a general defence review, Cameron maintained that any plan which addressed defence 'seriously' had to regard the 'Irish Free State with its armed forces as certainly a possible and really a probable enemy'. At the same time, while an earlier War Office appraisal had dismissed the Special Constabulary as so partisan as to be 'useless', Cameron maintained that their 'value in an emergency is clear'.[46]

The following March Cameron was informed that the Army Council now 'concurred' with his analysis. For the first time, perhaps, the War Office officially regarded a British dominion as a potential enemy. This fact later prompted Michael Farrell's sober observation that no matter how many times Free Staters proved their fidelity to the Treaty settlement, they would never be regarded as trustworthy by the British establishment.[47]

More immediately, the adoption of Cameron's recommendations raised serious questions should any government attempt to carry out a Boundary Commission award that was opposed by Ulster Unionists. When Craig's Cabinet suggested that the Specials should be mobilised to guard the boundary, Cameron endorsed the proposal despite Home Office reminders that border security was the sole responsibility of the British Army. Cameron's response was telling. There was little his forces could do alone, he replied, considering the 'great preponderance of numbers of Constabulary over troops'.[48]

---

45 Ibid., War Office 'Note on the Colonial Office Memorandum on Ireland', 11 June 1924. For more on Britain's defence problems at this time, see B. Bond, *British Policy Between the Two World Wars* (Oxford, 1980), pp. 1–160.

46 Ibid. 'Home Defence Scheme – Northern Ireland', 4 July 1924, WO 32/5313. Not surprisingly, Craig agreed that the Irish boundary should be regarded as a potentially hostile frontier. See *NI HC Deb*, vol. 4, cols 715–16, 6 May 1924.

47 Cubitt to Cameron, 12 Mar. 1925 [two letters], WO 32/5313. Farrell, *Arming the Protestants*, p. 229. This mistrust was rife throughout Whitehall. See Canning, *British Policy*, pp. 112–13.

48 Blackmore to Tallents, 11 Aug. 1924; Maxwell to War Office, 18 Aug. 1924; and Cameron to Creedy, 13 Jan. 1925, WO 32/5313.

Before the end of 1924, the Home Office was forced to concede that Specials might be used as auxiliaries to army units. Cameron took this acceptance and turned it on its head. Instead of the army defending the frontier, he informed the War Office that his troops 'would naturally be employed to support the Constabulary'. Only then would a military officer take charge of the combined force. This decision reflected the desire of Craig's ministers to keep control of the Specials out of British hands. Incredibly, the War Office not only abdicated responsibility for border security but further agreed that 'command of the combined forces should only pass to the General Officer Commanding at the request of the Northern Government'.[49] No one, it seems, considered what the army would do if the Specials put up armed resistance to a Boundary Commission award ceding large tracts of Northern Ireland to the Free State.

ARTICLE 12'S 'ALLEGED AMBIGUITY'

At the end of April, Lord Birkenhead delivered a speech to the Liverpool Conservative Club in which he declared that only minor readjustments to the Irish border could be expected from the Boundary Commission.[50] Although this was not the first time that Birkenhead had made such remarks, his speech hit a raw nerve in Dublin. On 6 May, Kevin O'Higgins hit back. Article 12 had been Craig's choice, not theirs, O'Higgins told an audience in Howth. While the Free State would not coerce 'that portion of North-East Ulster which is homogeneously Orange and Unionist', neither would it allow Craig's government to coerce those 'units which are predominantly Nationalist and desirous of being within the jurisdiction of our State'.[51]

Behind the scenes, O'Higgins saw Birkenhead's speech as a warning. '[W]e cannot allow . . . an alleged ambiguity in Article 12', he told Cosgrave, 'to be left to . . . a Chairman appointed by the British Government.' O'Higgins wanted the matter settled at once. Did MacDonald and Thomas agree with Birkenhead that the Boundary Commission was only empowered to make minor border readjustments? If there was any question between the two governments about Article 12, O'Higgins insisted, 'we must have the ambiguity cleared up before the Boundary Commission sits', possibly by arbitration.

Hugh Kennedy, the Free State's attorney-general, disagreed. Whatever Birkenhead claimed, none of the four British governments that had been in

49 Ibid., Anderson to Creedy, 16 Dec. 1924; Cameron to Creedy, 13, 27 Jan. 1925; 'Copy of Memorandum sent to Prime Minister Northern Ireland on 21st January 1925'; Cubitt to Cameron, 12 Mar. 1925 [two letters].

50 See chapter 7 below for more on this speech.

51 'Statement by Minister for Home Affairs, Howth, 6th May 1924', D/T, S 1801/R.

office since the signing of the Treaty had raised this issue, and there was no reason for the Irish to get 'tied up' by the conclusions of an arbitrator. Moreover, O'Higgins's strategy was 'based on the assumption that there is some ambiguity which we have always denied and cannot now admit'. Both governments had repeatedly said that it was up to the Commissioners themselves to set their terms of reference. Why stir up a controversy where none might exist? If the issue arose, Eoin MacNeill could easily refer the matter to Dublin; then would be the time to settle any dispute.

Cosgrave also told O'Higgins that Curtis had answered Birkenhead's claim, pointing out that the British hardly were in a position to 'interpret an Article to which they were but one party of two'. O'Higgins agreed. But 'I go further', he wrote, 'what the British Government cannot do, the British nominee on the Boundary Commission ought not to be allowed to do.' Possibly, O'Higgins allowed, the two governments were at one on this question. But 'the tone of practically all the leading British newspapers' convinced him that it was foolish to allow this issue to remain unresolved.[52]

O'Higgins had good reason to be alarmed. At a Cabinet meeting on 5 May, Craig repeated to his colleagues Thomas's assurance that the Boundary Commission would restrict itself to 'an adjustment of the actual boundary.' A week later, a similar story reached James MacNeill in London, and he immediately relayed the information to Cosgrave.[53] Yet Kennedy's view prevailed. Just as British politicians wished to avoid the boundary issue generally, their Irish opposites averted their eyes from this specific question, hoping that it might go away on its own.

DELAY FOLLOWING DELAY

On 2 June, MacDonald formally notified Cosgrave and Craig that in the face of Belfast's continued defiance, it was unclear whether the Boundary Commission could function with only two members and, if not, whether London had the power to name Belfast's representative. These questions posed a constitutional dilemma that could only be answered by the Judicial Committee of the Privy Council.[54] Strangely, MacDonald's Cabinet did not

52   O'Higgins to Cosgrave; Kennedy to Cosgrave; and O'Higgins to Cosgrave, 7, 9, 10 May 1924, D/T, S 1801/R. 'The Irish Boundary', *The Times*, 2 May 1924. 'The Irish Boundary. Meaning of Clause 12', *Morning Post*, 7 May 1924.

53   Cabinet Conclusions, 5 May 1924, PRONI, CAB/4/112/12. MacNeill to Cosgrave, 13 May 1924, D/T, S 1801/H.

54   MacDonald to Cosgrave and to Craig, both 2 June 1924, Cmd 2166, nos 4 and 5.

ask, and the committee did not reach out to answer, the most important question: namely, was it within the power of Northern Ireland's subordinate Parliament to defy an agreement reached by the Imperial Parliament? Put another way: 'Have the King, Lords and Commons of Great Britain and the Six Counties any authority whatever in the Six Counties?'[55]

To ensure the widest possible backing for the committee's decision, the Cabinet decided that two of the panel members should be from the dominions. While a Canadian judge was being sought, it had already been arranged for the chief justice of Australia to sit on the committee. Given the distances that both men had to travel, it was obvious that some time would pass before a judgment could be rendered. The interval should not be wasted. In his June letters to Cosgrave and Craig, MacDonald announced that the British were about to name the Boundary Commission chairman. To spare everyone from the 'difficulties' that they now confronted, he again proposed that the chairman should be employed in one last attempt to reach 'an amicable settlement'.

If MacDonald thought this action would win any plaudits in Dublin he was mistaken. Even before his despatch reached the Irish capital, Healy informed Thomas that the Free State government wanted the Commission to be established, immediately. In both this letter and one written the following day by Cosgrave, the Irish all but openly accused Labour of deliberately frustrating the intentions of Article 12. '[D]elay follows delay', Cosgrave bitterly complained, and the appeal to the Judicial Committee looked like yet another 'device' designed to 'shelve the whole matter'. While this accusation was vigorously denied by both MacDonald and Thomas, the Irish were closer to the truth than they knew.[56]

In his 6 June letter to Cosgrave, MacDonald pointed out that no formal request to appoint a Boundary Commissioner had been put to Ulster's government until 29 April and that its formal refusal had not been sent until 10 May. True, the British knew that Craig's government 'might' refuse to appoint its representative. They did not know this for sure until mid-May, however, and, MacDonald argued, 'we should get into difficulties if we try to deal with contingencies before they have actually arisen'. But, as early as 2 April Thomas had informed the Cabinet that this contingency was 'almost certain'. Less than a week later, the government's law officers reported that without a Northern Ireland representative, the Boundary Commission could not in their view legally function.[57]

---

55 'Viewpoints', *Irish News*, 23 June 1924.

56 See Healy–Thomas and Cosgrave–MacDonald correspondence, 3, 4, 6, 12 June 1924, Cmd 2166, nos 6, 8, 11, and 12.

57 C 24 (24), 2 Apr. 1924, CAB 23/47. 'Boundaries of Ulster. Opinion of the Lord Chancellor and Law Officers of the Crown', CP 242(24), 7 Apr. 1924, TJ GG/2/20.

By contrast, from early May Ulster's government worked on the assumption that the issue would be sent to the Privy Council and Craig, in his own words, was soon 'endeavouring by hook or by crook' to influence its decision. If he succeeded and the Privy Council ruled out large-scale transfers of territory, the feeling in Belfast was that Cosgrave would 'take little further interest' in the boundary question. Were this to happen, Craig himself suggested that the Free Staters might then take advantage of the ensuing uproar to repudiate their financial obligations in Article 5 of the Treaty.[58]

Whatever Craig was getting up to behind the scenes, this latest development further strained relations between London and Dublin. Even if the best of intentions are attributed to British motives, the practical effect of not arranging for an early sitting of the Judicial Committee allowed the government to again put off the inevitable. As Lionel Curtis had earlier suggested, an appeal to the committee would buy the government a little more time.[59]

The irritation made plain in Cosgrave's 4 June letter to MacDonald reflected a growing mistrust of Labour among Free State politicians. Following the breakdown of the Chequers conference, Cosgrave and his colleagues had to show their supporters that their patience was at long last about to bear fruit. This could best be demonstrated, Healy informed Thomas on 3 June, by putting the new chairman and MacNeill to work ascertaining the wishes of the inhabitants in the border counties.

Dublin's proposal, O'Higgins pointed out, was 'within the Treaty and is preparatory to its enforcement'. MacDonald's idea of using the chairman as an intermediary was 'preparatory to its evasion'. Worse, the idea was fast gaining ground in Ireland that the British had no intention of taking account of the wishes of border-county Nationalists, that doing so was 'not within the sphere of practical politics'.[60]

'A MISERABLE FARCE'

In mid-June Cosgrave was forced to allow time for a Dáil debate on Britain's 'long series of evasions' regarding the Boundary Commission. This 'miserable long-drawn-out farce', complained one opposition TD, had allowed Unionists to create 'acute difficulties' for Northern Nationalists 'which did not exist

---

58 Tallents to Anderson, 8 May 1924, HO 144/3915/7. Craig to Spender, 14 July 1924, PRONI, PM/9/11.

59 'Appreciation of the Present Political Position in Ireland', 9 May 1924, CAB 21/281.

60 O'Higgins to Cosgrave, 10 June 1924, D/T, S 1801/H.

when the Treaty was signed in 1921'.[61] What so outraged these members of the Dáil was Craig's continuing assault on proportional representation.

Although the Northern Ireland Parliament abolished PR for local elections in 1922, Craig had found it politic to postpone implementing the legislation for county council and rural district council elections until 1924. He maintained that the postponement was necessary to allow for the redrawing of electoral boundaries, despite objections from grassroots Unionists.[62] In the meantime, the abolition of PR for municipal elections had already deprived Northern Nationalists of their majorities on urban councils in Londonderry, Enniskillen, and Downpatrick.[63]

This same outcome was about to be repeated at the county level and would have a huge impact on the boundary question. At a rally of Tyrone Nationalists, Cosgrave and his colleagues were accused of 'fiddling' while their co-religionists faced 'a war of extermination'. At this same meeting a reso-lution was passed protesting not only 'the grossly scandalous gerrymandering' that had occurred with the redrawing of electoral districts but also against 'the delay in settling our claim to form part of the Irish Free State'.[64]

These protests explain Cosgrave's repeated requests to the British that they establish the Boundary Commission before the end of May. Once Nationalists lost control of the local government councils that they had won thanks to PR, it would be far more difficult to press the Free State's claim to the border counties. Unfortunately for Northern Nationalists, the weapon with which they chose to demonstrate their opposition both to the abolition of PR and to redistricting played right into their opponents' hands. A Nationalist boycott of elections held on 1 June ensured Unionist victories. Significantly, the boycott did not have the support of the North-Eastern Boundary Bureau, which correctly forecast that the move would backfire.[65]

At the same time, the boycott won the Nationalists no sympathy in Whitehall. While it was admitted that the redistricting plans 'were most carefully thought out by the Unionists to secure them a majority', one Home Office official observed that Nationalists had only themselves to blame for

61   *Dáil Deb*, vol. 7, cols 2355, 2357, 2364, 2366, and 2630, 13 and 18 June 1924. It was during this debate that the government was also attacked for agreeing to suspend the Council of Ireland. See chapter 4 above.

62   'Local Elections in Northern Ireland', 22 Apr. 1924, DO 35/893/1/xii/123. Montgomery to Craig, 8 Sept. 1922, PRONI, CAB/9B/40/1.

63   See chapter 3 above.

64   'Tyrone Asks Fair Play', *Freeman's Journal*, 8 Apr. 1924. 'The Gerrymander Scandal', *Ulster Herald*, 12 Apr. 1924.

65   Phoenix, *Northern Nationalism*, p. 302.

their dilemma. According to this official, Nationalist refusal to participate in hearings on the redistricting plans, or their 'purely destructive criticism' of those plans when they did attend such meetings, robbed their objection of 'much of its force'.[66]

Meanwhile, Craig's government was busily creating what a later generation would call 'facts on the ground'.[67] As one TD predicted, these facts would make all the difference. Once the Unionists gained control of the county councils with the patronage that accompanied that control – and coupled these powers with the physical force of the Specials – they would have no problem in turning a large majority against them into a majority in their favour.[68]

'THE GRAVE OF REPUTATIONS'

On 5 June MacDonald informed the House of Commons that his government was at last ready to name the chairman of the Irish Boundary Commission.[69] Richard Feetham, a native of Monmouthshire, had made his reputation as a barrister in South Africa where only the year before he had been appointed to that country's Supreme Court. For his decision to go to South Africa in the first place, Feetham largely had one man to thank: Lionel Curtis. The two met while studying at Oxford and continued their association in South Africa, working in Alfred Milner's famous 'Kindergarten' of civil servants. Among other appointments, Feetham served as legal adviser to the future Tory Die-hard, Lord Selborne, when the latter was Britain's high commissioner in Pretoria. Feetham and Curtis maintained contact through the Round Table, a movement dedicated to promoting unity within the British empire. Ironically, Curtis had wanted his old friend to draft the final version of the Irish Treaty in 1921.[70]

He was not, however, the first choice for this job. As early as September 1922, Curtis had suggested to Churchill that the ideal candidate to chair the Boundary Commission would be former Canadian Prime Minister Sir Robert Borden.[71] When approached about the chairmanship nearly two years later,

---

66 'Local Elections in Northern Ireland', 22 Apr. 1924, DO 35/893/1/xii/123.

67 The phrase is often used to describe Israel's settlements policy, especially in and around Jerusalem.

68 *Dáil Deb*, vol. 7, col. 2366, 13 June 1924.   69 *HC Deb*, vol. 174, col. 1469, 5 June 1924.

70 Richard to Mary Feetham [his mother], 4 July 1924, RF, 6/1, ff. 18–19. Thomas to Selborne, 19 May 1924, Selborne Papers, MSS 84, ff. 165. Jones diary, 27 May 1924, vol. III, p. 232. Lavin, *Curtis*, p. 14, 19, 192, 223. G. Hand, 'MacNeill and the Boundary Commission', in F. X. Martin and F. J. Byrne, ed. *The Scholar Revolutionary: Eoin MacNeill, 1867–1945, and the Making of the New Ireland* (Shannon, Ireland, 1973), pp. 219–22.

71 Curtis to Churchill, 13 Sept. 1922, CO 739/7/45885.

Borden replied that he would accept only if both Irish governments appointed their own commissioners and 'if I am assured that my acting is desired by both'. As he later confessed to Lord Beaverbrook, he 'was not sorry that the North persisted in its refusal', taking him off the hook.[72]

Like Borden, Feetham's understanding of the Irish Question was rooted in an empire and Commonwealth framework.[73] Recent Irish historians have been decidedly reluctant to subject Feetham to harsh scrutiny. This may be an embarrassed reaction to the 'Feetham-cheat 'em!' abuse suffered by the chairman at the hands of Nationalist critics.[74] To be sure, there is no evidence that Feetham was vetted for his views on what he thought the Boundary Commission ought to achieve. But given his background and associations, there was no need. As Curtis later told Churchill, Feetham was selected precisely because he was a man of 'conservative temperament' who could be counted on to reject the sort of 'preposterous and extravagant claims' being made by the Free State. 'Feetham', he assured Churchill, 'is a chairman exactly of the kind you contemplated.' Quite so. On hearing of Feetham's appointment, Curtis sent his old friend a two-word telegram that was as revealing as it was cryptic: 'England expects'.[75]

MacDonald gave a similar assurance to Lady Londonderry. Any arbitrator, the British prime minister wrote, was bound to say that the Commission could do nothing more than make minor changes to the Irish border. 'I understand this is Feetham's view', MacDonald continued, though he admitted that his information was the product of 'mere gossip'.[76]

---

72 'Paraphrase Telegram, Governor General of Canada to Thomas', 7 May 1924, HO 45/12296/12. Borden to Beaverbrook, 9 Oct. 1924, BBK C/51.

73 J. E. Kendle, 'The Round Table Movement and "Home Rule All Round"', *Historical Journal*, vol. 1, no. 3, 1993, pp. 332–53.

74 Hand, 'MacNeill', pp. 221–2. Hand, *Report*, pp. x–xxi. According to Joseph Lee, Hand's 'dispassionate assessment of Feetham' retrieved 'the reputation of Irish scholarship'. See *Ireland*, p. 148, n. 411. While emphasising that Feetham was 'conscientious', Hand, pp. x–xi, notes that he was 'unimaginative' and his approach to the Commission 'was marked by a legalism and remoteness from political realities . . . it is just possible that he was not the right kind of man' for the job. The abuse hurled at Feetham was, in any event, scurrilous. Both Labour's Thomas Johnson, and Farmers' Party chief Denis Gorey suggested that Feetham's career depended on pleasing his English 'master'. See *Dáil Deb*, vol. 8, cols 2505, 2558, 15 Oct. 1924. For a dispassionate, though no less critical assessment of Feetham, see D. Gwynn, *The History of Partition* (Dublin, 1950), pp. 231–2.

75 Curtis to Churchill, 19 Aug. 1924, Curtis Papers, MSS 89, ff. 76–83. Hand, 'MacNeill', p. 220. Curtis's telegram was a reminder of Lord Nelson's famous order to the fleet just before the Battle of Trafalgar: 'England expects every man to do his duty'.

76 MacDonald to Lady Londonderry, 5 Aug. 1924, quoted in H. M. Hyde, *The Londonderrys: A Family Portrait* (London, 1979), pp. 159–60.

Feetham's appointment did not mean that MacDonald had 'abandoned hope' that the two Irish Governments might yet reach a mutual settlement.[77] Soon after his arrival in London, Feetham was dispatched first to Dublin and then to Belfast for informal talks with the two Irish governments. Curtis was under no illusions about Feetham's task. Solving the Irish problem, he pointed out to a mutual friend, had been 'the grave of reputations and also of old friendships'. But he was confident that Feetham would soon show the Irish, North and South, that he was 'a man who cannot be twiddled around anyone's finger'.[78]

Even so, Feetham's discussions with Cosgrave and Craig achieved nothing. Although the Irish president ruled out another conference before the Boundary Commission set to work, Feetham nevertheless suggested such a meeting when he met with Craig on 3 July. Ulster's prime minister was willing to consider another conference; he warned, however, that any proposal to transfer loyalists from the six counties on a 'large scale would not be tolerated'. Craig also danced around Free State demands for a plebiscite in the border areas, saying that 'he would not insult loyalists by asking their wishes, since he had no doubt what the replies would be'. Craig was incensed because London had failed to consult him before sending Feetham to Ireland, and he used their initial meeting to bring home to the South African judge 'the very grave dangers which would ensue' should he misinterpret his role as Boundary Commission chairman.[79]

If anyone had reason to worry after Feetham's first visit to Ireland, it should have been the Free Staters. During a second interview, Feetham questioned Cosgrave about his government's attitude regarding the transfer of territory from South to North. Cosgrave replied that his government 'had never admitted' that the Commission had a right to hand over Free State territory to Northern Ireland. Even so, just such an outcome clearly was on Feetham's agenda.[80]

After returning to England, Feetham visited Craig at his country home in Berkshire. 'We had a long heart-to-heart talk', Ulster's premier confided to Wilfrid Spender. Craig's earlier hostility had vanished and was replaced by a quiet confidence that Feetham now 'grasped more fully and clearly the difficulties that lie ahead'.[81] The contest over partition was still to be played out. But whereas Cosgrave and his Free State team were still warming up, the Ulster Unionists were positioning themselves to score the deciding goal.

77   *HC Deb*, vol. 174, col. 1259, 4 June 1924.

78   Curtis to Lady Selborne, 28 June 1924, Lady Selborne Papers, Eng. Lett. d. 430, ff. 52–4.

79   'Index to Dates and Conferences', 1–4 July 1924, D/T, S 1801/P. Cosgrave memorandum, 6 July 1924, D/T, S 1801/I. Cabinet Conclusions, 4 July 1924, PRONI, CAB/4/117/5.

80   Ibid., Cosgrave memorandum.

81   Craig to Spender, 14 July 1924, PRONI, PM/9/11.

SEVEN

HEADING FOR IRISH ROCKS

*. . . London is much excited over Ireland. Ulster and the Morning Post
are on the war-path; Ll. G. feels that 'all's right with the world' again, and
I am terribly gloomy. S.B. is either dishonest or he absolutely agrees with me,
but has he the clearness of conviction and the force of will to impress the
Ulstermen? It will be a miracle if we keep our ship off the rocks.*

AUSTEN CHAMBERLAIN[1]

—

Not long after his return from Dublin at the end of March, Tom Jones was
'startled' one morning to find the ex-prime minister of Great Britain standing
in his office doorway. So unexpected a visit was 'very like' Stanley Baldwin.
And so was Jones's reaction. Never one to miss an opportunity, he decided to
tell the Conservative leader about his recent visit to Ireland and 'the coming
trouble on the Boundary Commission'. A crisis was just over the horizon, and
Jones hoped that Baldwin might use his influence with Carson and Craig 'to
bring Ulster into a more reasonable mood'.[2]

Despite Labour's difficulties with the Irish boundary, Conservatives were
largely silent on the issue through the winter and spring of 1924. Even behind
the scenes, party leaders avoided the issue as much as possible.[3] But however
much they tried to steer their ship clear of Irish rocks, strong currents were
pulling them in that direction. It was true that the Conservative ship was not
the only one that might run aground. But though Labour was in office and the
Liberals, especially Lloyd George, had Irish skeletons of their own, the potential
for damage was greatest for the Tories.

For two of Austen Chamberlain's ex-Coalition partners the boundary
dispute was particularly dangerous. One, on the fringe of the Conservative
Party, the other desperate to get back in, both Birkenhead and Churchill
feared that the brewing trouble over Ulster would cause them 'considerable

---

1   Austen to Ivy Chamberlain, 1 Aug. 1924, AC 6/1/548.
2   Jones diary, 9 Apr. 1924, vol. I, pp. 275–6.
3   For a rare exception, see Bernard–Chamberlain correspondence, 18, 25 Feb. 1924, AC 35/4/7–8.

difficulty' if it again became a major political issue. Over the next 18 months they were to play increasingly prominent roles in creating the conditions that would contain the boundary question for the next half century. In the meantime, the stakes for themselves and for the Conservative Party were high and the crisis, when it erupted, would again threaten to make Ireland the 'disastrous and dominating issue' of Britain's political life.[4]

THE RETURN OF BIRKENHEAD AND CHURCHILL

Although the Tory high priests had been willing to 'kill the fatted calf' for Austen Chamberlain, there were no burnt offerings on Birkenhead's return to 'the true fold' after the 1923 election. His reinstatement in the Conservative leadership had been 'a more difficult proposition', allowed only because it was a case of 'Austen and F. E. or no Austen'. Party leaders hoped that once the two men were re-established in the Tory hierarchy, the 'very honourable though perverted chivalry' which bound them together would disappear. They could be patient and in time rid themselves of Birkenhead – if his 'drunkenness and loose living' did not do the job for them.[5]

The enmity which Conservatives felt for Birkenhead was nothing compared to the detestation they reserved for Churchill. Though officially a Liberal until Asquith allowed Labour to take office, rumours that Churchill was about to rejoin the Conservative Party had been circulating for over a year – a prospect that many stalwarts viewed 'without enthusiasm'.[6] Their rancour grew after each of his increasingly desperate efforts to regain a parliamentary seat, with or without Tory support.

In such a climate, neither Birkenhead nor Churchill could afford to see an issue as divisive as the Irish Question re-emerge. Churchill, edging his way back into the party of his father, was especially determined that 'this difficulty' should not become 'gravely embarrassing' to himself. It was imperative, he later told Lionel Curtis, to keep the boundary question out of Parliament. Once it became a domestic political issue, questions would be raised about 'the

---

4   Churchill to Birkenhead, 30 Apr. 1924, *Comp V, 1*, pp. 151–2. *HC Deb*, vol. 189, col. 360, 8 Dec. 1925.

5   Salisbury to Baldwin, 26 Jan. 1924, SB vol. 159, ff. 258–61. 'Memorandum of conversation with Mr Baldwin,' 4[?] Feb. 1924, AJB-S, GD 433/2/19, Reel 4. Baldwin to Salisbury, 25 Jan. 1924, S (4) 108/83–4. Chamberlain diary, 18 Nov. 1923, NC 2/21. The Ulster Unionists, though, could not forgive or forget. See Lady Carson's diary, 7, 9 Feb. 1924, D/1507/C/8.

6   Lady Spender's diary, 27 May 1923, D/1633/2/26.

meaning to be attached to Article 12' – and for Churchill, that could be very embarrassing indeed.[7]

'POLITICAL DYNAMITE'

It was Birkenhead, though, who discovered that the boundary question could still arouse passions. Speaking to the Liverpool Conservative Club at the end of April, the former lord chancellor boldly defended his decision to sign the Irish Treaty. Article 12 was written in 'plain language', he insisted, and the Commission was bound to make only minor readjustments to the border. Ulster's leaders had nothing to fear, and by appointing a representative they could save the country from the 'political dynamite' which their refusal might otherwise set off.[8]

Craig, after reading the speech, was incandescent. 'How any Britisher, any man with the blood of his forefathers in him, can contemplate such an outrageous action', he told the Ulster Association, 'passes my comprehension'.[9] He was equally scathing when, during an hour and a half meeting that same day, he told the Shadow Cabinet that he 'got more time and interest from the present Government on the Ulster question than he did from his own associates' in the Tory Party. To smooth over matters, it was agreed that Birkenhead, along with Carson and Sir Douglas Hogg, would act as a 'special committee' to co-ordinate strategy between the Tories and Ulster Unionists. In return, the Conservatives made it clear that 'it was of vital importance' for Ulster Unionist MPs to 'be in constant attendance at Westminster' in case their votes were needed by Baldwin. Despite this agreement, hard feelings remained. All of the Conservatives, Lady Carson wrote in her diary, 'except Lord Cave were rotten about Ulster'.[10]

At the same time, the Shadow Cabinet formed a separate committee to examine the legal implications arising out of Northern Ireland's refusal to appoint its Boundary Commissioner. The committee's report was far from reassuring. On the one hand, the committee's members – Birkenhead, Cave,

---

7   Winston to Clementine Churchill, 19 Aug. 1924, CSC 2/17/13–15. Churchill to Curtis, 15 Aug. 1924, WSC 2/570/18. According to John Ramsden, local Conservatives would not consider Churchill's candidacy in the West Toxteth by-election that spring 'because of his past attitude to Ulster'. See *Balfour and Baldwin*, p. 192.

8   'Ulster and the Boundary. Lord Birkenhead's Appeal', *The Times*, 1 May 1924.

9   'Ulster's Resolve', *The Times*, 2 May 1924.

10   LC Min. 1 (24), 1 May 1924, Cave Papers, Add. MSS 62,489, ff. 75–7. Cabinet Conclusions, 5 May 1924, PRONI, CAB/4/112/12. Lady Carson's diary, 3 May 1924, D/1507/C/8.

and Hogg – agreed that the Commission could not function unless Ulster was represented on the panel. That said, once the Commission was legally constituted, there was no certainty that it would limit itself to making minor changes to the Irish frontier. Quite the contrary, even a Boundary Commission award which transferred the whole of Fermanagh and Tyrone to the Free State 'could not be treated as bad in law or set aside by any Court.'[11]

The upshot of these events was to make the Conservatives even more anxious to steer clear of the boundary issue. Afterwards, it was decided that 'as far as possible party leaders should avoid making any public pronouncement on the Irish question'. Whatever the merits of this decision, it stymied discussion of the problem within the party's higher counsels and meant that the Tories would not be 'prepared to meet any probable eventuality'. As spring gave way to summer, Conservatives pinned their hopes on the idea that Labour might somehow solve the boundary dispute for them, even though the dangers to the party were obvious should Ireland again erupt as an issue in British politics.[12]

'BEASTLY AWKWARD': THE PRIVY COUNCIL DECISION

For Austen Chamberlain, the summer of 1924 seemed to drag on forever. 'The session is slowly petering out', he wrote to his wife from the House of Commons; 'everybody is bored and a holiday would be good for all.' By the end of July, Chamberlain was not the only MP longing to get away from London. Months of negotiations – with the Europeans on reparations, the Soviets on trade and, lately, with the Irish – had put MacDonald and his colleagues under a great strain. 'I am living in a perpetual succession of special Cabinet Meetings', one of them wrote, interrupted by 'sittings of the House . . . called at short notice'. It was agreed that Parliament would adjourn after the first week in August and would not reconvene until the end of October. 'Only Ireland is menacing', Chamberlain confided to his wife. 'Will there never be an end to that bitter chapter?'[13]

The menace referred to by Chamberlain was the report of the Judicial Committee of the Privy Council. The committee's decision was about to be issued, and as Jones confided to his diary it was 'beastly awkward'. Charles

---

11   LC 10 (24), 5 May 1924, Cave Papers, Add. MSS 62,464, ff. 69–72.

12   Robert Cecil to Salisbury, 9 May 1924, S (4) 109/44–7. LC Min. 2 (24), 5 (24), 6, 28 May 1924, Cave Papers, Add. MSS, 62,489, ff. 78–9, 91–3.

13   Austen to Ivy Chamberlain, 29 July 1924, AC 6/1/543. MacDonald diary, 2 and 6 Aug. 1924, JRM, PRO 30/69/1753/1. Olivier to Reading, 7 Aug. 1924, IO, MSS Eur. E. 238/7, no. 29.

Craig, who was also apprised of its contents, quickly sent word to his brother, James. In effect, the committee closed off any avenue the government might take to call the Boundary Commission into being without the passage of additional legislation. There could be no Commission without a representative from Northern Ireland; the Crown, acting on the advice of its British ministers, could not force Northern Ireland's governor-general to appoint a representative; nor, as Article 12 was written, could the government in London make the appointment on its own. Jones dreaded the prospect of Parliament passing an Irish boundary bill. Were that to happen, he wrote, 'Cosgrave's opponents would say that if the British Parliament could alter the Treaty, so could the Irish Free State.'[14]

At the end of July MacDonald finally heeded Jones's advice and invited other party leaders to discuss what had become a matter 'of serious Parliamentary importance.' Even before the invitations were sent, Jones was ordered to sound out Baldwin. What he got was a 'diehard reaction, more so than I ever remember having before from him'. Jones was surprised by Baldwin's attitude towards the Free Staters and shocked when his once and future master told him that it was 'difficult to forgive assassination and to forget their behaviour in the war'.[15]

Baldwin's reaction is easy to explain. Alarmed at the prospect of boundary legislation, he was, in effect, 'being asked to open up old wounds among his most loyal followers so that the Labour Party should be spared embarrassment'. Thomas confirmed as much when he informed Conservative and Liberal leaders that the government intended to pass a one-clause bill allowing it to name Northern Ireland's Boundary Commissioner. Furthermore, unless the other leaders 'had some better suggestion to make', Labour expected cross-party support for the legislation so that it could be enacted as quickly as possible.[16]

The participants at the 30 July meeting were well aware that Labour's attempt to bypass Craig's government would be thrown out by the House of Lords. In that case, Jones noted in his diary, 'Ireland will be back in our politics'. Baldwin, sensing the danger for himself and for his party, was 'for

---

14 Jones diary, 31 July 1924, vol. III, p. 233–4. Charles to James Craig, 30 July 1924, PRONI, CAB/9Z/3/2. Cmd 2214: *Report of the Judicial Committee of the Privy Council, as Approved by Order of His Majesty in Council, of the 31st July, 1924, on the Questions Connected with the Irish Boundary Commission Referred to the Said Committee*; 1924, xi, 351.

15 C 45 (24), 30 July 1924, CAB 23/48. Duff to Lloyd George, 30 July 1924, LG G/13/2/1. Besides Lloyd George, Asquith, Baldwin, Birkenhead, Austen Chamberlain, and Worthington-Evans were invited to the meeting. Jones diary, 29 July 1924, vol. III, p. 233.

16 Middlemas and Barnes, *Baldwin*, pp. 269–70. C 44 (24), 30 July 1924, CAB 23/48. For evidence that opposition leaders anticipated Labour's proposal, see Austen to Ivy Chamberlain, 29 July 1924, AC 6/1/543.

going very slow' before any final decision was made.[17] He adamantly opposed any suggestion that the adjournment might be postponed to rush the legislation through Parliament, telling one confidante that he would do his 'utmost to stave that off'.[18]

His nemesis, on the other hand, could not have been more pleased with this turn of events. Lloyd George was in his element, pledging Liberal support for the government's bill and urging its immediate passage. 'LlG. is just bursting with new-born hope', Chamberlain told his wife, while 'S.B. sees himself confronted with disaster.' Both men knew that if Tory peers rejected the legislation, Labour and the Liberals could then go to the country on a platform of 'the Lords versus the People'. In any such election, Chamberlain predicted, the Conservatives would suffer a 'smashing defeat'.[19] Other Tory leaders were equally pessimistic. Lord Derby thought that MacDonald would be 'rather glad' to see Parliament dissolved over the boundary question as Labour was 'in a peck of troubles' over a number of other issues.[20]

In fact, MacDonald was no more anxious to fight an election on Ireland than was Baldwin. At this same time, he was immersed in two delicate foreign policy issues: the struggle to resolve disputes over post-war reparations and, separately, an effort aimed at normalising relations with the Soviet Union. The MacDonald-led discussions to bring round both France and Germany to accept the Dawes Plan on reparations would not achieve success until mid-August. Meanwhile, negotiations with the Soviets were proving to be especially difficult.

The collapse of the Soviet talks, just as the crisis over the boundary bill erupted, was followed less than 24 hours later by the dramatic announcement that agreement with Moscow had been reached after all. On the same day that the Irish bill was given its first reading in the House of Commons, MPs were stunned to learn that British and Soviet negotiators had concluded two treaties: a trade agreement, along with a general treaty which held out the promise of government-backed loan guarantees to Moscow. Tory newspapers leapt onto this astonishing turn of events and pointed to it as proof of communist influence deep within the bowels of MacDonald's administration. Incredibly,

17   Jones diary, 31 July 1924, vol. III, p. 234.

18   Baldwin to Joan Davidson, 30 July 1924, Davidson Papers.

19   Austen to Ivy Chamberlain, 31 July 1924, AC 6/1/546. Neville Chamberlain called Lloyd George's reaction 'downright unpatriotic'. See Neville to Ida Chamberlain, 3 Aug. 1924, NC 18/1/446. Lord Londonderry also attacked Lloyd George for 'creating a false election issue'. See Londonderry to MacDonald, 9 Aug. 1924, Lord Londonderry Papers, D/3099/2/93.

20   Derby to Rawlinson, 15 Aug. 1924, quoted in R. Churchill, *Lord Derby, 'King of Lancashire': The Official Life of Edward, Seventeenth Earl of Derby, 1865–1948* (London, 1959), pp. 572–3.

at this very moment, the Cabinet then handed its critics yet further evidence which served to confirm these accusations.[21]

In late July, Britain's communist party newspaper, the *Workers' Weekly*, published an article calling on soldiers not to allow themselves to be used as strike-breakers. A warrant charging acting editor John Campbell with incitement to mutiny was duly issued, only to be suddenly dropped after a confused series of exchanges involving MacDonald, other members of the Cabinet and Labour backbenchers.[22] As with the Soviet treaties, this sudden turnaround fuelled charges of a 'red menace' within the government.

From Labour's point of view, then, the atmosphere was hardly propitious for a general election even if they could make Ireland and the Lords the main issues. Anyway, no one in the party leadership really wanted to revisit the Irish crisis. It was not their fight. Finally, MacDonald had as much reason as Baldwin for wanting to stop 'Lloyd George and his miserable minded following' from capitalising on the boundary dispute. 'This is a thing to settle between friends', MacDonald told Lady Londonderry. They should not allow themselves to be dragged down into a squabble between 'dishonest politicians and hard mouthed bigots'.[23]

Other Labour grandees felt that the party needed more time in office to prove itself, and this alone was reason for avoiding an early election. 'All depends on whether the P.M. pulls off a satisfactory settlement with France', Beatrice Webb wrote. 'If he does, the Labour Government is in for another nine months – until the next budget'. But, she feared, if 'neither the Russian loan nor Irish boundary business "comes off" we may be turned out in November.'[24]

On 2 August MacDonald, along with Thomas and Henderson, met with Cosgrave, Kennedy, Londonderry, and Pollock (Craig again being ill) to inform them of the government's plan of action. Privately, Cosgrave was told that although the boundary legislation would be introduced on 6 August, it would not be passed until Parliament reconvened in late autumn.

That was two months too long, the Irish president replied. His government's ten-vote majority in Dáil Éireann did not account for some 40 members who refused to take the Oath of Allegiance and, therefore, were denied their seats. Cosgrave believed that Thomas Johnson, the Dáil's Opposition leader, planned to argue that the Treaty had been broken by Britain's continued refusal to set up the Boundary Commission. That being so, the 40 abstentionist TDs could take their seats without submitting to the Oath – and if that happened, the Irish Republic would become a *fait accompli*.

21 Lyman, *First Labour Government*, pp. 192–6.

22 Jones diary, 6 Aug. 1924, vol. I, p. 287. Marquand, *MacDonald*, pp. 364–70.

23 MacDonald to Lady Londonderry, 5 Aug. 1924, quoted in Hyde, *The Londonderrys*, pp. 159–60.

24 Webb diary, 21 July 1924, vol. 38, 4096–4102. Also, see Gretton to Carson, 16 Sept. 1924, PRONI, CAB/9Z/3/2.

Despite this warning, MacDonald and his colleagues agreed that 'even this very serious risk was outweighed by the practical certainty that the Bill . . . would be rejected by the House of Lords; [and] that a General Election might have to be undertaken under unfavourable conditions'. According to a Free State account of the meeting, MacDonald warned Londonderry and Pollock of the 'possibility of constitutional changes' if the North persisted in its refusal to appoint a Commissioner and the House of Lords threw out Labour's bill. The implicit threat, to abolish what powers remained in the Lords, made no impression on either Unionist leader. Yet, even when faced with this stubborn reaction, MacDonald and Thomas still hoped that they might persuade the Ulstermen to name a Commissioner on their own. They were certain that only this could save them from an election on the boundary dispute.[25]

INFLAMING PASSIONS

Any doubts that Ireland still had the power to inflame passions were dispelled when Thomas rose to speak in the Commons on 1 August. His announcement of the proposed boundary bill 'completely overshadowed' all other business. Now that the Irish spectre had reappeared in the House of Commons, its presence confirmed Baldwin's worst fears. 'The old feeling', H. A. L. Fisher recorded in his diary, was 'very intense'. Clearly, a large body of Conservative MPs were ready to fight the legislation without considering the political damage this might do to them in the country at large. 'Disaster is staring you in the face!' one MP cried out at the government; but his words might better have served as a warning to the Opposition front bench.[26]

Five days later the boundary bill was given its first reading in the House of Commons. Unless Craig and his followers were prepared to appoint their own Boundary Commissioner, Thomas declared that there was no alternative but to pass a bill allowing the imperial government to do it for them. Pressed by Baldwin for a go-slow approach on the one hand, and the Free State's demand that the legislation be enacted immediately, Thomas split the difference and announced that Parliament would reconvene on 30 September to complete the bill's passage.[27]

---

25   C 46 (24), 4 Aug. 1924, CAB 23/48. Free State memorandum on 2 Aug. 1924 conference, undated, D/T, S 1801/J.

26   MacDonald to George V, 2 Aug. 1924, JRM, PRO 30/69/228. *HC Deb*, vol. 176, cols 2401–6, 1 Aug. 1924. H. A. L. Fisher diary, 2 Aug. 1924, MSS 19.

27   Ibid., cols 2930–2, 6 Aug. 1924. Cosgrave to MacDonald, 3 Aug. 1924, D/T, S 1801/J. C 48(24), 6 Aug. 1924, CAB 23/48.

What happened next 'produced one of the most interesting days of the Session'. Baldwin limited his remarks to the problems that would be entailed by Parliament's early recall. Sir John Simon, speaking for the Liberals, took a decidedly different course. Not only would his party back the boundary bill, Simon announced; it was also willing to extend Parliament's current sitting so that the measure could be enacted without delay. MacDonald called the speech a 'thinly disguised' attempt 'to inflame passion and political prejudice'. It did just that, provoking 'ominous cries' from Conservative and Unionist backbenchers and forcing the Speaker to intervene before the situation got completely out of hand.[28]

For those who recalled the pre-war Home Rule crisis, the scene was all too familiar. The 'Prince of Darkness', one contemporary journal noted, was again 'active in his old hunting ground'. This was territory many MPs had hoped they would never have to revisit. Yet they seemed to be set on a course taking them precisely in that direction, with the added danger of a third general election in less than two years at the end of the road.[29]

THE CONSERVATIVES' DILEMMA

Except for his brief intervention on the 6th, Baldwin had maintained a disquieting silence during the opening days of the boundary crisis. That evening, however, he lashed out. Speaking to Conservatives at Hemel Hempstead, Baldwin delivered a fighting speech, arguing that a pledge of honour to Ulster Unionists was implicit in the 1920 Act, a pledge as binding as any explicit promises made to Irish nationalists in the Treaty. He then turned on the Liberals 'who were prepared, apparently, to throw the whole of this subject back into the political arena' and to 'plunge the country into a crisis of the gravest character imaginable'. Conservative MPs, he promised, would fight any legislation to 'alter the Treaty by changing the character' of the Boundary Commission – a pledge which was in fact more ambiguous than his listeners might have realised.[30]

Baldwin was in a delicate position. Although Die-hards were the most vocal section of his party when it came to Ireland, few Tories wanted to risk electoral oblivion just because Ulster Unionists were unwilling to compromise. After all, Lord Derby pointed out, Labour's bill was 'only compelling them to

28   Ibid., cols 2934–7. MacDonald to George V, 7 Aug. 1924, JRM, PRO 30/69/228. *Annual Register: 1924*, pp. 86–8.
29   'The Devil and the Peace Treaties', *The Nation*, 9 Aug. 1924.
30   'Mr Baldwin on Irish Crisis', *The Times*, 7 Aug. 1924.

do what, legally, they are bound to do.' Rather than have these divisions burst into the open, the party's national executive even considered postponing the Conservatives' annual conference 'in view of the Political Situation which had arisen over the Irish Boundary question'.[31]

Even if Baldwin could keep these rifts from breaking into the open, the party still might be torn apart. Hints coming from Belfast held out the tantalising prospect that Craig's government privately might accept the boundary bill. But, as Baldwin explained to Edward Wood: 'The Lords are the crux'.[32] Tory members of the upper house were unwilling to 'incur the odium of letting the bill through' without public backing from the Ulstermen, and this step Craig and his colleagues were unwilling to take.[33] That meant that the Lords would block Labour's bill, Conservatives in the Commons would feel bound to support them, and Labour – and Lloyd George and the Liberals – would have a golden opportunity to smash the party.

To be sure, not every Tory leader felt that they were in such dire straits. Leo Amery admitted that the Tories might 'have to face the possibility of the Goat trying to lead a raging campaign against Ulster in the hope of bringing about a Liberal Socialist combination and swamping us'. But, he assured Baldwin, 'It won't come off.' Even if MacDonald could be tempted into such an alliance with Lloyd George, most Labour MPs would not stand for it. Nor was Amery convinced that British voters would turn against the Tories for backing the House of Lords. The 'country, sick of Ireland, as it is, is just as likely to be cross with those who force on an election'.[34]

Few of Amery's colleagues shared his optimism, however, and they did not include Baldwin. From the beginning, Austen Chamberlain felt that the party's 'only hope' would be for Baldwin to somehow persuade Craig to compromise. Otherwise, 'nothing but crushing disaster awaits us'. More than most, Chamberlain had already learned the bitter lesson that Ireland was 'a fatal influence in British politics.'[35]

---

31   Derby to Baldwin, 4 Sept. 1924, SB vol. 99, ff. 130–1. Executive Committee minutes, 9 Sept. 1924, NUA 4/1/4, ff. 101. The committee went ahead with its plans only after it was pointed out that postponement meant foregoing its venue for the conference at Newcastle – and after the party's chairman was given discretion to cancel the event if necessary.

32   Baldwin to Wood, 6 Sept. 1924, Halifax Papers, A4.410/14/1.

33   Salisbury to Baldwin, 25 Aug. 1924, SB vol. 99, ff. 122–5.

34   Amery to Baldwin, 3 Aug. 1924, SB vol. 99, ff. 118–19.

35   Austen to Ivy Chamberlain, 31 July 1924, AC 6/1/546. Also, see Birkenhead to Churchill, 21 Aug. 1924, WSC 2/570/48–9.

BALDWIN'S VISIT TO BELFAST

A week after Parliament recessed, Baldwin reluctantly decided that he must go to Belfast to impress upon Northern Ireland's Cabinet the gravity of the impending crisis. He was going against his better judgment, having earlier told Craig that he did not want to make the trip 'unless it is absolutely necessary'. Such a visit was bound to attract press speculation which 'might do harm'. Baldwin, though, was sure that the Labour government was about to fall. 'It is difficult to see how they can get over the Soviet treaty in early November', he confided to Joan Davidson. But before that could happen, there might still be 'a crash over Ireland', and to prevent such an accident he was willing to risk a visit to the six counties.[36]

For the better part of Sunday the 17th, Baldwin was involved in 'protracted discussions' with Craig and his colleagues. At the outset, their guest made it clear that there was little enthusiasm among Conservatives to do battle over the Irish boundary. Only two members of the Shadow Cabinet were inclined to pick a fight over the issue; the consensus, rather, was that 'it would be better to get the matter cleared up by this Government if Ulster would consent'.[37]

Craig, on the other hand, wanted his Tory allies to fight Labour's bill just short of forcing a general election on the issue. '[B]ut I showed him the snag', Baldwin explained in separate letters to Lord Salisbury and Edward Wood. Such a strategy was bound to fail, because the Lords would 'never assent' to the bill without an 'assurance of agreement' from the Ulster Unionists. Once the peers rejected the legislation, Labour might immediately call an election and 'we may be in a grave difficulty'.[38]

Despite this warning, Craig refused to give any such assurance. At most, he was willing to consider acquiescing to the boundary bill 'under duress'. In exchange, Baldwin gave the Northern Ireland government what amounted to a veto over any Boundary Commission award it did not like. 'If the Comn. should give away counties', he told Edward Wood, 'then of course Ulster couldn't accept it and we should back her.' At any rate, Baldwin was confident that this scenario would not occur. Labour would 'nominate a proper representative' to be Northern Ireland's Commissioner, he wrote, and 'he and Feetham will do what is right'.[39]

---

36 Baldwin to Joan Davidson, 14 Aug. 1924, Davidson Papers. Middlemas and Barnes, *Baldwin*, p. 270. As Baldwin suspected, his visit to Belfast did not remain secret for long. See 'Belfast's Farewell to Mr. Baldwin', *Morning Post*, 19 Aug. 1924.

37 Craig to Carson, 18 Aug. 1924, PRONI, CAB/9Z/5/1.

38 Baldwin to Wood, 6 Sept. 1924, Halifax Papers, A4.410/14/1. Baldwin to Salisbury, 2 Sept. 1924, S(4) 110/25.

39 Ibid., Baldwin to Wood.

After his return from Belfast, Baldwin was 'inclined to think' that the next election would not be on Ireland, after all. And, he hinted to Joan Davidson, 'there are strong forces working to that end'.[40] Baldwin had good reason to be optimistic. In the wake of this meeting, Craig suggested to Edward Carson that, perhaps, the time had come to confront the boundary problem, 'to face the music and have done with it'. Like Baldwin, Ulster's premier had concluded that it would be wise if the Unionists 'did not force a General Election' as it would be 'impossible to explain the intricacies of the Boundary question to audiences other than those which in any event would be likely to vote Conservative'. If Labour's bill was thrown out by the Lords, the election 'would be fought on whether the Commons or the hereditary peers were to prevail', and on that platform the Liberals and Labour would happily join forces. Ulster could expect 'little mercy' from a Lib–Lab government which might decide that they had 'a mandate to do what they liked.'[41]

Even if this nightmare scenario did not come to pass a Conservative victory, large or small, also posed a dilemma. Baldwin 'would be immediately faced with the problem of how to carry out the Treaty and this might possibly split the Conservative Party once more'. Aside from these considerations, Craig intimated that they had little to fear from MacDonald and Thomas. He was certain that Labour would nominate a 'safe person' to represent Northern Ireland on the Commission, who, with Feetham, could be trusted to 'override the Free State representative' if needs be.[42] None the less, Craig still refused to take the next step and make public his willingness to accept Labour's bill. Instead, because of his continuing ill-health, Ulster's premier let matters hang fire and set off on another three-week sea cruise.[43]

With Craig somewhere on the Baltic and Baldwin on holiday in France, matters were allowed to drift. An attempt by Salisbury to hammer out an agreement between Ulster Unionists and Conservatives went nowhere. Salisbury was emphatic that only a 'public expression' by Craig would enable Tory peers to pass the boundary bill. Anything less, he pointed out to Lord Cave, 'would rob us of the last atom of credit which the Irish question has left us'.[44] Fearing a sell-out, however, the Ulster Unionists still refused to budge.

40 Baldwin to Joan Davidson, 21 Aug. 1924, Davidson Papers.

41 Craig to Carson, 18 Aug. 1924, PRONI, CAB/9Z/5/1.

42 Ibid.

43 Ervine, *Craigavon*, p. 491.

44 Salisbury to Baldwin, 25 Aug., 5 Sept. 1924, SB vol. 99, ff. 122–5 and 132–3. Salisbury to Cave, 2 Sept. 1924, Cave Papers, Add. MSS 62,464, ff. 77–80.

THE BIRKENHEAD LETTER

These were the circumstances that led to the publication of Birkenhead's hitherto confidential letter to Arthur Balfour. Written in March 1922, the letter was intended to avert a political explosion that would have erupted had Balfour defected over the Irish Treaty.[45] At the beginning of this latest crisis, the Shadow Cabinet was informed that a deal, including Ulster Unionist consent, 'would be much easier' if it could be shown 'beyond dispute' that the Treaty's signatories never envisioned anything more than minor border readjustments when they agreed to Article 12. Winston Churchill believed that Birkenhead's letter was the answer to their prayers. The importance 'of such a document in the discussions to which we are now condemned', he pointed out to Balfour, could be decisive.[46]

Churchill hoped that by producing this letter he would finally be absolved of his role in the Irish settlement, thus paving the way for his return to the Tory fold. With an election in the offing, he was particularly anxious to be adopted as the candidate for a safe Conservative seat – a search that was quietly endorsed by Baldwin. In fact, party chairman Stanley Jackson approached a number of local Conservative associations about adopting Churchill; but, noted one party insider, 'they won't have him anywhere'.[47]

That Ireland was a stumbling block to Churchill's ambitions was made clear in a letter from Sir Harry Goschen, chairman of the Epping Conservative Association. Goschen would recommend Churchill's candidature in the constituency – but only on condition that he give his explicit backing to the party, its leader and its policies 'especially as regards Ireland'. The cost of the Epping seat was a pledge to back no change of the Irish boundary that did not have Northern Ireland's approval.

For Churchill, it was a price worth paying.[48]

On 19 August Churchill triumphantly sent Craig a copy of Birkenhead's 1922 letter. Given its contents, he hoped the Ulster government might now see that they had nothing to fear from the Boundary Commission and might even appoint their representative, rendering Labour's bill – and its likely veto by the

---

45 See chapter 3 for the letter's origins. The text is reprinted in Appendix III.

46 LC Min. 6 (24), 30 July 1924, Cave Papers, Add. MSS 62,489, ff. 95–6. Churchill to Balfour, 7 Aug. 1924, WSC 2/134/57.

47 Churchill to Jackson, 14 Aug. 1924, WSC 2/134/69. Gilbert, *Churchill*: vol. V, p. 29-30, 43–5. After the 1923 debacle, Baldwin told Robert Boothby: 'If and when I get back to power, there is one man I am going to have at my side – Churchill'. See R. Boothby, *I Fight to Live* (London, 1947), p. 36. Bayford diary, 29 July 1924, p. 216.

48 See Goschen–Churchill correspondence, 5, 11, 28 Aug. 1924, *Comp V*, 1, pp. 172–5, 183–4.

Lords – unnecessary. An autumn general election was all but certain, Churchill pointed out, and in the coming campaign 'we must not allow ourselves to be out-manoeuvred . . . when the forces of evil are so strong'.[49]

Despite the importance Churchill attached to Birkenhead's letter, it did not make the open-and-shut case he claimed. A series of letters between Churchill and Birkenhead, and one from Birkenhead to Chamberlain, hint that Birkenhead harboured deep misgivings about the Coalition's handling of the boundary issue during the Treaty negotiations. Moreover, the version of Birkenhead's 1922 letter that Churchill now proposed to publish may have been materially altered.

Although Birkenhead readily agreed with Churchill's plans to give the letter to the press, he raised a disquieting question about its authenticity. According to the published version, Birkenhead maintained that Collins's claim that the Boundary Commission would transfer whole counties to the Free State had 'no foundation whatever except in his overheated imagination'.[50] But, writing to Churchill on 20 August, Birkenhead pointed out that in the original draft of his letter he had 'qualified in it my reference to Michael Collins by a phrase which substantially ran "honest if hot-headed"'. In other words, Collins's claim might have been made in a moment of hot-headed anger, and it might have been at odds with the British interpretation of Article 12. But admitting that the claim was an honest one contradicts the dismissive assertion that it was purely the product of Collins's imagination. These words were now missing and, Birkenhead continued: 'I cannot understand their omission from the letter as sent'.[51]

Two days after he sent this letter to Churchill, Birkenhead wrote to Austen Chamberlain. This second letter paints a wholly unflattering picture of the conduct of the negotiations surrounding Article 12. 'The plain truth', he admitted, was that the Treaty never would have been signed had it not been for the promise of the Boundary Commission. As for the current crisis, Birkenhead observed, it boiled down to the simple question of whether or not the imperial government had the right to act on Northern Ireland's behalf to fulfil its Treaty obligation.

> In my opinion we possess such a power. . . . The Northern Government has in fact already so far recognised the Treaty as to avail itself of an option which only came into existence in virtue of the Treaty. In my judgment it is futile to reply that certain extremists in the South of Ireland, and many organs of the Press are

49 Churchill to Craig, 19 Aug. 1924, PRONI, CAB/9Z/8/1.
50 Appendix III.
51 Birkenhead to Churchill, 20 Aug. 1924, WSC 2/570/38.

making excessive and even absurd claims for the possession of Ulster territory. Every one of us knew that such claims had been made in the past and would be made in the future. We decided that they should be pronounced upon by a Commission. We decided upon the appropriate formula for reference to this Commission. Having satisfied ourselves that the words employed were only capable . . . of the meaning which we placed upon them we assented to the addition of other words at the earnest entreaty of the Irish negotiators. We should not have agreed to the insertion of these words if we had not believed that they were powerless to affect the meaning of the article taken as a whole. . . . In other words we agreed upon a reference to the Commission which many of us knew to be disputable but which we were certain could only be decided in one way. . . .[52]

Several conclusions can be made when this remarkable letter is read in conjunction with Birkenhead's 20 August note to Churchill. First, these letters contradict the assertion made in Birkenhead's 1922 letter, and elsewhere, that the extensive territorial claims made by the Free State were simply the product of one man's 'overheated imagination'. On the contrary, Birkenhead admits that the Irish Treaty delegates were led to believe that the Boundary Commission would substantially reduce Northern Ireland's territory.[53]

Second, the letter to Chamberlain provides damning evidence to substantiate the charge that the Irish negotiators were deceived when they were told that the Boundary Commission would ensure Ireland's 'essential unity' – Arthur Griffith's price for accepting Dominion status. As Birkenhead later admitted in the House of Lords, the Treaty 'never could have been signed, it never would have been signed, without Article 12'. If this was so, his letter to Chamberlain substantiates the conclusion reached by John Campbell that the Irish were indeed 'cheated' when they signed the Treaty.[54]

Third, and what may be most important, Birkenhead is explicit that after 6 December 1921, the 1920 Act was irrelevant when it came to determining Northern Ireland's frontier. It should be remembered that the first ten articles of the Treaty speak of Ireland as a whole. As Nicholas Mansergh has pointed out, the Treaty was between Great Britain and Ireland, not Southern Ireland or the 26 counties. Other historians tend to dismiss this point, calling it an attempt 'to reconcile the reality of partition with the imagination of unification'.[55]

52 Birkenhead to Chamberlain, 22 Aug. 1924, WSC 2/570/50–6.

53 Appendix III. The opposite claim is made in Curtis to Churchill, 19 Aug. 1924, Curtis Papers, MSS 89, ff. 76–83.

54 *HL Deb*, vol. 62, col. 1232, 9 Dec. 1925. Campbell, *F. E. Smith*, pp. 583–4.

55 Mansergh, *Unresolved Question*, p. 193. D. G. Boyce, *Ireland, 1828–1923: From Ascendancy to Democracy* (Oxford, 1992), p. 103. Also, see Pakenham, *Peace By Ordeal*, pp. 250–9. Fanning, *Independent Ireland*, p. 23.

But, on the contrary, Birkenhead made it plain that the Treaty and its ratifying legislation superseded the 1920 Act just as that legislation repealed the 1914 Home Rule Act before it. This admission undercuts one of the primary arguments in Birkenhead's earlier letter to Balfour. Article 12, Birkenhead had then claimed, 'contemplates the maintenance of Northern Ireland as an entity already existing' whose boundaries were 'defined by the Act of 1920'. On that basis, he argued, it was 'inconceivable' that the Boundary Commission had the power to make wholesale changes in a 'creature already constituted'.

But if Northern Ireland's Parliament gained the right to vote itself out of a single Irish state only through Article 12, the entity created by the 1920 Act was irrelevant, and so were its boundaries. If that were true, Birkenhead's assurances to Balfour were beside the point, meaning that the Boundary Commission was capable of making extensive changes to the size and shape of Northern Ireland.

Churchill was horrified by the implications of what Birkenhead had written to Chamberlain. 'I hope you will not show the letter you have written to Austen to anyone else, or allow him to show it to anyone else', Churchill begged his friend. The defeat of Labour, he reminded Birkenhead, was their primary concern and they must keep clear of 'Irish cross currents'. Their best hope was to ensure the timely publication of the 1922 letter which, Churchill advised his friend, would 'do you good among the Die-hards and Ulstermen'.[56]

On the Irish issue, at least, Churchill was clearly aligning himself with the Die-hard wing of the Conservative Party, working closely with Carson as well as with Balfour. Much as he wished the Ulster Unionists would appoint their Boundary Commissioner, Churchill now told Birkenhead that he would 'not in any circumstances oppose them'. He was well aware that he still had 'a lot of prejudice to overcome' among rank and file Conservatives.[57] The Irish Treaty may not have been his greatest transgression in Tory minds; but because it was again a live issue it was causing the most problems, and he was anxious to avoid it when at all possible. 'Do not, I pray you, stress unnecessarily the Irish question in any speeches', he asked Robert Horne, prior to their joint appearance at a Conservative gathering. 'It would only divide friends and unite enemies. The Russian issue is the one, and with good handling might well be decisive.'[58]

56 Churchill to Birkenhead, 19, 25, 30 Aug. 1924, WSC 2/570/65–6, 69–76, and 78–80.

57 Lady Carson's diary, 28–29 Aug. 1924, D/1507/C/8. Churchill to Birkenhead, 25 Aug. 1924, WSC 2/570/69–76. Coote to Churchill, 4 Sept. 1924, WSC 2/134/117–18.

58 Churchill to Horne, 30 Aug. 1924, WSC 2/134/84–5.

LLOYD GEORGE COMES TO TERMS

Before Churchill could release Birkenhead's 1922 letter to the press, he had to be sure that it would not be disavowed by Lloyd George. As early as 19 August, Churchill had won a verbal commitment from the Welshman to endorse the contents of Birkenhead's letter. But he was careful to keep Lloyd George on board, lest his sometime friend, sometime rival be tempted by other considerations.[59]

As it happened, Lloyd George had reasons of his own for deciding that the Irish problem would not make such a good election issue after all. Although the two wings of the Liberal Party were reunited, deep suspicions and bitter animosities remained. In August Edward Grey let it be known that he might lead a breakaway faction of the party and that he might raise the boundary issue to wound Lloyd George.[60] 'The truth' about the Treaty negotiations, Herbert Gladstone conceded, 'is shrouded in the grim vapours of the past'; but that did not mean that Lloyd George should be allowed to escape the 'onus' for the deceitful tactics that he had practised with such reckless abandon.[61]

Certainly, the developing crisis was raising awkward questions about his handling of Ireland while at No. 10 Downing Street. Several months earlier, the *Daily Herald* spoke for many when it had called the boundary dispute 'one of the damnable legacies of Lloyd Georgeism'.[62] Neville Chamberlain also suspected 'that Ll.G. did give Michael Collins reason to think he would get Fermanagh and Tyrone and at the same time allowed Craig to believe that no such transfer would take place'. A gleeful John St Loe Strachey was sure that 'before we reach the end we shall see L.G. hopelessly discredited'.[63]

The Russian treaties, on the other hand, held no such dangers for Lloyd George and resurrected no embarrassing ghosts. On the contrary, by coming to a 'tacit arrangement' with the Conservatives, he hoped to position the Liberals so that they could recapture their place as the country's acceptable party of the left. At the same time, he deliberately withheld support from Asquithian Liberals so that the coming election could be used to purge the party. His leadership unchallenged, Lloyd George would then be free to

59 Churchill to Birkenhead, 19, 30 Aug. 1924, WSC 2/570/65-66 and 78-80. Churchill to Balfour and Carson, 1 Sept. 1924, AJB-S, GD 433/2/19, Reel 4.

60 Grey to Maclean; and Pamela Grey to Maclean, 12, 25 Aug. 1924, Maclean Papers, Dep. c. 467, ff. 94–5, 110–13.

61 Gladstone to Maclean, 14 Aug. 1924, Maclean Papers, Dep. c. 467, ff. 96.

62 'Ulster Boundary Crisis. A Lloyd Georgeism Legacy', *Daily Herald*, 29 Apr. 1924.

63 Gladstone to Maclean, 14 Aug. 1924, Maclean Papers, Dep. c. 467, ff. 96. Neville to Ida Chamberlain, 3 Aug. 1924, NC 18/1/446. Strachey to Carson, 12 Sept. 1924, Strachey Papers, S/4/2/11.

reshape Liberalism in his own image. As one historian has put it: 'It might be said that Lloyd George decided to destroy the party in order to save it.' Finally, his endorsement of the Birkenhead letter also guaranteed his own safety in the forthcoming election, when he obtained a Conservative promise not to challenge him for his Caernarvon Boroughs seat.[64]

By the time Liberal Party leaders gathered in mid-September to discuss strategy, Lloyd George was all for directing their fire at Labour's Soviet policy. Asquith demurred, saying that 'important as was the Russian Treaty, the first, and perhaps the only, thing with which the House would deal would be Ireland'. But Lloyd George was better informed. As he told his colleagues, 'he had heard that there were grounds for hope' that the Irish issue would be contained after all. The Conservatives, Lloyd George said, 'were not anxious to make it an electoral issue, and the House of Commons men were doing their best to prevent the Lords rejecting the Bill.'[65] That, of course, was Baldwin's hope. 'If we get over this fence', he wrote to Wood while on holiday in France, 'it looks as though the Soviet Treaty would be the next big event: and on that we can join issue gaily.'[66]

PUBLICATION OF THE BIRKENHEAD LETTER

On 8 September, newspapers across Britain published Birkenhead's 1922 letter to Balfour. The *Daily News* summed up the reaction of most newspapers, calling the letter 'conclusive and irrefutable' proof that there had never been any intention to dismember Northern Ireland. The *Daily Express* went further, arguing that it would now be 'unthinkable' for the Boundary Commission to interpret Article 12 broadly.[67]

The Times magisterially observed that 'there has never, as a matter of fact, been any real doubt about the broad intentions of the Imperial Government'. Conveniently forgotten was the fact that less than a year before this same newspaper had reported that it was quite likely that Article 12 would result in a 'considerable modification of the present boundary'. In any event, *The Times* still felt that it was 'unreasonable to expect Northern Ireland to stake everything'

---

64 Churchill to Balfour and Carson, 1 Sept. 1924, AJB-S, GD 433/2/19, Reel 4. Cowling, *Impact of Labour*, pp. 404–5. Campbell, *Lloyd George*, pp. 87–9, 95–6, and 101–6.

65 'Narrative of the General Election 1924', Gladstone Papers, MSS. 46,480/310–11.

66 Baldwin to Wood, 6 Sept.1924, Halifax Papers, A4.410/14/1.

67 'Ulster's Right. The Proof', *Daily News*; and 'Boundaries Not Areas. Lord Birkenhead's Letter', *Daily Express*, both dated 8 Sept. 1924. The *Daily News* endorsement was particularly significant because it was the voice of Asquith's faction of the Liberal Party.

on the Commission and its chairman.[68] Nor was the press entirely unanimous in its verdict. Birkenhead's revelation was 'interesting', the *Manchester Guardian* commented, 'but it adds nothing new'.[69]

These comments aside, Churchill was delighted with the letter's overall reception. 'Politics are, I hope, moving towards a crisis', he reported to Lord Rosebery two days later and for that reason it was 'essential that the Irish issue should be got out of the way'.[70] It was soon evident, however, that Birkenhead's letter was not changing minds. While Die-hards might be glad that its contents had been made public, this did not mean they thought that Northern Ireland should now name its Boundary Commissioner. 'That step', one told Lord Salisbury, 'Ulster will not and cannot take'.[71] Nor had Birkenhead won any personal gratitude. As the *Belfast News-Letter* told its readers, the letter was yet another example of the kinds of tricks Birkenhead had performed at the behest of his erstwhile master in the Coalition.[72]

LLOYD GEORGE CONTRADICTS HIMSELF

Soon, the old master was himself in the thick of the controversy. On 10 September Lloyd George delivered what was billed as an 'important speech' on both the Russian treaties and the boundary question. As promised, he fully endorsed Birkenhead's correspondence with Balfour. 'I stand by the letter itself, and all that it contains', he told an audience in Wales. Ulster had nothing to fear from the Commission. Nor could he believe that its chairman would 'come to wild and unreasonable decisions which would tear up the territory of Ulster, and leave it as a province with nothing but an unconsidered remnant of its land and population'.

But as was so often the case with Lloyd George, what he gave with one hand, he took back with the other. Although most attention focused on his endorsement, the speech was in fact a gigantic contradiction. During the Treaty negotiations, Lloyd George explained, both sides agreed

---

68 'Irish Boundary. Lord Birkenhead on Article 12', and 'New Light on the Irish Deadlock', *The Times*, 8 Sept. 1924. 'The Ulster Boundary. An Embarrassing Situation', *The Times*, 11 Sept. 1923.

69 'Lord Birkenhead's Letter', and 'Lord Birkenhead on Article 12', *Manchester Guardian*; and 'Ireland's Boundaries. Wishes of the Inhabitants the Kernel of Article 12', *Daily News*, all dated 8 Sept. 1924. 'Events of the Week', *The Nation*, 13 Sept. 1924.

70 Churchill to Rosebery, 10 Sept. 1924, WSC 2/134/119–21.

71 R. S. Howe to Salisbury, 8 Sept. 1924, S (4) 110/29–30.

72 'Birkenhead Letter. Irish Views', *The Times*, 9 Sept. 1924.

that the boundaries of the Six Counties did not accurately represent the real division between North and South. . . . We then proposed that a Boundary Commission should be appointed with a view to arranging the fairest boundaries possible . . . which would hand over to the Southern States [sic] the Catholic parishes which were anxious to join them, but which would, on the other hand, transfer to the North those Protestant parishes which are now in the Free State. . . .[73]

While this sounds inconsequential, an award based on the wishes of the population in parishes, or poor law unions, did not mean the exchange of pockets here and there along the border. Based on memoranda presented by Arthur Griffith in 1921, along with evidence accumulated by the North-Eastern Boundary Bureau, it would mean that large portions of counties Tyrone, Fermanagh and Armagh would go to the Free State, as well as Derry City, Strabane and Newry – precisely what Unionists feared.

Next, Lloyd George disposed of the argument that the economic and geographical qualifications mentioned in Article 12 were intended to be equal counter-weights to the wishes of the inhabitants. '[T]here are islands of Catholics surrounded by Protestants, and islands of Protestants in the South surrounded by Catholics', Lloyd George observed. 'It was therefore further proposed that the boundaries should be based not only on the wishes of the inhabitants, but on geographical and economic considerations.' Dealing a further blow to Birkenhead's letter, Lloyd George explained that these qualifications were taken 'out of recent treaties where similar difficulties had to be faced in Central Europe'. Birkenhead's reference in his letter to the 1878 Treaty of Berlin was irrelevant. The Versailles Treaty and the boundary commissions provided in it were the only international guides to consider.

CRAIG REFUSES TO BUDGE

Despite the widespread publicity given to Birkenhead's letter, Churchill's effort failed to impress the one person at whom it was aimed. On his return from the Baltic, Craig told a crush of reporters that the letter made 'no difference whatever' to his views on the Boundary Commission.[74] This was later confirmed when the Northern Ireland Cabinet met at Cleeve Court, Craig's English residence at Streatley-on-Thames. The Cabinet, Craig told

73 'Irish Boundary. Mr. Lloyd George's Position', and 'The Birkenhead Letter. Mr. Lloyd George's Support', *The Times*, 11 Sept. 1924.
74 'Ireland. Sir James Craig's Return', *The Times*, 12 Sept. 1924.

Baldwin, felt 'bound to take every possible step to prevent the passage of the Bill revising the Treaty unless it is amended . . . to apply merely to an adjustment of the Boundary'.

Any hopes Baldwin had for avoiding a vote on the Irish bill were dashed. Craig made it clear that his first allegiance was not to the British Empire, and certainly not to the Tories, as he felt 'entitled to look to any political party' to 'safeguard our rights and privileges under the Act of 1920'. Even so, Craig shamelessly urged Baldwin to use every means at his disposal as Conservative Party leader to amend the bill in Northern Ireland's favour. 'If there is any constitutional difficulty in getting such a clause inserted', Craig wrote, 'I should of course be glad if the Bill could be rejected'. If, on the other hand, Tory leaders were

> convinced that I am merely asking them to provide against dangers which they consider to be purely imaginary and if they therefore feel unable to reject the amending Bill I rely upon you and them to give Ulster unqualified support later on should it prove that our fears are justified.[75]

None of the warnings given by Baldwin, Salisbury, and other Conservatives seemed to have made the slightest impression on Northern Ireland's prime minister. Even an appeal from George V was met with an unyielding response. 'I shall have to maintain a firm attitude to the end', Craig told the king's private secretary, 'else there would be no limit to the claims of the Free State'.[76]

Earlier, Lord Londonderry had confided to Salisbury that both he and Craig agreed that a general election fought over the House of Lords 'throwing out the Treaty would be disastrous'. Now, he was forced to admit that the Ulster Unionists were determined to defeat the bill, come what may. 'Our people are very headstrong', he ruefully admitted, 'and they can only think for themselves. They cannot take the long view of British politics which might be that an election on this point would not serve the interests of the Conservative Party.'[77]

Londonderry could have gone further. As far as Ulstermen were concerned, they had little reason to care about what happened to a good many Conservatives who, they believed, would as readily sell out Northern Ireland as any other group of English politicians. This mistrust was given an added boost when Eamon de Valera produced letters from Arthur Griffith written during the Treaty negotiations. At a speech in Cork on 14 September, de Valera quoted extensively from the letters to show that the Irish had accepted

75 Craig to Baldwin, 17 Sept. 1924, PRONI, CAB/9Z/3/1.
76 See Stamfordham–Craig correspondence, 17, 20 Sept. 1924, PRONI, CAB/9Z/3/2.
77 Londonderry to Salisbury, 8, 18 Sept.1924, S (4) 110/32 and 43–4.

Article 12 only on the understanding that it would cede vast tracts of Northern Ireland to the Free State.[78]

Griffith's letters caused no end of problems for ex-Coalition Tories. This revelation, one Unionist angrily told Sir Laming Worthington-Evans, 'hardly fits in with our ideas of what Ulster has been led to expect'.[79] Around any Conservative who took part in the Treaty negotiations, the suspicion still lingered that they had betrayed the cause before and might do so again. With so many of these same men in the party's front ranks, Unionists felt they had more reason than ever to be suspicious of the Tory leadership.

BALDWIN'S THREAT

The Ulster Unionist decision to oppose Labour's boundary bill meant that Baldwin was in exactly the same position he had been in when the crisis erupted in August. There was every danger that Conservative MPs might be swept up by an emotional impulse to join the fight and damn the consequences. Die-hards, not surprisingly, were doing all they could to push the party in that direction. They believed the time had come 'to destroy the Socialist Government' in general, and their Irish bill in particular, 'with the utmost determination'. John Gretton accused Baldwin of 'half-hearted' leadership, telling Carson there 'should be no talk of compromise or fear of facing a General Election'.[80]

Yet even Gretton was forced to admit that much as the party hated Labour's bill, few if any Tory MPs or parliamentary candidates actually wanted to fight the next election on Ireland and the Lords.[81] However much the Ulster cause could still pluck at the heartstrings of Tory regulars, its power to strike a chord among the British people at large had long since faded. Other Conservatives realised this. Edward Wood felt that the party would be flirting with disaster if it became associated for a second time with an Ulster revolt. Far from being one of the party's shining moments, Wood suspected that 'the British law-abiding temperament was more shocked than we always recognised by Carson's performance' during the 1912–14 crisis. In the new, post-war politics, 'Ulster will lose sympathy if she appears to be following that line'. And, of course, so would the Conservative Party.[82]

---

78   'No Boundary for Mr De Valera', *Morning Post*, 15 Sept. 1924.

79   Williamson to Worthington-Evans, ? Sept. 1924, W-E, MSS Eng. hist., c.914, ff. 194.

80   Gretton to Carson, 16 Sept. 1924, PRONI, CAB/9Z/3/2.

81   Ibid. Gretton sought to minimise this point, noting that his canvass of current and prospective Tory MPs was 'quite limited'.

82   Wood to Baldwin, 10 Sept. 1924, Halifax Papers, A4.410/14/1.

Tory moderates had an additional reason for wanting to avoid a fight over the boundary bill and to focus instead on the Russian treaties. As Churchill observed in a letter to Carson, no one could foretell the outcome of the next election, and there was every reason to believe that the results could be as close as the outcome of the 1923 race. This meant that the Conservatives might need the support of Lloyd George and the anti-Labour wing of the Liberal Party. The Tory leadership 'will have to come to some sort of terms with him', Churchill argued, 'if they are to turn the Socialists out'. That would be a lot less likely to happen if these same Liberals found themselves allied with Labour in a hard-fought battle over Ireland, only to be told that they were to switch sides to support the Conservatives against the Soviet agreements.[83]

Austen Chamberlain also doubted that the Conservatives were strong enough to beat Labour on their own. Once he was convinced that a general election was inevitable, he wrote with foreboding, 'then the deluge!'[84] Like Churchill, Chamberlain felt that an understanding of some kind with the Lloyd George Liberals might be the price of power. His brother, Neville, however, had reached a different conclusion. Even with the Irish Question looking 'insoluble', he felt that the Tories should 'risk a General Election' on the issue, believing the party would still come out of the race 'with a very narrow majority'.[85]

While the younger Chamberlain may have been willing to take such a gamble, it would be extraordinarily risky for the party's leader. Baldwin had 'wrecked his party once', the *Quarterly Review* reminded its readers. Were he to risk an election on a conflict between the two houses of Parliament over Ireland he would 'wreck his party again, and this time more effectively than before'.[86] Running a political party aground once had been a mistake. Doing so a second time would look careless. Almost certainly, it would be fatal to Baldwin's political career. Small wonder, then, that the Conservative leader was still 'anxious' about Ireland when Leo Amery saw him on the 19th.[87]

A week later, the Shadow Cabinet met to decide once and for all what position the party should take on the Irish legislation. 'The general conclusion was that we ought not to let the Lords wreck the bill', Amery wrote in his diary, but that the Conservatives should attempt an amendment defining the Boundary Commission's scope. Given that the chances of such an amendment passing were slim, the Shadow Cabinet decided it would then fall back

83 Churchill to Carson, 18 Sept. 1924, WSC 2/570/118–19.
84 Austen to Ida Chamberlain, 5 Oct. 1924, AC 5/1/334.
85 Neville to Hilda Chamberlain, 20 Sept. 1924, NC 18/1/452.
86 'Ireland Today', *Quarterly Review*, Oct. 1924, no. 484, p. 371.
87 Amery diary, 19 Sept. 1924, p. 386.

on a none-too-subtle threat. 'If over-ridden', Amery wrote, the Tories would warn Labour that they would 'resist any attempt to enforce against Ulster a decision based on what we regard as a false interpretation of the Treaty.'[88]

That did not go far enough for the Die-hards, who were ready to fight the boundary bill 'whatever our front bench may decide'.[89] What the Die-hards failed to see was the sheer brazenness underlying the Shadow Cabinet's state-ment. In effect, the Conservatives were handing to themselves – and through them, the Ulster Unionists – the right to veto any Boundary Commission award they did not like.

---

88   Ibid., 25 Sept. 1924, p. 387. Also, see annual party conference minutes, 2–3 Oct. 1924, NUA 2/1/40.
89   Gretton to Craig, 27 Sept. 1924, PRONI, CAB/9Z/3/2.

EIGHT

THE BOUNDARY BILL AND ITS AFTERMATH

Is not the present debate in this House absolutely unreal? What are
you thinking about? You are not thinking of the rights or wrongs
of this question at all. You are really thinking about the
General Election that is going to follow . . . .
LORD CARSON[1]

—

By the third week of September Beatrice Webb was beginning to think that
the boundary dispute would not bring down Britain's first Labour government after all. 'The Irish question has disappeared', she wrote in her diary, 'all
parties apparently having agreed to pass the Bill, and no sustained opposition
being expected from the Lords.'[2] Lord Olivier was equally confident. If the
Tory-dominated upper house refused to pass the Irish bill, 'there might be a
dissolution'; but he doubted that would happen. He even thought that the
government stood a good chance of surviving the furore over its Soviet policy.[3]

This mood reflected an unwarranted complacency within Labour's
hierarchy. None of the government's leaders principally responsible for Irish
policy – MacDonald, Thomas, and Henderson – seems to have paid much
attention to the boundary problem during Parliament's two-month recess.
MacDonald returned to his primary interests in foreign affairs; Thomas was
in South Africa for much of August and September; and Henderson involved
himself in arms reduction talks at the League of Nations.

Meanwhile, the government's critics turned their attention more and more
to the Russian treaties, so much so that by mid-September this issue 'engaged
the public attention almost equally' with the Irish boundary dispute. Although
Craig still urged Conservatives to put up a 'stiff fight' on the boundary bill, the
Tories clearly had decided to concentrate their fire on Labour's Soviet policy.
This, it seemed, rather than the Irish bill would be the issue on which 'the

---

1   *HL Deb*, vol. 59, col. 616, 8 Oct. 1924.
2   Webb diary, 20 Sept. 1924, vol. 38, 4111–16.
3   Olivier to Reading, 18 Sept. 1924, IO, MSS Eur. E. 238/7, no. 32.

Government would have to fight for its life'. And, crucially, questions about the government's handling of the Campbell mutiny case refused to go away.[4]

Nevertheless, MacDonald and his colleagues were wrong to think that they were safely out of the Irish bog. The saviour of Labour's boundary bill, when he came, would surprise everyone, including himself. Nor would any of these moves be enough to spare the country from its third general election in less than two years.

CRAIG BARGAINS WITH LABOUR

'Chilled and wretched' with a cold, MacDonald returned to London on the night of 28 September, little better rested than when Parliament had gone into recess eight weeks before. With the House of Commons scheduled to reconvene in two days' time, and Thomas not yet returned from South Africa, it fell to MacDonald to introduce the second reading of the Irish bill. Beforehand, he was involved in two long discussions on the Boundary Commission: first, with Craig and, later, in Cabinet – and in both cases, the details were as murky as they were revealing.

Why Craig made this last-minute approach to MacDonald is unclear. It is possible that the Ulster leader was attempting to play for time: Gretton had told him that from the Conservatives' point of view it was important that Parliament should not reconvene before the end of October.[5] Alternatively, Craig may have been trying to win concessions from Labour now that the government was so clearly under pressure from other directions.

As it was, he was getting little help from his friends in the Conservative Party. Craig tried to convince Baldwin to fight the boundary bill with a series of 'strong' amendments which, though they stood no chance of passing, were meant to 'satisfy the people of Ulster' and their supporters in Britain. The Shadow Cabinet's decision on 25 September ruled this out. Craig, in turn, bluntly told Baldwin that he and his followers would not 'tie ourselves to any party'. It is altogether likely that he was now looking to see if he could cut a deal with the government.[6]

---

4   Marquand, *MacDonald*, pp. 357–72. J. H. Thomas, *My Story* (London, 1937), pp. 78–9. Wrigley, *Henderson*, pp. 152–3. *Annual Register: 1924*, pp. 95–6, 100. Craig to Gretton, 17 Sept. 1924, PRONI, CAB/9Z/3/2.

5   MacDonald diary, 29 Sept. 1924, JRM, PRO 30/69/17531/1. Gretton to Craig, 16 Sept. 1924, PRONI, CAB/9Z/3/2.

6   Craig to Carson, 20 Sept. 1924, PRONI, CAB/9Z/5/1. Cabinet Minutes, 30 Sept. 1924, PRONI, CAB/4/122/1.

If that was the case, he played his hand badly. At the outset of their discussions, Craig informed MacDonald that his position on the Boundary Commission was 'unchanged'. Even so, he had come to London to ask for three 'concessions' from the imperial government. First, he wanted £1 million for the Special Constabulary, a sum promised by Neville Chamberlain shortly before the fall of Baldwin's first government. Next, he proposed amalgamating the British and Northern Irish unemployment insurance funds. Otherwise, he explained, 'Ulster would either have to reduce benefits or increase taxation'. Finally, Craig resurrected his demand, first put forward during their Chequers conference in May, that if the Boundary Commission's decision forced any Unionist to migrate, all relocation costs ought to be borne by the British government.

Supposing these points were conceded, MacDonald asked, would Ulster's government accept a frontier redrawn by the Boundary Commission? Craig refused to give any concrete assurance, promising only that 'he would accept the decision if it were not too foolish'.[7]

Unfortunately for Craig, the chancellor of the exchequer had just prepared a detailed summary of the extensive financial support that successive governments had already given to Belfast. 'Since 1921', this report began, 'the British Treasury has been subject to continual demands for money from Ulster'. To members of the Cabinet, who were given Snowden's report at the same time as they were told about Craig's conversation with MacDonald, the Ulster premier's demands simply looked like more of the same.[8]

On one point, however, Snowden was wrong. He dismissed Craig's proposal that the British Exchequer should underwrite any population transfer triggered by the Boundary Commission's award, writing that the idea 'has never been even informally mentioned to us'.[9] Quite the contrary, MacDonald had already committed the government to Craig's demand – the cost of which no one could begin to foretell – without bothering to tell his chancellor of the exchequer. Craig attached great importance to this promise, and it was one of a handful of factors that nearly persuaded him not to oppose Labour's Irish bill. The effects of any Boundary Commission award, he told Carson, would be 'greatly softened' because MacDonald had promised 'to generously compensate those Protestants who are now located in an area to be transferred to the South'.[10]

Craig's claim is supported by a Free State account of the 2 August meeting between MacDonald, Thomas, Cosgrave, and Londonderry. According to

7   C 51(24), 29 Sept. 1924, CAB 23/48.

8   Ibid. Snowden memorandum to MacDonald, 26 Sept. 1924, JRM, PRO 30/69/61.

9   Ibid.   10   Craig to Carson, 18 Aug. 1924, PRONI, CAB/9Z/5/1.

this version, however, MacDonald was willing to compensate any person whose home or business was transferred from one Irish jurisdiction to the other – not just Protestants who would find themselves in the Free State.[11]

At its 29 September meeting, the Cabinet did not discuss this proposal, and if MacDonald ever bothered to inform Snowden of the commitments he had made to the Irish, there seems to be no record of it. At any rate, before reaching a final decision on how to handle their Irish bill, Labour's ministers were given yet one more piece of curious information. Less than a quarter of an hour before the Cabinet was due to meet, MacDonald was informed that if the government appointed Carson to the Boundary Commission, Craig 'would give a pledge that he would accept its findings'. MacDonald was suspicious – 'I smelt rats!' he confided to his diary – but he felt that the proposal could not be dismissed out of hand.[12]

Where this idea originated is a mystery. The Carsons believed that it came from MacDonald, though this clearly was not the case.[13] At any rate, the list of suspects should not be confined to those in government. To anyone who wanted to get the Irish dispute out of British politics, the idea of putting Carson on the Commission was a stroke of genius. This surely would allay fears in Belfast and, as Churchill put it, what 'might have been a stumbling block will now pass out of the sphere of immediate action'.[14]

Although Craig was initially attracted to the idea, his Ulster Unionist colleagues were not. At a hastily arranged Cabinet meeting, one minister after another pointed out that once they accepted Carson's nomination they were, in effect, accepting that the Boundary Commission was legitimate. It would then be impossible for them to oppose an unfavourable award. Were that to happen, pointed out Richard Best, the attorney-general, 'we should not even have the Ulster people behind us'. Faced with what amounted to a revolt within his Cabinet, Craig backed down and urged Carson to reject any overtures that he join the Commission.[15]

Nor, in the end, was the British Cabinet willing to accede to any of Craig's demands. Whatever he had hoped to gain from his private talk with MacDonald was lost once Snowden's memorandum was presented to the Cabinet. There would be no last minute 'bargain with Ulster'; neither would

---

11　'Resume of the Proceedings of Conference in London, 2nd August 1924', undated, D/T, S 1801/J.

12　MacDonald diary, 29 Sept. 1924, JRM, PRO 30/69/1753/1. The Cabinet minutes are typically vague, saying only that a 'particular name' was mentioned. See C 51(24), 29 Sept. 1924, CAB 23/48.

13　Lady Carson's diary, 28 Sept. 1924, D/1507/C/8.

14　Churchill to Balfour, 2 Oct. 1924, AJB-S, GD 433/2/19, Reel 4.

15　Cabinet Minutes, 30 Sept. 1924, PRONI, CAB/4/122/1. Craig to Carson, 7 Oct. 1924, PRONI, CAB/9Z/5/1.

the Cabinet allow any further delays while it quibbled with Belfast over Carson's possible appointment to the Commission. The second reading of the government's amending bill would go ahead as planned.[16]

PASSAGE OF THE BOUNDARY BILL

'Not many years ago', MacDonald wrote to the king on 1 October, 'a debate on the Irish question would have provided a ready outlet for the superfluous energy which members had accumulated as a result of the holiday season. But', he continued, 'circumstances have changed.'[17] Provided that Conservative leaders could contain their extremists when it came to the Irish bill, it was clear that they meant to bring down the government over the Russian treaties. The difference between the two issues boiled down to a simple case of parliamentary arithmetic. As the *New Statesman* pointed out, while the government could rely on Liberal support to see through its boundary legislation, no such help could be expected for its policy towards the Soviet Union.[18]

However, neither the Russian treaties nor the Irish dispute was uppermost in the minds of MPs when they reconvened on 30 September. The 'explosion', when it occurred, was over the government's handling of the Campbell case – a prosecution, MacDonald sourly wrote in his diary, that had 'been foolishly entered upon but much more foolishly dropped'. Forced to watch as 'every political hypocrite' took the opportunity to denounce his government, MacDonald was compelled to schedule a debate on the incident before he could move onto the Irish bill. The outburst had one salutary effect. Having wasted so much of their 'superfluous energy' on the Campbell case, MPs had little left to expend on the boundary bill which, MacDonald told the king, was considered 'in a more sober and dispassionate manner' than might otherwise have been the case.[19]

MacDonald's distaste for the Irish legislation was obvious from the outset of his speech. 'I cannot say that I rise with any pleasure to move the Second Reading of this Bill', he told the House. Yet neither could he as prime minister walk away from a solemn commitment. 'I shall be delighted if any hon. Member has got the ingenuity to find a way out of this difficulty, only it must be an honourable way out', a mere contrivance of words would not do. 'We are bound to make Article 12 work', MacDonald continued, reminding his listeners

16   C 51(24), 29 Sept. 1924, CAB 23/48.

17   MacDonald to George V, 1 Oct. 1924, JRM, PRO 30/69/228.

18   'Comments', *New Statesman*, 20 Sept. 1924.

19   MacDonald to George V, 1 Oct. 1924, JRM, PRO 30/69/228. MacDonald diary, 30 Sept. 1924, JRM, PRO 30/69/1753/1.

that the Treaty had been given all-party support from the beginning. That support could not now be abandoned. Without it, Ireland would again tear apart British politics and all that had been achieved 'will have been destroyed once and for all'.[20]

Baldwin's reply was brief. Conservatives, he announced, would not oppose the bill's second reading. Instead, they would propose amendments during its committee stage, making it clear that the Commission was only meant 'to deal with the rectification of the Boundary'. But if these amendments were not accepted, what then? Then, Baldwin warned

> the responsibility for what is in the Bill must rest with the Government and with the Government alone; we can have no part in or responsibility for it, and we shall have to consider then what our action will be at a later stage.[21]

Later that night, MacDonald confided to his diary that the boundary bill 'is to go all right', seeming to believe that its passage was now a mere formality.[22] In fact, debate on the legislation was stormy and was marked by a number of bitter exchanges, so that 'the temper of the House remained on edge for the rest of the sitting'.[23] Determined to thwart a commitment they wished to see broken, the bill's opponents made any number of extraordinary assertions, which T. P. O'Connor rightly dismissed as a 'deluge of nonsense'.[24]

Central to the Die-hard case was their argument that once the Boundary Commission's chairman had been appointed, the imperial government had done all that it was legally bound to do. From that moment, it was up to Northern Ireland to decide whether or not the Commission could function, and the British were under 'no obligation either of honour or of legality' to pursue the matter any further. Moreover, according to the Ulster Unionist Hugh O'Neill, many MPs had earlier supported the Treaty only on the understanding that if Ulster did not like the agreement 'she need never appoint a Commissioner'.[25]

Although this claim was later denounced as the 'greatest roguery', it was by no means the most damaging admission made by the bill's opponents. Not the least of these was Sir Laming Worthington-Evans's disclosure that he and his former Coalition partners had in fact deceived the Sinn Féin delegates during the Treaty negotiations. Or, as Worthington-Evans himself put it: '[I]t is not always possible in the middle of negotiations to say fully and entirely what you would like to say . . . sometimes it is discreet to be silent.'[26]

20 *HC Deb*, vol. 177, cols 27, 37–40, 30 Sept. 1924.   21 Ibid., cols 41–5.

22 MacDonald diary, 30 Sept. 1924, JRM, PRO 30/69/1753/1.

23 *Annual Register: 1924*, p. 102.   24 *HC Deb*, vol. 177, col. 409, 2 Oct. 1924.

25 Ibid., cols 52, 57, 67, 223, 30 Sept.–1 Oct. 1924. 'In Honour to Ulster', *Morning Post*, 17 Sept. 1924.

26 Ibid., cols 156, 391–3, 1–2 Oct. 1924.

Elsewhere, Die-hard spokesmen actually conceded that if an award was based on the wishes of the inhabitants, 'we shall leave it in the power of the Commission to include in the Free State the whole of Tyrone, Fermanagh and a large portion of County Down'. This admission drew another stinging rebuke from O'Connor. 'Am I', he bitterly asked the House of Commons, 'at this date to defend the principle that men must be free to choose their own government?'[27]

The main contention of the bill's opponents was that, in Baldwin's words, Parliament had a 'double debt of honour'. Pledges had been made to Northern Ireland, as well as to the Free State, and these earlier commitments also had to be upheld.[28] But it was not the leader of the Opposition, nor any other Conservative for that matter, who espoused this view as unashamedly as did Lord Grey. According to Grey, Parliament was being asked to choose between 'an honourable understanding with Ulster in 1920 . . . [and] a definite engagement with the Free State'. Grey was for honouring the first commitment. 'I would rather face a demand from the Free State to be a Republic', he said, 'than see the understanding with Ulster broken.' Most peers heartily agreed.[29]

While Grey's speech was 'cheered in the House', those outside were left 'dumbfounded'. As *The Nation* pointed out, to accept Grey's reasoning meant that 'the understanding [with Northern Ireland] should override the definite engagement [with the Free State], because it preceded it in point of time'. Did the noble Lord, asked the journal, 'give no weight to the superior status of a definite engagement, concluded in the form of a Treaty, and ratified, as the understanding never was, by Parliament?'[30]

Coming from a former foreign secretary, Grey's claim was, indeed, astonishing – until the state of Liberal Party politics is recalled. As he had earlier intimated to Donald Maclean, Grey was prepared to use the boundary dispute as a defining issue with which he might separate himself from the rest of the Liberal leadership – and from Lloyd George in particular.[31] His speech was an attempt to do just that.

Although Baldwin had promised that Conservatives would propose a series of amendments to the boundary bill, their attempt to alter the legislation boiled down to a single proposed change. This would have limited the Boundary Commission's award to one not 'substantially altering the area of Northern Ireland as fixed by the Government of Ireland Act, 1920'.[32] Despite Thomas's warning that the Conservative amendment could cost lives, lead to

27 Ibid., cols 365–7, 412, 2 Oct. 1924.   28 Ibid., cols 43, 30 Sept. 1924.

29 *HL Deb*, vol. 59, cols 550–3, 7 Oct. 1924.   30 'The Scales of Lord Grey', *The Nation*, 11 Oct. 1924.

31 Grey to Maclean, 12 Aug. 1924, Maclean Papers, Dep. c. 467, ff. 94–5.

32 *HC Deb*, vol. 177, col. 363, 2 Oct. 1924. Two other amendments were proposed by Ulster Unionist MP David Reid. The first would have forbidden the transfer of any territory between the two parts of Ireland 'without the consent of the Parliament to whom jurisdiction over that territory has been

war, and 'shake the foundations of the Empire', observers were surprised when it was defeated by a comparatively slim margin of 50 votes.[33]

One of those who voted for the motion was a debonair MP, new to the Commons: Anthony Eden. Until then an obscure backbencher, Eden seized the opportunity when called upon to speak after Lloyd George attacked the Conservatives' amendment. Much as Lloyd George had done when himself was a young MP, Eden turned the tables on the elder statesman with a swift, scathing dismissal of his arguments. He then warned against 'any decision which might take away from Ulster large slices of her territory'. The speech marked Eden's emergence as a rising star in Conservative ranks; he himself was particularly pleased with the report of his remarks in *The Times*, 'the best that there has been so far', he wrote.[34]

Because the committee stage of the boundary bill ended earlier than expected, Thomas proposed that its third reading should be considered that night. So it was that, because Baldwin was not in London, it fell to Austen Chamberlain to explain why the Conservative Party was not prepared to carry on its fight against Labour's Irish bill. Although only the day before he had attacked the boundary legislation as 'one-sided', Chamberlain now conceded that its rejection 'at this stage of the proceedings' would be unwise. Instead, he appealed to Thomas to appoint to the Boundary Commission 'a man as Ulster itself might have chosen had it been willing to do' so. He also called on the government to compensate anyone displaced by the Commission's award.[35]

Thomas willingly assured Chamberlain that his first concern would be met but refused to 'bind the Government' on the matter of compensation. With the boundary bill now assured of passage in the Commons, its highest hurdle was yet to come in the House of Lords. 'I do not know what the fate of this Bill may be', Thomas solemnly declared, but the government had no intention of seeing the measure passed in the lower house, only to have it defeated elsewhere. The boundary bill, unamended, must be enacted immediately. Labour would 'stand or fall by that position'.[36]

32 *cont.*   granted by the Imperial Parliament'. See Col. 50, 30 Sept. 1924. His second amendment, that 'the expression "in accordance with the wishes of the inhabitants" in that Article [i.e., Article 12] means the consent of the Parliament of the Irish Free State and of the Parliament of Northern Ireland' was ruled out of order. See col. 423, 2 Oct. 1924.

33   Ibid., cols 386, 419–24, 2 Oct. 1924. *Annual Register: 1924*, p. 103.

34   Ibid., *HC Deb*, cols 402–4. Rhodes James, *Eden*, p. 82. 'Irish Boundary Bill. Unionists and the Commission', *The Times*, 3 Oct. 1924.

35   Ibid., *HC Deb*, cols 169 and 465–7, 1–2 Oct. 1924.

36   Ibid., cols 468–74, 2 Oct. 1924. The final vote was 251 to 99 in favour of the bill.

SALISBURY'S 'SAFETY VALVE'

Though it was never likely that the Conservatives would succeed in amending the boundary bill in the House of Commons, party leaders waited until the last minute before deciding what they would do if the unamended legislation was sent to the House of Lords. Convinced that an election was now unavoidable, Austen Chamberlain believed that even the Unionists wanted to get this issue out of the way. 'My own conviction', he told one of his sisters, 'is that Ulster or at least the Ulster members, are glad to see the Boundary Bill through.' In that case, there was simply no reason for the party to risk a fight in Parliament's upper house. 'If the Lords are wise', he continued, 'they won't touch the Bill, but then they are not wise enough for that!'[37]

It is not the least of ironies in this story that the saviour of the Irish boundary bill turned out to be a man who, in other circumstances, would have been one of its fiercest opponents. With no letter from Craig to absolve Tory peers of their commitment to Ulster, it fell to Lord Salisbury to extricate his colleagues in both Parliament and the Conservative Party from the corner into which they had painted themselves. He did not relish the task and, throughout, feared that he would pay a heavy price for performing this service.[38]

During the Lords' debate, Salisbury made it clear that any attempt on their part to amend the boundary legislation 'would amount to the rejection of the bill'. Once they did that, the matter would be out of their hands entirely and 'would be transferred from Parliament to the hustings'. That was 'the last thing' any friend of Ulster should want, as the average British voter had little interest in, and even less understanding of, Irish affairs. To link the Irish dispute with a debate on the powers of the House of Lords, Salisbury maintained, was simply foolish.[39]

As an alternative to amending the government's bill, Salisbury proposed that the Lords should instead attach a non-binding resolution. This would make clear that the Boundary Commission was created only to facilitate 'a readjustment of the boundaries' and that in their opinion 'no other interpretation would be acceptable' – or could be enforced. His suggestion proved to be decisive. 'By the use of this safety-valve', the *Round Table* explained to its readers, 'the Lords avoided the risk of bursting their own boiler'.[40]

Even so, it was not certain that Salisbury's compromise would win through until the House heard from Lord Carson. Although he had decided to 'acquiesce'

---

37   Austen to Ida Chamberlain, 5 Oct. 1924, AC 5/1/334.

38   Brumwell to Salisbury, 11 Oct. 1924, S (4) 110/92.

39   *HL Deb*, vol. 59, cols 596–600, 8 Oct. 1924.

40   Ibid., cols 600–3. 'The Irish Boundary Question', *Round Table*, Dec. 1924, No. 57, p. 39.

in the resolution, Carson proceeded to deliver a withering speech, one at least as bitter as his assault on the Irish Treaty delivered three years earlier. There was no point in opposing the boundary bill, Carson told the House, because even if the Tories held office they would propose similar legislation. 'And why? Because all the eminent men of the Conservative Party are up to their neck in the original Treaty', which had led to this crisis in the first place. In fact, Carson admitted a grudging respect for the Labour government, for he doubted that Tory ministers 'would show the same amount of courage' in dealing with Ulster's grievances.

Most of all, Carson was outraged that Ulster Unionists were being sacrificed at the altar of British politics. 'Is not the present debate in this House absolutely unreal?' he asked. 'You are not thinking of the rights or wrongs of this question at all. You are really thinking about the General Election that is going to follow upon another question.' Carson's grudging acceptance, combined with Lord Londonderry's endorsement, ensured the bill's passage, although 38 peers still could not be reconciled.[41]

Salisbury's compromise saved the boundary bill and ensured that Ireland would not be an issue in the upcoming election. Now, however, it was becoming a race against time to get the boundary bill onto the Statute Book before the government collapsed. For while the House of Lords was busy debating the Irish legislation, MacDonald's government was falling apart.

THE FALL OF LABOUR

'I have no inside news to tell you', Sidney Webb wrote to his wife on 2 October, 'but it is generally assumed that "our number is up"'. Like most of his colleagues, Webb expected to survive in office a few more weeks, if only because for both Tories and Liberals 'it would be unsatisfactory to defeat the Government before the Irish Bill is disposed of'.[42] Throughout the first week of October, however, 'the air was full of impending crises' around Westminster. 'Nerves are on edge', MacDonald reported to the king, and 'even a bill which raises such grave issues as the Irish bill occupies only a secondary position in that it does not seem to contain the germs of a domestic crisis.'[43] Soon, in fact, it would be hard to remember that the Irish boundary question had even been an issue in British politics.

41 Ibid., cols 615–16, 650–1, and 664.
42 Sidney to Beatrice Webb, 2 Oct. 1924, Passfield Papers, 2/3/1/18/191–3.
43 MacDonald to George V, 3 Oct. 1924, JRM, PRO 30/69/228.

Faced with a Conservative motion censuring the Cabinet's handling of the Campbell case, and a Liberal motion condemning the Russian treaties, Labour's first government was already teetering on 8 October. Matters were further complicated by a Liberal amendment to the Conservative motion which, instead of censuring the government, called for a Parliamentary select committee to investigate the Campbell affair. MacDonald announced that he would consider a vote for either the motion or the amendment as a vote of no confidence in his government and, if defeated, he would immediately call a general election.

The debate then took what one contemporary called 'a dramatic turn'. It was obvious, Baldwin told the House, that MacDonald planned to defeat the Liberal amendment by relying on Conservative votes, only to then appeal to Liberal MPs to defeat the Conservative motion 'and so ride off in triumph'. Before he would allow that to happen, Baldwin announced that the Conservatives would vote for the Liberal amendment to their own motion, thus ensuring Labour's defeat. MacDonald was left with no choice and, early on the morning of 9 October, he asked George V to dissolve Parliament that very afternoon and call the third general election in two years.[44]

MacDonald's 'extreme haste' in dissolving Parliament very nearly brought the boundary bill crashing down. Once the House of Lords accepted Salisbury's resolution, no one in the government thought that there would be any more trouble with Ireland. They did not count on Carson, who saw in this sudden turn of events a chance to kill off the Boundary Commission once and for all. At the bill's third reading on 9 October, Carson sought to insert a proviso that the boundary bill would come into operation only after it was confirmed by Northern Ireland's Parliament, as well as by Dáil Éireann. The effect of Carson's amendment, the Earl of Mayo noted, 'simply wrecks this bill' and, if passed, would put Ireland and the House of Lords squarely at the forefront of British politics. A contemporary account was certain that if Carson's amendment had been put to a vote it 'would no doubt have been carried'. Once again, Salisbury intervened and saved the day. Carson withdrew his proposed change with the not altogether convincing claim that it was made merely 'to emphasise my protest against the coercion of Ulster.' With that, Labour's contribution to settling the Irish Question went onto the Statute Book at 6 p.m., just hours ahead of Parliament's dissolution.[45]

44   *Annual Register: 1924*, pp. 105–7.
45   *HL Deb*, vol. 59, cols 667–9, 9 Oct. 1924. *Annual Register: 1924*, p. 108.

THE ELECTION OF 1924

The election of 1924 was brought about because of 'a matter which the public understood but vaguely and in which it was little interested'.[46] But if the Campbell case was not explosive enough on its own, when combined with outrage surrounding the Russian treaties, it proved to be a lethal concoction in the hands of Conservative propagandists. Very quickly the campaign degenerated into one dominated by charges of Bolshevik influence inside the Labour Party, while the Liberals were held responsible for allowing the 'red menace' ever to take office. The Irish boundary dispute had no place in such a campaign. In fact, it was no longer discernible on Britain's political landscape, which was where most politicians wanted Ireland to be. 'It was quite evident as soon as I got up to London', Churchill wrote to Balfour, 'that the Irish question was not going to be any trouble.'[47]

The election, held on 29 October, gave the Tories a victory 'beyond their wildest expectations'. With no fewer than 413 members, Baldwin led a Commons majority of 211 against all other parties combined. He had won the greatest single-party victory in twentieth-century British politics; only the National Government landslide of 1931 would be larger.[48] In contrast, MacDonald saw Labour reduced from 191 to 151 members.

But it was the Liberal Party for whom the 1924 election was a catastrophe. The Liberals went into the campaign with 159 MPs. Afterwards, the once proud party was reduced to only 40 seats in the House of Commons depleted 'beyond hope of recovery'. Lloyd George's opponents within the party later blamed him for their annihilation, claiming that he had planned all along to use the election to purge them before refashioning Liberalism in his own image. Whether or not this is true, Lloyd George could not have foreseen the disaster which occurred, a disaster which was 'wholly unexpected' and which meant the 'practical disappearance . . . of the Liberal Party from Parliamentary life'.[49]

---

46 *Annual Register: 1924*, p. 109.

47 Churchill to Balfour, 2 Oct. 1924, AJB-S, GD 433/2/19, Reel 4.

48 *Annual Register: 1924*, pp. 116–17. The results of the century's other major victories were: 1906 – Liberal majority of 130; 1918 – Lloyd George Coalition majority of 249; 1931 – National Government Coalition majority of 554; 1935 – National Government majority of 242; 1945 – Labour majority of 146; 1959 – Conservative majority of 100; 1983 – Conservative majority of 144; 1997 – Labour majority of 179. See Butler and Freeman, *British Political Facts*, pp. 140–4. G. Foote, *A Chronology of Post War British Politics* (London, 1988), pp. 4, 84, 123, and 243. 'The History Man', *The Guardian*, 3 May 1997.

49 *Annual Register: 1924*, pp. 116–17. Olivier to Reading, 30 Oct. 1924, IO, MSS Eur. F. 118/63(a), ff. 1–6. Campbell, *Lloyd George*, p. 101–6.

THE DEFEAT OF THE NORTHERN NATIONALISTS

It was not the Liberals, however, who suffered most as a result of the 1924 election. While the Irish boundary dispute played no role in British politics, in one corner of the United Kingdom it was not just the main issue, it was the only issue. This was true even in constituencies far from the border. 'Our enemies seek to sell us into Sinn Fein bondage', ran one typical Unionist appeal, 'by endeavouring to deprive us of large tracts of our territory'. Working-class loyalists in Belfast were further warned that independent Labour candidates, as well as Nationalists, were working against their real interests. 'My Socialistic opponent asks for the solid Roman Catholic vote', R. J. Lynn told voters in this same election address. 'I ask for none but rely entirely upon the Protestants to return me triumphantly at the head of the Poll.'[50]

So far as Nationalists were concerned, Labour's fall gave them yet another opportunity to use the ballot box to demonstrate their desire to join the Free State. For all practical purposes, the election would be a plebiscite, a 'test vote in the border counties' is the way one journal put it, which neither the British government nor the Boundary Commission could ignore.[51]

No one in the Nationalist camp, however, counted on Eamon de Valera.

Twice before, during the general elections of 1922 and 1923, Nationalists had combined to elect T. J. S. Harbison and Cahir Healy to represent the two-member constituency for Fermanagh–Tyrone.[52] On both occasions, de Valera had held that anyone participating in any election in the six counties – never mind actually standing as a candidate – was guilty of an act of treason against the Irish Republic. Now, he declared that Sinn Féin candidates would stand for election in several constituencies, including Fermanagh–Tyrone, as this was 'the only means available of making the wishes of the people clearly known'.[53]

There was, however, much more behind de Valera's *volte-face*. Having decided that he must lead his followers out of the wilderness into which they had condemned themselves in the Civil War, de Valera was setting off on the

---

50 R. J. Lynn 'To the Electors of West Belfast', 16 Oct. 1924, PRONI, PM/10/13. Craig's own address to Ulster voters struck the same notes, if less stridently. See 'To the Loyalists of Northern Ireland', 22 Oct. 1924, same file.

51 *Annual Register: 1924*, pp. 145–7. 'Comments', *New Statesman*, 18 Oct. 1924.

52 Phoenix, *Northern Nationalism*, pp. 262–4, 297–302. On his release from internment, Healy joined Harbison at Westminster to fight the Nationalist cause. He also wrote a series of newspaper articles to put their case directly to the British people. See, e.g., 'Will the Free State Fall?', *The People*, 23 Mar. 1924.

53 'Comments', *New Statesman*, 18 Oct. 1924. Lord Longford and T. P. O'Neill, *Eamon de Valera* (London, 1970), p. 238.

long road back into constitutional politics. Among the many twists and turns in that road, he would, within two years, split Sinn Féin and establish his own republican party, Fianna Fáil. More immediately, he had to face down accusations that he and his followers had, in his words, 'smashed the possibility' of Ireland's reunification by bringing on the Civil War. 'We will have to be very careful as to that', he told a meeting of anti-Treaty TDs. 'The Ulster problem will remain for us and it will be a very difficult problem'.[54]

To get round this problem, de Valera began to nurture the myth that he had opposed the Treaty mainly out of a desire to prevent Ireland's partition. At public appearances in the South in mid-August, he declared that if he had been responsible for negotiating the Treaty, 'he would never have signed it until the boundary question was settled'. These speeches, one historian has written, vividly illustrated de Valera's propensity for 'deliberately twisting the truth'.[55]

Fortunately for Sinn Féin's leader, it was at this moment that Craig's government then stepped in to lend a helping hand. Arrested after he crossed the border to deliver a speech in Londonderry, just days before voters went to the polls, de Valera was sentenced to a month in solitary confinement. News of his incarceration in a Belfast jail reinvigorated the republican cause in the South where, in a matter of weeks, Sinn Féin would score spectacular gains in a series of by-elections held in the Free State.[56]

These victories came at a price, however, and it was paid by the Nationalists of Fermanagh and Tyrone. Although the joint constituency was considered a Nationalist stronghold when MacDonald called the 1924 election, de Valera had 'willed otherwise' by insisting that Sinn Féin candidates should stand for the seats. The *New Statesman* called the move an act of unimaginable 'folly', because it placed Free State supporters north of the border in an impossible position. Reversing roles with de Valera, pro-Treaty Nationalists called on their followers to abstain from the election and demand a plebiscite to show their desire for inclusion in the Free State. With Nationalist opinion bitterly divided, the only likely winners would be the Unionist candidates for the two seats. Nor would that be all. Were the Unionists to score such a victory, *The Nation* predicted, Craig's government would use the election 'as fresh proof of

54   Minutes of meeting of Comhairle na dTeachtaí [Council of Deputies], 7 Aug. 1924, reprinted in J. A. Gaughan, *Austin Stack: Portrait of a Separatist* (County Dublin, 1977), p. 335.

55   'Mr de Valera and Final Success', *Morning Post*, 25 Aug. 1924. T. R. Dwyer, *De Valera: The Man & the Myths* (Swords, Ireland, 1992), p. 136.

56   That said, de Valera had no desire ever to repeat this experience. In an extraordinary exchange with one of his captors, he admitted that his detention in 'Belfast was the worst' as well as the most 'depressing and disheartening' of his prison ordeals. See Kelly to Wilkin, 29 Nov. 1924, PRONI, CAB/9Z/2/2.

the homogeneity of "Ulster", and [it] may have a prejudicial effect on the Boundary Commission' – which, in the event, is exactly what happened. On election day, Northern Nationalists stayed away from polling stations in droves and, when the votes were counted, both Unionist candidates took the seats with overwhelming majorities.[57]

Unionists could not believe their luck. '[W]e have actually gained in Tyrone and Fermanagh', a stunned Lady Craig wrote in her diary. She attributed the triumph directly to the split created by de Valera's decision and, 'coming at this time, when the Boundary question is so acute, it is of tremendous import and assistance, and enormously strengthens J.'s hand'.[58]

Writing in her own diary that same day, Lady Carson was no less overjoyed. 'It's too thrilling', she wrote, and her husband could 'think of nothing else' once he had heard the news. With the taking of these two seats, the Conservative and Unionist victory of 1924 was complete. After the election, there could be no question but that Fermanagh and Tyrone would remain in Unionist hands. 'Now', Lady Carson wrote, 'no one will dare touch those counties.'[59]

'A FATAL POLICY ATTENDED BY DISASTER'

With the election of 1924 what Winston Churchill called 'two years of insensate faction' finally came to an end. The country turned a corner or, to be more precise, it at last returned to the security of two-party politics. The Lloyd George Coalition left in its wake three roughly equal parties each vying for a place in a system designed for only two major players. From either end of the political spectrum it was agreed that this could not continue indefinitely. 'The basic fact', one journal told its readers, was this: 'there is no room in this country for three parties'. By the end of 1924, most voters agreed. As the third campaign in just two years drew to a close, *The Nation* was not surprised that what seemed to be uppermost in everyone's mind was 'the desire to put an end to this plague of annual elections'.[60]

Once Labour established itself as the party of the left, the contest boiled down to a bid over who would lead the country's anti-socialist forces. Even in 1924 it was by no means certain that Lloyd George and the Liberals were

---

57 *Annual Register, 1924*, pp. 146–7. 'Events of the Week', *The Nation*, 25 Oct. 1924. 'Comments', *New Statesman*, 18, 25 Oct. 1924. Craig to Andrews, 31 Oct. 1924, PRONI, PM/10/13.

58 Lady Craig's diary, 31 Oct. 1924, D/1415/B/38. Because of Nationalist abstentions, the Fermanagh–Tyrone result was called a 'farce'. See 'Events of the Week', *The Nation*, 8 Nov. 1924.

59 Lady Carson's diary, 31 Oct. 1924, D/1507/C/8.

60 Rhodes James, *British Revolution*, p. 477. Ramsden, *Balfour and Baldwin*, pp. 199–202.

going to lose in this competition, nor that Baldwin and the Conservatives were going to emerge to dominate British politics. Austen Chamberlain was convinced that years would pass before his party would again hold office, and by then he would 'be too old to take up the burden of leadership'.[61] A number of factors working in the Conservatives' favour – not least, dissension within the Liberal Party's top echelon, and pure luck – were beyond their control. What was within Baldwin's power was his decision not to play the 'orange card' but rather, 'the red card of anti-socialism', and this proved to be decisive.[62]

Baldwin was walking a tightrope when he decided that his party's interests would not be served by picking a fight over the Irish boundary. With so much hanging in the balance, he could not risk alienating Tory Die-hards; but neither could he ignore the consequences that would accompany their demand of unquestioning support for the Ulster Unionists. These dangers were made clear, ironically, during an exchange between J. H. Thomas and Lord Hugh Cecil, when the latter insisted that the government should threaten to use force against the Free State in the boundary dispute. Thomas agreed that the British people would actively oppose the establishment of an Irish republic or abolition of the Oath of Allegiance. But, he continued, 'believe me when I say I don't believe you could hold one-half your present seats on the question of the boundary'.[63] Even if Thomas was exaggerating to drive home his point, he was probably close to the truth. The point is that Baldwin also recognised this risk and he was unwilling to take it, even if his Die-hards were.

Instead, the Conservative leader opted for a less confrontational approach. The party allied with Ulster Unionists to wage a deft campaign, assiduously cultivating the popular press and promoting their point of view in the Irish dispute.[64] By its own reckoning, during the 'acute stage of the boundary controversy' the Ulster Association, 'in addition to articles in the press', distributed over 300,000 pamphlets and over 20,000 bulletins 'stating the Ulster case'. The result, according to the association, was a 'considerable change which has taken place in public opinion regarding Ulster affairs'.[65] Down the road, this swing in popular opinion could be used to the Conservatives' advantage if they had to face any trouble from Dublin on the boundary issue. Closer to the moment, the Tories found themselves in the happy position where they were

---

61   Austen to Ida Chamberlain, 10 Mar. 1923 and 5 Oct. 1924, AC 5/1/268 and 334. Also, see Spender to Maclean, 2 Oct. 1924, Maclean Papers, Dep. c. 467, ff. 134–5. Cowling, *Impact of Labour*, p. 419.

62   Cowling, *Impact of Labour*, pp. 411, and 419–21. Ramsden, *Balfour and Baldwin*, p. 199.

63   Exchange written on the back of an envelope, 30 Sept. 1924, Quickswood Papers, 33/12.

64   See, e.g., Harmsworth to Baldwin, 28 Aug. 1924, SB vol. 159, ff. 209–10. Churchill to Carson, 8 Sept. 1924, WSC 2/570/115.

65   Ulster Association to Salisbury, 19 Mar. 1925, S (4) 112/119–20.

seen to be giving their utmost support to the Unionists but at no real risk to themselves. Thus, Baldwin was able to contain his Die-hards while, at the same time, sidelining the Irish threat. Once this was accomplished, the Conservatives were able to concentrate on the anti-communist scare, and they were the ones who rode off in triumph.

Still, it came very close to being otherwise.

When the Irish crisis erupted in early August, MacDonald predicted that Baldwin and his colleagues faced 'a most critical decision on which the fortunes of their Party for the next few years may depend'. Later, he reported to George V that because the Conservatives had decided to direct all of their fire on the Campbell case, the Irish bill 'received an easier passage through its remaining stages than might have been anticipated in normal circumstances'.[66] These letters raise two intriguing, if ultimately unanswerable, questions: namely, if there had been no Campbell case, if there had been no Russian treaties, what then would have happened to Labour's boundary bill? More broadly, what would have been the course of British politics if Ireland and the power of the House of Lords had been the main issues of the 1924 election?

It is surely more than mere speculation to say that in both instances what might have been would have been very different from what actually occurred. Without the diversion of the communist scare used so effectively by Baldwin and his lieutenants, it would have been impossible, as Edward Wood put it, to 'extricate us from the cul-de-sac' of Ireland.[67] The boundary bill almost certainly would have met furious Conservative resistance in the House of Commons and would likely have been shot down in flames in the Lords. That would have brought on the general election so feared by Baldwin, a campaign whose focus would have been on the power of the peers versus the power of the people, the sort of campaign in which Lloyd George would have thrived.

It is impossible to know how such an election would have turned out, but it seems hardly likely that the Conservatives would have emerged with one of the greatest landslides of the century. Defeat would have cast Baldwin into outer darkness, his career one of shortest and most curious of those who have reached the pinnacle of British politics. There would have been no 'Baldwin–MacDonald Regime' – as Churchill called it – to govern, or misgovern, Britain during the inter-war years.[68] Under Lloyd George, the Liberals might have been revitalised; or, MacDonald's Labour Party might have won an outright Parliamentary majority, a goal that eluded him for the rest of his political life.

66 MacDonald to George V, 2 Aug., 3 Oct. 1924, JRM, PRO 30/69/228.
67 Wood to Baldwin, 10 Sept. 1924, Halifax Papers, A4.410/14/1.
68 Churchill, *Gathering Storm*, p. 21.

Instead, Baldwin was established as the dominating figure in British politics for the next thirteen years.

More immediately, this meant that the new British government would take a very narrow view of what was to be achieved by the Ulster clauses of the Irish Treaty. Theirs would be the interpretation that counted, and this included any redrawing of the frontier, whatever the Boundary Commission itself might decide. The final chapter of the Irish Question would be written by men who had opposed the Treaty's Ulster clauses from the beginning or, if they had been responsible for them, had long since learnt the price of going against Conservative opinion on this issue. They would not make that same mistake again. But this boldness, this certainty of a firm policy on Ireland, was not the result of Tory commitments to the Ulster Unionists. What made it possible was the fundamental change that had taken place in British politics.

During the peers' debate on the boundary bill, Lord Londonderry wondered aloud if MacDonald and his colleagues had any real Irish policy to speak of, and decided that they did not:

> I feel myself forced to the conclusion that the present Government, like the Coalition Government, is clinging to the slender hope that, by keeping the framework of the Treaty in being and by the avoidance of anything which might give offence to one or other of the parties concerned, a solution will be found in some indefinable way which will relieve them of their responsibilities and bring about a settlement in the process of time. That, in my judgment, is a fatal policy . . . [and] . . . can only be attended by disaster.[69]

Although Londonderry's remarks were directed at MacDonald and Lloyd George, his charge applied with equal – perhaps more – justice to Bonar Law and Baldwin. The unstable condition of British politics between the fall of Lloyd George and the 1924 election was bound to affect any attempt to settle the Irish Question. No party could afford to take on such a divisive issue. The risks were simply too great in such an uncertain political climate and that is why Jones's concept of 'indefinite postponement' was so attractive to all politicians, especially the Conservatives.[70] It is true that the Tories would have fought any large-scale boundary change whatever the outcome of the 1924 election. However, Craig himself was afraid that even if Baldwin won the election a fight over Ireland 'might possibly split the Conservative Party once more'.[71]

69   *HL Deb*, vol. 59, col. 565, 7 Oct. 1924.
70   Jones diary, 10 June 1923, vol. III, p. 221.
71   Craig to Carson, 18 Aug. 1924, PRONI, CAB/9Z/5/1.

What made the difference was the scale of the party's victory. Baldwin and his colleagues could confidently settle the Irish Question on their own terms because they could rely on a massive and united Parliamentary majority to back them. They need not reckon with the views of any other party on this issue. The Liberals counted for nothing, and Labour for not much more. No government, including the Coalition, had been in such a position since 1910.

During its brief first term in office, however, Labour played a crucial role in settling the boundary dispute. That this role is seldom acknowledged may have much to do with the ambivalence Labour has felt about Ireland since the party's inception, an ambivalence personified by its first prime minister.

On the day that MacDonald tendered his resignation to the king, Lady Lavery wrote to tell him of the Free State government's gratitude for his 'courage and fairness in dealing with a problem that was not of your making'. Given MacDonald's feelings about the Irish, it is doubtful that he would have responded in kind. Between them there had never been any empathy nor understanding. As Lavery was forced to admit in this same letter, the Free Staters were 'conservative in their sentiments'. Their goals were not MacDonald's, and his goals were not theirs.[72]

In any case, it no longer mattered. MacDonald's first, unhappy encounter with the Irish was at an end. His next major confrontation with them would be in the person of Eamon de Valera; but nearly eight years were to elapse in between – time enough for MacDonald to prepare himself for that supreme ordeal. He would never become entangled in the boundary question again.[73]

Ireland did not figure as a chief concern when MacDonald decided that Labour should take office. But of all the issues that he encountered during those tumultuous nine months, the Irish boundary dispute had proved to be the most intractable, the most impervious to compromise, and remained so to the very last hours of his first government. With evident relief, MacDonald turned his back on the Irish and their bitter quarrel. Having walked away from this and all the other tribulations of high office, he wrote in his diary: 'And tonight as I go into a new world, the dead come to me and in companionship I have spent an hour with them.'[74]

72 Lavery to MacDonald, 4 Nov. 1924, JRM, PRO 30/69/1433/73–4. 'I think', O'Higgins once told the Dáil, 'that we were probably the most conservative-minded revolutionaries that ever put through a successful revolution'. See White, *O'Higgins*, p. 145. Also, see McCoole, *Lavery*, p. 117.

73 Dwyer, *Man and Myths*, pp. 165–9. Thomas delivered Labour's response to the boundary agreement the following year. See *HC Deb*, vol. 189, cols 321–6, 8 Dec. 1925.

74 MacDonald diary, 9 Oct. 1924, JRM, PRO 30/69/1753/1.

NINE

'NOT AN INCH!'

It was a merit of the Treaty that it retained this Council of Ireland.
It was an all-Ireland body, and with it disappears the last
hope of unity in our time.
CAHIR HEALY[1]

—

Shortly after dawn on the morning of 9 December 1924, three 'rather appre-hensive looking' men stepped from a train at a stop just north of the Irish frontier. Almost three years to the day after its conception, the Irish Boundary Commission was at long last ready to begin its work. 'We drove rapidly to Armagh', Stephen Tallents reported, where the Commissioners, their retinue of assistants, and 'their extensive luggage' were housed in the local judge's lodgings, 'without even a dog to watch them'. No one in the town seemed to notice, or care, about the Commission's arrival. 'When I came away at noon', Tallents wrote, 'Armagh still preserved its customary air of languid boredom.'[2]

Given the passions aroused by the Boundary Commission since its incep-tion, its members must have been surprised that their arrival was met with such indifference. In fact, a shift of opinion was taking place. Among Free Staters bitter resignation had replaced earlier expectations that the Commission would reunite their country. Having demanded the boundary tribunal for so long, Northern Nationalists were beginning to realise that it might not produce the desired outcome after all. 'They have asked for their pound of flesh', one correspondent wrote to Lord Salisbury, 'and now apparently they do not like the prospect of receiving it.'[3]

This bitterness contrasted with the benign indifference and, in some cases, growing confidence, felt by leading border-county Unionists. 'I found the proposed visit to be regarded by them as more a matter of routine than I had expected', Tallents reported to the Home Office. One prominent County

---

1   'Agreement Signed in London', *Ulster Herald*, 12 Dec. 1925.
2   Tallents to Maxwell, 9 Dec. 1924, HO 267/179.
3   *Dáil Deb*, vol. 8, cols 2502–68, 15 Oct. 1924. Brumwell to Salisbury, 11 Oct. 1924, S(4) 110/92.

Fermanagh landowner (and future Northern Ireland prime minister), Sir Basil Brooke, told Tallents that he was not at all worried about the Commission's proposed tour, which he viewed 'with equanimity'.[4]

This view was not, however, shared in Belfast. Although Sir James Craig entertained hopes that the Commission might actually expand his domain to include Unionist East Donegal, he nonetheless set out to frustrate its work within his jurisdiction.[5] On hearing of the proposed tour, Craig fired off a letter to Britain's new home secretary, Sir William Joynson-Hicks, warning of 'considerable alarm' about the impending visit. Ulster's premier found it particularly galling that Eoin MacNeill, a man he accused of taking part 'with Roger Casement and the German Government' in the Easter Rising of 1916, should be allowed 'to venture at any time into the heart of a loyalist population'. If the Commissioners wanted to take evidence from anyone living in the border counties, Craig's advice was that the witnesses ought to be invited to London to give their testimony – and at British expense. Not surprisingly, Baldwin's new government deemed his suggestion 'undesirable'.[6]

Such incidents were to characterise much of the Boundary Commission's work over the next year.[7] Buoyed by the results of the 1924 election, Ulster Unionists felt they had little to fear from the tribunal. While Craig might not always get his way, his supporters were safe in the knowledge that a Conservative government in London would not enforce any Boundary Commission award unless it had Belfast's blessing.

Nationalists, on the other hand, were increasingly apprehensive. 'We thought we knew what Conservative ministers meant by Article 12', wrote the Irish high commissioner to London. But after what these same men had said during the fight over Labour's boundary bill, Free Staters could no longer justify that belief. Now, these same Tories filled the top ranks of Baldwin's new government; men who, according to James MacNeill, would refuse 'to be honourably bound by any decision which the Six County Government would likely resist'.[8]

For their part, Free State supporters north of the border saw themselves as increasingly isolated. Despite solemn vows from Dublin that they were kith and kin, in a year's time Northern Nationalists would accuse Cosgrave's government of throwing them 'unceremoniously to the wolves'.[9] There would be a good deal of truth in that accusation.

4   Tallents to Anderson, 28 Nov. 1924, HO 45/12296/55(a).

5   Cabinet Minutes, 22 Oct. 1924, PRONI, CAB/4/126/16.

6   See Craig–Joynson-Hicks correspondence, 25, 26, 28 Nov. 1924, PRONI, CAB/9Z/3/2.

7   See, e.g., Tallents to Bourdillon, 2 Dec. 1924, CAB 61/18. Spender to Tallents, 9 Feb. 1925, HO 267/210.

8   MacNeill to FitzGerald, 31 Oct. 1924, D/T, S/1801 K.

9   '"Callously Betrayed."', *Ulster Herald*, 12 Dec. 1925.

BALDWIN'S SECOND GOVERNMENT

Although some Tories might claim that the 1924 election was a vindication of the 'old "Die-Hard" movement', the Conservative landslide actually freed Baldwin from these supporters and allowed him to remake the party in his own image.[10] This he proceeded to do, and the result was to have a profound impact on the settling of Ireland's boundary question. While old allies were rewarded for their loyalty, former Coalitionists were at the same time given prominent roles in the government. Austen Chamberlain became foreign secretary. Lord Birkenhead, much to the consternation of Die-hards who still called him a 'traitor', took over the India Office. 'It's all very exciting', Lady Carson wrote in her diary; 'some people have again started to grumble.'[11]

But these objections were nothing compared to the astonishment triggered by Baldwin's decision to make Winston Churchill chancellor of the exchequer.[12] Though the appointment did not sit well with a number of Conservatives and Ulster Unionists, Craig immediately realised that it was a stroke of luck for his cause. Churchill was, in effect, on probation. 'It would be up to him to be loyal', Baldwin remarked to Tom Jones – 'if he is capable of loyalty.' In such a position, it is not surprising that Churchill, as Baldwin's biographers later wrote, 'was evidently prepared at this moment to go a long way to conciliate his new-found colleagues'.[13]

Given the behind-the-scenes role Churchill had played in the autumn boundary crisis, along with his earlier support while at the Colonial Office, Craig surmised that the new chancellor was as anxious to re-establish his Unionist, as he was his Conservative, credentials. For while Baldwin might be willing to overlook the past, it rankled influential Conservatives that his Cabinet contained 'too many ministers identified with the Coalition's cowardly surrender to Sinn Fein . . . in the so-called "Treaty"'.[14] Churchill need not be told that he figured prominently on that list.

Craig wasted no time putting the new chancellor to the test. In a letter congratulating Churchill on his appointment to the Treasury, Ulster's leader let it be known that he wished to discuss 'a certain number of matters still

---

10   Gretton to Baldwin, 1 Nov. 1924, SB vol. 36, ff. 22–4. Tyrrell to Baldwin, same date, SB vol. 42, ff. 226–7. According to Maurice Cowling, the election enabled Baldwin to 'command all the forces Lloyd George had tried to lead from 1920 onwards'. See *Impact of Labour*, pp. 414–15.

11   W. J. Rhodes, Liverpool Protestant Electoral Federation, to Craig, 28 Oct. 1924, PRONI, PM/10/13. Lady Carson's diary, 6 Nov. 1924, D/1507/C/8.

12   Gilbert, *Churchill:* vol. v, pp. 58–62.

13   Jones diary, 8 Nov. 1924, vol. I, p. 303. Middlemas and Barnes, *Baldwin*, p. 290.

14   'Episodes of the Month', *National Review*, Apr. 1925, p. 200.

outstanding' between the two governments. Although Churchill's response included a gentle reminder that the success of Baldwin's government depended on 'sound finance', he wrote assuring: 'I shall support you in essentials.'[15]

This exchange set off alarm bells at the Treasury, where officials saw themselves in an ongoing struggle to ward off Ulster Unionist raids on the British exchequer. The 'matters' that were on Craig's mind were the same three issues that had bedevilled relations between the Treasury and the Belfast government since 1921: funding of the Ulster Special Constabulary; amalgamation of the British and Ulster unemployment insurance funds; and Craig's attempts to lower Northern Ireland's imperial contribution.[16]

In the run-up to Churchill's meeting with Craig, Otto Niemeyer, along with two other senior Treasury officials, G. C. Upcott and P. J. Grigg, attempted to persuade the new chancellor to take a tough line with his guest. The trio concentrated on Craig's request for an additional £1 million grant for the Special Constabulary, a claim that he had been pressing on the Treasury since the fall of Baldwin's first government. Britain could give in to Craig's demands, they argued, only at the cost of 'breaking the Treaty' since Belfast was supposed to be responsible for funding its security forces.

More immediately, the existence of the Specials had a direct bearing on the boundary question. For these reasons, Upcott and Grigg pointed out, Churchill's predecessor had resisted Craig's demand for the money. Niemeyer added that if Craig's government rejected the Boundary Commission's findings, it was altogether likely that it would use the British-funded force to prevent implementation of the award. Such a development, Niemeyer wrote with considerable understatement, would be *'very awkward'*.[17]

Churchill was having none of this. 'The Free State have got Home Rule', he truculently responded, 'but since when has Great Britain lost the right to do what she chooses within her own borders'. Writing separately to Niemeyer, he staked out the Treasury's new position:

Nothing in the Treaty gives the Free State any right to complain of any measures wh. we may choose to take for maintaining the peace and security of Northern Ireland. It is our duty to sustain the Northern Govt. effectually either by subvention or by troops, or by both during the difficult period through wh. they are now passing – through no fault of their own. The fact that the boundary commission

15   See Craig–Churchill correspondence, 8, 10 Nov. 1924, T 160/131/F.4855/02/1.

16   Ibid., Niemeyer to Churchill, 15 Nov. 1924.

17   Ibid., 'Claims of Northern Ireland', Upcott memorandum; and Niemeyer to Churchill, which includes notes by Grigg and Churchill, 14, 15 Nov. 1924.

is sitting makes it all the more necessary that the Northern Govt. should be solidly supported . . . .[18]

For the moment, the three officials were more successful at convincing Churchill to resist Craig's appeals for reconsideration of the first Colwyn Committee award and his insistence that Northern Ireland's unemployment insurance fund should be linked to its British counterpart.[19]

But on the immediate issue, Churchill stood firm. 'I shall certainly agree to the Million grant at once', he wrote. Craig's paramilitary force was safe for the present and, perhaps, even longer. A future grant to the Specials should not be ruled out, Churchill informed Niemeyer, but would be decided upon once 'we see what the Boundary Commission award and what is the state of affairs thereafter'[*sic*].[20]

At their second meeting, Baldwin's new Cabinet not only approved the £1 million grant for the Specials, it also authorised an immediate advance of an additional £250,000 at the chancellor's discretion. More importantly, the Cabinet put Churchill back at the centre of Irish affairs. He, not the home secretary, was to be the 'medium of communication' with Craig on all financial questions.[21] With this direct line into the Treasury, Craig could rest assured that his pleas for assistance would be heard by a chancellor who was anxious, if not always able, to help.

That said, the government's decision to fund the Specials was coolly received by the House of Commons. Critics pointed out that Parliament was expected to fund a paramilitary force whose exact numbers it did not even know – Churchill could only say that there were 'something like 35,000'. If these numbers were correct, one Liberal MP pointed out, Craig had at his command an armed force that was larger than the armies of Austria or Bulgaria. The most damaging allegation was made by Snowden, who told the House that the proposed grant was nothing but a roundabout attempt by Craig, with Churchill's collusion, to help Northern Ireland's unemployed.[22] Despite Parliament's evident distaste for underwriting the Specials, Baldwin's overwhelming majority ensured that Churchill had his way. According to one opposition MP, the chancellor of the exchequer obviously meant to 'redeem his past in the matter of Ireland'. Craig was delighted.[23]

18 Ibid., Niemeyer–Churchill correspondence, 15 Nov. 1924.

19 The new minister of labour was also opposed. See Steel-Maitland to Churchill, 19 Nov. 1924, T 160/187/F.7136/2.

20 Churchill to Niemeyer, 15 Nov. 1924, T 160/131/F.4855/02/1.

21 C 60(24), 19 Nov. 1924, CAB 23/49.   22 *HC Deb*, vol. 180, cols 1651–86, 23 Feb. 1925.

23 Ibid., col. 1673. Lady Craig diary, 23 Feb. 1925, D/1415/B/38.

THE BOUNDARY COMMISSION SETS TO WORK

At the same time that Baldwin was busy forming his new government, in another part of London the Boundary Commission was itself setting to work. With offices in the Strand at 6 Clement's Inn, Eoin MacNeill, the Free State's representative, and Richard Feetham, the Commission's chairman, were joined by Joseph R. Fisher, the man at long last appointed to represent Northern Ireland.[24]

Fisher has been called the 'shadowy figure' of this story, a man whose views 'were not generally known outside his own circle'.[25] That is not really true. As a barrister and later as editor of the *Northern Whig*, Fisher had already played a prominent role in the Ulster Unionist cause. Earlier than most of those in the movement, he had advocated partition, not as a means of thwarting Home Rule, but as an end in itself.[26]

After the signing of the 'Midnight Treaty', as he called the 1921 agreement, Fisher argued that if there must be a Boundary Commission, it should not be hindered by 'ancient county boundaries'.[27] Implicitly, he suggested that the Commission might be used to copper-fasten partition for all time by restructuring Northern Ireland's frontier. In a private letter to Craig, he explained what he meant. 'Ulster can never be complete without Donegal', he wrote, and with 'North Monaghan *in* Ulster and South Armagh *out*', the Belfast government 'would take in a fair share of the people we want and leave out those we don't want'. As has been noted elsewhere, Fisher, far from being opposed to a substantial revision of the Irish border, was all for it – 'albeit in one direction'.[28]

Fisher's selection as Northern Ireland's Boundary Commissioner is something of a mystery, and there is debate over whether or not Craig was allowed to do behind the scenes what he refused to do in public. More important is the question of whether or not Craig was telling the truth when he maintained

---

24 Hand, 'MacNeill', p. 232.

25 Hand, *Report*, p. xi. Gwynn, *History of Partition*, p. 232.

26 Buckland, *Documentary History*, nos 152, 199, 229. Gwynn, *History of Partition*, pp. 229–30. In one of many articles promoting the Unionist cause, Fisher compared the Ulster counties that wished to remain a part of the United Kingdom with the counties of Virginia opposed to that state's secession during the American Civil War. The comparison is revealing as these counties were themselves partitioned to form the state of West Virginia. See J. R. Fisher, 'The "Unreasonableness" of Ulster', *Nineteenth Century*, May 1918, pp. 1088–91.

27 'Irish Boundaries. The "Principal Act"', *The Times*, 4 Feb. 1924.

28 Ervine, *Craigavon*, pp. 481–2. Phoenix, *Northern Nationalism*, p. 267. Publicly, Craig also favoured the incorporation of Donegal into his state. See '"The Proper Border"', *Irish Independent*, 27 Mar. 1925.

that he knew 'nothing whatever' of the Commission's deliberations.[29] Recently released documents confirm what some have long suspected: from the beginning, Fisher regularly sent reports to Craig via the Ulster Unionist MP, David Reid.[30]

The importance of this secret line of communication is impossible to underestimate. At the Commission's first meeting, all three members agreed to a strict code of secrecy; they would neither 'consult any of the Governments concerned as to the work of the Commission' nor would any member discuss his work with 'any individual without first consulting his colleagues'.[31] Feetham observed this agreement; so did MacNeill, much the chagrin of his colleagues in Dublin and to the annoyance of Northern Nationalists. Long before the Commission finished its work, the activities of Ulster's representative on behalf of his fellow Unionists was an open secret. 'Fisher keeps them well informed', one Nationalist complained to Ernest Blythe.[32] Yet, no one – either from the Free State government or the Boundary Commission – ever seems to have confronted Fisher about his abuse of trust.

Although he was not a member of the Boundary Commission as such, F. B. Bourdillon, the tribunal's secretary, played a key role in its deliberations. Having served on the commission that determined the German–Polish border in Upper Silesia, Bourdillon came to the attention of Lionel Curtis after writing an article criticising the Free State's case as put forward in the Boundary Bureau's *Handbook of the Ulster Question*. Curtis was so impressed that he ordered copies of the article for all senior civil servants responsible for British policy on the boundary dispute.[33] It is likely that on the basis of this work, Bourdillon was asked to become secretary to the Commission sometime in early 1924.[34] That his views influenced the Commission, or more particularly the Commission's chairman, cannot be proved. But it is noteworthy that

29 Bryan Follis, e.g., maintains that Craig took no part in Fisher's appointment. See *State Under Siege*, pp. 164, 173, 180. For the opposite view, see Canning, *British Policy*, p. 102, 105. For Craig's claim, see *NI HC Deb*, vol. 6, col. 1118, 7 Sept. 1925.

30 The correspondence is found in PRONI, CAB/9Z/2/2.

31 Commission Minutes no. 1, 6 Nov. 1924, CAB 61/1.

32 MacNeill later explained that in his view he 'was not purely and simply the representative of a government nor was I an advocate for a particular point of view'. See *Dáil Deb*, vol. 13, col. 796, 24 Nov. 1925. His 'vow of silence was particularly exasperating to the Free State government'. See White, *O'Higgins*, p. 207. Ironically, the British Cabinet took it for granted that MacNeill kept his colleagues informed of the Commission's deliberations. See I.A.(25)-1st Minutes, 23 Nov. 1925, CAB 27/295. Coyle to Blythe, 15 Sept. 1925, EB, P24/497/3–4.

33 Bourdillon to Curtis; Bourdillon article; Curtis to Whiskard; and Curtis to Bourdillon, 28 Nov., 7, 13, and 19 Dec. 1923, CO 739/25/60802.

34 Bourdillon to Curtis, 25 Jan. 1924, CO 739/27/13299.

Bourdillon's interpretation of Article 12 bears a striking resemblance to the one later outlined by Feetham.[35]

Irish Nationalist fears that Feetham did not share their ideas about the Boundary Commission's mandate were confirmed before the end of 1924.[36] The Commission's December tour of the border counties, the one that began in Armagh, was billed as a preliminary excursion, to allow the panel to 'acquaint' itself with the region. No evidence was taken and there were no formal sittings; those would occur at a later date.[37]

Before the panel left Londonderry, however, Feetham stunned Free State supporters by announcing that the Commission had no power to call a plebiscite to ascertain the wishes of the inhabitants.[38] In the wake of this pronouncement, E. M. Stephens reported that many Nationalists were now unwilling to give evidence to the tribunal if they lived in 'areas which have very little hope of coming into the Free State'. There was, in fact, a growing belief among Northern Nationalists that the Commission was 'unwilling, or unable, to carry out its work'.[39]

Why MacNeill did not protest against Feetham's statement is unclear. As a Free State minister, he was well aware of the Executive Council's insistence that as a 'first step' the Boundary Commission should hold plebiscites in the Poor Law Unions of each of Northern Ireland's border counties.[40] Nor was this the first blow that Feetham had delivered to the Nationalist case. In the run-up to its December visit, the Commission heard evidence from a Free State legal panel headed by Attorney-General John O'Byrne. Over the course of two days O'Byrne and his colleagues argued that 'the onus is not on us to prove how much of Northern Ireland should be in the Free State, but on Northern Ireland to show how much of it should remain out of the Free State'.[41]

Feetham made it plain that he did not share this view.[42] As he later wrote, to accept Dublin's arguments meant that the Boundary Commission would 'be entitled to abolish Northern Ireland altogether and include the whole of its

35   Hand, *Report*, 'Chairman's Memorandum', pp. 32–68.

36   O'Doherty to Collins, 19 Aug. 1924, JHC, D/921/2/4/20. Also, see *Dáil Deb*, vol. 8, cols 2424–6, 2431–9, 7 July 1924.

37   'The Irish Commission. Tour of the Border Next Week', *Manchester Guardian*, 8 Dec. 1924.

38   'Index to Dates and Conferences', 22 Dec. 1924, D/T, S 1801/P.

39   Stephens to O'Higgins, 21 Jan. 1925, D/T, S 1801/L.

40   C.2/128, 5 Sept. 1924, D/T, G 2/3. O'Higgins memorandum, 3 Sept. 1924, D/T, S 1801/J.

41   'The Irish Boundary. Free State's View of Article 12', *Manchester Guardian*, 8 Dec. 1924. Also, see 'Statement by the Irish Free Government', 20 Nov. 1924, D/T, S 1801/L.

42   Hand, *Report*, Appendix I, pp. 8–9 and, especially, Feetham's exchange with Serjeant Hanna, pp. 16–21.

area within the territory of the Irish Free State'. Whatever the Commission's award might be, it must enable Northern Ireland, as well as the Free State, to 'retain its own identity'.[43] Here, he was emphatic:

> The term 'Northern Ireland' as used in Article XII, clearly means not some vague indefinite area in the north of Ireland, but the Northern Ireland established and defined by the Government of Ireland Act, 1920, and it is the boundary between this 'Northern Ireland' and 'the rest of Ireland' which is to be 'determined,' or . . . redetermined.[44]

Without saying so, Feetham had accepted the Unionists' main point: namely, that the 1920 Act took precedence over the Treaty. Even worse for the Dublin government, the Free State, according to Feetham's interpretation of Article 12, could expect to lose as well as gain territory from the Commission's award.[45]

How Feetham reached these sweeping conclusions has never been explained. They suggest, however, the influence of Lionel Curtis, an influence easiest to identify in the decision not to hold plebiscites. Shortly before leaving the Colonial Office, Curtis reiterated his opposition to a vote in the border counties in a memorandum that found its way into Feetham's hands. A whole host of problems would arise from such a request, including the need for enabling legislation to allow the vote to take place. It should be pointed out to Feetham, Curtis suggested, 'that it is, for obvious reasons, extremely inadvisable to bring the proceedings of the Commission into the arena of Parliamentary discussion if it can possibly be avoided'.[46]

Feetham proceeded to heed his old friend's advice. A large part of the testimony delivered by the Free State's legal experts was taken up by questions about how the Boundary Commission should ascertain the 'wishes of the inhabitants', with Feetham steadily chipping away at the Irish position. Might there not, he wondered, be other ways to glean the same information, say by looking at election results, census returns (which included statistics on religious affiliation), or by asking 'what the representative people of districts say'?[47]

O'Byrne rejected the first two suggestions, arguing that they could give nothing more than a 'rough indication' of the person's political preference. As for Feetham's last idea, the Irish attorney-general pointed out that it was the Commission's duty to consult the wishes of all the people, not merely the region's leading citizens. In any case, such an idea would have been wholly unacceptable to Northern Nationalists, given recent election results.

43 Hand, *Report*, 'Chairman's Memorandum', pp. 34, 49.   44 Ibid., p. 37.
45 Ibid., pp. 36–7.   46 'Plebiscites', Curtis memorandum, 18 Sept. 1924, RF, 7/2, ff. 1.
47 Hand, *Report*, Appendix I, pp. 22–41.

David Lloyd George

Cannes conference, January 1922, with Lloyd George seated second from left, with Lord Riddell next to him holding a cigar. Tom Jones is standing on the left. Lord and Lady Curzon are seated left and right. Frances Stevenson standing on the right.

(*left to right*) Austen Chamberlain, Stanley Baldwin and Winston Churchill, following the 1924 general election

Arthur James Balfour

Lord Birkenhead

Lord Beaverbrook

James Ramsay MacDonald

Lord and Lady Carson (*centre*). To their left (*standing*) is Sir James Craig.
Andrew Bonar Law is seated with the child and Lady Craig is to his left

Northern Ireland's first Cabinet: left to right, E. M. Archdale, Richard Dawson Bates, Marquess of Londonderry, Sir James Craig, H. M. Pollock, and J. M. Andrews. Seated in the rear is the Cabinet's secretary, Sir Wilfrid Spender.

Dublin Castle officials, 1920. Standing from left: Basil Clarke, G.N. Crutchley, L.N. Blake Odgers, M.T. Loughnane, J.P. Fairgrieve. Seated, from left: Geoffrey Whiskard, Alfred Cope, John Anderson, Mark Sturgis

Michael Collins

Arthur Griffith

Eamon de Valera (*centre*) with anti-Treaty TDs, 1922

William Cosgrave

Kevin O'Higgins

The Irish Boundary Commission: *left to right* F.B. Bourdillon (secretary), J.R. Fisher, Richard Feetham, Eoin MacNeill, C. Beerstecher (private secretary to Richard Feetham)

These exchanges revealed yet another blow to the Free State's case. Throughout, O'Byrne had argued that the Boundary Commission should consider conditions as they were when the Treaty was signed – not as they might now find them. Feetham hinted that he took a dim view of this position. Here, the years of delay most clearly took their toll on the Free State's case. As Feetham later wrote, partition had given rise to 'certain vested . . . interests . . . during the four years which have now elapsed since it [the Treaty] first took effect'. These interests, he judged, 'should not be lightly interfered with'.[48] It is perhaps not surprising that, as Free State officials were well aware, Curtis held the same view.[49]

In less than two months the Boundary Commission had travelled a long way down the road towards its final conclusions. In every respect, Feetham made it clear that the main elements of the Free State's case – that the Commission was empowered to make sweeping territorial changes, based on conditions as they were in 1921; that it had a right, if not a duty, to call a plebiscite in the border region; and that it had no mandate to transfer territory from the South to the North – were views that he did not share. Seven months earlier, O'Higgins had warned Cosgrave of just such a possibility if the two governments did not reach an understanding on the meaning of Article 12. His advice was ignored, not least because Curtis had assured the Free State president that the British government could not be the sole interpreter of an article of the Treaty. Instead, as O'Higgins had predicted, the Irish effectively handed that power to the British-appointed chairman.[50] The competition over the interpretation of Article 12 was the crucial match; by failing to face the issue head-on, Cosgrave and his colleagues scored the deciding own goal.

And the Commission had not even heard its first witness.

'NOT AN INCH': NORTHERN IRELAND'S 1925 ELECTION

Despite the Commission's importance to the future of Northern Ireland, Craig and his Cabinet adopted an official policy of non-co-operation with the tribunal.[51] Unofficially, they enlisted the Ulster Unionist Council to act in the government's place with Herbert Dixon, chief whip of the Ulster Unionist Parliamentary Party, co-ordinating operations. Dixon was ideally placed for the job. As parliamentary secretary to the Ministry of Finance, he reported

48   Ibid., pp. 27–31; 'Chairman's memorandum', p. 54.
49   MacCartan to Stephens, 11 March 1924, NEBB Box 27.
50   O'Higgins to Cosgrave, 7 and 10 May 1924, D/T, S 1801/R.
51   Cabinet Minutes, 10 Nov. 1924, PRONI, CAB/4/129/20.

directly to the Cabinet where he could at the same time report on the boundary issue. Thus, in private Craig and his colleagues could direct Unionist strategy while in public they remained 'free to take action' if the tribunal produced an award that they disliked. As with the Treaty, Craig could then say that his government had not been consulted and thus was not bound by the report.[52]

This co-ordination between Craig's government and the UUC took on more sinister tones at a different level. Throughout the winter and spring of 1925, RUC detectives regularly reported on meetings at which Northern Nationalists discussed the evidence they planned to lay before the Boundary Commission. These reports, which included lists of participants, were then forwarded to Craig's office, where they were in turn handed over to the UUC. It is difficult to escape the conclusion that this information was then used to intimidate Nationalists, and contributed to the Boundary Bureau's 'difficulty in obtaining witnesses' for the Commission hearings.[53]

On 3 March the Boundary Commission returned to Armagh, at long last ready to take evidence from the people of the border counties. Days later its work was overshadowed when Craig suddenly dissolved Northern Ireland's Parliament and called an election on the boundary question. He freely admitted that he had deliberately called the election, scheduled for 3 April, 'while the Commission is sitting in [our] midst'. Feetham might be hesitant about taking a vote; Ulster's premier was not – albeit on his terms. The result, Craig confidently predicted, would demonstrate Northern Ireland's continued and overwhelming support for partition to everyone, not least to the Commission.[54]

It is likely that Craig hoped his sudden move would allow him to play on continuing Nationalist divisions as had occurred during the 1924 election. To avoid another such debacle, a convention of Devlinites and pro-Treaty Sinn Féiners nominated eleven candidates to stand in the election. Despite the effort to create a united front, Eamon de Valera announced that his party, too, would put forward candidates. In the event, the Republicans were all but marginalised; as Cahir Healy acidly noted, 'for the Nationalists in the north-east, it is not a question of Free State versus Republic; unfortunately they had neither'.[55]

52   Spender to Hungerford, 11 Dec. 1924; Dixon to Hungerford, 3 Feb. 1925, PRONI, CAB/9Z/2/2. Spender to Hungerford, 2, 12 Feb. 1925, UUC D/1327/24/3. Follis, *State Under Siege*, pp. 166–7.

53   See, e.g., Gilfillan reports, 27 Jan., 5 Feb. 1925; Blackmore–Hungerford correspondence, 25, 27 Feb. and 18, 19 May 1925, PRONI, CAB/9Z/2/2. Stephens to O'Higgins, 21 Jan. 1925, D/T S/1801/L.

54   *NI HC Deb*, vol. 5, col. 19, 10 Mar. 1925.

55   Kennedy, *Widening Gulf*, p. 137. Phoenix, *Northern Nationalism*, pp. 317–21. Press statement, 20 Mar. 1925, FLK, de Valera Papers, File No. 347.

In the run-up to the election, Craig's allies in the British press were confident that the results would prove once and for all that Northerners had no wish to be 'cast into the outer darkness' of the Irish Free State. That indeed is how Craig interpreted the results. April's vote, he told Northern Ireland's newly elected House of Commons, proved that residents of the border counties had 'no desire to break their connection' with Belfast.[56]

In fact, Nationalists stood their ground in most of these counties. In two constituencies, Fermanagh–Tyrone and Londonderry, Nationalist candidates polled the most first preference votes. In Armagh and Fermanagh–Tyrone, the final results were evenly split between Unionists and anti-partition candidates who took an equal number of seats in both constituencies. Only in Down were the Unionists overwhelmingly triumphant – and there all of the candidates ran unopposed, including both Craig and de Valera. As one contemporary journal noted, whatever Craig might tell his supporters, the election 'showed that on the partition issue things remained very much as they were in 1920'.[57]

Overall, Craig's party was sharply rebuffed. Official Unionists held on to only half of Belfast's 16 seats, while overall they were reduced from 40 to 32 seats in the new Parliament. Thanks to proportional representation, ten Nationalists were elected to the assembly, along with four Independent Unionists, two anti-Treaty Sinn Féin candidates, and one tenant farmers' representative.[58]

Most worrying for Craig and his followers was the election of all three Labour candidates to the new Parliament. The Unionist campaign slogan – 'Not an inch!' – rang hollow for working-class Protestants held in the grip of an economic depression. It would be wrong to say that Northern Ireland's Labour Party was in any sense 'anti-partitionist'. But as party leader Sam Kyle later explained, what mattered to his followers was 'housing, wages, unemployment insurance, national health insurance, old-age pensions, [and] education'. Comparatively speaking, the boundary was not 'a matter of very much importance'.[59]

Put another way, it was becoming increasingly difficult for the Unionist Party to play the sectarian card so long as proportional representation gave working-class Protestants a viable alternative. PR had to be abolished once and for all. As Herbert Dixon bluntly wrote: 'There is no room in Ulster for

56 'Episodes of the Month', *National Review*, April 1925, p. 201. *NI HC Deb*, vol. 6, cols 24–5, 15 Apr. 1925.

57 Follis, *State Under Siege*, Appendix 2, pp. 198–200. *Annual Register*. 1925, p. 134.

58 Follis, *State Under Siege*, Appendix 2, pp. 198–200

59 *NI HC Deb*, vol. 6, cols 1115–16, 7 Sept. 1925.

diversities of opinions, and the people have got to learn this sooner or later.'[60] By the time elections were next held for Northern Ireland's Parliament, PR was indeed abolished and with telling results. In the 1929 election, only one Labour MP managed to hold on to his seat. Craig had learned his lesson well. Sectarianism kept him in power and he would resort to it to the end.[61]

At the same time, Craig recognised that sectarian politics had its limits, and that his government had to appear more responsive to rank and file Unionist concerns. During a tour at the height of the 1925 campaign, he vowed that so long as he was prime minister the 'B' Specials would not be disbanded. As well as reassuring Unionists over the boundary dispute, his promise appealed to working-class Protestants who were associated most closely with this branch of the Constabulary.[62] Behind the scenes meanwhile, Craig redoubled his efforts to persuade London to amalgamate the Ulster and British unemployment insurance funds.

SOLVING NORTHERN IRELAND'S FINANCIAL CRISIS

However much Unionists might claim that Ulster was 'not financially dependent upon Great Britain', its drain on the British Treasury was impossible to ignore by 1925. It was 'obvious', one journal reported, 'that the Government of Northern Ireland is really living on the charity of England, and giving very little but trouble in return'.[63]

Northern Ireland's economic problems were deep-seated and reached to the creation of the state itself. As far as possible the Ulster Unionists had modelled their six-county state after its British parent. But as Churchill noted, when it came to the provision of social services this model could properly function only if it was based on a 'sufficiently large area and large numbers of trades'.[64] Even in the best of times, this could not be said of Northern Ireland. Hence, it was unrealistic to expect that social services provided in the six counties would ever be on a par with those offered elsewhere in the United Kingdom.

Nor could they be, if Craig and his colleagues were to stay within the bounds of the Colwyn awards.[65] In its second report, delivered in December

60 Dixon to Spender, 23 Aug. 1924, PRONI, CAB/9B/101.

61 Morgan, *Labour and Partition*, p. 323. P. Buckland, *James Craig: Lord Craigavon* (Dublin, 1980), p. 97.

62 "'The Proper Border'", *Irish Independent*, 27 Mar. 1925.

63 See, e.g, 'Imperial Ulster', undated, DFA, Box 4, 37/D, which also contains other pamphlets presenting the Unionist case for partition. 'Events of the Week', *The Nation*, 4 Apr. 1925.

64 Churchill to Steel-Maitland, 13 Mar. 1925, T 160/187/F.7136/4.

65 See chapter 4.

1924, the Colwyn panel held that the imperial contribution should be determined only after Northern Ireland's government had paid for 'actual and necessary expenditure'. The catch was that Belfast could not count any government service as 'necessary' if it did not exist in the rest of the United Kingdom, or if the service provided was of 'a higher average standard than exists in Great Britain'. On this second point, it further held that this 'average standard' rule would be broken if Ulster officials did not take into account Northern Ireland's lower cost of living. This meant that disparities between social services provided in the two parts of the United Kingdom were bound to occur.[66]

Given a choice between staying within the bounds of the Colwyn rules or mollifying working-class Protestants, Craig and his colleagues decided to break the rules. The 'plain truth', Ulster's minister of labour later wrote, 'is that we cannot carry on as a Government here unless our working classes enjoy the same social standards as their brother Trade Unionists in Great Britain'.[67] While disaffected Protestants had no desire to join the Free State, once they became disillusioned with Belfast rule they might combine with Nationalists to support reintegration into the United Kingdom. That would put Ulster Unionists back where they were before 1920 – forever at the mercy of British governments which might one day do a deal with Dublin over their heads.

The only way out, Craig and his colleagues decided, was reintegration with Britain's social services beginning with unemployment insurance. In effect, the Northern Ireland government decided to destroy the 1920 Government of Ireland Act in order to save it. For, as Sir John Anderson pointed out to a colleague in the British Ministry of Labour, amalgamation would be an admission that the 1920 Act was 'unworkable'.[68]

RE-AMALGAMATION

On becoming chancellor of the exchequer, Churchill had resisted pleas to bail out Northern Ireland's unemployment insurance fund, reasoning that the province's reduced imperial contribution made any additional help unnecessary.[69] The Treasury was not alone in opposing amalgamation of the unemployment funds. Although Craig might have expected the support of Cabinet Diehards, Joynson-Hicks scolded the Unionists for wanting 'to be relieved of the consequences of self-government in so far as those consequences may be to

---

66 Cmd 2389, p. 4. Lawrence, *Northern Ireland*, pp. 43–8.
67 Andrews to Londonderry, 14 May 1925, PRONI, CAB/9C/1/6.
68 Anderson to Wilson, 17 Dec. 1924, HO 45/13743/6.
69 Churchill to Niemeyer, 15 Nov. 1924, T 160/131/F.4855/02/1.

their disadvantage'. Worse, this request was not intended to cover a special emergency. Rather, it was 'a claim for continuous assistance' and if used to bail out the unemployment insurance programme could be applied to any of the other services for which the Belfast government had been made responsible.[70]

Craig, it seems, forced matters by making amalgamation an issue in the Northern Ireland elections.[71] Writing to Churchill the day after he dissolved Parliament, he maintained that his supporters 'never would have consented to accept self-government' in 1920 had there been any suggestion but that 'living in Ulster was to be on a parallel with Great Britain'. For added emphasis, he resorted to his tried and true threat of resignation if these 'very definite pledges' were not carried through.[72] Whatever caused the shift, in late March Baldwin's Cabinet reversed itself and decided that 'on the grounds of equity' Britain should directly assist Northern Ireland in its 'difficulties' with the unemployment insurance fund.[73]

The problem was how. In the Cabinet committee set up to examine the issue, both Churchill and Lord Cave, the committee's chairman, swung behind Craig's plea for reamalgamation. Otherwise, Churchill later explained to Tom Jones, Ulster's voters might begin to question the wisdom of partition, placing 'Ulster at the mercy of the Free State'.[74]

Steel-Maitland still opposed the idea precisely because it meant 'a complete reversion to the position prior to the Government of Ireland Act'.[75] Even if the Free Staters did not object, the government might face a revolt from its own backbenchers who, despite economic hardship throughout Britain, were being told that prudence required continuing reductions in government spending. Yet here was Baldwin's Cabinet toying with an open-ended commitment far greater than the annual grants for Ulster's Special Constabulary which had caused so much resentment when Parliament last debated that issue in February.[76]

The issue was again raised in Cabinet at the end of May after another of Craig's threats to resign over the issue.[77] Rather than allow that, Baldwin and his colleagues appointed a sub-committee of civil servants under the

70   CP 53(25), 2 Feb. 1925, T 160/187/F.7136/3.   71   CP 167(25), 17 Mar. 1925, CAB 27/279.

72   Craig to Churchill, 11 Mar. 1925, T 160/187/F.7136/4.

73   C 17(25), 20 Mar. 1925, CAB 23/49.

74   Churchill to Steel-Maitland, 13 Mar. 1925, T 160/187/F.7136/4. 'Ulster Unemployment Insurance', 25 May 1925, T 160/187/F.7136/2. Jones diary, 17 May 1925, vol. I, p. 316.

75   CP 167(25), 17 Mar. 1925, CAB 27/279.

76   'Ulster Unemployment Insurance'; and Niemeyer to Bowers, both dated 25 May 1925, T 160/187/F.7136/2.

77   'Minute of discussion' between Baldwin and Craig, 26 May 1925, PRONI, CAB/9C/1/6.

chairmanship of Sir John Anderson to examine the practical problems of amalgamation. For the first time, apparently, the Cabinet was warned that what they were doing was a 'departure from the spirit, if not the terms, of the [Irish] Treaty'. But 'the Cabinet did not accept this view'.[78] One member was not so coy. In arguing for amalgamation, Churchill conceded that such a scheme involved a 'substantial modification' of the 1920 Government of Ireland Act; he even accepted that once word of the plan was made public it 'would be resented by the Irish Free State'. But this would be a good thing, he declared, if it gave the southern Irish 'an object lesson in the value of the British connection'.[79]

In mid-July, however, Anderson's sub-committee decided that full amalgamation of the two unemployment funds was impossible without raising 'difficult questions as to the constitutional relationships between Great Britain, Northern Ireland and the Irish Free State'. The problem was that the Treaty prevented any British government from extending the powers of Northern Ireland as this 'would be a blow to the cause of reuniting the country and a clear violation of the spirit of the Treaty'. By the same token, Dublin could object that any '*diminution*' of the powers and responsibilities of Northern Ireland's government was also a violation of the Treaty if it led to 'the ultimate re-inclusion of Northern Ireland in the political system of Great Britain'. Anderson and his colleagues could not be sure if Cosgrave's government would make such a claim, but they deemed it 'in the highest degree undesirable' that 'the issue should ever be raised'.[80]

Instead, the sub-committee devised a complicated 're-insurance scheme' which became the basis of the 1926 Unemployment Insurance Agreement. To stay within the letter, if not the spirit, of the Irish Treaty the British and Ulster unemployment insurance funds remained technically separate. To guarantee that the benefits offered by both funds would be the same, the Northern Ireland government agreed to contribute a yearly 'equalization payment' to its own unemployment fund. If, after this payment was made, the Ulster fund was still short of the amount needed to offer benefits equal to those given to British workers, the Treasury in London would provide up to three quarters of the additional amount needed. In addition, Craig's government had to accept sole responsibility for paying off the deficit already incurred by the Northern

---

78 C 27(25), 28 May 1925, CAB 23/50. This last remark was struck from the minutes and replaced by a far more ambiguous explanation: 'the Cabinet did not feel that the consideration of this aspect of the matter would be prejudiced by the proposed investigation'.

79 NIU (25) – 2nd, 26 May 1925, CAB 27/279.

80 NIU (25) 4, 15 July 1925, CAB 27/279.

Ireland fund – £3.6 million, a staggering sum when it is realised that the Ulster government's entire budget amounted to just over £5 million.[81]

Not surprisingly, the Ulster Unionists were less than happy with this arrangement.[82] But in the circumstances, this was the best they were going to get. Although the reinsurance scheme was approved by the British Cabinet on 7 August, Baldwin was in no hurry to put the matter before the House of Commons where it was 'certain to be most controversial'.[83] Elaborate measures were taken to 'shorten Parliamentary discussion' of the proposed legislation, and it was not until the following March that the agreement became law.[84] In the interim, Baldwin and his colleagues had plenty of other Irish problems to keep them occupied.

THE BOUNDARY COMMISSION HEARINGS

While Craig was busy renegotiating Northern Ireland's financial relations with the British government, the Boundary Commission had been taking evidence in the border counties. Beginning again in Armagh, the Commission held its first hearing on 3 March; its last sitting took place in Omagh, County Tyrone on 2 July.[85] To expedite the hearings, those giving evidence were cross-examined by the Commissioners themselves. The Commission also decided to bar newspaper coverage of its sessions and instead issued statements 'from time to time'. The consequences of this last decision were far reaching, once it was learned that the Commission did not propose to say publicly how it was interpreting the powers given to it by Article 12. In an atmosphere thick with rumour, this proved to be the Commission's undoing.[86]

There are several accounts of the Boundary Commission's hearings and only a brief summary is necessary here.[87] Initially, things seemed to go well for the Northern Nationalists. Their witnesses in County Down, for example,

---

81 Cmd 2588: *Unemployment Insurance (Northern Ireland Agreement): Memorandum Explaining Financial Resolution* ; 1926, xxii, 115, pp. 3–4. Lawrence, *Northern Ireland*, pp. 50–2.

82 Spender to Anderson, ? July 1925, HO 267/174.

83 C 44(25), 7 Aug. 1925, CAB 23/50. Upcott to Newsam, 19 Nov. 1925, HO 45/13743/22.

84 'Northern Ireland Unemployment Insurance', Upcott memorandum, 28 Oct. 1925, T 160/187/F.7136/5. C 51(25), same date, CAB 23/51.

85 For the panel's itinerary, see 'Index to Dates and Conferences', D/T, S 1801/P.

86 Hand, *Report*, pp. 14–15. Commission Minutes no. 1, 6 Nov. 1924, CAB 61/1. Bourdillon to O'Hegarty, 2 Feb. 1925, D/T, S 1801/L. 'The Boundary Commission. Armagh City's Claim for Transfer', *Tyrone Constitution*, 13 Mar. 1925.

87 See, e.g., Hand, 'MacNeill', pp. 236–46. Phoenix, *Northern Nationalism*, pp. 316–17, 322–8.

were 'splendidly organised', so that by the end of the hearings E. M. Stephens was confident that Newry would be transferred to the South.[88] In fact, the Boundary Bureau's secretary told Dublin, across the North 'hopes of the Free State supporters were rising'. He also found it encouraging that prominent Unionists such as Sir Basil Brooke had come round to accepting that the Commission's award 'would be binding, and would probably be upheld by the British Government'.[89]

By the time the Commission wound up its proceedings in Londonderry, however, Stephens was far less confident. '[J]udging by the nature of the questions asked', he felt that 'the chairman was adopting a view adverse to the Nationalist claim.' In one exchange, Feetham suggested that transferring Derry to the Free State would be a 'serious surgical operation', clearly implying that he was reluctant 'to make any change' in the status quo. On the other hand, Stephens noted that Londonderry's Unionists 'were becoming very anxious as to the fate of the city'.[90]

While the Free State government had to sort through these often conflicting dispatches, Craig could rely on a more reliable source of information. Acting as a go-between, David Reid passed along a steady stream of reports from Fisher, or 'our friend' as he was sometimes referred to, detailing the Commission's work. As early as 7 July, Fisher was able to tell his friends that the Free State's 'extreme claims' of territory had been rejected.

The problem was Newry. '[T]here is no question that the balance of population is against us', Reid admitted in one letter. Only at the end of October was Fisher in a position to report that Unionists would 'retain or gain control of the essential waterways', the Foyle, the Erne and Carlingford Lough; Newry, in other words, was safely in their hands. At one time or another, Fisher told his friends, all had been 'in danger'.[91]

Despite these assurances, Ulster Unionist leaders were afraid that they might yet be in for a nasty surprise. Craig at any rate was unwilling to commit himself to accepting the Commission's award so long as Newry was still in play. These concerns intensified when, in late August, the *Sunday Express* reported that the Commission would hand over 'considerable territory' to the Free State.[92] The article sparked two months of fevered, and often contradictory,

---

88 Stephens to O'Higgins, 24 March 1925, NEBB Box 28. At the same time, though, Feetham observed that the present border of 'Carlingford Lough might be regarded as a good natural boundary', not a good sign for Nationalists.

89 Ibid., Stephens to O'Higgins, 19 Feb. 1925.   90 Ibid., Stephens to O'Higgins, 22 May 1925.

91 See Reid–Craig correspondence, July–Oct. 1925, PRONI, CAB/9Z/2/2.

92 'New Border Puzzles in Ireland', *Sunday Express*, 23 Aug. 1925. For Fisher's assurance, see Reid to Craig, 1 Sept. 1925, PRONI, CAB/9Z/2/2.

speculation in newspapers on both sides of the Irish Sea.[93] One newspaper reported that leave had been cancelled for all Free State soldiers; another said that the British Army had established an outpost deep within County Fermanagh, indicating that a large part of the county was about to be ceded to the Free State. Donegal Nationalists were warned that a part of their county was about to be handed over to Northern Ireland. Unionists were told that South Armagh and parts of South Down were to be transferred to the Free State. Appeals were made for another conference of the two Irish governments. Ministers in Belfast warned that 'not one inch of Northern territory would be transferred . . . without the sanction of the people of Ulster'. Their prime minister, meanwhile, maintained a stony silence.[94]

Craig's refusal, either in public or in private, to 'commit himself in any way', left his friends in London in a 'politically impossible' position. Like Northern Ireland's government, Baldwin's administration had declined to give evidence to the Boundary Commission and had kept contact with the tribunal to a minimum. This meant that officials in London knew even less about the situation than their counterparts in Dublin. All sides were aware, however, that the Commission would soon issue its report, and both Amery and Joynson-Hicks were keen to give Craig prior notice of its contents. Otherwise, the Conservatives would be open to accusations that they had treated their Ulster friends as cavalierly as had Lloyd George during the Treaty negotiations. Senior government advisers adamantly opposed this idea. Speed, they pointed out, was essential if the award was to be implemented with a minimum of trouble, whereas details of the award would 'certainly leak out' once in Craig's hands.[95]

Tom Jones also spotted the danger. 'Once you begin to discuss', he warned Baldwin, 'you are in the Irish bog again.'[96] Jones also felt that the Boundary Commission's award should be implemented as soon as it was issued, and he pressed Baldwin to use his 'personal courage' to force this view on the Cabinet. But he failed. 'The moment the subject was mentioned at the Cabinet', Baldwin told his assistant secretary, 'they all got excited; Salisbury and Jix were bursting their buttons with eagerness to talk'. The meeting became fractious as its members were 'plunged into the regular Irish atmosphere'. Everyone was 'talking excitedly and most of them irrelevantly'.[97] To soothe nerves, Baldwin

---

93   For a running account of these reports, see 'Index to Dates and Conferences', Aug.–Oct. 1925, D/T, S 1801/P.

94   Ibid., 27 Aug., 1, 14, 21,and 22 Sept. 1925. *NI HC Deb*, vol. 6, cols 1117–18, 7 Sept. 1925.

95   CP 445(25), 26 Oct. 1925, CAB 24/175. Waterhouse to Bourdillon, 18 Nov. 1924, in Hand, *Report*, p. 6. Amery diary, 22 Oct. 1925, p. 424.

96   Jones to Baldwin [memorandum excerpt], 28 Oct. 1925, vol. III, p. 236.

97   Ibid., 29[?] Oct. 1925, p. 236. 'Jix' was a nickname for Joynson-Hicks. Amery diary, 28 Oct. 1925, p. 424.

offered to see the Boundary Commission's chairman privately. But Feetham, mindful of the agreement with his colleagues not to discuss their deliberations with anyone else, could not be drawn. In any event, by the time Baldwin informed the Cabinet that no meeting had taken place, events had already taken a dramatic, and very public, turn.[98]

FEETHAM'S MEMORANDUM ON ARTICLE 12

After its last hearing in County Tyrone in early July, the Boundary Commission continued its work in near total isolation for the better part of four months. Only a two-day hearing with Free State lawyers in late August interrupted their labours.[99] 'I am as much alone here as if I was living at the North Pole', MacNeill wrote to his wife on 10 September.[100] The following day both he and Fisher received a memorandum in which Feetham outlined his interpreta-tion of Article 12. On this foundation, the Boundary Commission's report would stand.[101]

From Article 12's 'maddeningly few words', Feetham drew a 'wealth of meaning'. As he had hinted to Free State lawyers the previous December, the Commission's chairman would not consider wholesale changes of the border, nor would he countenance a transfer of territory where there was 'no sufficient reason' for doing so.[102]

Under the criteria laid down by Feetham, providing a sufficient reason would be no small task. First, he threw out the idea that the Commission's main task was to draw a boundary 'in accordance with the wishes of the inhabitants'. These wishes were a 'primary consideration', but they were not 'paramount'. A 'substantial majority' must desire change, a term he vaguely defined, and which became vaguer still when he added that the greater the change demanded 'the higher the percentage of inhabitants . . . should be required to justify it'. Even then, the Commission had a 'duty' to 'overrule' those wishes if they might cause 'economic or geographic inconvenience'.[103]

Feetham reiterated his opposition to the holding of plebiscites, arguing that as the word did not appear in Article 12 'it was not the intention of the parties to the Treaty that the Commission should ascertain the wishes of the inhabitants in that manner'. Instead, the Commission should rely on the

98 Waterhouse to Baldwin, 31 Oct. 1925, SB vol. 99, ff. 235–7. C 52(25), 11 Nov. 1925, CAB 23/51.
99 Hand, *Report*, pp. 13–14; and Appendix IV, pp. 55–72.
100 Eoin to Agnes MacNeill, 10 Sept. 1925, EM-UCD, LA1/H/123(19).
101 Hand, *Report*, 'Chapter III', pp. 25–32; 'Chairman's memorandum', pp. 32–68.
102 Ibid., p. xiii; 'Chairman's memorandum', p. 52.   103 Ibid., pp. 49, 52–5.

returns of the 1911 Census, assuming that Protestants would desire to live in Northern Ireland and Roman Catholics in the Free State. He then rejected applying these figures to whole counties or poor law unions and, instead, opted for 'the smallest area' which could be regarded separately in any given place.[104] Finally, he held that the Commission was fully within its rights to transfer portions of the Free State to Northern Ireland, as well as the other way round.[105]

In effect, Feetham claimed that the Commission had been handed a blank cheque, allowing it to do pretty much as it pleased, even if this meant that the criteria used to determine the boundary in one area contradicted the reasons used to determine it in another. Or, as Feetham himself wrote, it was 'impossible I think to lay down any precise rule as to the requirements which must be fulfilled in the case of individual areas'.[106]

The sight of this memorandum ought to have shaken MacNeill to his bones. If this was to be the basis for the Commission's findings, it was obvious that the award would be disastrous for the Free State. Surely MacNeill did not need to be, as he later put it, 'a better politician . . . , if you like a better strategist' to see that.[107] If ever there were a time for him to signal to Feetham and Fisher that he could not possibly be a party to a report based on these assumptions, this would have been the time to do so.

Given the course of later events, MacNeill's action, or inaction, bears some consideration. According to the Free State's Commissioner, there were 'profound differences . . . between the chairman and myself as to the funda-mental principles upon which an award ought to proceed'. MacNeill claimed that early on he realised that Feetham had 'imported' a new 'dominant condition' into the Commission's mandate: namely, that Northern Ireland must be preserved as a separate political entity even if this meant that the tribunal must 'override the wishes of the inhabitants'. Nor, he complained, was there 'consistent application' of the Commission's principles. Feetham had made it possible 'in one part of our award, for us to make economic considerations dominant and, in another place, to make the wishes of the inhabitants dominant'.[108]

Yet far from confronting Feetham about these matters, MacNeill refused in any way to challenge 'the commanding position held by the Chairman'.[109] Later, when the crisis forced him to resign not only from the tribunal but from Cosgrave's government as well, MacNeill blamed his inaction on the fact

104 Ibid., pp. 59–60, 61–4.   105 Ibid., pp. 36–7, 40.

106 Ibid., p. 51.   107 *Dáil Deb*, vol. 13, col. 802, 24 Nov. 1925.

108 Ibid., cols 799–801. MacNeill returned to this latter point throughout his Dáil speech.

109 MacNeill to Cosgrave, 10 Oct. 1925, EM-UCD, LA1/H/119(1).

that he was, in effect, a part-time Commissioner. Throughout the tribunal's deliberations, he had continued to work as the Free State's minister of education, making it impossible for him to see what was happening until it was too late. 'The details came before us in a very gradual and a very piecemeal manner', he said of the Commission's work, and only over time did he come to the 'conclusion that when those parts of the award were put together . . . it would not be possible for me to defend them'.[110]

This explanation is hard to square with the fact that MacNeill had to know where Feetham was headed once he read the September memorandum. In fact, at the time MacNeill did respond to the paper – but not with a wide-ranging critique like the one in his later speech to the Dáil. Instead, he only questioned the Commission's right to transfer territory from the Free State to Northern Ireland (and concluded that it could not).[111]

A vital opportunity was lost. Because MacNeill raised no serious objections to Feetham's memorandum, the Boundary Commission chairman, and Fisher too, assumed that their Free State colleague accepted these guidelines. Given that MacNeill did not resign from the Commission until 20 November, both men were justified in later telling the press that his decision 'came as a complete surprise'.[112] In any event, during a series of meetings held in mid-October, the three men gave final shape to their award.[113] In sum, 31,319 people and 183,290 acres were transferred to the Free State; 7,594 people and 49,242 acres were transferred to Northern Ireland. Dublin gained more people and territory – 23,725 people, and 134,048 acres – than Belfast. The boundary itself was shortened by 51 miles.[114]

Fisher was elated. 'I am well satisfied with the result', he wrote to Carson, which would 'not shift a stone or a tile of your enduring work for Ulster.'

> No centre of even secondary importance goes over, and with Derry, Strabane, Enniskillen, Newtownbutler, Keady and Newry in safe keeping your handiwork will endure.
>
> If anybody had suggested twelve months ago that we could have kept so much I would have laughed at him . . . .
>
> On the balance the number of Protestants in Ulster has been increased – the number of R.C's materially decreased: – which will put an end to certain political difficulties in Tyrone and Fermanagh.[115]

110 *Dáil Deb*, vol. 13, 24 Nov. 1925, cols 802–3.

111 Unsigned memorandum, 19 Sept. 1925, EM-UCD, LA1/119/(7–25).

112 MacNeill quoted their statement in *Dáil Deb*, vol. 13, cols 797–8, 24 Nov. 1925.

113 Hand, 'MacNeill', p. 248. Commission Minutes, nos 20–4, 13–17 Oct. 1925, CAB 61/1, though, provide no details.

114 C 55(25), 30 Nov. 1925, CAB 23/51. Hand, *Report*, Appendix V, pp. 73–109.

115 Fisher to Carson, 18 Oct. 1925, Carson Papers, D/1507/A/44/52.

In this same letter, Fisher told Carson that another six weeks would elapse before the Boundary Commission's award would be ready for publication. He also let slip that he had told at least one other person about the report. Fisher had been indiscreet, and it was to cost him and Feetham their triumph.

THE 'MORNING POST' REPORT

On 6 November Bourdillon informed Hankey that the Boundary Commission would soon be ready to issue its report and that the imperial and Irish governments should waste no time making arrangements to put the award into effect.[116] Early the following day both governments were rocked by the *Morning Post*'s dramatic publication of a forecast of the Commission's award. The tone of the article is best demonstrated by its comparison of Unionist gains in County Donegal, which would be 'of great commercial assistance', to Free State gains in County Armagh which, at best, was 'wild and very beautiful country'. In other words, the Ulster Unionists had lost nothing of value. Armagh's 'principal towns . . . including the much discussed Newry' would remain under Belfast's jurisdiction. What was most striking about the article was the precision of the map that accompanied it.[117]

Without warning, this single newspaper report had put 'the fat in the fire'.[118]

Although he denied it, Fisher has long been held responsible for the *Post*'s scoop.[119] What is not in doubt is that the article left Cosgrave's government dangerously exposed. '[N]ot since partition was introduced', commented one pro-government newspaper, 'has feeling run so high.' Although Boundary Bureau representatives did their best to play down the forecast, J. H. Collins reported that Free State supporters in the North 'were very angry'.[120]

On Thursday, the 19th, MacNeill returned to London and, the following afternoon, stunned Feetham and Fisher by resigning from the Commission. A few days later, at O'Higgins's instigation, he was forced out of the Free State Cabinet as well. It seems that MacNeill, along with other members of the Irish government, thought that this first resignation at any rate would make it impossible for the Boundary Commission to issue its award and thus the Free

116 Bourdillon to Hankey, 6 Nov. 1925, HO 45/12296/88.

117 The article is reproduced in J. H. Andrews, 'The "Morning Post" Line', *Irish Geography*, vol. IV, no. 2, 1960, pp. 99–106.

118 'Episodes of the Month', *National Review*, Jan. 1926, p. 675. Baldwin later blamed the report for having 'precipitated a crisis'. See 'Irish Bill. Debate in the Commons', *The Times*, 9 Dec. 1925.

119 Reid to Craig, 7 Nov. 1925, PRONI, CAB/9Z/2/2. Mansergh, *Unresolved Question*, p. 236.

120 Hand, 'MacNeill', p. 254. Collins to Stephens, 13 Nov. 1925, JHC, D/921/2/4/121.

Staters would steer clear of disaster. Instead, Bourdillon informed the Free State government that as far as the two remaining Commissioners were concerned, MacNeill's resignation was not 'valid or effectual'. More worrisome, from Dublin's standpoint, the Commission had 'continued its labours' and would soon 'be in a position to deliver the Award'.[121]

Before he would allow that to happen, Cosgrave asked to see his British counterparts. A hastily arranged meeting was held on the 26th with Baldwin, Austen Chamberlain, Joynson-Hicks, Amery and Tom Jones at which the Free State president warned of dangers, including 'a danger of bloodshed', if the Commission's award was implemented. At the very least, he faced an imminent revolt within his own party and, if de Valera took Sinn Féin's abstentionist TDs into Dáil Éireann, Cosgrave would find himself 'in a tight corner'. Worse, though the Free State president may not have known it, elements within the Irish Army had decided that they would resist any transfer of Free State territory to the North. It was obvious, Chamberlain later observed, that Cosgrave, though 'anxious for peace', did not 'know how to deal with the situation'.[122]

Despite these warnings, Cosgrave's suggestion that 'the Boundary Commission should not issue their award either now or at any time' was coldly rebuffed. Chamberlain, in particular, gave vent to his feelings. 'I took great risks' for the Treaty he told Cosgrave, far understating the price he had paid. Less candidly, he claimed that the Tories had been prepared to 'impose' the Commission's award on Craig's government 'whatever it might be'. So far as Chamberlain was concerned, if the Free Staters were looking for a way out of a dilemma of their own making, they would have to turn to Craig for a solution. '[W]e cannot offer it.'[123]

Baldwin was equally unyielding. All three governments wanted peace, he pointed out. But the Free Staters had to remember that they had forced the British to impose the Boundary Commission on their Northern Irish allies. Then Baldwin went in for the kill. 'If this unhappy disclosure had not been made [i.e., the *Morning Post* forecast], and had the report been favourable to you, you would have expected us to impose it on Ulster.'

'Yes', Cosgrave replied.

---

121 Ibid., Hand, pp. 254–9, 274. Commission Minutes, nos 28 and 35, 20, 28 Nov. 1925, CAB 61/1. Bourdillon to O'Hegarty [two letters], 24 Nov. 1925, CAB 61/17. Craig, at least initially, also thought that resignation could be used to thwart a Commission award. See Cabinet Minutes, 30 Sept. 1924, PRONI, CAB/4/122/1.

122 IA (25)-3rd Minutes, 26 Nov. 1925, CAB 27/295. Jones diary, 25 [*sic*] Nov. 1925, vol. III, p. 237. Farrell, *Arming the Protestants*, pp. 247, 357, n. 47.

123 CA/H/48–1st Minutes, 26 Nov. 1925, CAB 27/295.

'It might have been such as to lead to Civil War', Baldwin observed. Now, however, the southern Irish expected the Boundary Commission's award to be quashed simply because it gave them less than they expected. No, no this was not good enough. 'We cannot compel Ulster in any direction', he told Cosgrave.[124] The British government could not 'deprive Ulster of the benefit of a decision by the Commission because it proved more favourable to Ulster than the Free State had expected'.[125] The best that the British prime minister was willing to promise was that he would ask Craig to meet with Cosgrave that afternoon. Perhaps a deal could be worked out between the two Irish leaders.

Birkenhead, for one, was not 'sanguine' about the prospects for such a meeting. 'It seems to me', he wrote that morning, 'that the differences which sunder Moslems from Hindus are not as bitter or as unbridgeable as those which divide Orangemen from the rest of Ireland.'[126]

THE CRISIS WIDENS

As the boundary crisis edged to its climax Craig, at some point in mid-November, decided that the moment had arrived for him to become directly involved in the boundary negotiations. As he told his wife: 'All that matters in regard to Ulster's future is at stake, (financial), and I well know that if I left here, decisions would be come to behind my back, as on the famous occasion of the Treaty'. That, he vowed, would not happen again.[127]

This might have been the beginning of what Craig saw as a golden opportunity to get rid of more problems than just the Boundary Commission.[128] Earlier in the month, he had intimated to Joynson-Hicks that he might be prepared to accept the Commission's award. The offer was only good, though, if financial compensation was provided for any Unionist whose home or business was transferred out of Northern Ireland, and if the imperial government was willing to meet his funding demands for the Specials.[129]

Craig later detailed what he had in mind. First, he wanted Northern Ireland's imperial contribution suspended for the next two years followed by a further readjustment of future payments. Next, he suggested creating a

124 Ibid.

125 IA (25)-3rd Minutes, 26 Nov. 1925, CAB 27/295.

126 Birkenhead to Reading, 26 Nov. 1925, IO, MSS Eur. E. 238/8, no. 17.

127 Lady Craig's diary, 23 Nov. 1925, D/1415/B/38.

128 Sir John Anderson believed this was what Craig was up to. See notes from a meeting of civil servants, ? Nov. 1925, CO 537/1104/545043.

129 Joynson-Hicks to Baldwin, with memorandum, 4 Nov. 1925, SB vol. 99, ff. 238–41.

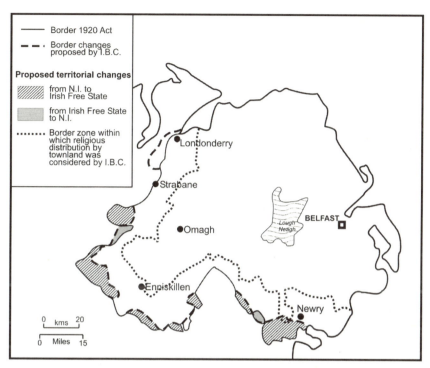

Border changes considered by the Irish Boundary Commission

tribunal (to be chaired by Fisher, interestingly) to adjudicate claims for financial 'compensation to Protestants' arising out of the Commission's award or for damages caused by its implementation. No such compensation would be offered to inhabitants transferred to the North against their will nor for any damages caused in areas transferred to the Free State. Craig estimated that the compensation package would cost £4 million – roughly equal, conveniently, to Northern Ireland's imperial contribution for the next two years. Separately, he called for abolition of the Council of Ireland.[130]

Churchill was incandescent. These 'claims are outrageous', he told his Cabinet colleagues. As it was, the Treasury had already promised Ulster £650,000 for its unemployment fund, along with another £500,000 for the Special Constabulary. 'This last vote will be extremely unpopular in the House of Commons', Churchill pointed out, 'and I shall have to face a storm of abuse on account of it'. Craig's continuing demands, of which this 'astonishing document' was just the latest, could not go on. Perhaps, the chancellor

130 IA (25)2 and 5, 16, 23 Nov. 1925, CAB 27/295. Churchill memorandum with proposed letter to Craig, 26 Nov. 1925, WSC 22/55/21–2.

of the exchequer suggested, it was time to 'undeceive' Northern Ireland's prime minister.[131]

The dispute came to a head on the 26th, at a meeting of a Cabinet committee formed in the wake of the *Morning Post* report.[132] Churchill poured cold water on Craig's proposals, suggesting instead that there were really only two solutions to the developing crisis. The lesser of the two was that the Commission's award should be implemented. It was not 'injurious to Ulster' and the Free Staters had no grounds for setting it aside. The other alternative, 'which would be preferable if it were practicable', was this: 'leave the Boundary question as it was for a term of say 25 years'. In the interim, the two Irish governments could 'endeavour to build up either in the[ir] Senate[s] or on the Council of Ireland some plan for joint action between the North and South where common interests were affected'.[133]

Craig would have nothing to do with this idea. More than that, he now declared that it would be 'impossible' for him to meet with Cosgrave on the boundary question, until the committee addressed his claims for compensation and suspension of the imperial contribution.

At this point, it seemed that tempers would flare. According to the minutes, Churchill, obviously irritated by Craig's demands, told the committee that they 'clearly showed that the real aim was a general easement of Ulster finance'. He was no more willing to do that 'than he would be prepared to give up the financial advantages of Article 5 of the Treaty, though', he caustically added, 'he had no doubt that he would be invited to do' just that. Baldwin, who was sitting in on the meeting, intervened and urged Craig to meet with Cosgrave. If, in the end, a financial concession would smooth the way to an agreement, Baldwin promised that he would shoulder responsibility for it. Only then did Ulster's leader agree to meet with his Free State counterpart.[134]

In the event, their encounter solved nothing. Cosgrave had hoped that in return for leaving the boundary in place, Craig might be persuaded to release a number of Nationalists held captive in the North. Craig offered to release only 30 IRA prisoners held since 1922, leaving Cosgrave with no other choice but to return to Dublin to lay this offer before the Executive Council.[135]

---

131 Ibid., Churchill memorandum.

132 The committee, chaired by Austen Chamberlain, included Churchill, Joynson-Hicks, Amery, Lords Salisbury and Birkenhead, Worthington-Evans, and Sir Douglas Hogg. See C 52 (25), 11 Nov. 1925, CAB 23/51.

133 IA (25)-3rd Minutes, 26 Nov. 1925, CAB 27/295.

134 Ibid. Craig's demands were 'put in a form well calculated to upset Winston'. See Amery diary, 26 Nov. 1925, p. 428.

135 Farrell, *Arming the Protestants*, p. 248. Amery diary, 26 Nov. 1925, p. 428.

There, it was given short shrift by O'Higgins. As he later told Craig and Baldwin, the offer would have caused the Irish government 'to fall at once'.[136] Instead, O'Higgins himself was dispatched to London to see what he might work out. Craig, meanwhile, was growing ever more confident. 'It is a delicate, tedious, and nervy job', he told his wife. But 'I have a feeling in my bones that the *present* boundary will be allowed to stand . . . if I can bring off "Not an Inch", I will be very pleased.' He predicted one more thing. Article 5, that part of the Treaty dealing with the Free State's debt to the British Treasury, would be 'washed out' too.[137]

THE SIGNIFICANCE OF ARTICLE 5

Although Article 5 never sparked the same passions as Article 12, its potential consequences were nearly as significant. The two clauses were similar in that, like Article 12, an independent tribunal was to determine the Free State's share of Britain's public debt after taking into account claims that Ireland had been over-taxed since the Act of Union. Ulster Unionists saw this as yet another attempt to coerce them into an all-Ireland government, because while their imperial contribution was to be fixed the South's was open to negotiation. Craig scored one of his first successes against the Treaty when he won a commit-ment from the Coalition to lower Northern Ireland's imperial contribution should the Irish claims prove to be successful.[138]

Both London and Dublin had agreed to delay negotiations on Article 5 until the boundary question was settled. Free State officials argued that it was impossible to determine their financial liabilities so long as the extent of their jurisdiction over the island of Ireland was unresolved.[139] However, periodic press complaints about Dublin's failure to come to the 'relief of the long-suffering British taxpayer' ensured that the issue never entirely went away.[140]

Because of such complaints, perhaps, in April 1925 members of Baldwin's second government began to press for discussions.[141] Shortly thereafter, an outline of the British case was sent to Dublin, but at the end of November the Treasury was still waiting for a brief of the Irish counter-claims.[142] By then,

136 IA (25) 7, 29 Nov. 1925, CAB 27/295.   137 Lady Craig's diary, 27 Nov. 1925, D/1415/B/38.

138 Mansergh, *Unresolved Question*, pp. 192–3, 198–9. PGI 48, undated [? Jan. 1922], CAB 27/154.

139 See Churchill's statement to this effect in CA/H/48–2nd Minutes, 1 Dec. 1925, CAB 27/295.

140 See, e.g., 'Boundaries in Ireland', *The Times*, 8 May 1924. 'Ireland Today', *Quarterly Review*, no. 484, Oct. 1924, p. 362.

141 R. Fanning, *The Irish Department of Finance: 1922–58* (Dublin, 1978), p. 157.

142 Niemeyer memorandum to Churchill, 30 Nov. 1925, T 176/15.

Cosgrave and his colleagues had every reason to be skittish about facing this issue. With the Boundary Commission crisis breaking over their heads, de Valera was broadening his attack on the Free State government. If anyone was still foolish enough to believe in the Treaty, he declared in one interview, they would be finally disillusioned when 'that *other commission* provided for in the "Treaty" – the Financial Commission – is set up and comes to deliver its award'.[143]

This is where matters stood when O'Higgins, along with Free State Commerce Minister Patrick McGilligan and Attorney-General John O'Byrne, arrived at Chequers on the weekend of 28–29 November. From the outset, Baldwin made it clear that only three options were on the table: accept the Boundary Commission's award; accept the existing boundary; or attempt another boundary conference with Craig, though no one seemed enthusiastic about that idea. Personally, Baldwin confided to his guests, he could not 'see how even an angel could devise a boundary which would be agreed'.[144]

O'Higgins replied that the Boundary Commission's award was unacceptable in any shape or form. As far as the Free Staters were concerned, the tribunal had taken the line of 'least resistance', influenced not by the wishes of the inhabitants but by 'the truculent utterances' of Craig's Cabinet. Newry was 'the acid test'. Any award leaving this Nationalist-dominated town within Belfast's jurisdiction was not worth having. Moreover, Britain had allowed the Commissioners to be 'terrorised' by the Specials and for that reason it might be time to take the boundary question to the League of Nations.[145] Nor, O'Higgins told the British prime minister, could the Free State government accept the offer Cosgrave had taken back to Dublin on Thursday. It was simple fantasy to suggest that the Irish president should tell Dáil Éireann, 'We are very sorry but the old line shall stand and in return Sir James Craig will give up 24 prisoners.' The moment that happened, McGilligan added, Cosgrave and his colleagues would 'disappear politically'.[146]

It fell to Tom Jones to suggest a way out. During their Saturday discussions, O'Higgins repeatedly raised the plight of Northern Nationalists, arguing that the abolition of proportional representation and electoral redistricting had made them 'politically impotent' while they were 'kept down by an army of Special Constables paid and maintained by the British Government'. If, Jones asked, the boundary was left untouched but, at the same time, the situation for Northern Nationalists was alleviated, could the Free Staters then 'ride the storm'?

143 De Valera interview, 24 Nov. 1925, FLK, de Valera Papers, File No. 347.
144 IA (25)-6, 28 Nov. 1925, CAB 27/295.
145 IA (25)-7, 29 Nov. 1925, CAB 27/295.
146 IA (25)-6, 28 Nov. 1925, CAB 27/295.

O'Higgins believed they might. Such a settlement would benefit Nationalists living far from the border who never had any hope of 'rescue' by the Boundary Commission's award in any case. Their satisfaction 'would be some set-off against the disappointment of people who had been hoping that the award would get them out' of Northern Ireland.[147] At no time during the Saturday talks was Article 5 an issue.

Most of these matters were covered again when, on Sunday, Craig joined the discussions. Though he accepted the Free Staters' analysis of the boundary dispute, Ulster's leader would give no ground on demands that Belfast get rid of the Specials, reinstate PR, and reapportion its electoral districts. O'Higgins later quoted Craig as saying that 'he could not re-enact what he had repealed, nor repeal what he had enacted'.[148]

Only then did Article 5 emerge as a major element in the negotiations. According to Craig, the article came up during an after-lunch conversation between himself and the Free State vice-president. As Baldwin later told the Cabinet, Craig was 'satisfied that what was at the bottom of the whole difficulty was Article 5 of the Irish Treaty . . . and if that could be waived altogether the Free State might ride the storm and stand on the present boundary.'[149] This was shading the truth, because the Free Staters would have much preferred concessions for the Northern Nationalists. Only when it was plain that Craig was unwilling to budge on this issue did the southern Irish turn to Article 5 as a 'safety valve' to channel outrage over the impending deal.[150]

The idea of such a trade-off was not new.[151] What may have made it attractive now was Craig's reputed offer to help the Free Staters against the British. While he was unwilling to 'surrender an inch of Northern territory', Craig promised 'to help you all I can to get as much as you can out of these fellows'. And, of course, if the Free State was to be excused from its imperial contribution, why not Ulster too?[152] The result, according to Birkenhead, was 'a greater degree of cordiality between Southern and Northern Ireland than has ever existed', as the two Irish sides happily joined together 'in the task of plundering us'.[153] However, Craig's help came at a price: the Free Staters also had to accept abolition of the Council of Ireland.[154]

147 Ibid.   148 CA/H/48–2nd Minutes, 1 Dec. 1925, CAB 27/295.

149 C 55(25), 30 Nov. 1925, CAB 23/51.   150 CA/H/48–2nd Minutes, 1 Dec. 1925, CAB 27/295.

151 See, e.g., 'Irish Boundary Commission. Free State and the Treaty', *Morning Post*, 14 Sept. 1923.

152 Ervine, *Craigavon*, p. 502. O'Byrne was the source for this story. Spender to Blackmore, 26 Nov. 1925, PRONI, CAB/9Z/2/2.

153 Birkenhead to Reading, 3 Dec. 1925, IO, MSS Eur. E. 238/8, no. 18.

154 Jones diary, 29 Nov. 1925, vol. III, p. 242.

Whatever hopes remained for the Northern Nationalists disappeared once Cosgrave joined the negotiations on 1 December. Craig's promise to 'sift . . . to the bottom' of any Nationalist complaints of maltreatment was, in the end, all that the Free Staters got for their Northern allies. O'Higgins again pressed for the restoration of proportional representation and was again rebuffed. 'I can't stick PR', Craig told him. 'Does not seem to be British. Too Continental.' Cosgrave, who was having his own problems with this method of elections, agreed that he too would like to get rid of proportional representation in the Free State.[155]

Even more astounding, Craig's willingness to discuss steps to make joint Free State–Northern Irish Cabinet meetings a formal part of the agreement was dropped because Cosgrave 'foresaw great difficulties' with the idea. It has been said that the Irish president disliked the proposal because it would have been 'tantamount to recognition of the legitimacy of the Northern government'. But that is no explanation at all; the Free Staters had recognised the Ulster government's equal status by entering into these negotiations.[156] So it was that yet another opportunity to bring about what Churchill now called 'unity in Ireland' was allowed to slip away.[157] The grievances of Northern Nationalists were disposed of once and for all the next day when Cosgrave accepted that Craig could not 'deliver the goods' on improving conditions for Northern Nationalists and, as Churchill put it, the 'only question remaining to be discussed was that of finance'.[158]

Although Baldwin's government was just as anxious as the Free State to bury the Boundary Commission report, its concessions on Article 5 'were not so readily forthcoming as is generally supposed'.[159] Baldwin's Cabinet colleagues were only willing to agree to a moratorium on the Free State's assumption of its share of the imperial debt until 1933, when repayment of Britain's war loans to the United States were due to increase.[160] To resolve the problem, Churchill, Birkenhead and Salisbury were given the job of hammering out an agreement with the Free State delegates. Both Churchill and Salisbury were inclined to take a 'fairly stiff stand' on Ireland's obligations, and this was the line the

155 Ibid., 1 Dec. 1925, pp. 243–4.

156 Mansergh, *Unresolved Question*, p. 238. Wall, 'Partition', p. 89.

157 CA/H/48–4th Minutes, 1 Dec. 1925, CAB 27/295. Not surprisingly, Craig began to back away from the idea when Churchill spoke of it in these terms.

158 CA/H/48–5th Minutes, 2 Dec. 1925, CAB 27/295.

159 Birkenhead to Reading, 3 Dec. 1925, IO, MSS Eur. E. 238/8, No. 18.

160 C 55(25), 30 Nov. 1925, CAB 23/51. The American connection was made by Churchill may have hoped that the Irish would use their influence in Washington so that the United States might become 'less rigid' on the war debts issue. If so, he hinted, none too subtly, the British would be 'in a position to deal more generously' with the Free State. See CA/H/48–3rd Minutes, 1 Dec. 1925, CAB 27/295.

chancellor of the exchequer pursued when negotiations resumed.[161] The British could not simply waive Article 5, Churchill told the Free Staters, not least because it would lead to demands 'to reduce or abolish the Northern Irish contribution', as well.[162]

What seemed to turn matters round was the strong impression made by Cosgrave when he outlined his country's economic plight. In such circumstances, Birkenhead thought it was senseless to pursue payments which the Dublin government 'could not possibly hope to discharge'.[163] If, as he argued at a meeting of British officials, they now had the chance 'to round the corner' on the Irish Question, the financial sacrifices involved in such an agreement would be well worth it.[164] Despite objections from Salisbury, Birkenhead brought Churchill and, eventually, the entire Cabinet to the same conclusion. By the end of an urgently held meeting, Baldwin's associates agreed 'by a large majority' to the framework of the 1925 settlement.[165]

In essence, the agreement covered four points: first, the boundary between the two parts of Ireland was to remain unchanged. Second, the cases of republican prisoners held by Northern Ireland would be reviewed by British officials and their decisions would be accepted by Craig. Third, the Council of Ireland was abolished and its powers relating to Northern Ireland were transferred to Belfast. Instead, both governments agreed to meet 'as and when necessary' to work together on matters of common interest. The British Cabinet was also told that Craig and the Free Staters had reached a 'personal understanding' that would lead to 'more friendly co-operation' but, interestingly, 'this could not be put in writing'.[166]

Solving the financial question proved to be somewhat less straightforward, until Cosgrave mooted a proposal that proved to be the breakthrough on this issue.[167] Article 5 was dropped. In its place, the Free State agreed to repay the British government for compensation payments that it had made for malicious property damage incurred during the Anglo-Irish War of 1919–21. In addition, the Dublin government promised to increase by 10 per cent its payments for malicious property damage that occurred within its jurisdiction during the Irish Civil War of 1922–23.[168] As O'Higgins explained, this arrangement was preferable because it enabled the Free Staters 'to say that they were prepared to shoulder their own burdens arising out of the disturbances in Ireland'.[169]

161 IA (25) 9, 2 Dec. 1925, CAB 27/295.   162 CA/H/48–2nd Minutes, 1 Dec. 1925, CAB 27/295.

163 CA/H/48–6th Minutes, 2 Dec. 1925, CAB 27/295.

164 IA (25) 9, 2 Dec. 1925, CAB 27/295.   165 C 56(25), 2 Dec. 1925, CAB 23/51.

166 Ibid. For the text of the agreement, see CP 511(25), 4 Dec. 1925, CAB 27/295.

167 CA/H/48–6th Minutes, 2 Dec. 1925, CAB 27/295.

168 C 56 (25), 2 Dec. 1925, CAB 23/51.   169 CA/H/48–7th Minutes, 2 Dec. 1925, CAB 27/295.

By early evening, the deal was done. Cosgrave told Churchill that the settlement would 'promote goodwill between North and South' and 'would go far to cement the friendship' of Irish and British peoples. O'Higgins added that the Dublin government would use its influence to 'induce the Nationalist members in Ulster to take their place in the Northern Parliament'.[170] The following day O'Higgins made one last attempt to include in the agreement a clause promising Anglo-Irish co-operation should the two parts of Ireland ever wish to unite politically. Such a statement, he thought, would 'have a sentimental and political value'. Churchill was leery. Such a statement, he told the Irish, might lead to the 'possible opposition of eminent Ministers' in the British Cabinet. Cosgrave also agreed that this difficult point 'should not be pressed'.[171]

There remained, however, the Boundary Commission itself. Technically, no one could stop the Commission from issuing its award, and Feetham was particularly keen to see its publication as the 'good faith of the tribunal was at stake'.[172] It took a meeting with Baldwin, Churchill, Cosgrave and Craig to persuade him to give up. Churchill admitted that the two Commissioners were being asked to make 'a great sacrifice'. They should know however, that due to their 'secret labours' this 'miracle of peace had come about'. Perhaps as 'an historical document', their report 'might some day appear'. But not now.[173]

Against such formidable opposition, the Boundary Commission's chairman could not stand. As a consolation, Feetham was to be granted a personal audience with George V. Baldwin also promised that a statement outlining the Commission's interpretation of its mandate could be published – but only after the 1925 agreement 'became an accomplished fact'.[174]

At 7.50 p.m., the leaders of the three governments met one last time to sign the new boundary agreement. There followed a dinner, hastily arranged by Churchill and Amery, before the Free Staters had to leave to catch the 8.45 train from Euston. At one point earlier in the evening, Cosgrave turned to Craig and said, 'One of us no doubt will hear from the other?' In fact, they never met again.[175]

Later that same evening, in a House of Commons swelled to its 'utmost capacity', Baldwin was cheered triumphantly as he entered to report the terms of the agreement.[176] Almost immediately, the negotiations were compared with that other great diplomatic triumph of the day, the Locarno treaties. 'To

---

170 Ibid.   171 CA/H/48–8th Minutes, 3 Dec. 1925, CAB 27/295.
172 CP 503(25), 3 Dec. 1925, CAB 27/295.   173 Ibid.
174 Ibid. Feetham to Mary Feetham, 16 Dec. 1925, RF, 6/1, ff. 61–3.
175 Ibid. CA/H/48–10th Minutes, 3 Dec. 1925, CAB 27/295. Amery diary, 2–3 Dec. 1925, p. 429.
Ervine, *Craigavon*, p. 508.
176 'Irish Peace. A Threefold Agreement', *The Times*, 4 Dec. 1925.

the "midnight Treaty", hastily negotiated in 1921', *The Times* commented, 'the new agreement stands as the Treaty of Locarno to the Treaty of Versailles, a proof of the growth of appeasement and conciliation.'[177] Arthur Balfour cast rather a more cynical eye over the settlement. For 'all their talk about the horrors of leaving a Roman Catholic population in the North and a Protestant population in the south', he observed, the two Irish governments found it more convenient to leave the border unchanged after all. The entire crisis, he told his sister, had been 'exquisitely comic'.[178]

THE PARLIAMENTARY DEBATES

Late on the afternoon of 8 December, MPs gathered at Westminster to ratify the Irish agreement. The 'general tone' of the Commons debate, wrote one reporter, was in the main 'quiet and peaceful' and stood 'in striking contrast to the fiery animosity of 1913, and also to the mournful apathy of 1920'. Northern Ireland's MPs were there 'in force'. But Lloyd George was absent. So was Ramsay MacDonald.[179]

Baldwin set the mood. The work of the Boundary Commission had not been in vain; simply put, it had proved to be 'beyond the power of mortal man' to devise a new arrangement. Ireland's border was 'an accident of history', he admitted, but accident it would stay. As for the Commission's report, it would be kept under lock and key. Only when the Irish boundary aroused 'about as much excitement in Ireland as Offa's Dyke or Hadrian's Wall' aroused in Britain would it see the light of day.[180]

Few words were spoken against the pact, and these focused mainly on the agreement to waive Article 5. J. H. Thomas's single contribution to the debate was that 'Irishmen, North and South, only agree when they are getting something from England.'[181] Another MP, Rosslyn Mitchell, attacked the government itself. Recalling the 'havoc, the tragedies, the misery, the woe and want'

---

177 'The Irish Agreement', *The Times*, 5 Dec. 1925. The Locarno treaties, named after the Swiss town in which they were signed, were a series of agreements aimed at stabilising Europe in the aftermath of the First World War. The most important of these treaties provided for an Anglo-Italian guarantee of the borders of France, Belgium, and Germany. See Dutton, *Chamberlain*, pp. 230–58.

178 A. J. to Alice Balfour, 4 Dec. 1925, AJB-S, GD 433/2/76, Reel 8.

179 'Irish Bill. Debate in the Commons', *The Times*, 9 Dec. 1925.

180 *HC Deb*, vol. 189, cols 309–21, 8 Dec. 1925. This last remark was a reference to two ancient boundaries, the first dividing England from Wales, the second England from Scotland. The Boundary Commission's report was released to the public on 1 Jan. 1968.

181 Ibid., cols 321–6.

that Conservatives had wrought by playing politics with the Irish Question, Mitchell said that Baldwin should have offered the agreement as an act of penance on behalf of his party.[182]

These 'sour and malignant reflections', Churchill told the Commons, did not befit the hour. It was, instead, time to look forward to a new day in Anglo-Irish relations. The agreement was ratified that same evening.[183]

Although Northern Ireland's Parliament was not required to approve the December pact, a debate was held on Craig's return to Belfast. Ulster's MPs were not as uncritical of the boundary agreement as is sometimes supposed. Aside from disappointment that East Donegal would not be transferred into Northern Ireland, Craig also had to announce the end of Britain's subsidy for the Special Constabulary. While the part-time 'B' Specials would be retained, the full-time 'A' and voluntary 'C-1' Specials would be abolished completely. This, said one MP, was 'the great drawback' of the agreement.

It was 'a matter of unspeakable regret to have to part with these men', Craig agreed, but they had no choice and were lucky for the settlement they had got. An additional £1.2 million would be contributed by the Treasury towards demobilisation of the force; at the same time, the British were forgiving a £700,000 loan for equipment. There was no hiding the fact that, given the ongoing depression, prospects for the Specials would be bleak. The most Craig could offer was a hope that businessmen in the province would recognise their 'moral responsibilities' to the disbanded constables. Barring that, he suggested that the former Specials might consider emigrating to the British dominions.[184]

Ulster's premier tried to sugar this bitter pill by making a general announcement about the Unemployment Re-insurance Scheme which had been negotiated the previous July. The effect was spoiled, though, because Craig could not divulge any details about the plan (the legislation had still not been introduced in the British Parliament) and because what he did say was, at best, ungracious. The imperial government, he told Ulster's assembly, had 'arranged to bear – I will not say a satisfactory share – because I am very hard to satisfy, but at all events a generous share of the burden which has been thrust upon us'. Hardly a ringing endorsement.[185] In any case, MPs were more interested in knowing why Craig had not pressed for a reduction or abolition of Northern Ireland's imperial contribution. It hardly seemed fair, Labour's Sam Kyle pointed out, that while their contribution remained in place, the Free State was totally absolved of its share of the British debt.[186]

182 Ibid., cols 330–1.

183 Ibid., cols 356–63. The agreement was ratified by the House of Lords the next day. See *HL Deb*, vol. 62, col. 1271, 9 Dec. 1925.

184 *NI HC Deb*, vol. 6, 1858–60, 1872–3, 9 Dec. 1925.

185 Ibid., cols 1860–2.   186 Ibid., cols 1865–9.

'THIS BARREN QUESTION': THE DÁIL DEBATE

Whatever criticism Craig faced in Belfast was nothing compared to the storm that awaited Cosgrave and his colleagues when they returned to Dublin. Demands for a referendum on the settlement were avoided only when Cosgrave declared that passage of the agreement was necessary to preserve public safety. Under the Free State's Constitution, this precluded such a vote from taking place.[187]

According to one contemporary estimate, those who opposed the agreement could expect to muster no more than 66 votes in the Dáil – and that included the abstentionist TDs from Sinn Féin. At least 74 TDs, meanwhile, were expected to back the government. But it was also noted that Cosgrave 'would not be satisfied with anything less than a two-thirds majority'. Failing that, 'a general election may become inevitable'.[188]

In other words, for the boundary agreement to be approved much depended on the course de Valera chose to take. A statement issued by the Sinn Féin leader assailed what he called this 'meditated crime', made worse because the Free Staters had 'sold our countrymen for the meanest of all considerations – a money consideration'.[189] However, there were considerations that de Valera himself thought worth bargaining over. In the wake of the agreement, he suggested that the Boundary Commission's award might indeed be worth trading – not for Article 5, but for those hated elements of the Treaty: the oath and the crown.[190] De Valera, then, had his own price when it came to selling out the Northern Nationalists.

Because the abstentionist TDs did not enter Dáil Éireann even at this crucial moment, the American consul in Dublin reported that debate on the 1925 agreement lacked 'the edge of final conviction'.[191] De Valera's official biographers later maintained that it would not have mattered if the abstentionist TDs had participated; in the Dáil's crucial vote on 10 December, the government won by a majority of 71 votes to 20.[192] The addition of Sinn Féin's 47 votes, however, would have taken the opposition to within a whisker of defeating the government. Given that William Magennis and a handful of other Cumann na nGaedheal TDs had already defected from the party, is it mere fancy to suppose that the dramatic entry of de Valera and his followers might have swayed other, former colleagues to join them in fighting the agreement?

---

187 Mansergh, *Unresolved Question*, p. 238.   188 Republican Activity', *The Times*, 9 Dec. 1925.

189 'Speech at Dublin', 6 Dec. 1925, FLK, de Valera Papers, File No. 347.

190 J. Bowman, *De Valera and the Ulster Question: 1917–1973* (Oxford, 1982), p. 91.

191 Mansergh, *Unresolved Question*, p. 238.

192 Longford and O'Neill, *Eamon de Valera*, p. 241. *Annual Register: 1925*, p. 141.

The suggestion cannot be dismissed out of hand. Even if it meant taking the oath, Austin Stack, that bitterest of abstentionists, 'was inclined to favour the idea . . . if our going in would defeat the proposal'. Would it not, he asked de Valera, 'be the end of the Free State?' And what better issue on which to defeat their opponents 'than Irish territorial integrity?'[193]

Instead, Sinn Féin's leader opted for a policy of wilful impotence. On 7 December, de Valera and 38 other Republican TDs held a joint meeting with Magennis, Labour's Tom Johnson and other members of the Dáil opposed to the settlement. Cahir Healy, T. J. Harbison and several Northern Irish priests also attended. Although 'strong pressure' was brought to bear on the Republicans, they steadfastly refused to take the fight into the Dáil itself. As Cosgrave had earlier predicted, this proved to be the Free Staters 'one safeguard – de Valera's lack of political foresight'.[194]

No matter what Sinn Féin's president might say, Ireland's unity meant less to him than party unity. 'For a united Ireland', de Valera had declared at the height of the boundary crisis, he and his followers 'would have been willing to go very far'[195] – but not that far, it seems, if it meant crossing the threshold of Leinster House.

Once Sinn Féin's entry into Dáil Éireann was no longer an issue, it was all over bar the shouting. According to one contemporary account, the Dáil's debate on the boundary agreement was 'equalled in intensity of feeling only by the historic Treaty debate of 1921'.[196] But even as the old arguments were being resurrected, Cosgrave summed up the feelings of many TDs when he declared that it was time 'to put this barren question of the boundary behind us once and for all'. Those who opposed the settlement were, in the end, brought up against one unalterable fact: they had no alternative.[197]

Beyond de Valera's own lack of resolve, what saved Cosgrave and his colleagues, at least for the moment, was sheer weariness. The people, declared one TD, 'are sick of these political and border questions. Should we not get back to business . . . when we are faced with problems of unemployment and bad trade in the country? In face of these matters, is it really not time to get back to our ordinary work?'[198]

---

193 Stack to de Valera, 4 Dec. 1925, FLK, de Valera Papers, File No. 1521.

194 'Irish Republican Activity', *The Times*, 9 Dec. 1925. Jones diary, 25 Nov. 1925, vol. III, p. 237.

195 'Speech at Dublin', 6 Dec. 1925, FLK, de Valera Papers, File No. 347.

196 'Executive's Hopes Exceeded', *The Irish Times*, 12 Dec. 1925.

197 *Dáil Deb*, vol. 13, col. 1306, 1314, 7 Dec. 1925.

198 *Dáil Deb*, vol. 13, col. 1964, 15 Dec. 1925.

'A LAST WORD'

On 18 December Richard Feetham boarded RMS *Saxon* to begin the long journey back to South Africa. That same day his justification of the Boundary Commission's work was published in newspapers throughout the British Isles. *The Times* called his defence 'a dignified and impressive answer' to the months of abuse hurled at the Boundary Commission and at its chairman in particular. Although the Commission's report was suppressed, the newspaper was glad that Feetham had been given the 'solace' of having 'a last word' in this chapter of Irish history.[199]

Feetham's wounded pride had, indeed, been soothed. Writing to his sister while on board ship, he noted triumphantly, 'I did get a little say in the end.'[200] Not everyone, though, was so charitable about Feetham's 'elaborate summary', or about the tribunal he had led. 'Peace', the *Morning Post* told its readers, 'can best be promoted now by forgetting that the Boundary Commission ever existed.'[201]

Whatever regrets Feetham may have harboured about his involvement with the Boundary Commission were nothing compared with the feelings of Northern Nationalists. 'Not a thought was given to the denial of our civil rights', a group of their representatives protested. 'Not a word about our political prisoners, our educational difficulties, or our social disabilities' was in the agreement. What Cosgrave and O'Higgins had signed in London, Cahir Healy later said, was 'a betrayal' of every promise made to the Ulster Nationalists since 1921. He was bitter most of all at the loss of the Council of Ireland, believing that with it 'the last hope of unity' in his lifetime had disappeared.[202]

The loss of the Council of Ireland has been called 'an unmitigated disaster' for Northern Nationalists.[203] But even if Craig had not raised the issue, the British probably would have, as they were also anxious to be rid of the forum.[204] At the same time, it would be wrong to dismiss the promise of joint Irish Cabinet meetings as an empty gesture. When recommending the settlement to their respective parliaments, all three leaders plainly expected that the conferences would be a part of Ireland's political landscape.[205] Others agreed.

---

199 'Irish Boundary. Commissioners on Their Task'; and 'The Boundary Commission – A Last Word', *The Times*, 18 Dec. 1925.

200 Richard to Mary Feetham, 22 Dec. 1925, RF, 6/1, ff. 63a–63d.

201 'Mr. Justice Feetham's Apologia', *Morning Post*, 18 Dec. 1925.

202 '"Callously Betrayed"' and 'Agreement Signed in London. Present Boundary Line to Remain', *Ulster Herald*, 12 Dec. 1925.

203 Phoenix, *Northern Nationalism*, p. 332.

204 'Irish Boundary', Whiskard memorandum, 26 Nov. 1925, CO 537/1106/54045.

205 *NI HC Deb*, vol. 6, col. 1863, 9 Dec. 1925. *HC Deb*, vol. 189, cols 318–19, 8 Dec. 1925. *Dáil Deb*, vol. 13, col. 1313, 7 Dec. 1925.

Sam Kyle, for instance, hoped that the meetings would lead to 'reciprocal arrangements' to promote employment, while *The Times* told readers that 'any impulse to partition was more than counterbalanced by the new provisions as to mutual consultations'.[206] Perhaps most tellingly, civil servants on both sides of the border worked for some time on the assumption that the conferences would take place.[207]

What was lacking was both the will and the machinery to make this part of the agreement work. Once the crisis was over, there was little incentive in Dublin, and even less in Belfast, to build on the idea, while there were a good many reasons for walking away from it. Cosgrave saw nothing attractive in an arrangement that might infringe Irish sovereignty, while Craig found it easier to placate extremists by turning down even ceremonial invitations to visit the Free State capital.[208] Even if these hurdles could have been overcome, the mutual suspicion and jealousy between both sides might have been insurmountable. The meetings were supposed to take place 'as and when necessary', fine words so long as Belfast and Dublin agreed on what constituted a matter for joint action. But what if they differed?

What is harder to defend is that the Free Staters allowed the focus of the talks to shift entirely from the effects of partition to the question of Article 5. Cosgrave apparently convinced himself that the tribunal charged with apportioning Ireland's share of Britain's debt would leave the Free State crippled by years of payments to the imperial Treasury. To be sure, until the very end Churchill was adamant that the British would not waive Article 5.[209] Yet the Free Staters had a rough and ready answer to these demands. Simply put, one Irish civil servant wrote in September, 'we have no contribution to give them'.[210] Even Balfour, a man of little sympathy when it came to the Irish, recognised that conditions in the Free State were such that 'she could not pay her debts to us' even if Cosgrave and his colleagues wanted to.[211]

Craig was equally sceptical. 'You'll never get a bob under clause 5', he told Baldwin at one point during the negotiations.[212] Ulster's leader was, of course, working towards his own ends in suggesting that the British give up on Article 5.

206 Ibid., *NI HC Deb*, cols 1865–6. 'Irish Bill. Debate in the Commons', *The Times*, 9 Dec. 1925.

207 Stephens to O'Hegarty, 12 Jan. 1926, D/T, S 4743(A). Quekett to Martin-Jones, 15 Mar. 1926, HO 45/12341/2.

208 Lyons, *Ireland Since the Famine*, p. 487. Fanning, *Independent Ireland*, p. 92. Mansergh, *Unresolved Question*, p. 238.

209 CA/H/48–2nd and 5th Minutes, 1 and 2 Dec. 1925, CAB 27/295.

210 Fitzgerald to Brennan, 8 Sept. 1925, quoted in Fanning, *Irish Department of Finance*, p. 163.

211 A. J. to Alice Balfour, 4 Dec. 1925, AJB-S, GD 433/2/76, Reel 8.

212 Jones diary, 29 Nov. 1925, vol. III, p. 242.

In any case, once negotiations began to concentrate on these financial questions attention shifted away from the boundary and from the plight of Northern Nationalists. For if they and, to a lesser extent, the Free Staters were the big losers in the 1925 agreement, then Ulster Unionists – and especially Craig – were its biggest winners. Craig was certainly pleased with what he had got, knowing that he had given nothing in return. He told hiswife that 'in his wildest dreams he had never expected to be able to keep Ulster completely intact, without some give and take'.[213]

For that he had Churchill to thank. Craig knew as much, telling Churchill that he had 'done the right thing in a big way'.[214] Others agreed that the outcome of the talks had hinged on the chancellor of the exchequer. 'Winston really did all the work', Amery wrote. Tom Jones's assessment was much the same. 'Chamberlain was important at the early and Churchill at the later meetings', he confided in his diary. 'Birkenhead' was 'always big and helpful', Amery and Joynson-Hicks less so.[215] Salisbury's contribution was almost wholly negative. On at least one occasion, he bolted from the talks rather than be a party to the decisions being reached.[216]

By solving the boundary dispute, Churchill may have saved the Conservative Party from another Irish disaster. Ever since Bonar Law's acceptance of the Treaty on becoming prime minister in 1922, successive Conservative governments had been torn between their legal obligations to carry out the settlement and their 'moral obligation' to the Ulster Unionists.[217] These conflicting responsibilities could be ignored so long as the British were able to delay facing up to the boundary question. But when that was no longer possible, doubts over whether the Tories would implement the Boundary Commission's award actually made matters worse. Unionists came to believe that if they protested 'loudly enough' no Conservative government would dare face them down. This impression, one civil servant warned, made it certain that the Unionists would 'not merely protest against, but [would] resist' changes to the boundary – with the Specials to back them up.[218]

---

213 Lady Craig's diary, 3 Dec. 1925, D/1415/B/38.   214 IA (25) 11, 3 Dec. 1925, CAB 27/295.

215 Amery diary, 2–3 Dec. 1925, p. 429. Jones diary, 3 Dec. 1925, vol. III, p. 245. P. J. Grigg praised Birkenhead's 'balanced and cool judgment'. See *Prejudice and Judgment* (London, 1948), p. 209.

216 CA/H/48–6th Minutes, 2 Dec. 1925, CAB 27/295. Also, see Ervine, *Craigavon*, p. 503. Nevertheless, Salisbury was angry that he was not asked to sign the final agreement. See Baldwin to Salisbury, 3 Dec. 1925, S(4) 115/92.

217 Amery was particularly sensitive about this issue. See IA (25) 3, 18 Nov. 1925, CAB 27/295.

218 'Irish Boundary Commission', Whiskard memorandum, ? Nov. 1925, CO 537/1096/50285. British officials considered disarming the Specials prior to the Commission's report, only to discover that they were powerless to do so. See Tallents to Buckland, 10 Oct. 1925, HO 45/12296/80(a).

In that case, Lord Beaverbrook outlined what might have happened next: 'the British government would have had to enforce the new boundary against violent Ulster resistance; and 90% of the English Conservatives would have backed Ulster against their own leaders'. If, as many at the time were predicting, Fermanagh and Tyrone were handed over to the Free State – then, Beaverbrook wrote, Baldwin's second 'ministry would have fallen'.[219]

However much this was wishful thinking on Beaverbrook's part, the danger was real enough. Speaking in the House of Lords on 9 December, Birkenhead admitted that everyone who had signed the Treaty of 1921 knew 'that in Article 12 there lurked the elements of dynamite'.[220] For over four years this bomb, in the form of the Boundary Commission's award, had threatened to go off in their midst wreaking havoc in British affairs. At long last, the bomb had been defused. As Churchill said after the 1925 agreement was signed, the boundary question 'which has always hung over us', which baffled governments since before the Great War, 'this boundary question is absolutely settled'.[221] The passions and bitterness that Ireland had aroused in the bosom of British politics were gone. Forever.

But Baldwin was taking no chances. The papers on the boundary negotiations were bundled together and put in the care of the ever-trustworthy Tom Jones. Before shelving the Irish Question away, for all time he hoped, Jones scrawled a warning to himself and to anyone else who might be tempted to re-open this Pandora's box: 'S. B asked me to keep these papers from his sight', Jones wrote – 'and from everybody else's'.[222]

---

219 Beaverbrook to Brisbane, 30 Nov. 1925, BBK C/64.
220 *HL Deb*, vol. 62, col. 1232, 9 Dec. 1925.
221 'Irish Peace. A Threefold Agreement', *The Times*, 4 Dec. 1925.
222 'Boundary Commission', ? Dec. 1925, TJ GG/4/1.

EPILOGUE

'THE HARVEST GATHERED IN'

We must not expect too much. . . . But neither, I think, need we expect to
see too little. There very probably are members here in this chamber
now who will live in a new Parliament to see the harvest gathered in,
and who will find at the side of Britain a free and united Ireland.
WINSTON CHURCHILL[1]

—

Towards the end of 1928, Britain's chancellor of the exchequer was hard at work, writing the last volume of his history of the First World War. Before going to print with *The Aftermath*, however, Winston Churchill asked Sir John Anderson to peruse its contents. 'I have read and re-read your Irish Chapters', Anderson replied from his perch in the Home Office, 'and have refreshed my own recollection of events which, though they are only a few years old, now seem quite remote'.[2]

Anderson was not the only one who was surprised at how quickly the parishes of Fermanagh and Tyrone had, in Churchill's own memorable phrase, 'faded into the mists and squalls of Ireland'.[3] Viewed from London, it was indeed amazing that the dispute that had dominated British politics for forty years was so soon a distant memory. No one felt this transformation more keenly than did Stanley Baldwin. Just weeks after signing the 1925 boundary agreement, he reported that the House of Commons was now able 'to spend many hours discussing Irish affairs in an atmosphere of calm and moderation'. The change, he told George V, 'is a pleasant contrast compared with former times'.[4]

Even so, it would have been no more true to say that Baldwin 'conjured' the Irish Question out of existence than had Lloyd George.[5] Ireland dominated British public life for so long because the country's politics had fractured. This was true not only of the left, of the struggle between Labour and the Liberals

1   *HC Deb*, vol. 189, col. 363, 8 Dec. 1925.   2   Anderson to Churchill, 29 Nov. 1928, HO 317/70.
3   Churchill, *World Crisis*: vol. 1, p. 205.
4   Baldwin to George V, 23 Feb. 1926, SB vol. 61, ff. 498–503.   5   Taylor, *English History*, p. 161.

and, in the latter case, between the supporters of Asquith and Lloyd George. Until 1924, the cleavage in the Conservative Party was no less a threat to its long-term survival. As Maurice Cowling has pointed out, had the Tories split into two parties at the 1922 election, 'almost anything might have happened'.[6]

Instead, following his party's landslide two years later, Baldwin emerged as the first prime minister since 1910 to command an overwhelming, and loyal, parliamentary majority. That was something that never could have been said about the topsy-turvy world of the Lloyd George Coalition. At the same time, when it came to its Irish policy, Baldwin's government faced no real opposition in or out of Parliament. Labour was ambivalent about Ireland's problems, and after 1924 it did not much matter where Liberals stood on the question. This explains Baldwin's triumph.

Yet the settlement fashioned between 1920 and 1925 did not resolve the Irish Question so much as sweep it to one side. As a practical solution to the dispute between Irish nationalists and Ulster Unionists, partition ultimately failed. Left behind, left unreconciled, was 'an uncomfortably large Catholic minority' within the six counties. This minority was not small enough to be absorbed into Northern Ireland's wider community, nor was it large enough to force the Belfast government to deal with it on equal terms. The Boundary Commission's failure to address this issue only made matters worse, leaving behind 'deep scars on the landscape and in the human mind'.[7]

Nor did the events of this period really settle the other critical problems that separated Dublin from Belfast, and Belfast from London. This was clear from the very beginning. For, despite his pledge to 'promote cordial relations' with the Free Staters, it was soon evident that Craig was up to his old tricks.[8]

When outlining the December boundary agreement to Ulster's Parliament, Craig had announced that 'as an act of grace' he had agreed to a British review of the convictions of Nationalists imprisoned by his government.[9] Cosgrave understood this to mean that the prisoners would be released in time for Christmas, as a gesture of goodwill. Yet, despite the fact that the Free State president had himself delivered a list of prisoners' names when the issue was raised as far back as August, on 23 December Leo Amery had to tell James MacNeill that Belfast authorities had still not turned over the promised

6　Cowling, *Impact of Labour*, pp. 419–20.

7　J. Neville, H. Douglas, and P. A. Compton, 'The Northern Ireland–Irish Republic Boundary', *Espace, Populations, Sociétés*, no. 2, 1992, p. 218. For a contrary view, see Clare O'Halloran's *Partition and the Limits of Irish Nationalism: An Ideology Under Stress* (Dublin, 1987), in which she argues that partition was inevitable – the result of history, sectarian hostility and, even, different climates in North and South.

8　Craig to Baldwin, 21 Dec. 1925, SB vol. 99, ff. 287.

9　*NI HC Deb*, vol. 6, col. 1858, 9 Dec. 1925.

reports.[10] Officials in Amery's own department also took a lackadaisical approach to the prisoners' release. After all, one civil servant in the Dominions Office wrote, Craig had not agreed to an 'amnesty' but only to a 'review' of the disputed cases. 'An amnesty', this official pointed out, 'could of course be effected by a stroke of the pen, but a review, however sympathetic, must necessarily take a little time'.[11]

Any goodwill that might have been gained from the prisoners' release was lost by the time they were finally set free in late January.[12] And, but for Baldwin's personal intervention, the gesture would have been further undermined by Northern Ireland's home minister. On their release, Richard Dawson Bates intended to serve exclusion orders on the freed prisoners, prohibiting them from living in the six counties.[13] Baldwin was incensed when word of the proposal reached him. Without waiting to consult his Cabinet colleagues, he fired off a telegram to Craig telling him that the exclusions were 'in effect a further penalty' on the detainees and, as well, were 'inconsistent both with the professions contained' in the December agreement 'and with the exercise of royal clemency'.[14] S. G. Tallents personally delivered the telegram to Craig who, reading it 'with a twinkle in his eye', seems to have expected Baldwin's reaction. According to Ulster's premier, the exclusion orders were conceived by Dawson Bates and himself 'chiefly for the protection' of the detainees. If the orders were not to be issued, that was fine by them. They simply wished to free the Northern government from responsibility 'in case any untoward events here followed the releases'.[15]

Craig, however, seems to have realised that he had overstepped his bounds. The next day he wrote to Baldwin to deny that he had any intention of 'cutting across' the December agreement and again stressed that the exclusion orders had been proposed for the protection of the soon-to-be-released prisoners. With 'our meagre police forces', he claimed, 'we are quite unable to afford personal protection to so large a number of marked men'.[16] This argument neatly underscored Craig's insistence that the Ulster Special Constabulary was needed to secure law and order in the province; perhaps, he was saying in effect, disbanding large sections of the force was not such a good idea after all. As it was, dissolving the Special Constabulary had proved to be more difficult

10 Amery to MacNeill, 23 Dec. 1925, SB vol. 99, ff. 18.
11 Whiskard to Waterhouse, 24 Dec. 1925, SB vol. 99, ff. 15.
12 Whiskard to Waterhouse, 9 Jan. 1926, SB vol. 99, ff. 27–8.
13 Magill to Anderson, CP 18(26), 20 Jan. 1926, CAB 24/178.
14 Ibid., Baldwin to Craig, 21 Jan. 1926.
15 Tallents to Anderson, 22 Jan. 1926, HO 267/191.
16 Craig to Baldwin, 22 Jan. 1926, SB vol. 99, ff. 32.

than Craig anticipated. While disbanding of the 'C-1' force took place without trouble, opposition within the ranks of the 'A' Specials verged on mutiny
before they accepted the inevitable.[17]

Significantly, while these two branches of the Special Constabulary were
abolished, the 'B' Specials were not. As Michael Farrell has pointed out, this
branch of the Specials was the one most resented by Northern Nationalists
and, therefore, the one Free State leaders would have been most anxious to see
disbanded.[18] Throughout the boundary negotiations, O'Higgins in particular
complained about the Specials, going so far as to say that abolishing the force
was a more immediate concern to Northern Nationalists than reinstituting
proportional representation. Since the 'B' force constituted far and away the
largest segment of the Special Constabulary, it is fair to assume that they were
the ones O'Higgins had uppermost in his mind.[19] It is true that Craig had
declared the previous April that the 'B' Specials would remain in being so long
as he was prime minister.[20] Nevertheless, it was Churchill's understanding,
which he repeated to the Free Staters on more than one occasion, that all of
the Specials would be disbanded once the boundary crisis was resolved.[21] No
exception was made for the 'B' Specials then or later when, as chancellor of the
exchequer, he asked Parliament to appropriate £1.2 million for 'the winding up
of the Special Constabulary'.[22] Once again, there seemed to be less to Craig's
promises than met the eye.

Churchill may have been willing to overlook Craig's sleight-of-hand when
it came to the 'B' Specials. It was, after all, no longer a Treasury concern once
maintaining the force was left solely to Ulster's government. He was not
willing to turn a blind eye, however, when it came to Britain's subsidy of
Northern Ireland's unemployment insurance fund. On 3 February 1926,
Churchill had to report that data supplied by Northern Ireland's Ministry of
Labour, information on which the Cabinet had approved Anderson's re-
insurance scheme the previous August, 'had proved wholly fallacious'. Instead
of an unemployment rate of 20 per cent, the ministry now claimed the figure

17   Lady Craig's diary, 14 Dec. 1925, D.1415/B/38. Farrell, *Arming the Protestants*, pp. 252–75.

18   Farrell, *Arming the Protestants*, p. 254.

19   CA/H/48-3rd Minutes, 1 Dec. 1925, CAB 27/295. Also, see IA (25)) 6, 28 Nov. 1925; and
CA/H/48-2nd and 5th Minutes, 1–2 Dec. 1925, CAB 27/295. The Free Staters drew a clear distinction
between the 'A' Specials, which they largely regarded as a professional force, and the 'B' and 'C-1'
Specials, which they did not. See 'Notes of a Meeting at the Dominions Office', 28 July 1925, HO
45/12296/75(b).

20   See chapter 9.

21   CA/H/48-3rd and 5th Minutes, 1–2 Dec. 1925, CAB 27/295.

22   *HC Deb*, vol. 189, cols 361–2, 8 Dec. 1925. The 'B' Specials would not be disbanded until 1970, half
a century after they were created to relieve British troops engaged in the Anglo-Irish War.

was 24 per cent. Moreover, Churchill had budgeted no more than £600,000 to cover the Treasury's first contribution to the fund, and had only agreed to Anderson's scheme on the understanding that any subsidy of the Ulster fund would never exceed £650,000 in any given year. Yet Belfast officials now claimed they would need at least £1.3 million for the present year, and over £800,000 for the year after that. It was inexplicable, Churchill told his colleagues, 'how the comparatively small percentage increase in unemployment' could account for this 'sudden and alarming increase' in the British Treasury's liability.[23]

Churchill was not the only one who was suspicious. The Cabinet committee charged with handling this problem warned their Northern Ireland counterparts that unless 'a satisfactory explanation' could be given to explain the discrepancy, British support for Northern Ireland's unemployment fund would be reconsidered.[24] The threat worked. Several days later, Churchill was able to report that instead of the £1.3 million initially asked for, Craig had agreed to request no more than Churchill's maximum offer of £650,000. Beyond that, the Ulster leader also had to agree that if his government ever again put forward a request for more than £1 million in any given year, officials in London would have the right to reconsider British subsidy of the fund.[25]

Shortly before this agreement was reached, Northern Ireland's finance minister confidently predicted to Churchill that Ulster's unemployment fund would 'show a great improvement in future years'.[26] In fact, Northern Ireland's economy would not spring to life until the Second World War. At Stormont, it was admitted that partition played a large role in exacerbating these conditions. Before the erection of the Free State's customs barrier in 1923, markets in the South had been of 'paramount importance' to a number of Ulster businesses. 'In the course of the succeeding 15 years', one official wrote, 'Northern Ireland now finds herself virtually excluded from the Irish Free State market', making the prospects for finding work in the province that much more bleak.[27]

As Ulster's unemployment fund lurched about in the worsening economic conditions of the 1930s, it was kept afloat only because of continuing increases of the British subsidy.[28] This result, however, should have surprised no one. Ulster officials had themselves argued to the Colwyn Committee that the

23 NIU (26)-1st Conclusions, 3 Feb. 1926, CAB 27/279.

24 Ibid.

25 'Unemployment Insurance (Northern Ireland) Agreement', CP 47(26), 8 Feb. 1926, CAB 27/279.

26 Pollock to Churchill, 6 Feb. 1926, HO 45/13743/24.

27 'Note by the Government of Northern Ireland', ? Jan. 1938, T 160/747/F.14026/04/1.

28 Mansergh, *Unresolved Question*, p. 247. Even so, Craig continued to deny that the province was a drain on the imperial exchequer. Quite the reverse. See, e.g., 'Ulster and the Empire. Lord Craigavon on Loyalty', *The Times*, 27 Aug. 1934.

province's unemployment rate was, as it had been 'for many years, at least 50% more than in Great Britain'.[29] Given this record, only a miracle would have enabled Northern Ireland to pay its own way when it came to providing these services. Craig's demand for parity in social service provision was meant to serve a larger purpose: namely, to satisfy 'the desire of the government and people of Northern Ireland to remain in the closest possible association with Great Britain'.[30] Or, to put it another way, to differentiate the six counties as much as possible from the rest of Ireland.

Craig's efforts in this field must be counted a resounding success, a success that can be gauged by the reactions that it provoked not only at the time but long after he was dead. Sir Warren Fisher, who by 1938 was Whitehall's most senior civil servant, seldom missed an opportunity to point out that British finances would 'gain greatly from the termination of the present wholly uneconomic partition' of Ireland.[31] Three and a half decades later, Fisher's words would be repeated almost verbatim when the then-Cabinet Secretary noted that if 'the six counties ceased to be British . . . the net saving to public expenditure would be considerable'.[32]

When it came to his other efforts to entrench partition, Craig's legacy was rather more equivocal. In 1929 the last vestiges of proportional representation were abolished, this time for elections to Northern Ireland's parliament. Earlier, Joe Devlin bitterly denounced the decision in a speech to his fellow Ulster MPs. Abolition, he warned, would '[m]aintain and foster our divisions, keep alive the old religious rancours and hatreds' and continue 'all those evils that have cursed Ireland for the last century'.[33]

But Craig was as unmoved by Devlin's speech as he was by similar pleas for fairness from Protestant Labour MPs. Ulster's premier was determined to have a two-way fight in his parliament. Or, as he put it: 'What I want to get in this House . . . under the old-fashioned plain and simple system, are men who are for the Union on the one hand or who are against it and want to go into a Dublin Parliament on the other.'[34] Left unstated, at least by Craig, was the fact that in any such fight his party was bound to win. All the time.

29 Clark to Piercy, 5 Sept. 1923, W-E, MSS Eng. hist., c. 913, ff. 123–6.

30 'Memorandum Submitted by the Government of Northern Ireland Who Ask to be Included in the British Scheme', ? June 1925, SSA (25)-2, CAB 27/279. Also, see Londonderry to Churchill, 6 May 1938, WSC 2/347/13.

31 See Fisher note written at the bottom of S. D. Waley memorandum, 14 Jan. 1938, T 160/747/F.14026/04/1.

32 O. Bowcott, 'Heath was Urged to Share Ulster with Dublin', *The Guardian*, 1 Jan. 2002.

33 *NI HC Deb*, vol. 8, col. 2278, 25 Oct. 1927.

34 Ibid., col. 2276.

Even sympathetic writers have had to admit that Craig's abolition of PR was 'a major act of misgovernment'. As it soon became clear that a majority of constituencies would always return Unionist candidates and a minority would always return Nationalists, the number of uncontested elections shot up. Elections soon became a mere 'formality', as occurred in 1933, when 27 of the 52 seats to Ulster's House of Commons were uncontested by anti-government candidates. The crude reality, two historians of the later 'Troubles' pointed out, was that Craig's party had won the election 'before a vote was cast'. Condemned to perpetual opposition, it is hardly surprising that over time some Nationalists and, even, some Protestant Labour politicians, began to question whether it was 'worth while treading a constitutional path'.[35]

Ensuring Unionist control at all levels of government meant the drawing and redrawing of electoral boundaries to favour the party's candidates. This insistence on electoral domination came from grassroots Unionists as well as from those in the higher echelons of the party. Some demands were so egregious that implementing them, Dawson Bates admitted, would have made the government liable to a charge of 'indecent gerrymandering'.[36] Simply put, Unionists were unwilling to accept 'the consequences of being in a minority'. This was nowhere more true than in Londonderry. There, a government-backed scheme in 1936 guaranteed that roughly 10,000 Nationalist voters elected no more than eight city councillors, while roughly 7,500 Unionists elected 12 councillors to Derry's governing body.[37]

Ironically, Craig's determination to create in Northern Ireland a politics based on a clear – if unequal – choice between Unionism and nationalism proved to be its own undoing. Retaining control of local government necessitated widespread discrimination. This was particularly true when it came to housing, since the right to vote in local elections was based on home-ownership. All of these issues – housing discrimination, limitations on the right to vote, and gerrymandered electoral districts – would play a crucial role in igniting the civil rights movement that exploded in the late 1960s.

Nor, in the end, was Craig ultimately successful in burying proportional representation. After the resumption of direct rule from London, PR was reintroduced for local elections in 1973. Foremost among the guarantees of the

---

35 Buckland, *Factory of Grievances*, pp. 227–8. D. McKittrick and D. McVea, *Making Sense of the Troubles: The Story of the Conflict in Northern Ireland* (Chicago, 2002), p. 9. According to John Coakley, 'At the 12 elections from 1921 to 1969 the Unionist majority in the House of Commons averaged 69.9% of the membership of the house and never fell below 61.5%'. See J. Coakley, ed. *Changing Shades of Orange and Green: Redefining the Union and the Nation in Contemporary Ireland* (Dublin, 2003), p. 8.

36 Dawson Bates to Craig, 24 July 1934, PRONI CAB/9B/13/2.

37 Buckland, *Factory of Grievances*, pp. 232, 245.

Good Friday Agreement of 1998 was the establishment of a Northern Ireland Assembly, whose members would also be elected by PR. More than that, the Agreement created a ten-member Executive which would itself be composed on a proportional basis.[38]

For the better part of the twentieth century, however, partition distorted public life throughout Ireland. The existence of an issue 'of such apparent importance' often meant that other troubling problems (e.g., unemployment) could be 'squeezed off the agenda' by politicians schooled in the arts of Civil War politics in the South or sectarian politics in the North.[39]

As it happened, the Boundary Commission debacle did not convince all Free State politicians that the time had come to abandon their hopes for some form of Irish union. While attending the Imperial Conference in London at the end of 1926, Kevin O'Higgins privately approached several leading Conservatives and Unionists with an alternative to partition.[40] As outlined by Leo Amery, O'Higgins proposed creating a dual monarchy similar to the Austro-Hungarian model, with the king of Great Britain crowned separately in Dublin as king of a united Ireland. O'Higgins had, in essence, resurrected the very same idea that Arthur Griffith had put forward as long ago as 1904 and which was the original programme advocated by Sinn Féin. Initially, Amery felt that the proposal ought to be explored. As he pointed out in a letter to Craig, a united Irish state 'strengthened by the cooperation of Ulster would be better than the present division', both for Ireland and for the empire as a whole. The Free Staters, he told Baldwin separately, 'want the union of Ireland more than anything else in the world and that means that Craig can dictate his terms'.[41]

But Craig was having nothing to do with 'these mischievous proposals' which, he was certain, 'would set Ulster ablaze' if made public. Whatever the imperial government might think, Craig's 'considered opinion' was that 'the interests of Ulster, Ireland as a whole, Great Britain and the Empire' were best served by his country's continued partition. Time, the Ulster Unionist leader declared, 'has only strengthened me in this attitude'.[42]

---

38   J. Ruane and J. Todd, ed. *After the Good Friday Agreement: Analysing Political Change in Northern Ireland* (Dublin, 1999), p. 14. Also, see 'The Electoral System of Northern Ireland', Oct. 1970, HO 221/180.

39   D. Pringle, 'Partition, Politics and Social Conflict', in Carter and Parker, *Ireland*, p. 48.

40   According to Terence de Vere White, O'Higgins initially approached Carson about this idea, 'acting on impulse and without disclosing his plan to anyone'. See *O'Higgins*, pp. 225–6.

41   Amery to Craig, 11 Dec. 1926, PRONI, CAB/9Z/8/1. Amery to Baldwin, 13 Dec. 1926, SB vol. 101, ff. 210–11.

42   Craig to Baldwin, 16 Dec. 1926, PRONI, CAB/9Z/8/1.

Aside from these objections, O'Higgins's scheme ran into determined opposition within the British Cabinet, not least from Austen Chamberlain. Having just accepted the idea that the Dominions were equal in status but still linked to Great Britain through the bond of a common monarchy, Chamberlain protested that O'Higgins's proposal ran 'directly counter to all that was said and done at the imperial conference'.[43]

That finished the matter. Amery beat a hasty retreat, washing his hands of the entire idea. In January the concept of a dual monarchy was disposed of once and for all, with Baldwin assuring the Cabinet that 'nothing more was likely to be heard of this proposal'.[44] He was closer to the truth than he knew. Six months later, O'Higgins was gunned down by Republicans while walking to church. Ironically, the first person to reach him was Eoin MacNeill, whose political career had been ruined when O'Higgins used the Boundary Commission crisis to force him out of the Free State government.[45]

The offer of a dual monarchy was the last serious attempt by any Free State leader to reunify Ireland. The question that begs to be asked, even if it can never adequately be answered, is this: Would the outcome have been any different if the state's two founders, Griffith and Collins, had lived? The ghosts of both men haunted the Dáil's debate on the 1925 boundary agreement, as both opposition and government attempted to claim their support from beyond the grave.[46] Certainly, the two would have been better placed to fight their country's corner than were any of their successors. As neither Cosgrave nor O'Higgins had participated in the Treaty negotiations, any claims they made about pledges given in 1921 were easily dismissed by the British as hearsay. At the same time, claims made by Austen Chamberlain, Birkenhead, and Churchill as to what was intended by the Treaty's clauses on Northern Ireland went virtually unchallenged by the Free State's leaders.[47] Even before the Boundary Commission debacle, Thomas Johnson had put his finger on the problem. The weakness of Cosgrave's government was that it 'tended to interpret the Treaty not in the manner that was promised in the Dáil debates of 1921 and 1922, but . . . in the manner desired by the British signatories rather than the Irish signatories'.[48]

43 'Note by the Secretary of State for Foreign Affairs', CP 423(26), 18 Dec. 1926, DO/117/51/13477.
44 C 4 (27), 26 Jan. 1927, CAB 23/54.
45 M. Tierney, *Eoin MacNeill: Scholar and Man of Action, 1867–1945* (Oxford, 1980), pp. 358–9.
46 *Dáil Deb*, vol. 13, 7–10 Dec. 1925. See, e.g., cols 1371, 1426, 1433–6, 1470–1, 1480, 1605, 1641, 1670, 1692–4, 1716, 1750, 1758, 1759.
47 See, e.g., CA/H/48-1st and 2nd Minutes, 26 Nov., 1 Dec. 1925, CAB 27/295.
48 *Dáil Deb*, vol. 8, col. 2557, 15 Oct. 1924.

The historian Nicholas Mansergh once observed that Collins was 'psycho-
logically committed' to Northern Nationalists, while Eamon Phoenix has
written that 'Collins stands out as the only Sinn Féin leader for whom partition and the plight of the Northern Nationalists were major concerns'.[49] The
same should be said of Griffith in both instances. Their commitment stands
in marked contrast to the 'indifferent' attitude of their successors, a change
noted as early as 1923.[50] It is hard to imagine either man sitting still had they
been alive to hear Cosgrave claim that the Boundary Commission was never
meant 'to do more than relieve the situation of some of its difficulties'.[51]

Having said all that, it is by no means clear that Griffith or Collins would
have been any more successful in their attempts to bring about Irish unity.
Two of the policy options that they might have pursued (the erection of
economic barriers and the Boundary Commission) were tried, and failed.[52] As
a third option, Collins might have been willing to risk war with the North, the
direction in which he was headed until the onset of the Civil War. Indeed,
Collins told members of the Northern IRA that he would never recognise
partition, 'even though it might mean smashing the Treaty'.[53] Had a war
strategy been pursued, however, it is certain that the conflict would have
involved Britain long before the Free Staters could have achieved any of their
goals. In the meantime, conditions for Ulster's Catholics, especially those
living in Belfast, would have been far worse than anything they had already
experienced during the violent spring of 1922.[54]

If, somehow, all-out resumption of the Anglo-Irish War could have been
avoided, Collins might have sparked yet another crisis by threatening to declare
a republic when, finally, his patience had worn out over delays at settling the
boundary question. But, again, it is hardly likely that such a threat would have
done anything to bring about Irish unity, especially if Bonar Law was by then
head of the British government. So far as the 26 counties were concerned,
Bonar Law 'saw no objection to their establishing a republic'.[55] On the contrary, the fact that such a move would have further widened the gap between

49 Mansergh, *Unresolved Question*, p. 225. Phoenix, *Northern Nationalism*, p. 395.

50 Watt to Spender, 13 April 1923, PRONI, CAB9B/182.

51 *Dáil Deb*, vol. 13, col. 1300, 7 Dec. 1925. Also, see col. 1716, 10 Dec. 1925.

52 For Collins's belief that a tariff policy would end partition, see Collins to Walsh, 7 Feb. 1922, D/T,
S 9241.

53 'Report of 2nd Northern Division in 1922', 8 Apr. 1925, Thomas Johnson Papers, MSS 17,143.
Also, see Woods to Mulcahy, 29 Sept. 1922, RM, P7/B/287.

54 Phoenix, *Northern Nationalism*, pp. 395–6, holds Collins responsible for the Provisional
Government's 'complicated and confusing policy' towards the North.

55 Borden to Beaverbrook, 9 Oct. 1924, BBK C/51.

his beloved Ulster and the rest of Ireland, as indeed happened when the Irish republic was declared in 1949, would have pleased Bonar Law very much.

Griffith and Collins failed themselves and their country by assuming that they and their British counterparts in the Treaty negotiations would be around long enough to implement the settlement that they had hammered out. No one, of course, could have foreseen that less than a year after the Treaty was signed both Griffith and Collins would be dead, the Coalition toppled, and southern Ireland torn apart by a vicious civil war. That said, too much of what was agreed in London was based on understandings with the Coalition's leaders and a belief that the Ulster question would be settled sooner rather than later. Any delay was bound to be fatal to this strategy because it was based on conditions as they were in December 1921. The Irish negotiators were well aware that speed was essential. Standing on Britain's shifting political ground, 'they had no guarantee that in 12 months Bonar Law might be P.M. and the promised Boundary Commission [would] be put into the waste paper basket with all other promises'. That is why they were adamant that the Ulster Unionists should have only one month to decide whether or not they would join a single Irish government.[56]

Once it became clear that legal necessities would stretch this month into a full year, Collins sought to bypass the British entirely and embarked on his ultimately futile pact negotiations with Craig. Collins rightly suspected that the longer the boundary question was left in limbo, the greater the chances that the Ulster Unionists would 'create new facts on the ground'.[57] This explains his repeated objections to the financial assistance given to Belfast and, especially, his bitter opposition when Craig abolished proportional representation in local government elections.[58]

Perhaps the last word on Griffith's and Collins's attempts to reunify their country should be given to Robert Barton, their colleague-turned-foe. Imprisoned in Mountjoy Jail during the Civil War, Barton heard a rumour that British law advisers were about to declare Article 12 invalid. 'Poor A. G. would turn in his grave', Barton wrote of Griffith. 'He looked upon the Boundary Commission as the grave of Carsonism'.[59]

By O'Higgins's own admission, the boundary crisis left Cosgrave's government 'politically bankrupt'.[60] In its wake, Free Staters turned their backs on

56 Sturgis diary, 6 Dec. 1921, PRO 30/59/5. Also, see 'Minutes of Conferences with Irish Ministers', 22/N/60(5), 6 Feb. 1922, CAB 21/249.

57 This phrase is often used to describe Israel's settlements policy after the 1967 Six-Day War.

58 See, e.g., Collins to Churchill, 24 Mar. 1922, PRONI, CAB/6/75.

59 Barton to 'Adj. General'[?], 24 Feb. 1923, FLK, de Valera Papers, File No. 1296.

60 CA/H/48-2nd Minutes, 1 Dec. 1925, CAB 27/295.

the North, opting instead to build the foundations of a politically conservative 26-county state. With their emphasis on Ireland's Gaelic tradition to the exclusion of all others, and by allowing the Roman Catholic Church to take control of social questions, Cosgrave and his colleagues did much to extend the already large gulf that separated their state from Northern Ireland. There is a good deal of truth in R. F. Foster's observation that while Sinn Féin and its successor movements won the Anglo-Irish War, 'they lost the peace'.[61]

By forfeiting the Ulster question, Cosgrave's government allowed Eamon de Valera and his new political party, Fianna Fáil, to become the rhetorical standard-bearers of Irish unity. In 1927, following Kevin O'Higgins's assassination, de Valera and the other Fianna Fáil TDs took their seats in Dáil Éireann. The hated oath of fidelity was dismissed as an 'empty political formula' – a rhetorical wave of the hand which, though clever, could not so easily wave off de Valera's responsibility for those who were killed in the Civil War.

In any case, hopes that de Valera would lead a campaign to reunify Ireland were soon dashed as it became clear that Fianna Fáil's anti-partitionism was purely '*aspirational* in character'.[62] This was made plain at the party's inaugural meeting, where de Valera told his supporters that 'cutting the bonds of foreign interference' must be their first task. Only then should they tackle 'the problem of successfully bringing in the North'.[63] Once in office, he never wavered from the course he had laid out. While his 1937 Constitution made southern Ireland a republic in all but name, its celebrated claim of jurisdiction over the six counties was rightly dismissed by Cosgrave as pure 'make-believe'.[64]

Craig was equally unimpressed by Articles 2 and 3 of de Valera's Constitution, saying they made 'not a pin of difference' so far as Northern Ireland was concerned. There was not a man alive, Craig told an audience in London, who could govern the whole of Ireland and, were the attempt ever made, he predicted a civil war lasting more than a hundred years.[65] As Leo Amery earlier told the British Cabinet, Craig 'was entirely opposed *ab initio* to

---

61   Foster, *Modern Ireland*, pp. 518–19, 530–5. Collins was no less committed to the creation of an exclusively 'Gaelic Ireland'. See, e.g., M. Collins, *The Path to Freedom* (Dublin, 1922), pp. 9–32.

62   Phoenix, *Northern Nationalism*, p. 370. Bowman, *De Valera*, p. 108.

63   Address at La Scala Theatre, Dublin, 16 May 1926, in M. Moynihan, ed. *Speeches and Statements by Eamon de Valera: 1917–1973* (Dublin, 1980), p. 135.

64   'No Increase of Privileges. Mr. Cosgrave and Partition', *The Irish Times*, 3 May 1937. Also, see 'Re-Integration', the newspaper's leader, same date.

65   'Ulster and Free State. Lord Craigavon's View', *Belfast News-Letter*, 6 May 1937. Craig's indifference about Articles 2 and 3 stands in marked contrast to later Unionist objections. Ian Paisley, for example, denounced them as a 'cancer' in Irish politics. See Bowman, *De Valera*, p. 328.

any form of union with the Free State'.[66] Even when pressed to concede the principle of unity to enlist southern Irish support for the British war effort in 1940, Northern Ireland's prime minister still maintained that he knew what was best for the empire. 'The wisdom of "Partition"', he told reporters, 'has been fully justified'.[67] For many Britons, Ulster's strategic importance during the Second World War would bear out this claim.[68]

Craig spent much of his later years warning fellow Unionists that they would have to be on their guard 'for all time' against those at Westminster who wished to abandon them to a single Irish government.[69] In fact, after 1925 few British politicians wished to go anywhere near the partition question or to become involved in Ulster's sectarian politics. The lesson of the previous five years was that to delve too deeply into Irish affairs was to play with fire. 'Ireland is a country of surprises', Anthony Eden told the House of Commons. If there were any British men or women who wished to bring about Irish unity, he suggested that the best service they could render 'in the light of history, is to keep silent on the subject'.[70]

No one was better practised at maintaining this vow than William Joynson-Hicks, even when as home secretary he was responsible for Northern Irish affairs. At the end of 1928, Joynson-Hicks informed Craig that a delegation had unexpectedly come to see him to protest about the abolition of PR for elections to Northern Ireland's Parliament. His letter continued: 'I don't know whether you would care at any time to discuss the matter with me; of course, I am always at your disposal. But beyond that "I know my place", and don't propose to interfere'.[71]

While Joynson-Hicks knew his place, and was happy to stay there, it was impossible for other British politicians to so easily wash their hands of Ireland and its problems. On several occasions in the 1930s, both Baldwin and MacDonald found themselves facing de Valera across the negotiating table. The Irish leader, Baldwin later told an interviewer, was 'impossible to deal with', a sentiment shared by MacDonald.[72] By the time he assumed the premiership a second time, MacDonald's animosity toward the Irish was even more pronounced than was the case in 1924. Despite evidence to the contrary,

66 'Note by the Secretary of State for Dominion Affairs', 22 Dec. 1926, CP 425(26), DO 117/51/13477. Also, see 'Ulster and the Empire. Lord Craigavon on Loyalty', *The Times*, 27 Aug. 1934.

67 'Statement for Press Conference', 7 July 1940, copy with Lady Craig's diary, D/1415/B/38.

68 Foster, *Modern Ireland*, pp. 558–9.

69 'Orange Demonstrations in Ulster. "No Return to Westminster"', *The Times*, 13 July 1934.

70 *HC Deb*, vol. 189, col. 344, 8 Dec. 1925.

71 Joynson-Hicks to Craig, 14 Dec. 1928, PRONI, CAB/9B/13/1.

72 Bowman, *De Valera*, pp. 4–5, 110.

he became convinced that Britain's unemployment problems and crime rate could only be alleviated by the forced repatriation of Irish immigrants to the Free State.[73] 'We should not', he wrote on one occasion, 'be a dumping ground of Dominion refuse'.[74]

About de Valera, at least, both men found themselves on common ground with their old nemesis, Lloyd George. After one of their early meetings, Lloyd George famously said that negotiating with de Valera was 'like trying to pick up mercury with a fork'. To which de Valera had tartly replied: 'Why doesn't he use a spoon?'[75] But that was all in the past. After the boundary crisis of 1924–25, Lloyd George tended to avoid Irish troubles. Following his death two decades later, Frank Pakenham described Lloyd George as 'an elemental force of nature beyond the categories of good and evil'. Ireland, Pakenham wrote, 'saw him at his worst'.[76] It is a harsh, though not altogether unfair estimation of a life that deeply affected, and was deeply affected by, the attempt to reconcile Ireland's two traditions.

True to his 'celebrated discretion',[77] the man who had served all three of these prime ministers remained forever reluctant to discuss his role in Irish affairs. Years later, Tom Jones was asked to recall the part that he and others in Lloyd George's secretariat had played in the Treaty negotiations. Characteristically, he replied that he did not 'think that much if anything should be said about those of us who were civil servants'.[78] Only the publication of his diaries some 15 years after his death, revealed the extent of Jones's role in devising Britain's Irish policy.

Although Jones was reticent about discussing his role in Irish affairs, others were quick to give him his due, in particular Lord Birkenhead. Years of dissipation and money problems finally caught up with 'F. E.' during Baldwin's second government, where his tenure at the India Office was but a coda to an earlier, more brilliant career. After putting his name to the Irish Treaty in the early hours of 6 December 1921, Birkenhead told Collins that he had just signed his political death warrant. He probably had. Even so, to the end Birkenhead was proud of the part he had played in bringing about the Irish settlement. 'When you recall the state of affairs which existed only four years ago', he pointed out to Edward Wood, now Lord Irwin, 'I think you will agree that the Irish settlement is working better than in our most extravagant hopes

---

73 Canning, *British Policy*, pp. 116–17.

74 See MacDonald note written on Vincent memorandum, 14 Aug. 1931, JRM, PRO 30/69/358.

75 Pakenham, *Peace by Ordeal*, p. 74.

76 'The Changing World', *Irish Press*, 30–31 Mar. 1945, in O Lúing Papers, MSS 23,516.

77 Ellis, *T.J.*, p. 248.

78 Jones to Shakespeare, 16 January 1948, TJ WW/26/ 30.

we could have anticipated'.[79] On his retirement, Birkenhead singled out the Treaty as one of his greatest achievements. 'We have gone through a great deal together', he wrote to Tom Jones after resigning from Baldwin's Cabinet. 'Ireland was a triumph and no one helped more than you'.[80]

There were, of course, plenty of Conservatives who disagreed with this assessment, none more so than Lord Hugh Cecil. Like many Die-hards, Cecil was never fully reconciled with those in his party who had signed the 1921 agreement and he never hesitated to rekindle memories of their betrayal. After one 'bitter personal attack' on Churchill early in 1929, Austen Chamberlain wrote to his wife: 'The fact is that Hugh cannot forgive Winston his position or his share in the Irish Treaty'.[81]

No British politician, however, paid a higher price for the role he had played in this story than Chamberlain himself. Nearly a decade after the fact, he confided to one of his sisters that the Marquess of Salisbury still 'had not forgiven me my part in the Irish settlement'.[82] Ireland scarred Chamberlain's relations with a number of leading Conservatives; he was destined to be one of only two of the party's leaders in the twentieth century who did not eventually become prime minister.[83] Lord Carson was particularly unforgiving towards his one-time colleague. In time, the old Irish Unionist was reconciled with both Birkenhead and Churchill. Not Chamberlain. Asked for his opinion of the men who had made the Irish settlement, Carson's rebuke of Chamberlain was as scathing as it was brief. 'Austen's a coward', was all he would say.[84]

Churchill never suffered anything approaching such reprobation. In fact, within a matter of weeks after the 1925 agreement he was back in the bosom of his old Ulster Unionist friends. At the end of February 1926, Churchill and his wife travelled to Northern Ireland as personal guests of the Craigs. Churchill was 'very excited' about the visit, as it included an invitation to speak at Belfast's Ulster Hall, a place from which he had been barred during the Home Rule Crisis in 1912.[85] 'It is strange how kind Ulster men have been to me', Churchill wrote to Carson a year after his visit. 'I think they have treated me better than I have been treated by anybody else in public life – & I might almost say better than they have treated anyone else who is not one of themselves'. No one was

79 Birkenhead to Irwin, 4 Nov. 1926, IO, MSS Eur. C 152, no. 18.

80 Birkenhead to Jones [letter excerpt], 17 Oct. 1928, vol. II, p. 150.

81 Austen to Ivy Chamberlain, 20 Feb. 1929, AC 6/1/745.

82 Austen to Hilda Chamberlain, 11 Aug. 1930, AC 5/1/511.

83 The other was William Hague, party leader from 1997 to 2001.

84 H. M. Hyde, *Carson* (London, 1953), pp. 486–7.

85 Lady Craig's diary, 31 Dec. 1925, D/1415/B/38. Ervine, *Craigavon*, pp. 510–11. M. C. Bromage, *Churchill and Ireland* (Notre Dame, Indiana, 1964), pp. 107–8.

more surprised by this twist of fate than Churchill. As he admitted to Carson, far from being at one with the Ulster Unionists, 'I was indeed at one time very much the contrary'.[86]

Unlike his hosts, though, Churchill still looked forward to the day when Ireland would be 'united within itself and united to the British Empire'. Even after the passage of two decades and yet another world war, and as he watched the component parts of that empire 'falling away like autumn leaves', he told the House of Commons: 'Strange as it may seem, I still cherish that dream'.[87]

Instead, less than five years after Churchill's death, Northern Ireland was again plunged into conflict. The post-1969 'Troubles' proved be particularly disruptive – as well as dangerous – for those living in the border counties. This was true for both communities, but for Unionists most of all. One result of the violence was a large-scale demographic shift in the province so that, by 1995, the Roman Catholic population west of the River Bann had increased by 25 per cent, as Protestants fled to strongholds along Ulster's east coast. By the mid-1990s, many of the areas argued over in front of the Boundary Commission were incontestably Catholic, if not Nationalist, in their make-up.[88] This was not least true of south Armagh, an area that elected Michael Collins as its first MP to Northern Ireland's Parliament in 1921, and that remained 'fiercely nationalist' to the end of the century. Had this area, known to the British military as 'bandit country', been ceded to the Free State, as many as 200 lives might have been spared between 1969 and the mid-1990s.[89]

What is striking about recent attempts to cut Ulster's Gordian knot is the way in which successive British governments have found themselves resorting to the same solutions that were devised between 1920 and 1925. The abortive Sunningdale Agreement of 1973 resurrected the Council of Ireland which, like its predecessor, never met. One of the major components of the 1998 Good Friday Agreement was the creation of a North–South Ministerial Council which, both in its composition and terms of reference, in many ways echoed the 1920s Council of Ireland.[90]

---

86   Churchill to Carson, 28 Feb. 1927, *Comp V, Part I*, p. 956.

87   See *HC Deb*, vol. 457, cols 246–8, 28 Oct. 1948, in which Churchill quoted from his 1926 speech.

88   'Canute of North Down', *The Guardian*, 13 June 1995. According to the 1991 census, Catholics made up a majority in local government districts such as Londonderry (73 per cent), Strabane (64 per cent), Omagh (67 per cent), Dungannon (58 per cent), Newry and Mourne (77 per cent), Down (60 per cent) and all of County Fermanagh (57 per cent). At the same time, Protestants made up a majority in such east coast local government districts as Larne (76 per cent), Carrickfergus (92 per cent), and North Down (90 per cent).

89   B. Cathcart, 'It all Began with a Line on a Map', *Independent on Sunday Magazine*, 22 May 1994.

90   McKittrick and McVea, *Making Sense of the Troubles*, pp. 95–7, 105. Ruane and Todd, *After the Good Friday Agreement*, p. 14.

Desperate to end the violence that had engulfed Northern Ireland by the summer of 1972, officials in Edward Heath's Conservative government seriously considered forced population transfers followed by an extensive redrawing of the boundary.[91] William Whitelaw, Heath's first Northern Ireland Secretary, also considered a 'plebiscite on the Border' – the very idea that Lionel Curtis worked so hard to scupper in 1924.[92] At the same time that these ideas were being considered privately, redrawing the Irish frontier was publicly advocated by Oswald Mosley, still active half a century after he had first denounced Lloyd George's Irish policies in the House of Commons.[93]

While Heath and his advisers ultimately rejected proposals for reconfiguring Ireland's frontier, the idea never quite went away. Even Margaret Thatcher toyed with creating a new Boundary Commission, although her minister in charge of Northern Ireland in the mid-1980s asserts that it was nothing more than 'an idea in conversation'.[94] So bold an initiative was unlikely in any case, given the past. One of Austen Chamberlain's successors, both as party leader and as foreign secretary, summed up the dilemma with words that could have been Chamberlain's own. 'Our own parliamentary history', Alec Douglas-Home lamented, 'is one long story of trouble with the Irish'.[95]

And so the boundary described by Lady Spender in her diary has survived, a legacy of political struggles in both Britain and Ireland from an earlier time.

One mid-summer's morning in 1923, a motorcade sped along the back roads of Northern Ireland bound for the Irish frontier, running into it many times as happened at Clady, where 'here again the Boundary was an imaginary line across the middle of the river bridge'.[96] One morning five decades later, Kenneth Smyth, a Protestant, and Daniel McCormick, a Catholic, were shot to death by the IRA on these same back roads – their deaths also a legacy to the political struggles from that earlier time and the failure to resolve them.[97]

---

91 'Redrawing the Border and Population Transfer', 22 July 1972, PREM 15/1010.

92 Sir Burke Trend memorandum to Heath, 13 Sept. 1972, PREM 15/1013.

93 Skidelsky, *Mosley*, p. 519.

94 Douglas Hurd to the author, 11 Nov. 1998.

95 Douglas-Home to Heath, 13 Mar. 1972, PREM 15/1004.

96 Lady Spender's diary, 25 June 1923, D/1633/2/26.

97 D. McKittrick, S. Kelters, B. Feeney, and C. Thornton, *Lost Lives: The Stories of the Men, Women and Children Who Died as a Result of the Northern Ireland Troubles* (Edinburgh, 2001), p. 128.

Appendix 1

Biographical Notes

The material below was compiled from biographies, monographs and from successive volumes of

British Political Facts, 1900–67
A Dictionary of Irish History
The Dictionary of National Biography
The Oxford Companion to Twentieth-Century British Politics
Who Was Who

*   *   *

ADDISON, CHRISTOPHER (1869–1951). British politician. Born: Lincolnshire. Education: Trinity College, Harrogate; St Bartholomew's Hospital, London. Doctor and distinguished lecturer of anatomy. Political career: MP (Liberal), 1910–22; MP (Labour), 1929–31 and 1934–35; first Minister of Health, 1919–21; as Minister without Portfolio, 1921, he resigned from the Coalition over his housing scheme.

AMERY, LEOPOLD STENNETT (1873–1955). British politician. Born: Gorakhpur, India. Education: Harrow; Balliol College, Oxford. Journalist and barrister; served in First World War. Political career: MP (Conservative-Unionist), 1911–45; Assistant Secretary to the War Cabinet and Imperial War Cabinet, 1917; staff member of the War Council at Versailles and a member of the personal staff of the Secretary of State for War, 1917–19; Parliamentary Under-Secretary for the Colonies, 1919–21; Parliamentary and Financial Secretary to the Admiralty, 1921–22; First Lord of the Admiralty, 1922–24; Colonial Secretary, 1924–29; Dominions Secretary, 1925–29; Secretary of State for India and Burma, 1940–45.

ANDERSON, SIR JOHN (1882–1958). British civil servant and politician. Born: Midlothian, Scotland. Education: George Watson's College, Edinburgh; Edinburgh and Leipzig universities. Entered the Colonial Office, 1905 and held several positions before being appointed Joint Under-Secretary to the Lord Lieutenant of Ireland, 1920; Permanent Under-Secretary of State, Home Office, 1922–32; Governor of Bengal, 1932–37. Political career: MP (Independent National), 1938–50; Lord Privy Seal, 1938–39; Home Secretary and Minister of Home Security, 1939–40; Lord President of the Council, 1940–43; Chancellor of the Exchequer, 1943–45. Created 1st Viscount Waverley, 1952.

ANDREWS, JOHN MILLER (1871–1956). Ulster politician. Born: County Down. Education: Belfast Academical Institute. A prominent member of the Ulster Unionist Council, the Orange Order and, with Sir Edward Carson, one of two non-Labour members of the Ulster Unionist Labour Association, 1918. Political career: MP, Northern Ireland Parliament, (Unionist), 1921–53; Minister of Labour, 1921–1937; Minister of Finance, 1937–40; Prime Minister of Northern Ireland, 1940–43.

ANTROBUS, MAURICE EDWARD (1895–1985). British civil servant. Education: Winchester; Trinity College, Cambridge. Served in First World War. Assistant Principal, Colonial Office, 1920–27, after which he served as both a private and political secretary to UK High Commissioners in South Africa, Éire, Australia, and New Zealand; appointed Assistant Secretary, Commonwealth Relations Office, 1945–55.

ARCHDALE, EDWARD MERVYN (1853–1943). Ulster politician. Education: Naval School, Portsmouth. Royal Navy, 1866–80. Political career: MP (Conservative-Unionist), 1898–1903 and 1916–21; MP, Northern Ireland Parliament, (Unionist), 1921–37; Minister of Agriculture and Commerce, 1921–25; Minister of Agriculture, 1925–33.

ASQUITH, HERBERT HENRY (1852–1928). British politician. Born: Yorkshire. Education: City of London School; Balliol College, Oxford. Political career: MP (Liberal), 1886–1918 and 1920–24; supported Gladstone in the first Home Rule crisis; Home Secretary, 1892–94; Chancellor of the Exchequer, 1905–8; Prime Minister, 1908–16. Created 1st Earl of Oxford and Asquith, 1925.

BALDWIN, STANLEY (1867–1947). British politician. Education: Harrow; Trinity College, Cambridge. Political career: MP (Conservative-Unionist), 1908–1937; Financial Secretary to the Treasury, 1917–21; President of the Board of Trade, 1921–22; Chancellor of the Exchequer, 1922–1923; Prime Minister 1923–24, 1924–29 and 1935–37; Lord Privy Seal, 1932–34; Lord President of the Council, 1931–35. Created 1st Earl Baldwin of Bewdley, 1937.

BALFOUR, ARTHUR JAMES (1848–1930). British politician. Born: East Lothian, Scotland. Education: Eton; Trinity College, Cambridge. Political career: MP (Conservative), 1874–1922; joined Lord Randolph Churchill and others to form the 'Fourth Party' of Conservative Party dissidents; Private Secretary to his uncle, the 3rd Marquess of Salisbury when the latter was Secretary of State for Foreign Affairs, 1878–80; President of Local Government Board, 1885–86; Secretary for Scotland; Vice-President of Committee of Council on Education for Scotland, 1886–87; Chief Secretary for Ireland, 1887–91; nicknamed 'Bloody Balfour' for his handling of the Irish Land War and suppression of the National League; led Conservative campaign to 'kill Home Rule with kindness' by instituting reforms such as Congested Districts Board, 1890, and the Land Purchase Act, 1891; Leader of the House of Commons and First Lord of the Treasury, 1891–92; Opposition Leader, 1892–95; Conservative Leader in the House of Commons, 1895–1905; Prime Minister, 1902–5; Opposition Leader, 1906–11; First Lord of the Admiralty, 1915–16; Foreign Secretary, 1916–19; Lord President of the Council, 1919–22 and 1925–29; head of the British Mission to America, 1917; led British Mission to Washington Conference, 1921–22. Created 1st Earl of Balfour, 1922.

BARTON, ROBERT CHILDERS (1881–1975). Irish politician. Born: County Wicklow; cousin of Erskine Childers. Education: Rugby; Christ Church, Oxford. Served with British forces in First World War. Political career: MP/TD (Sinn Féin), 1918–23; Minister of Agriculture, 1919–21; Secretary for Economic Affairs, 1921–22; took part in Irish Treaty negotiations, 1921; voted against the Treaty; joined Irregular forces; captured and imprisoned; retired from politics a the end of the Civil War.

BATES, RICHARD DAWSON (1876–1949). Ulster politician. Born: Belfast. Qualified as a solicitor. Political career: Vice-President of the Ulster Unionist Council; founder-member of the Ulster Volunteer Force, 1913; MP, Northern Ireland Parliament, (Unionist), 1921–43; Minister for Home Affairs, 1921–43.

BAYFORD, IST BARON, ROBERT ARTHUR SANDERS (1867–1940). British politician. Born: Isle of Wight. Education: Harrow; Balliol College, Oxford. Barrister. Political career: MP (Conservative-Unionist), 1910–23 and 1924–29; Treasurer of the Household, 1918–19; Junior Lord of the Treasury, 1919; Under-Secretary for War, 1921–22; Minister of Agriculture and Fisheries, 1922–24. Created 1st Baron Bayford of Stoke Trister, 1929.

BEAVERBROOK, IST BARON, WILLIAM MAXWELL AITKEN (1879–1964). British newspaper owner and politician. Born: Ontario, Canada. Education: Public (Board) School, Newcastle, New Brunswick. Acquired political influence through his ownership of Britain's *Express* newspapers; confidant of Andrew Bonar Law. Political career: MP (Conservative-Unionist), 1910–16; Chancellor of the Duchy of Lancaster and Minister of Information, 1918; Minister for Aircraft Production, 1940–41; Minister of State, 1941; Minister of Supply, 1941–42; Lord Privy Seal, 1943–45. Created Baron Beaverbrook, 1917.

BIRKENHEAD, IST EARL OF, FREDERICK EDWIN SMITH (1872–1930). British politician. Born: Birkenhead. Education: Birkenhead School; Wadham College, Oxford. Barrister. Political career: MP (Conservative), 1906–19; principal assistant to Sir Edward Carson during the pre-war Home Rule Crisis, earning the nickname 'Galloper Smith'; served with the Indian Corps in France, 1914; Solicitor-General, 1915; Attorney-General, 1915–19; Lord High Chancellor of Great Britain, 1919–22; took part in Irish Treaty negotiations, 1921; Secretary of State for India, 1924–28. Created 1st Earl of Birkenhead, 1922.

BLACKMORE, SIR CHARLES HENRY (1880–1967). Northern Irish civil servant. Formerly Private Secretary to Parliamentary Secretary, Ministry of Pensions, and

Financial Secretary, Admiralty; Secretary to the Prime Minister of Northern Ireland; also Secretary to the Cabinet of Northern Ireland and Clerk of Privy Council of Northern Ireland, 1925–39.

BLYTHE, ERNEST (1889–1975). Irish politician. Born: County Antrim. Education: National School. Political career: MP/TD (Sinn Féin and Cumann na nGaedheal), 1918–33; Provisional Government Minister for Trade and Commerce, 1921–22; Irish Free State Minister for Local Government, 1922–23; Minister of Finance, 1923–32; Minister of Posts and Telegraphs, 1927–32; Vice-President of the Executive Council, 1927–32. Member of Seanad Éireann, 1934–36. Later, Director of Abbey Theatre, Dublin, 1943–67.

BONAR LAW, ANDREW (1858–1923). British politician. Born: New Brunswick, Canada. Returned to Scotland after his mother's death where he was raised by relatives. Education: Gilbertfield School, Hamilton and Glasgow High School. Political career: MP (Conservative-Unionist), 1900–23; Parliamentary Secretary to the Board of Trade, 1902; supported Joseph Chamberlain's campaign for tariff reform and Imperial Preference; Conservative Party leader, 1911–23; Colonial Secretary, 1915–16; played a crucial role in toppling Asquith and replacing him with Lloyd George as Prime Minister; Chancellor of the Exchequer, 1916–19; Lord Privy Seal and Leader of the House of Commons, 1919–21; Prime Minister, 1922–23.

BOURDILLON, FRANCIS BERNARD (1883–1970). British academic. Education: Charterhouse; Balliol College, Oxford. Lecturer in German, University College, Reading, 1908–1914; Modern Languages Lecturer, Balliol College, Oxford, 1913–16; Naval Intelligence Division, 1916–19; assisted the British delegation to the Versailles Peace Conference, 1919; member of the Upper Silesian Commission 1920–22; Secretary to the Irish Boundary Commission, 1924–25; Secretary of the Royal Institute of International Affairs, 1926–29; worked for the Foreign Office Research Department, 1943–49.

BRIDGEMAN, WILLIAM CLIVE (1864–1935). British politician. Education: Eton; Trinity College, Cambridge. Political career: MP (Conservative-Unionist), Shropshire, 1906–29; held various government offices before becoming Home Secretary, 1922–24 and First Lord of the Admiralty, 1924–29. Created 1st Viscount Bridgeman, 1929.

BROOKE, BASIL STANLAKE (1888–1973). Ulster politician. Born: County Fermanagh. Education: Winchester; Sandhurst. Served in First World War; active in the creation of Ulster Special Constabulary, 1920. Political career: MP, Northern Ireland Parliament, (Unionist), 1929–63; Minister of Agriculture, 1933–41; Minister of Commerce, 1941–45; Prime Minister of Northern Ireland, 1943–63. Created 1st Viscount Brookeborough of Colebrooke, 1952.

CARSON, SIR EDWARD HENRY (1854 –1935). Irish Unionist politician. Born: Dublin. Education: Portarlington School; Trinity College, Dublin. Barrister – Irish Bar, 1889; English Bar, 1894. Political career: MP (Conservative-Unionist), 1892–1921;

Solicitor-General for Ireland, 1892; Solicitor-General, 1900–6; Ulster Unionist leader, 1910–21; Attorney-General, 1915; First Lord of the Admiralty, 1917; Member of the War Cabinet without Portfolio, 1917–18; Lord of Appeal in Ordinary, 1921–29. Created Baron Carson of Duncairn (life peerage), 1921.

CAVE, GEORGE (1856–1928). British politician. Born: London. Education: St John's College, Oxford. Barrister, 1880. Political career: MP (Conservative), 1906–18; Solicitor-General, 1915–16; Home Secretary, 1916–19; Lord Chancellor, 1922–24 and 1924–28. Created Viscount Cave of Richmond, Surrey, 1918.

CECIL, LORD EDGAR ALGERNON ROBERT (1864–1958). British politician. Brother of the 4th Marquess of Salisbury and Lord Hugh Cecil. Education: Eton; University College, Oxford. Private secretary to his father, the 3rd Marquess of Salisbury. Called to the Bar, 1887. Political career: MP (Conservative), 1906–10 and (Independent Conservative), 1911–23; Parliamentary Under-Secretary for Foreign Affairs, 1915–16; Minister of Blockade, 1916–18; Assistant Secretary of State for Foreign Affairs, 1918; Lord Privy Seal, 1923–24; Chancellor of the Duchy of Lancaster, 1924–27. Created 1st Viscount Cecil of Chelwood, 1923.

CECIL, LORD HUGH RICHARD HEATHCOTE (1869–1956). British politician. Brother of the 4th Marquess of Salisbury and Lord Robert Cecil of Chelwood. Education: Eton; University College, Oxford. Private Secretary to his father, the 3rd Marquess of Salisbury. Lieutenant, Royal Flying Corps, 1915. Political career: MP (Conservative), 1895–1906 and 1910–37. Created 1st Baron Quickswood, 1941.

CHAMBERLAIN, ARTHUR NEVILLE (1869–1940). British politician. Born: Birmingham; second son of Joseph Chamberlain; half-brother of Austen Chamberlain. Education: Rugby; Mason College, Birmingham. Political career: Birmingham City Council, 1911; Lord Mayor of Birmingham, 1915–16; Director-General of National Service and member of the War Cabinet, 1916–17; MP (Conservative-Unionist), 1918–40; Postmaster-General, 1922–23; Paymaster-General, 1923; Minister of Health, 1923, 1924–29, and 1931; Chancellor of the Exchequer, 1923–24 and 1931–37; Chairman of the Conservative Party, 1930–31; Prime Minister, 1937–40; Lord President of the Council, 1940.

CHAMBERLAIN, SIR JOSEPH AUSTEN (1863–1937). British politician. Born: Birmingham; eldest son of Joseph Chamberlain; half-brother of Neville Chamberlain. Education: Rugby; Trinity College, Cambridge. Political career: MP (Liberal-, later Conservative-Unionist), 1892–1937; Civil Lord of the Admiralty, 1895–1900; Financial Secretary to the Treasury, 1900–2; Postmaster-General, 1902–3; Chancellor of the Exchequer, 1903–5; Secretary of State for India, 1915–17; Minister without Portfolio and member of the War Cabinet, 1918–19; Chancellor of the Exchequer, 1919–21; Lord Privy Seal and Leader of the House of Commons, 1921–22; leader of the Conservative Party, 1921–22; took part in the Irish Treaty negotiations, 1921; Foreign Secretary, 1924–29; First Lord of the Admiralty, 1931.

CHARTRES, JOHN SMITH (1862–1927). Irish journalist and political activist. Born: Birkenhead, England, the son of Irish parents. Education: Wellington College, Berkshire; London University. Admitted to the English Bar, 1908; economics correspondent, *Daily Graphic*, 1914–15. Worked as an analyst for the Ministry of Munitions and Ministry of Labour before transferring to the latter ministry's Irish Department, 1920. Converted to Irish republican cause after meeting Arthur Griffith and, later, Michael Collins, possibly as early as 1917; arms purchaser for the IRA in Germany, 1921; joint chief secretary, with Erskine Childers, to the Irish Treaty delegation, 1921; Provisional Government publicity agent, 1921–22; transferred to the Free State's Department of Industry and Commerce, 1922–27.

CHURCHILL, SIR WINSTON LEONARD SPENCER (1874–1965). British politician, soldier, and writer. Born: Blenheim Palace, England. Education: Harrow; Sandhurst. Entered the Army, 1895; served in India and, later, in the Boer War; commanded 6th Royal Scots Fusiliers, 1916–17. Political career: MP (Conservative), 1900–4, (Liberal), 1904–18, (Coalition Liberal), 1918–22, and (Constitutionalist, then Conservative), 1924–64; Under-Secretary of State for Colonies, 1906–8; President of the Board of Trade, 1908–10; Home Secretary, 1910–11; First Lord of the Admiralty, 1911–15; Chancellor of the Duchy of Lancaster, 1915; Minister of Munitions, 1917; Secretary of State for War and Air, 1919–21; Colonial Secretary, 1921–22; took part in Irish Treaty negotiations, 1921; Cabinet minister with primary responsibility for Irish policy, 1922; Chancellor of the Exchequer, 1924–29; Cabinet minister charged with solving the Irish Boundary Commission Crisis, 1925; First Lord of the Admiralty, 1939–40; Prime Minister and Defence Minister, 1940–45; Opposition Leader, 1945–51; Prime Minister, 1951–55; Defence Minister, 1951–52.

CLARK, SIR ERNEST (1864–1951). Northern Irish civil servant. Education: King's College, London. Barrister, 1894. Assistant Secretary, Inland Revenue, 1919; Secretary, Royal Commission on Income Tax, 1919–20; Assistant Under-Secretary for Ireland, 1920–21; Secretary, Treasury of Northern Ireland, 1921–25; later a member of the Joint Exchequer Board of Great Britain and Northern Ireland, and Governor of Tasmania.

COLLINS, JOHN HENRY (1880–1952). Northern Irish solicitor and nationalist. Born: County Down. Education: Christian Brothers School, Newry. Solicitor, 1910; senior partner, Collins & Collins; legal adviser to North-East Boundary Bureau for County Down. Political career: MP, Northern Ireland Parliament, (Nationalist), 1929–33.

COLLINS, MICHAEL (1890–1922). Irish soldier and politician. Education: Lissvaird and Clonakilty National Schools. Emigrated to London to work as a clerk; joined the Irish Republican Brotherhood, 1909; took part in the Easter Rising and interned at Frognoch Prison, Wales, 1916. On his release, Collins set about reorganising the republican movement as Secretary of the Irish National Aid and Irish Volunteer Dependents' Fund and as Adjutant General of the Irish Volunteers. Political career: MP/TD (Sinn Féin), 1918–22; MP, Northern Ireland Parliament (Sinn Féin), 1921–22; Minister of Home Affairs, 1919; Minister of Finance, 1919–21; organised the National Loan; President of the Supreme Council of the IRB, 1919–22; IRA Director of Organisation and of Intelligence, 1919–21; Acting President of Dáil Éireann, 1920; took part in the Irish Treaty negotiations; led pro-Treaty side in Dáil debates; Chairman of the Provisional Government, 1922; resigned as chairman to become commander-in-chief of the Free State Army, July 1922; killed in action.

COLWYN, 1ST BARON, FREDERICK HENRY SMITH (1859–1946). British rubber and cotton manufacturer. Director of Martin's Bank, Ltd. Served on various government committees, notably the Northern Ireland Special Arbitration Committee, which he chaired. Created 1st Baron Colwyn, 1917.

COPE, SIR ALFRED WILLIAM (1877–1954). British civil servant. Born: London. Entered government service as a boy clerk; joined the detective branch, Customs and Excise, 1896; Second Secretary, Ministry of Pensions, 1919–20, where his administrative skills brought him to the attention of Lloyd George; Assistant Under-Secretary for Ireland and Clerk of the Irish Privy Council, 1920–22. At Dublin Castle, Cope was charged with sounding out Sinn Féin leaders on the possibility of a negotiated end to the Anglo-Irish War. Retired from the civil service to become General Secretary, National Liberal Organisation, 1922–24; abandoned politics when, according to *The Dictionary of National Biography*, he 'found close co-operation with Lloyd George impossible'.

COSGRAVE, WILLIAM THOMAS (1880–1965). Irish politician. Born: Dublin. Education: Christian Brothers Schools. Joined the Irish Volunteers; took part in the Easter Rising; condemned to death but his sentence was later commuted; released, Dec. 1916. Political career: member of Dublin Corporation, 1909–22; Alderman, 1920; MP (Sinn Féin), 1917–18; MP/TD (Sinn Féin, later Cumann na nGaedheal, then Fine Gael), 1918–44; Minister for Local Government, 1919–22; supported the Treaty; member, and later Chairman of the Provisional Government, 1922; President of Dáil Éireann, 1922; first President of the Executive Council of the Irish Free State, 1922–32; while President, held portfolio of Minister of Finance, 1922–23, and Minister of Defence, 1924; founded Cumann na nGaedheal Party, 1923; founder-member and joint vice president of Fine Gael Party, 1933; Fine Gael president, 1935–44.

CRAIG, CHARLES CURTIS (1869–1960). Ulster politician. Born: County Down; brother of Sir James Craig. Education: Clifton College. Served in First World War with the Ulster Division; wounded and taken prisoner. Political career: MP (Unionist), 1903–29; Parliamentary Secretary to the Ministry of Pensions, 1923–24.

CRAIG, SIR JAMES (1871–1940). Ulster Unionist politician. Born: Belfast. Education: private and Merchiston Castle, Edinburgh. Worked as a stockbroker in Belfast and London; founder-member of the Belfast Stock Exchange, 1892; served in the Boer War; quartermaster general of the 36th (Ulster) Division, 1914–15. Political career: MP (Conservative-Unionist), 1906–21; MP, Northern Ireland Parliament (Unionist), 1921–27; Parliamentary Secretary to the Minister for Pensions, 1919–20; Parliamentary and Financial Secretary to the Admiralty, 1920–21; leader of the Ulster Unionist Party and first Prime Minister of Northern Ireland, 1921–40. Created 1st Viscount Craigavon, 1927.

CURTIS, LIONEL GEORGE (1872–1955). British civil servant. Education: Haileybury; New College, Oxford. Called to the Bar; served in the Boer War; member of Lord Milner's 'Kindergarten' of civil servants; Town Clerk of Johannesburg; Assistant Colonial Secretary to the Transvaal for Local Government; member of the Transvaal Legislative Council; British Secretary to the Irish Treaty Conference, 1921; Colonial Office Adviser on Irish Affairs, 1921–24.

CURZON, GEORGE NATHANIEL (1859–1925). British politician. Born: Derbyshire. Education: Eton; Balliol College, Oxford. Political career: MP (Conservative), 1886–98; Under-Secretary of State for India, 1891–92; Under-Secretary of State for Foreign Affairs, 1892–98; Viceroy of India, 1898–1905; Lord Privy Seal, 1915–16; President of the Air Board, 1916; Lord President of the Council and member of the War Cabinet, 1916–19; Leader of the House of Lords, 1916–24; Foreign Secretary, 1919–24; broke with the Coalition and joined the Bonar Law government; Lord President of the Council, 1924–25. Created Earl, 1911, later Marquess Curzon of Kedleston, 1921.

DAVIDSON, FRANCES JOAN (1894–1985). British politician. Born: London; wife of J. C. C. Davidson and confidante of Stanley Baldwin. Education: Kensington High School and in Germany. Political career: MP (Conservative), 1937–59. Created Baroness Northchurch (life peerage), 1963.

DAVIDSON, JOHN COLIN CAMPBELL (1889–1970). British politician. Born: Aberdeen, Scotland. Education: Westminster; Pembroke College, Cambridge. Called to the Bar, 1913. Political career: MP (Conservative-Unionist), 1920–23 and 1924–37; Parliamentary Private Secretary to Bonar Law as Leader of the House of Commons, 1920–21; to Stanley Baldwin as President of the Board of Trade, 1921–22; and to Bonar Law as Prime Minister, 1922–23; Chancellor of the Duchy of Lancaster, 1923–24; Parliamentary Secretary to the Admiralty, 1924–27; Chancellor of the Duchy of Lancaster, 1931–37. Conservative Party Chairman, 1927–30. Confidant of Bonar Law and Baldwin. Created 1st Viscount Davidson of Little Gaddesden, 1937.

DERBY, 17TH EARL OF, EDWARD GEORGE VILLIERS STANLEY (1865–1948). British politician. Born: London. Education: Wellington College. Lieutenant, Grenadier Guards, 1885–95; Aide-de-camp to the Governor-General of Canada, 1889–91; served in the Boer War. Political career: MP (Conservative) , 1892–1906; a Lord of the Treasury, 1895–1900; Financial Secretary to the War Office, 1900–3;

Postmaster-General, 1903–5; Director-General of Recruiting, 1915–16; Under-Secretary for War, 1916; Secretary of State for War, 1916–18 and 1922–24; Ambassador to France, 1918–20.

DE VALERA, EAMON (1882–1975). Irish politician. Born: New York; reared in County Limerick. Education: Christian Brothers School, County Cork; Blackrock College; University College Dublin. While a teacher of mathematics, de Valera joined the Gaelic League in 1908 and became involved in Nationalist politics. Joined the Irish Volunteers and took part in the Easter Rising as commandant of the 3rd Brigade at Boland's Mill. Sentenced to death, his execution was commuted to life imprisonment on account of his American citizenship; released, 1917. Political career: MP/TD (Sinn Féin, later Fianna Fáil), 1917–59; MP, Northern Ireland Parliament, (Sinn Féin), 1921–29; Sinn Féin President, 1917–26 and of the Irish Volunteers, 1917–22; President of Dáil Éireann, 1919; toured the United States of America in an attempt to secure official recognition of the Irish Republic and to raise funds for Sinn Féin, 1919–21; elected 'President of the Irish Republic' by the Dáil, 1921. Led opposition to the Irish Treaty and resigned as President and joined the anti-Treaty IRA; arrested and imprisoned by the Free State government at the end of the Civil War, 1923–24; split with Sinn Féin over his call for the party's entry into Dáil Éireann; founder-president of Fianna Fáil, 1926; formed coalition government with Irish Labour Party, 1932; President of the Free State, later Taoiseach of Éire, 1932–48, 1951–54, and 1957–59; drafted new Irish Constitution, 1937; President of the Republic of Ireland, 1959–73.

DEVLIN, JOSEPH (1871–1934). Northern Irish politician. Born: Belfast. Education: Christian Brothers School, Belfast. Journalist, the *Irish News*, 1891–93. Political career: MP (Nationalist), 1902–22 and 1929–34; MP, Northern Ireland Parliament (Nationalist), 1921–34. A leading figure in the regeneration of the Ancient Order of Hibernians, 1905–34; organised Ulster units of the Irish Volunteers, 1913; member of the Irish Convention, 1917–18.

DEVONSHIRE, 9TH DUKE OF, VICTOR CHRISTIAN WILLIAM CAVENDISH (1868–1938). British politician. Education: Eton; Trinity College, Cambridge. Political career: MP (Liberal-Unionist), 1891–1908; Treasurer of His Majesty's Household, 1900–3; Financial Secretary to the Treasury, 1903–5; a Civil Lord of the Admiralty, 1915–16; Governor-General of Canada, 1916–21; Colonial Secretary, 1922–24.

DILLON, JOHN (1851–1927). Irish politician. Born: County Dublin. Education: Catholic University and Royal College of Surgeons. Political career: MP (Nationalist), 1880–83 and 1885–1918; broke with Charles Stewart Parnell during the leadership crisis of 1890–1; supported John Redmond as leader of the reunified Irish Parliamentary Party, 1900; Leader of the IPP, 1918; led the party's withdrawal from the British House of Commons to protest conscription in Ireland, April

1918; defeated by Eamon de Valera in the general election of 1918 and retired from politics.

DUFFY, GEORGE GAVAN (1882–1951). Irish politician and lawyer. Education: French schools and Stonyhurst. Solicitor; prepared the defence for Sir Roger Casement in his trial for treason, 1916. Political career: MP/TD (Sinn Féin), 1918–23; helped to draft the Irish Declaration of Independence, 1919; Irish representative at the Versailles Peace Conference, 1919; Irish envoy to Italy, 1920; took part in the Irish Treaty negotiations, 1921; reluctantly recommended Treaty to Dáil Éireann; Minister for Foreign Affairs, 1922; resigned from the Dáil on its refusal to treat captured Irregulars as prisoners of war, 1923; High Court judge, 1936; President of the High Court, 1946.

DUGGAN, EAMON (1874–1936). Irish politician. Born: County Meath. Education: Dublin schools. Qualified as a solicitor, 1914. Joined the Irish Volunteers; took part in the Easter Rising, 1916; interned, 1916–17; Director of Intelligence, Irish Volunteers, 1918. Political career: MP/TD (Sinn Féin, later Cumann na nGaedheal), 1918–33; took part in the Irish Treaty negotiations, 1921; supported the Treaty in Dáil Éireann; Provisional Government Home Affairs Minister, 1922; Minister without Portfolio, 1922–23; Parliamentary Secretary to the President of the Executive Council and to the Ministry of Defence, 1927–32; member of Seanad Éireann, 1933–36.

DUGGAN, GEORGE CHESTER (?–1969). Northern Irish civil servant. Education: The High School, Dublin; Trinity College, Dublin. Entered the civil service, 1908; Admiralty, 1908–10 and 1914–16; Ministry of Shipping, 1917–19; Chief Secretary's Office, Dublin Castle, 1910–14 and 1919–21; Assistant Secretary (1922–25), later Principal Assistant Secretary, Northern Ireland Ministry of Finance.

FEETHAM, RICHARD (1874–1965). South African jurist. Born: Monmouthshire, Wales. Education: Marlborough; New College, Oxford. Called to the Bar, 1899. Emigrated to South Africa. Feetham was a Johannesburg town clerk and member of the Transvaal Legislative Council, 1907–10, as well as Legal Adviser to the British High Commissioner to South Africa (Lord Selborne), 1907, before being elected to South Africa's Legislative Assembly, 1915–23. He was a Justice of the Supreme Court of South Africa, 1923–30; Chairman of the Irish Boundary Commission, 1924–25; and later Chancellor of the University of Witwatersrand, Johannesburg; opposed apartheid.

FISHER, HERBERT ALBERT LAURENS (1865–1940). British politician and historian. Born: London. Education: Winchester; New College, Oxford. Political career: MP (Liberal and National Liberal), 1916–26; President of the Board of Education, 1916–22; British delegate to the League of Nations Assembly, 1920–22.

FISHER, JOSEPH R. (1855–1939). Ulster journalist. Born: County Down. Education: Royal Belfast Academical Institute; Queen's University, Belfast; also studied in

Germany and France. Foreign editor, the *Daily Chronicle*, 1881; assistant editor, *The Standard*, 1883–91; editor and managing editor of the *Northern Whig*, 1891–1913. Northern Ireland's representative on the Boundary Commission, 1924–25.

FISHER, SIR NORMAN FENWICK WARREN (1879–1948). British civil servant. Born: London. Education: Winchester; Hertford College, Oxford. Entered the civil service and eventually rose to the position of Permanent Secretary to the Treasury and Head of the Civil Service, 1919–39.

FITZGERALD, DESMOND (1889–1947). Irish politician. Participated in Easter Rising. Political career: MP/TD (Sinn Féin, later Cumann na nGaedheal), 1918–32; Dáil Éireann Director of Publicity and editor of *The Irish Bulletin*; Provisional Government Minister of Foreign Affairs, 1922; Irish Free State Minister of External Affairs, 1922–27; Minister of Defence, 1927–32; member of Seanad Éireann, 1938–47.

FRENCH, SIR JOHN DENTON PINKSTONE (1852–1925). British soldier. Born: Kent. French commanded the British Expeditionary Force, 1914–15; he was later Lord Lieutenant of Ireland, 1918–1921. Created Earl of Ypres, 1922.

GREENWOOD, SIR HAMAR (1870–1948). British politician. Born: Ontario, Canada. Education: Public School, Whitby, Canada. Served in First World War. Political career: MP (Liberal), 1906–22 and (Conservative), 1924–29; Under-Secretary of State for Home Affairs, 1919; Secretary for Overseas Trade, 1919–20; Chief Secretary for Ireland, 1920–22. Created 1st Baron Greenwood of Holbourne, 1937.

GRETTON, JOHN (1867–1947). British politician. Political career: MP (Conservative), 1895–1906, 1907–43. Gretton renounced the party whip when the Coalition began its negotiations with Sinn Féin and became a leading Die-hard MP.

GREY, SIR EDWARD (1862–1933). British politician and diplomat. Education: Winchester; Balliol College, Oxford. Political career: MP (Liberal), 1885–1916; Under-Secretary for Foreign Affairs, 1892–95; Foreign Secretary, 1905–16; Temporary Ambassador to the USA, 1919. Created 1st Viscount Grey of Fallodon, 1916.

GRIFFITH, ARTHUR (1871–1922). Irish politician and journalist. Born: Dublin. Education: Christian Brothers School, Dublin. Apprentice printer. A founder-member of the Celtic Literary Society, Griffith also belonged to the Gaelic League and, for a time, the Irish Republican Brotherhood. Emigrated to South Africa, where he supported the Boer cause; returned to Ireland to organise Irish opposition to the war and to edit the *United Irishman*. Published *The Resurrection of Hungary: A Parallel for Ireland*, advocating a dual monarchy for Ireland and Great Britain, 1904; founded Sinn Féin ('Ourselves Alone'), 1907; opposed the Third Home Rule Bill but joined the Irish Volunteers and participated in the Howth gun-running incident, 1914; persuaded by its leaders not to take part in the Easter Rising, Griffith was nevertheless imprisoned as a result of the rebellion, 1916–17. Political career: MP/TD (Sinn Féin), 1917–22; MP, Northern Ireland Parliament (Sinn Féin), 1921–22; Minister of Home Affairs and Acting President of Dáil

Éireann, 1919–20; led Irish delegation in Treaty negotiations, 1921; elected President of Dáil Éireann, 1922; died as the result of a cerebral haemorrhage due to overwork. Griffith was the first modern Irish leader to be buried as a head of state.

GRIGG, EDWARD WILLIAM MACLEAY (1879–1955). British politician and political adviser. Education: Winchester; New College, Oxford. Joined the editorial staff of *The Times*, 1903; served in First World War; military secretary to the Prince of Wales, 1919; private secretary to Lloyd George, 1921–22. Political career: MP (National Liberal), 1922–25 and (National Conservative), 1933–45; Parliamentary Secretary to the Ministry of Information, 1939–40; Financial Secretary, War Office, 1940; Joint Parliamentary Under-Secretary of State for War, 1940–42; Minister Resident in the Middle East, 1944–45. Created 1st Baron Altrincham, 1945.

GRIGG, SIR PERCY JAMES (1890–1964). British civil servant. Education: Bournemouth School; St John's College, Cambridge. Joined the Treasury, 1913; Principal Private Secretary to successive Chancellors of the Exchequer, 1921–30; later Permanent Under-Secretary of State, for War, 1939–42. Political career: MP (National), 1942–45; Secretary of State for War, 1942–45.

GUEST, FREDERICK EDWARD (1875–1937). British politician. Served in the Boer War before becoming private secretary to his cousin, Winston Churchill. Political career: MP (Liberal), 1910–22, 1923–29 and (Conservative) 1931–37. Guest served as a junior minister before becoming Chief Government Whip, 1917–21; he was Secretary of State for Air, 1921–22. Called 'Lloyd George's evil genius'.

HANKEY, SIR MAURICE PASCAL ALERS (1877–1963). British civil servant. A Royal Marines officer, Hankey was secretary to the Committee of Imperial Defence, 1912–38, as well as to several other wartime ministerial committees, 1914–18. In 1916, he was appointed Cabinet secretary by Lloyd George. In this capacity, Hankey created the Cabinet Secretariat, which had a fundamental impact on the shaping of modern British government. Created Baron Hankey, 1939.

HAWTREY, SIR RALPH GEORGE (1879–1975). British civil servant. Education: Eton; Trinity College, Cambridge. Entered the Admiralty civil service, 1903; Treasury, 1904–45; Director of Financial Enquiries, 1919–45.

HEALY, CAHIR (1877–1970). Northern Irish politician. Born: County Donegal. Political career: MP (Sinn Féin, later Nationalist), 1922–24 and 1950–55; MP, Northern Ireland Parliament, (Nationalist), 1925–65. Interned by the Northern Ireland government, 1922–24; interned by the British government, 1941–42.

HEALY, TIMOTHY MICHAEL (1855–1931). Irish politician. Born: County Cork; uncle of Kevin O'Higgins. Education: Christian Brothers School, Fermoy. Called to the Irish Bar, 1884. Political career: MP (Nationalist), 1880–83, 1885–1918; took a leading role in destroying Charles Stewart Parnell's career and splitting the Irish Parliamentary Party, 1890–91; rejoined the IPP, 1900; sympathised with Sinn Féin and stood down in 1918 general election; first Governor General of the Irish Free State, 1922–28.

HENDERSON, ARTHUR (1863–1935). British trade union leader and politician. Born: Glasgow. Political career: MP (Labour), 1903–18, 1919–22, 1923, 1924–31, and 1933–35; chairman of the Parliamentary Labour Party 1908–10 and 1914–17; Labour Party Chief Whip, 1914, 1921–24, and 1925–27; Paymaster-General and Labour Adviser, 1916; Minister without Portfolio and member of the War Cabinet, 1916–17; member of the British Mission to Russia, 1917; Home Secretary, 1924; Foreign Secretary, 1929–31; President of the World Disarmament Conference, 1932–33.

HEWART, GORDON (1870–1943). British politician and jurist. Education: Manchester Grammar School; University College, Oxford. Called to the Bar, 1902. Political career: MP (Conservative), 1913–22; Solicitor-General, 1916–19; Attorney-General, 1919–22; attended Versailles Peace Conference, 1919; took part in the Irish Treaty negotiations, 1921; Lord Chief Justice of England, 1922–40. Created 1st Viscount Hewart of Bury in County Lancaster, 1940.

HOARE, SIR SAMUEL JOHN GURNEY (1880–1959). British politician. Born: London. Education: Harrow; New College, Oxford. Assistant Private Secretary to the Colonial Secretary, 1905. Political career: MP (Conservative), 1910–44; Conservative Party Treasurer, 1930–31; Secretary of State for Air, 1922–24 and 1924–29; later held various Cabinet positions, including Secretary of State for India, Foreign Secretary, First Lord of the Admiralty, Home Secretary, Lord Privy Seal and, again, Secretary of State for Air; Ambassador to Spain on Special Mission, 1940–44. Created 1st Viscount Templewood, 1944.

HORNE, SIR ROBERT STEVENSON (1871–1940). Born: Stirlingshire, Scotland. Education: George Watson's College, Edinburgh; University of Glasgow. Called to the Scottish Bar, 1896. Political career: MP (Conservative-Unionist), 1918–37; Minister of Labour, 1919–20; President of the Board of Trade, 1920–21; Chancellor of the Exchequer, 1921–22. Created 1st Viscount Horne of Slamannan, 1937.

JONES, THOMAS (1870–1955). British civil servant. Born: Monmouthshire, Wales. Education: Pengam County School; University College, Aberystwyth; Glasgow University. Career: Barrington Lecturer in Ireland, 1904–5 before becoming a professor of economics at Glasgow University and Queen's University, Belfast. He was Deputy Secretary to the Cabinet, 1916–30.

JOHNSON, THOMAS (1872–1963). Irish trade unionist and politician. Born: Liverpool; immigrated to Ireland, 1892; founder-member of the Irish Labour Party, 1912; Vice-Chairman of the party's executive, 1912–23; member of the Mansion House Conference to co-ordinate opposition to conscription, 1918; to avoid a split of the nationalist vote, Johnson agreed to the Labour Party's abstention from the general election of 1918; co-authored the Democratic Programme adopted by the first Dáil Éireann. Political career: TD (Labour), 1922–28; Opposition Leader, 1922–27; resigned as Labour Party Secretary, 1928; represented Labour in Seanad Éireann, 1928–36; founder-member of the Labour Court, 1946.

JOYNSON-HICKS, SIR WILLIAM (1865–1932). British politician. Born: Canonbury, England; nicknamed, 'Jix'. Trained as a solicitor. Political career: MP (Conservative), 1908–10 and 1911–29. Parliamentary Secretary to the Overseas Trade Department, 1922–23; Financial Secretary to the Treasury, 1923; Minister of Health, 1923–24; Home Secretary, 1924–29. Created Viscount Brentford of Newick in Sussex, 1929.

KENNEDY, HUGH (1879–1936). Irish jurist. Born: Dublin. Education: University College, Dublin; Royal University of Ireland. Called to the Irish Bar, 1902. Member of the committee which drafted the Irish Free State Constitution, 1922; Law Officer of the Irish Provisional Government, 1922; first Attorney-General of the Irish Free State, 1922–24. Political career: TD (Cumann na nGaedheal), 1923–24; member of the first Free State delegation to the League of Nations, 1923.

LAVERY, LADY (HAZEL) (1880–1935). Born: Chicago, Illinois. Society hostess and confidante of British and Irish politicians. Married Irish artist Sir John Lavery, 1910. During the Irish Treaty negotiations, the Laverys' London home became an informal meeting place for the Irish and British delegates; her biographer suggests that she may have had romantic affairs with Michael Collins and, later, with Kevin O'Higgins. A portrait of Lady Lavery, by her husband, graced Ireland's paper currency from 1928 to 1977.

LLOYD GEORGE, DAVID (1863–1945). British politician. Born: Manchester; reared in Llanystumdwy, Wales. Education: Llanystumdwy Church School and privately. Solicitor. Political career: MP (Liberal, later Independent Liberal), 1890–1945; President of the Board of Trade, 1905–8; Chancellor of the Exchequer, 1908–15; Minister of Munitions, 1915–16; unsuccessfully attempted to negotiate a deal on Irish self-government in the wake of the Easter Rising, 1916; Secretary of State for War, 1916; Prime Minister, 1916–22; led British delegation during the Irish Treaty negotiations. Created 1st Earl Lloyd George of Dwyfor, 1945.

LONDONDERRY, 7TH MARQUESS OF, CHARLES STEWART HENRY VANE-TEMPEST-STEWART (1878–1949). Ulster politician. Cousin of Winston Churchill. Education: Eton; Sandhurst. Served in First World War. Political career: MP (Conservative-Unionist), 1906–15; Under-Secretary for Air, 1920–1921; First Commissioner of Works, 1928–29 and 1931; Secretary of State for Air, 1931–35; Lord Privy Seal and Leader of the House of Lords, 1935. Political career, Northern Ireland: Minister of Education and Leader of the Northern Ireland Senate, 1921–26.

LONG, WALTER HUME (1854–1924). British politician. Born: Bath. Education: Harrow; Christ Church, Oxford (did not take a degree). Political career: MP (Conservative), 1880–92, 1893–1921; Parliamentary Secretary to the Local Government Board, 1886–1905; President of the Board of Agriculture, 1895–1900; Chief Secretary of Ireland, 1905; Irish Unionist leader, 1906–10; President of the Local Government

Board, 1915–16; Under-Secretary of State for the Colonies, 1916–19; opposed Lloyd George's Irish negotiations, 1916; chaired Irish Situation Committee, 1918; First Lord of the Admiralty, 1919–21; chaired committee charged with framing the 1920 Government of Ireland Act, 1919–20. Created 1st Viscount Long of Wraxall, 1921.

LOUGHNANE, NORMAN GERALD (1883–1955). British civil servant. Education: London University. Career: Barrister; Colonial Office representative in the Irish Free State, 1923–24; member of the Financial Commission of Enquiry, Mauritius, 1931; member of the British Food Mission in North America, 1943.

MACDONALD, JAMES RAMSAY (1866–1937). British politician. Born: Morayshire, Scotland. Education: Board School. Secretary, Labour Representation Committee, 1900–12; chairman of the Independent Labour Party, 1906–9; Labour Party leader, 1911–14. Political career: MP (Labour, later National Labour), 1906–18 and 1922–37; Labour Party and Opposition Leader, 1922–24; first Labour Prime Minister and Foreign Secretary, 1924; Prime Minister, 1929–35; split the Labour Party with the formation of the National Government, 1931; Lord President of the Council, 1935–37.

MACLEAN, DONALD (1864–1932). British politician. Born: Tiree. Solicitor. Political career: MP (Liberal), 1906–22 and 1929–31; Deputy Chairman of Committees, 1911–18; knighted, 1917; led anti-Coalition Liberal MPs following the 1918 general election until Asquith's return in 1920; joined the National Government as President of the Board of Education, 1931.

MACNEILL, EOIN (1867–1945). Irish politician and historian. Born: County Antrim; brother of James MacNeill. Education: St Malachy's College, Belfast. Founder-member and first vice president of the Gaelic League, 1893; appointed first Professor of Early and Medieval Irish History, University College Dublin, 1908; founder-member and Chief of Staff of the Irish Volunteers, 1913–16; opposed calls for the Volunteers to join the British Army at the outbreak of First World War; also opposed plans for the Easter Rising; imprisoned, 1916–17. Political career: MP/TD (Sinn Féin, later Cumann na nGaedheal), 1918–27; MP, Northern Ireland Parliament (Sinn Féin), 1921–25; first Minister of Finance, 1919; Minister for Industries, 1919–21; supported the Treaty; acted as Ceann Comhairle (Speaker) during the Treaty debates; Minister without Portfolio in the Provisional Government, 1922; Minister of Education, 1922–25; head of Irish delegation at the League of Nations, 1923. MacNeill's son, Brian, joined the Irregulars and was killed during the Civil War. Free State representative to the Boundary Commission, 1923–25; the crisis surrounding the Commission's award effectively ended his political career. Headed the Irish Manuscripts Commission, 1927.

MACNEILL, JAMES (1869–1938). Irish diplomat. Born: County Antrim; brother of Eoin MacNeill. Education: Belvedere School; Blackrock College, Dublin; Emmanuel College, Cambridge. Entered the Indian Civil Service, 1890; later posted as an immigration investigator to the West Indies and Fiji; Chairman of Dublin County Council, 1922; member of the committee which drafted the Irish Free State Constitution, 1922; Free State High Commissioner, 1922–28; succeeded Timothy Healy, as Free State Governor-General, 1928–32; was forced to resign following a dispute with Eamon de Valera and the first Fianna Fáil government.

MACREADY, GENERAL SIR CECIL FREDERICK NEVIL (1862–1946). British soldier. Born: Aberdeen, Scotland. Education: Marlborough; Cheltenham. Commissioned, 1881; commanded British military forces in Ireland, 1920–21; served as an adviser to British negotiators during the Treaty negotiations; oversaw the withdrawal of British forces from southern Ireland, 1922; retired from active service, 1923.

MASTERTON-SMITH, SIR JAMES (1878–1938). British civil servant. Education: Harrow (Scholar); Hertford College, Oxford (Scholar). Entered Home Civil Service, Admiralty, 1901; Private Secretary to Second Sea Lord, 1904–8, to the Permanent Secretary, 1908–10, and to successive First Lords of the Admiralty (Reginald McKenna, Winston Churchill, Arthur Balfour, Edward Carson, and Eric Geddes), 1910–17; Assistant Secretary, Ministry of Munitions, 1917–1919; Assistant Secretary (Additional), War Office and Air Ministry, 1919–20 ; Joint Permanent Secretary, Ministry of Labour, 1920–21; Permanent Under-Secretary of State for the Colonies, 1921–24.

MCGILLIGAN, PATRICK (1889–1979). Irish politician. Born: County Londonderry. Education: St Columb's College, Derry City; Clongowes Wood College, Dublin; University College Dublin. Called to the Bar, 1921. Political career: secretary to Kevin O'Higgins, 1919–23; TD (Cumann na nGaedheal, later Fine Gael), 1923–51; Minister for Industry and Commerce, 1924–32; member of the Free State delegation that agreed the tripartite agreement ending the Boundary Commission crisis, 1925; also Minister of External Affairs, after the assassination of Kevin O'Higgins, 1927–32; led Free State delegation to the Imperial conferences which drafted the Statute of Westminster, 1931; Minister for Finance, 1948–51; Attorney General, 1954–57.

MCNEILL, RONALD (1861–1934). British politician. Born: County Tipperary. Political career: MP (Conservative), 1911–27; Under-Secretary of State, Foreign Office, 1922–24 and 1924–25; Financial Secretary to the Treasury, 1925–27; Chancellor of the Duchy of Lancaster, 1927–29. Created Baron Cushenden, 1927.

MONTAGU, EDWIN SAMUEL (1879–1924). British politician. Education: City of London School; Trinity College, Cambridge. Political career: MP (Liberal and Coalition Liberal), 1906–22; Parliamentary Secretary to the Chancellor of the Exchequer, 1906–08; Parliamentary Under-Secretary of State, India Office, 1910–14; Financial Secretary to the Treasury, 1914–1915 and again in 1916; Chancellor of the Duchy of Lancaster, 1915; Minister of Munitions and member of the War Committee, 1916; Secretary of State for India, 1917–22.

MOSLEY, OSWALD ERNALD (1896–1980). British politician. Son-in-law of Lord Curzon. Education: Winchester; Sandhurst. Served in Second World War. Political career: MP (Conservative-Unionist), 1918–22 (Independent), 1922–24 (Labour), 1924 and 1926–31; Chancellor of Duchy of Lancaster, 1929–30. Founded British Union of Fascists 1932; interned during Second World War.

MULCAHY, GENERAL RICHARD JAMES (1886–1971). Irish soldier and politician. Born: Waterford. Education: Christian Brothers School, Thurles. Joined the Irish Republican Brotherhood and Irish Volunteers, 1913; participated in the Easter Rising; imprisoned, 1916–17; Chief of Staff, Irish Republican Army, 1918–21. Political career: MP/TD (Sinn Féin, later Cumann na nGaedheal and Fine Gael), 1918–43 and 1944–61; acting Minister for Defence, 1919; supported the Treaty; Provisional Government Minister of Defence, 1922; Chief of Staff, Free State Army, 1922; Commander-in-Chief, 1922–23; Minister of Defence, Irish Free State, 1922–24; resigned in the wake of the Army Mutiny. Returned to office as Minister for Local Government, 1927–32. Founder-member of Fine Gael; party leader, 1944–59; Minister of Education, 1948–51 and 1954–57.

NIEMEYER, SIR OTTO ERNST (1883–1971). British civil servant and banker. Born: London. Education: St Paul's School; Balliol College, Oxford. Entered the Treasury civil service, 1906–27; Controller of Finance, 1922–27. Later served on numerous financial missions for the British government to Australia, New Zealand, Brazil, Argentina, India, and China.

O'BRIEN WILLIAM (1852–1928). Irish politician, journalist and land agitator. Born: County Cork. Education: Cloyne Diocesan School; Queen's College, Cork. Political career: MP (Nationalist), 1883, 1887, 1892–1909 and 1910–18. An anti-Parnellite, he was leading force in the reunification of the Irish Parliamentary Party, 1900 but broke with its leadership on several occasions; did not contest seat in 1918 general election and retired from active politics.

O'BYRNE, JOHN (1884–1954). Irish jurist. Born: County Wicklow. Education: University College Dublin; Royal University of Ireland. Called to the Irish Bar, 1911; member of the committee that drafted the Irish Free State Constitution, 1923; member of the Judiciary Committee, 1923; Delegate to the League of Nations, 1924; Attorney-General, 1924–26; Judge of the High Court of Justice, 1926–40; Judge of the Supreme Court of Justice, 1940–54.

O'CONNOR, TIMOTHY POWER (1848–1929). Irish politician. Born: Athlone. Education: Queen's College, Galway. Political career: MP (Irish Nationalist), first for a Galway constituency and then, for the Scotland Division of Liverpool, 1883–1929.

O'HIGGINS, KEVIN CHRISTOPHER (1892–1927). Irish politician. Born: Queen's County (Laois); nephew of Timothy Healy. Education: Clongowes Wood College, Maynooth (expelled); University College, Dublin. Called to the Bar, 1923. Political career: MP/TD (Sinn Féin, later Cumann na nGaedheal), 1918–27; Assistant

Minister for Local Government, 1919–22; Provisional Government Minister for Economic Affairs, 1922; played a leading role in drafting the Irish Free State Constitution, 1922; Free State Minister of Home Affairs, 1922–27; Minister of Justice, 1924–27; later Minister of External Affairs and Vice President of the Executive Council. His father was murdered by Irregulars during the Civil War. O'Higgins took part in the tripartite negotiations that led to the shelving of the Boundary Commission Report, 1925; represented the Free State at the Imperial Conference, 1926. Assassinated.

O'SHIEL, KEVIN (1891–1970). Irish Nationalist political organiser and lawyer. Born: County Tyrone. Career: called to the Irish Bar, 1915. Sinn Féin leader in Ulster, 1916–19; Republican Court Judge, 1919–22; Secretary, North-Eastern Boundary Bureau, 1922–23; Land Commissioner, 1923–63.

PEEL, 2ND VISCOUNT, WILLIAM ROBERT WELLESLEY (1867–1937). British politician. Education: Harrow; Balliol College, Oxford. Called to the Bar, 1893. Political career: MP (Conservative), 1900–06 and 1909–12. Among the offices he held, Peel was Under-Secretary of State for War, 1919–21 and Chancellor of the Duchy of Lancaster and Minister of Transport, 1921–22, before he became Secretary of State for India, 1922–24 and 1928–29. Created Earl Peel, 1929.

PIERCY, WILLIAM (1886–1966). British businessman and financier. Secretary to the Colwyn Committee, 1923–4; Director of the Bank of England, 1946–56. Created 1st Baron Piercy of Burford, 1945.

POLLOCK, HUGH MCDOWELL (1852–1937). Ulster politician. Born: County Down. Education: Bangor Endowed School. Chairman, Belfast Chamber of Commerce. Political career: represented Belfast Chamber of Commerce in the Irish Convention, 1917–18; MP, Northern Ireland Parliament, (Unionist), 1921–37; Finance Minister and Deputy Prime Minister, 1921–37.

REDMOND, JOHN (1856–1918). Irish politician. Born: County Wexford. Education: Clongowes Wood College; Trinity College, Dublin. Called to the English Bar, 1885; to the Irish Bar, 1887. Political career: MP (Nationalist), 1881–1918. Reunited the Irish Parliamentary Party after its split over the leadership of Charles Stewart Parnell; forced Liberal Prime Minister H. H. Asquith to commit his government to Irish Home Rule in return for Nationalist backing of the Parliament Act of 1911. Redmond's authority was undermined when the Liberals immediately suspended the 1914 Home Rule Act and he was further estranged from the Irish nationalists as First World War dragged on.

RIDDELL, GEORGE ALLARDICE (1865–1934). British journalist and newspaper proprietor. Confidant of David Lloyd George. Chairman, News of the World, Ltd; represented British press at the Paris Peace Conferences, 1919–22 and at Washington Conference on Disarmament, 1921–22. Created 1st Baron Riddell, 1920.

SALISBURY, 4TH MARQUESS OF, JAMES EDWARD HUBERT GASCOYNE-CECIL (1861–1947). British politician. Born: London; elder brother of Robert and Hugh Cecil. Education: Eton; University College, Oxford. Political career: MP (Conservative), 1885–92 and 1893–1903; Under-Secretary for Foreign Affairs, 1900–3; Lord Privy Seal, 1903–5; President of the Board of Trade, 1905; Lord President of the Council, 1922–24; Chancellor of the Duchy of Lancaster, 1922–23; Lord Privy Seal, 1924–29; Leader of the House of Lords, 1925–29.

SALVIDGE, SIR ARCHIBALD TUTTON JAMES (1863–1928). British political activist. Education: Liverpool Institute. Managing Director, Bent's Brewery Co. Ltd. Liverpool Alderman; Leader of Liverpool City Council; Chairman of the Council of the National Unionist Association of Conservative and Liberal Unionist Organisations, 1913; President, Liverpool Constitutional Association.

SCOTT, CHARLES PRESTWICH (1846–1932). British journalist. Education: private; Corpus Christi College, Oxford. Editor, the *Manchester Guardian*, 1872–1929. Political career: MP (Liberal), Lancashire, 1895–1906; long-time confidant of David Lloyd George.

SELBORNE, 2ND EARL OF, WILLIAM WALDEGRAVE PALMER (1859–1942). British politician. Brother-in-law of the 4th Marquess of Salisbury and of Lords Robert and Hugh Cecil. Education: Winchester; University College, Oxford. Assistant Private Secretary to the Secretary of State for War and Chancellor of Exchequer, 1882–85. Political career: MP (Liberal, later Liberal Unionist), 1885–95; Under-Secretary of State for the Colonies, 1895–1900; First Lord of the Admiralty, 1900–5; Governor of Transvaal and High Commissioner for South Africa, 1905–10; President of the Board of Agriculture, 1915–16.

SIMON, SIR JOHN ALLSEBROOK (1873–1954). British politician. Education: Fettes College, Edinburgh; Wadham College, Oxford. Barrister. Served in the Royal Flying Corps, 1917–18. Political career: MP (Liberal, later Liberal National), 1906–18, 1922–31, and 1931–40; Solicitor-General, 1910–13; Attorney-General, 1913–15; Home Secretary, 1915–16; Foreign Secretary, 1931–35; Home Secretary and Deputy Leader of the House of Commons, 1935–37; Chancellor of the Exchequer, 1937–40; Leader of the Liberal National Party; Lord Chancellor, 1940–45. Created 1st Viscount Simon of Stackpole Elidor, 1940.

SNOWDEN, PHILIP (1864–1937). British politician. Born: Yorkshire. Education: Board School. Civil servant, 1886–93; journalist and lecturer. Political career: chairman of the Independent Labour Party, 1903–6 and 1917–20; MP (Labour), 1906–18 and 1922–31; first Labour Chancellor of the Exchequer, 1924 and 1929–31; Lord Privy Seal, 1931–32. Created 1st Viscount Snowden of Ickornshaw, 1931.

SPENDER, LADY (LILIAN), *née* DEAN (1880–1968). Ulster Unionist supporter and diarist. Born: London. Education: Reading Agricultural College. Married Wilfrid Spender, 1913.

SPENDER, SIR WILFRID BLISS (1876–1960). Northern Irish civil servant. Education: Winchester College; Staff College, Camberley. Career: Joined the Royal Artillery, 1897; resigned over the Ulster Question, 1913; founder-member of the Ulster Volunteer Force, 1913; served in the Ulster Division during First World War; founder-member of the British Legion; re-established and commanded the Ulster Volunteer Force, 1919; first Secretary to the Northern Ireland Cabinet, 1921–25; Permanent Secretary, Ministry of Finance, and Head of Northern Ireland's Civil Service, 1925–44; member of the Joint Exchequer Board, 1933–54.

STACK, AUSTIN (1880–1929). Irish politician. Born: County Kerry. Founder-member of the Irish Volunteers, 1913; arrested and imprisoned at the outbreak of the Easter Rising, 1916–17. Political career: MP/TD (Sinn Féin), 1918–23; Deputy Minister for Home Affairs, 1919–21; Minister of Home Affairs, 1921–22. Opposed the Irish Treaty and joined the Irregulars. Uncompromising in his republican views, he remained in Sinn Féin after de Valera split the party to create Fianna Fáil.

STEEL-MAITLAND, SIR ARTHUR HERBERT DRUMMOND RAMSAY (1876–1935). British politician. Education: Rugby; Balliol College, Oxford. Political career: MP (Conservative), 1910–35; Conservative Party chairman, 1911; Parliamentary Under-Secretary for the Colonies, 1915–17; Joint Parliamentary Under-Secretary of State for the Foreign Office and Parliamentary Secretary to the Board of Trade in his capacity as Head of the Department of Overseas Trade (Development and Intelligence) 1917–19; Minister of Labour, 1924–29.

STEPHENS, EDWARD MILLINGTON (1888–1955). Irish civil servant. Born: Dublin. Career: secretary to the committee that drafted the Irish Free State Constitution, 1922; Secretary, North-Eastern Boundary Bureau, 1923–26; later Assistant Registrar to the Supreme Court and Registrar of the Court of Criminal Appeal; nephew and biographer of Irish playwright, J. M. Synge.

STEVENSON, FRANCES (1888–1972). British Cabinet secretary. Born: Worthing, England. Education: London University. Private secretary to David Lloyd George, 1912–43. Married Lloyd George, 1943.

STRACHEY, JOHN ST LOE (1860–1927). British journalist and barrister. Education: Balliol College, Oxford. Editor and proprietor of *The Spectator* until he retired, 1925.

STURGIS, SIR MARK BERESFORD RUSSELL (1884–1949). British civil servant. Private secretary to H. H. Asquith, 1906–10; Special Commissioner of Income Tax, 1910; Chairman, Treasury Selection Board, 1919–20; Joint Assistant Under-Secretary for Ireland, 1920–22; Assistant Under-Secretary of State for Irish Services, 1922–24. Took by deed poll additional surname of Grant, 1935.

TALLENTS, SIR STEPHEN GEORGE (1884–1958). British civil servant. Education: Harrow; Balliol College, Oxford. Joined the Board of Trade, 1909–14; served in First World War and wounded; returned to the civil service, in which he rose to the rank of Private Secretary to Viscount Fitz-Alan, Lord-Lieutenant of Ireland, 1921–22, and Imperial Secretary, Northern Ireland, 1922–26. Tallents subsequently worked as Secretary to the Empire Marketing Board and was BBC Controller for Overseas Services, among other positions.

THOMAS, JAMES HENRY (1874–1949). British trade union leader and politician. Born: Newport. Education: Council schools. Began working at nine years of age; General Secretary of the National Union of Railwaymen, 1918–24 and 1925–31. Political career: MP (Labour, later National Labour), 1910–36; Vice-Chairman of the Parliamentary Labour Party, 1921; Colonial Secretary, 1924 and 1931; Lord Privy Seal and Minister of Employment, 1929–30; Dominions and Colonial Secretary, 1935–36.

TYRRELL, WILLIAM GEORGE (1866–1947). British civil servant. Born: Naini Tal, India. Education: Balliol College, Oxford. Entered the Foreign Service, 1889; private secretary to Sir Edward Grey, 1907–15; Assistant Under-Secretary of State for Foreign Affairs, 1919–25; Permanent Under-Secretary of State for Foreign Affairs, 1925–28; Ambassador to France, 1928–34. Later President of the British Board of Film Censors, 1935–47. Created Baron Tyrrell of Avon, 1929.

UPCOTT, SIR GILBERT CHARLES (1880–1967). British civil servant. Born, Cullompton, Devon. Education: Marlborough; Corpus Christi College, Oxford. Joined the Treasury, 1903; Treasury Deputy Controller, 1921–31.

WATERFIELD, SIR ALEXANDER PERCIVAL (1888–1965). British civil servant. Education: Westminster; Christ Church, Oxford. Joined the Treasury, 1911; Treasury Remembrancer in Ireland, 1920–22; later, Deputy Secretary, Ministry of Information and Civil Service Commissioner.

WATT, SAMUEL (1876–1927). British civil servant. Born: County Down. Education: Trinity College, Dublin. Entered the civil service, working first in the Public Record Office, Dublin, before eventually becoming Private Secretary to successive Chief Secretaries for Ireland, 1918–20. Transferred from the Irish Office to work for the new Northern Ireland government, 1921. According to his obituary in *The Times*, his 'experience was invaluable in this stormy period'.

WEBB, MARTHA BEATRICE (1858–1943). British social reformer and Labour Party organiser. An indefatigable worker, Webb and her husband, Sidney, wrote numerous articles and books to promote their ideas. They were founder-members of the Fabian Society (1884) to promote their vision of a gradualist, democratic, and parliamentary path to socialism. They later helped found the London School of Economics (1895) as well as the *New Statesman* magazine (1913).

WEBB, SIDNEY JAMES (1859–1947). British social reformer and Labour Party organiser. Education: Birkbeck Institute; City of London College. Political career: MP (Labour), 1922–29; President of the Board of Trade, 1924; Dominion and Colonial Secretary, 1929–30; Colonial Secretary, 1930–31. Created Baron Passfield, 1929.

WHISKARD, SIR GEOFFREY GRANVILLE (1886–1957). British civil servant. Education: St Paul's School; Wadham College, Oxford. Joined the Home Office, 1911; Assistant Secretary, Chief Secretary's Office, Dublin Castle, 1920–22: Colonial Office, 1922–25; Dominions, Office. 1925–29. Whiskard later served as High Commissioner to Australia.

WILSON, FIELD MARSHAL SIR HENRY HUGHES (1864–1922). British soldier and politician. Born: County Longford. Education: Marlborough School. Served in the Boer War; brigadier general, 1907; Director of Military Operations, War Office, 1910–14; Lieutenant-General, 1914; secretly backed the Curragh Mutiny, 1914; Deputy Chief of Staff, 1914; Chief Liaison Officer for the British Expeditionary Force to the French Army, 1915; allied himself with Lloyd George's war policies; Chief of the Imperial General Staff, 1918–22; Field Marshal, 1919; became estranged from Lloyd George over Versailles Treaty and government policy towards Ireland, 1919–21. Political career: MP (Unionist), 1922; Security Adviser to the Northern Ireland government, 1922. Assassinated by Irish republicans, June 1922.

WOOD, EDWARD FREDERICK LINDLEY (1881–1959). British politician. Education: Eton; Christ Church and All Soul's, Oxford. Political career: MP (Conservative-Unionist), 1910–25; Parliamentary Under-Secretary for the Colonies, 1921–22; President of the Board of Education, 1922–24; Minister of Agriculture, 1924–25; Viceroy of India, 1926–31; President of the Board of Education, 1932–35; Secretary of State for War, 1935; Lord Privy Seal, 1935–37; Leader of the House of Lords, 1935–38 and 1940; Lord President of the Council, 1937–38; Foreign Secretary, 1938–40; British Ambassador to Washington, 1941–46. Created 1st Baron Irwin, 1925, and 1st Earl of Halifax, 1944.

WORTHINGTON-EVANS, SIR LAMING (1868–1931). British politician. Qualified as a solicitor. Political career: MP (Conservative), 1910–31; Controller, Foreign Trade Department, Foreign Office, 1916; Parliamentary Secretary to the Ministry of Munitions, 1916–18; Minister of Blockade, 1918; Minister of Pensions, 1919–20; Minister without Portfolio, 1920–21; assisted Walter Long with piloting the 1920 Government of Ireland Act through Parliament; Secretary of State for War, 1921–22 and 1924–29; Postmaster-General, 1923–24.

YOUNGER, GEORGE (1851–1929). British political leader. Education: Edinburgh Academy. Chairman of George Younger & Son Ltd, brewers; Conservative and Unionist Party chairman, 1916–23; party Treasurer, 1923–29. Created 1st Viscount Younger of Leckie, 1923.

Appendix II

Articles of Agreement for a Treaty
between
Great Britain and Ireland

ARTICLE I

Ireland shall have the same constitutional status in the Community of Nations known as the British Empire as the Dominion of Canada, the Commonwealth of Australia, the Dominion of New Zealand, and the Union of South Africa with a Parliament having powers to make laws for the peace, order, and good government of Ireland, and an Executive responsible to that Parliament, and shall be styled and known as the Irish Free State.

ARTICLE II

Subject to the provisions hereinafter set out the position of the Irish Free State in relation to the Imperial Parliament and Government and otherwise shall be that of the Dominion of Canada, and the law, practice and constitutional usage governing the relationship of the Crown or the representative of the Crown and of the Imperial Parliament to the Dominion of Canada shall govern their relationship to the Irish Free State.

ARTICLE III

The representative of the Crown in Ireland shall be appointed in like manner as the Governor-General of Canada and in accordance with the practice observed in the making of such appointments.

ARTICLE IV

The oath to be taken by Members of the Parliament of the Irish Free State shall be in the following form:

I . . . do solemnly swear true faith and allegiance to the Constitution of the Irish Free State as by law established and that I will be faithful to His Majesty King George V., his heirs and successors by law, in virtue of the common citizenship of Ireland with Great Britain and her adherence to and membership of the group of nations forming the British Commonwealth of Nations.

ARTICLE V

The Irish Free State shall assume liability for the service of the public debt of the United Kingdom as existing at the date hereof and towards the payment of war pensions as existing at that date in such proportion as may be fair and equitable, having regard to any just claims on the part of Ireland by way of set-off or counter-claim, the amount of such sums being determined in default of agreement by the arbitration of one or ignore independent persons being citizens of the British Empire.

ARTICLE VI

Until an arrangement has been made between the British and Irish Governments whereby the Irish Free State undertakes her own coastal defence, the defence by sea of Great Britain and Ireland shall be undertaken by His Majesty's Imperial Forces, but this shall not prevent the construction or maintenance by the Government of the Irish Free State of such vessels as are necessary for the protection of the revenue or the fisheries.

The foregoing provisions of this article shall be reviewed at a conference of representatives of the British and Irish Governments to be held at the expiration of five years from the date hereof with a view to the undertaking by Ireland of a share in her own coastal defence.

ARTICLE VII

The Government of the Irish Free State shall afford to His Majesty's Imperial Forces:

(a) In time of peace such harbour and other facilities as are indicated in the Annex hereto, or such other facilities as may from time to time be agreed between the British Government and the Government of the Irish Free State; and

(b) In time of war or of strained relations with a foreign power such harbour and other facilities as the British Government may require for the purposes of such defence as aforesaid.

ARTICLE VIII

With a view to securing the observance of the principle of international limitation of armaments, if the Government of the Irish Free State establishes and maintains a military defence force, the establishments thereof shall not exceed in size such proportion of the military establishments maintained in Great Britain as that which the population of Ireland bears to the population of Great Britain.

ARTICLE IX

The ports of Great Britain and the Irish Free State shall be freely open to the ships of the other country on payment of the customary port and other dues.

ARTICLE X

The Government of the Irish Free State agrees to pay fair compensation on terms not less favourable than those accorded by the Act of 1920 to judges, officials, members of police forces and other public servants who are discharged by it, or who retire in consequence of the change of government effected in pursuance hereof.

Provided, that this agreement shall not apply to members of the Auxiliary Police Force or to persons recruited in Great Britain for the Royal Irish Constabulary during the two years next preceding the date hereof. The British Government will assume responsibility for such compensation or pensions as may be payable to any of these excepted persons.

ARTICLE XI

Until the expiration of one month from the passing of the Act of Parliament for the ratification of this instrument the powers of the Parliament and the Government of the Irish Free State shall not be exercisable as respects Northern Ireland, and the provisions of the Government of Ireland Act of 1920 shall, so far as they relate to Northern Ireland, remain of full force and effect, and no election shall be held for the return of members to serve in the Parliament of the Irish Free State for constituencies in Northern Ireland, unless a resolution is passed by both Houses of the Parliament of Northern Ireland in favour of the holding of such elections before the end of the said month.

ARTICLE XII

If before the expiration of the said month an address is presented to His Majesty by both Houses of the Parliament of Northern Ireland to that effect, the powers of the Parliament and the Government of the Irish Free State shall no longer extend to Northern Ireland, and the provisions of the Government of Ireland Act of 1920 (including those relating to the Council of Ireland), shall, so far as they relate to Northern Ireland, continue to be of full force and effect, and this instrument shall have effect subject to the necessary modifications.

Provided, that if such an address is so presented, a Commission consisting of three persons, one to be appointed by the Government of the Irish Free State, one to be appointed by the Government of Northern Ireland, and one who shall be Chairman, to be appointed by the British Government, shall determine, in accordance with the wishes of the inhabitants, so far as may be compatible with economic and geographic conditions, the boundaries between Northern Ireland and the rest of Ireland, and for the purposes of the Government of Ireland Act of 1920, and of this instrument, the boundary of Northern Ireland shall be such as may be determined by such Commission.

ARTICLE XIII

For the purpose of the last foregoing article, the powers of the Parliament of Southern Ireland under the Government of Ireland Act of 1920 to elect members of the Council of Ireland shall, after the Parliament of the Irish Free State is constituted, be exercised by that Parliament.

ARTICLE XIV

After the expiration of the said month, if no such address as is mentioned in Article XII hereof is presented, the Parliament and Government of Northern Ireland shall continue to exercise as respects Northern Ireland the powers conferred on them by the Government of Ireland Act of 1920, but the Parliament and Government of the Irish Free State shall in Northern Ireland have in relation to matters in respect of which the Parliament of Northern Ireland has not power to make laws under that Act (including matters which under the said Act are within the jurisdiction of the Council of Ireland) the same powers as in the rest of Ireland, subject to such other provisions as may be agreed in manner hereinafter appearing.

ARTICLE XV

At any time after the date hereof the Government of Northern Ireland and the provisional Government of Southern Ireland, hereinafter constituted, may meet for the purpose of discussing the provisions, subject to which the last foregoing Article is to operate in the event of no such address as is therein mentioned being presented, and those provisions may include:

(a) Safeguards with regard to patronage in Northern Ireland;

(b) Safeguards with regard to the collection of revenue in Northern Ireland;

(c) Safeguards with regard to import and export duties affecting the trade or industry of Northern Ireland;

(d) Safeguards for minorities in Northern Ireland;

(e) The settlement of the financial relations between Northern Ireland and the Irish Free State;

(f) The establishment and powers of a local militia in Northern Ireland and the relation of the defence forces of the Irish Free State and of Northern Ireland respectively; and if at any such meeting provisions are agreed to, the same shall have effect as if they were included amongst the provisions subject to which the powers of the Parliament and the Government of the Irish Free State are to be exercisable in Northern Ireland under Article XIV hereof.

ARTICLE XVI

Neither the Parliament of the Irish Free State nor the Parliament of Northern Ireland shall make any law so as either directly or indirectly to endow any religion or prohibit or restrict the free exercise thereof or give any preference or impose any disability on account of religious belief or religious status, or affect prejudicially the right of any child to attend a school receiving public money without attending the religious instruction at the school, or make any discrimination as respects State aid between schools under the management of different religious denominations, or divert from any religious denomination or any educational institution any of its property except for public utility purposes and on payment of compensation.

ARTICLE XVII

By way of provisional arrangement for the administration of Southern Ireland during the interval which must elapse between the date hereof and the constitution of a Parliament and Government of the Irish Free State in accordance therewith, steps shall be taken forthwith for summoning a meeting of members of Parliament elected for constituencies in Southern Ireland since the passing of the Government of Ireland Act of 1920, and for constituting a provisional Government, and the British Government shall take the steps necessary to transfer to such provisional Government the powers and machinery requisite for the discharge of its duties, provided that every member of such provisional Government shall have signified in writing his or her acceptance of this instrument. But this arrangement shall not continue in force beyond the expiration of twelve months from the date hereof.

ARTICLE XVIII

This instrument shall be submitted forthwith by His Majesty's Government for the approval of Parliament and by the Irish signatories to a meeting summoned for the purpose of the members elected to sit in the House of Commons of Southern Ireland and, if approved, shall be ratified by the necessary legislation.

Signed on behalf of the British delegation:

LLOYD GEORGE,
AUSTEN CHAMBERLAIN,
BIRKENHEAD,
WINSTON S. CHURCHILL,
L. WORTHINGTON-EVANS,
HAMAR GREENWOOD,
GORDON HEWART.

On behalf of the Irish delegation:

ART O GRIOBHTHA   (ARTHUR GRIFFITH),
MICHEAL O COILEAIN   (MICHAEL COLLINS),
RIOBARD BARTUN   (ROBERT C. BARTON),
E. S. O DUGAIN   (EAMON J. DUGGAN),
SEORSA GHABHAIN UI DHUBHTHAIGH   (GEORGE GAVAN DUFFY).

6th December 1921.

ANNEX

1. The following are the specific facilities required:

Dockyard Port at Berehaven
(a) Admiralty property and rights to be retained as at the date hereof. Harbour defence to remain in charge of British care and maintenance parties.

Queenstown
(b) Harbour defences to remain in charge of British care and maintenance parties. Certain mooring buoys to be retained for use of His Majesty's ships.

Belfast Lough
(c) Harbour defences to remain in charge of British care and maintenance parties.

Lough Swilly
(d) Harbour defences to remain in charge of British care and maintenance parties.

Aviation
(e) Facilities in the neighbourhood of the above ports for coastal defence by air.

Oil Fuel Storage
(f) Haulbowline ⎰ To be offered for sale to commercial companies
    Rathmullen ⎱ under guarantee that purchasers shall maintain
                 a certain minimum stock for Admiralty purposes.

2. A Convention shall be made between the British Government and the Government of the Irish Free State to give effect to the following conditions:

(a) That submarine cables shall not be landed or wireless stations for communication with places outside Ireland be established except by agreement with the British Government; that the existing cable landing rights and wireless concessions shall not be withdrawn except by agreement with the British Government; and that the British Government shall be entitled to land additional submarine cables or establish additional wireless stations for communication with places outside Ireland.

(b) That lighthouses, buoys, beacons, and any navigational marks or navigational aids shall be maintained by the Government of the Irish Free State as at the date hereof, and shall not be removed or added to except by agreement with the British Government.

(c) That war signal stations shall be closed down and left in charge of care and maintenance parties, the Government of the Irish Free State being offered the option of taking them over and working them for commercial purposes subject to Admiralty inspection and guaranteeing the upkeep of existing telegraphic communication therewith.

3. A Convention shall be made between the same Governments for the regulation of Civil Communication by Air.

Appendix III

House of Lords, S.W.1.

March 3rd, 1922.

<u>Secret</u>.

My dear Balfour,

I understand that you wish to be reassured as to the meaning of the clause in the Articles of Agreement which relates to the determination of the boundary between Northern Ireland and the rest of Ireland.

It seems to me right in the first place to set out the exact words used in the Treaty, and to draw attention to the context in which they appear.

They appear in the form of a proviso to Article 12 of the Treaty. The main purpose of that Article is to preserve to Northern Ireland, if the Parliament of Northern Ireland desire, the maintenance of the provisions of the Government of Ireland Act, 1920, so far as they relate to Northern Ireland. The Article contemplates the maintenance of Northern Ireland as an entity already existing – not as a new State to be brought into existence upon the ratification of the Articles of Agreement. It is regarded as a creature already constituted, having its own Parliament and its own defined boundaries.

The Article then proceeds (by way of proviso, as I have said) to provide for the modification of those boundaries, and it does so in the following form (leaving out immaterial words):–

"Provided that ..... a Commission ..... shall
"determine, in accordance with the wishes of the
"inhabitants, so far as may be compatible with
"economic and geographic conditions, the boundaries
"between Northern Ireland and the rest of Ireland,
"<u>and for the purposes of the Government of Ireland</u>
"<u>Act, 1920</u>, and of this instrument, the boundary
"of Northern Ireland shall be such as may be
"determined by such Commission."

We have, therefore, a territory, namely, that of Northern Ireland, the boundaries of which are defined by the Act of 1920, and we have an Agreement that those boundaries should be subject to determination by a Commission in accordance with certain conditions set out in the Treaty.

This seems to me to differ in no way from the ordinary precedents set in innumerable Treaties between European States during the 19th century. Compare, for example, the establishment of the Principality of Bulgaria by the Treaty of Berlin. Article 2 of that Treaty sets out in detail the territories to be comprised within the new Principality just as the Government of Ireland Act sets out in detail the territories to be comprised within Northern Ireland.

The Article of the Berlin Treaty proceeds (I translate myself for clearness sake):–

"This delimitation will be fixed on the spot by
"the European Commission on which the signatory
"Powers will be represented. It is understood –

  "(1) That this Commission will take into
  "consideration the necessity of His
  "Imperial Majesty the Sultan being able
  "to defend the frontiers of the Balkans
  "of Eastern Rumania.
  "(2) That no fortifications can be
  "erected in a zone ten kilometres
  "round Samakow."

The only difference, as it seems to me, between the governing instruments in the two cases is that in one case (that of Bulgaria) the fixing of the territory and the power of rectifying the boundary of the territory so fixed are included in one document, and that in the other case (that of the Irish Treaty) the Government of Ireland Act, to which express reference is made in the Treaty, and the Treaty itself must be read together. Of course different considerations are set out in the two cases as those which the Commission is to apply as criteria, but this constitutes no difference in principle.

It appears to me inconceivable that any competent and honest arbitrator could take the opposite view. If the Article had meant what Craig now apprehends that it does, quite obviously the Agreement would have been drafted in very different words. I might remark incidentally that I can hardly suppose that in that case the duty would have been committed to a Commission. The natural course would have been that the Governments concerned should retain everything but details in their own hands, in accordance again with the precedents of Treaties. But assuming that it was intended that a Commission should operate which might conceivably wholly change the character of Northern Ireland by enormous reductions of its territory, I think it would have been necessary to say:

> "A Commission shall determine in accordance with
> "the wishes of the inhabitants, etc., what portions
> "of Ireland shall be included in the Irish Free
> "State and what portions shall be included in
> "Northern Ireland, and shall fix the boundary
> "between the portions thus allotted."

That my own view is well founded is made even clearer by the attitude of Carson and Craig during the earlier debates on the Treaty. This particular clause is the only one which can interfere with the status of Ulster as fixed by the Act of 1920, and it therefore focuses the whole searchlight of the controversy. Yet until Collins made the suggestion, no living soul in either House ever suggested that the clause was capable of the fantastic meaning of which Craig now professes himself to be apprehensive.

In the debates of December, Carson was seeking eagerly for any basis upon which he could establish his charge of treachery to Ulster. If you read his speech, you will not find a word suggesting that he then took this view. The real truth is that Collins, very likely pressed by his own people and anxious to appraise at their highest value the benefits which he had brought to them, in a moment of excitement committed himself unguardedly to this doctrine, and that it has no foundation whatever except in his overheated imagination.

If and when Collins and Griffiths obtain a majority and a sane Parliament, I think it highly probable that they will come to terms with Craig. If this does not happen, I have no doubt that the Tribunal, not being presided over by a lunatic, will take a rational view of the limits of its own jurisdiction and will reach a rational conclusion.

Yours as ever,
(Sgd.) BIRKENHEAD

Bibliography

PRIMARY SOURCES

MANUSCRIPTS

ENGLAND

Birmingham
University of Birmingham Library
    Austen Chamberlain Papers
    Neville Chamberlain Papers and Diary

Cambridge
Cambridge University Library
    Stanley Baldwin Papers
    Marquess of Crewe Papers
    Viscount Templewood (Samuel Hoare) Papers

Churchill College
    Clementine Spencer Churchill Papers
    Winston Spencer Churchill Papers
    Maurice Hankey Diary and Papers

Hatfield
Hatfield House
    Lord Quickswood Papers
    Lord Salisbury Papers

London
British Library
    Arthur James Balfour Papers
    Viscount Cave Papers
    Robert Cecil Papers
    Herbert Gladstone Papers
    Walter Long Papers
    C. P. Scott Papers

Oriental and India Collection
 Marquess of Curzon Papers
 Lord Irwin Papers
 Lord Reading Papers

House of Lords Record Office
 Lord Beaverbrook Papers
 Andrew Bonar Law Papers
 J. C. C. Davidson Papers
 David Lloyd George Papers
 Frances Lloyd George Papers
 John St Loe Strachey Papers

Imperial War Museum
 Sir John French Papers
 Sir Henry Wilson Papers

London School of Economics and Political Science
 Labour Party Conference Reports
 Passfield Papers
  Beatrice Webb Diary
  Sidney-Beatrice Webb Correspondence
 William Piercy Papers

Public Record Office
 Official Papers
  Cabinet Minutes & Papers
  Colonial Office Papers
  Dominions Office Papers
  Home Office Papers
  Lord Chancellor's Office
  Records of the Prime Minister's Office
  Treasury Papers
  War Office Papers
 Private Papers
  J. Ramsay MacDonald Papers
  Lord Midleton Papers
  Mark Sturgis Diary
  William E. Wylie Papers

Oxford
Bodleian Library
    Organisation Papers
        National Unionist Association Papers
    Private Papers
        H. H. Asquith Papers
        Lionel Curtis Papers
        H. A. L. Fisher Papers and Diary
        Sir Edward Grigg Papers
        J. L. L. Hammond Papers
        Donald Maclean Papers
        Earl of Selborne Papers
        Lady Selborne Papers
        Sir Laming Worthington-Evans Papers

Rhodes House Library
    Richard Feetham Papers

Sittingbourne
Viscount Davidson Collection (Private)
    J. C. C. and Joan Davidson Correspondence

York
Borthwick Institute, University of York
    Lord Halifax Papers

REPUBLIC OF IRELAND

Dublin
National Archives
    Dáil Éireann Papers
    Department of Foreign Affairs Papers
    Department of the Taoiseach Papers
    North-Eastern Boundary Bureau Papers

National Library
    Organisation Papers
        Sinn Féin Standing Committee Minutes
    Private Papers

Joseph Brennan Papers
Michael Collins Papers
George Gavan Duffy Papers
Timothy Healy Papers
Thomas Johnson Papers
Kathleen MacKenna Napoli Papers
Eoin MacNeill Papers
Art O'Brien Papers
J. J. O'Connell Papers
Sean T. O'Kelly Papers
Sean O Luing Papers
Sean O'Mahony Papers
John Redmond Papers
Celia Shaw Papers

Trinity College Archives
Erskine Childers Papers
John Dillon Papers
E. M. Stephens Papers

University College Dublin Archives
Ernest Blythe Papers
Michael Hayes Papers
Eoin MacNeill Papers
Richard Mulcahy Papers

Killiney
Franciscan Library
Eamon de Valera Papers
(Note: These papers are now at University College Dublin Archives.)

NORTHERN IRELAND

Belfast
Public Records Office of Northern Ireland
Official Papers
Cabinet Minutes and Papers
Department of Finance Papers
Department of Prime Minister's Correspondence

Organisation Papers
    Irish Unionist Alliance Papers
    Ulster Unionist Council Papers
Private Papers
    Edward Carson Papers
    Lady Carson's Diary
    John Henry Collins Papers
    Lady Craig's Diary
    Frederick H. Crawford Papers
    Cahir Healy Papers
    Marchioness of Londonderry Papers
    Marquess of Londonderry Papers
    Hugh de F. Montgomery Papers
    Lady Spender's Diary
    Wilfrid Spender Papers

SCOTLAND

Edinburgh
Scottish Record Office
    Arthur James Balfour Papers
    Lord Lothian (Philip Kerr) Papers

WALES

Aberystwyth
National Library
    George M. Ll. Davies Papers
    Thomas Jones Papers
    David Lloyd George Papers
    A. J. Sylvester Papers

NEWSPAPERS AND JOURNALS

ENGLAND

London
Contemporary Review
Daily Chronicle
Daily Express
Daily Herald
Daily Mail
Daily Mirror
Daily News
Daily Telegraph
Evening Standard
Independent on Sunday
Morning Post
The Nation
National Review
New Statesman
Nineteenth Century
The Observer
Pall Mall & Globe
The People
Popular View
Quarterly Review
Round Table
The Spectator
Sunday Express
The Times
Westminster Gazette

Liverpool
Liverpool Post

Manchester
Manchester Guardian

Yorkshire
Yorkshire Post

REPUBLIC OF IRELAND

Dublin
Freeman's Journal
Irish Independent
The Irish Times
Eire

NORTHERN IRELAND

Belfast
Belfast News-Letter
Belfast Telegraph
Irish News

Omagh
Ulster Herald
Tyrone Constitution

WALES

Cardiff
Western Mail

PARLIAMENTARY PAPERS

GREAT BRITAIN

Parliamentary Debates. House of Commons. Fifth Series (London, 1912–26).

Parliamentary Debates. House of Lords. Fifth Series (London, 1919–26).

Parliamentary Papers:

Cd 8310: *Headings of a Settlement as to the Government of Ireland*; 1916, xxii, 415.

Cmd 63: *Outrages (Ireland)*; 1920, xl, 799.

Cmd 645: *Government of Ireland Bill – Outline of Financial Provisions*; 1920, xl, 771.

Cmd 786: *Government of Ireland Bill – Basis of Financial Estimates*; 1920, xl, 787.

Cmd 1108: *Documents Relative to the Sinn Fein Movement*; 1921, xxix, 429.

Cmd 1326: *Intercourse Between Bolshevism and Sinn Fein*; 1921, xxix, 489.

Cmd 1560: *Articles of Agreement for a Treaty Between Great Britain and Ireland*; 1921, Sess. II, i, 75.

Cmd 1561: *Correspondence Between His Majesty's Government and the Prime Minister of Northern Ireland Relating to the Proposals for an Irish Settlement*; 1921, Sess. II, i, 83.

Cmd 1773: *Irish Free State (Consequential Provisions Bill – Memorandum on Financial Provisions)*; 1922, Sess. II, iii, 739.

Cmd 2032: *The Irish Grants Committee: Second Interim Report*; 1924, xi, 357.

Cmd 2072: *First Report of the Northern Ireland Special Arbitration Committee*; 1924, xi, 341.

Cmd 2155: *Irish Free State and Northern Ireland: Correspondence Between His Majesty's Government and the Governments of the Irish Free State and Northern Ireland Relating to Article 12 of the Agreement for a Treaty Between Great Britain and Ireland*; June 1924, xviii, 69.

Cmd 2166: *Irish Free State and Northern Ireland: Further Correspondence Relating to Article 12 of the Articles of Agreement for a Treaty Between Great Britain and Ireland*; June 1924, xviii, 97.

Cmd 2214: *Report of the Judicial Committee of the Privy Council, as Approved by Order of His Majesty in Council, of the 31st July, 1924, on the Questions Connected with the Irish Boundary Commission Referred to the said Committee*; 1924, xi, 351.

Cmd 2264: *Irish Boundary: Extracts from Parliamentary Debates, Command Papers, etc., Relevant to Questions Arising Out of Article XII of the Articles of Agreement for a Treaty Between Great Britain and Ireland, Dated 6th December, 1921*, 1924, xviii, 113.

Cmd 2389: *Final Report of the Northern Ireland Special Arbitration Committee*, 1924–25, xiv, 125.

Cmd 2588: *Unemployment Insurance (Northern Ireland Agreement): Memorandum Explaining Financial Resolution*, 1926, xxii, 737.

Cmnd 5460: *Royal Commission on the Constitution, 1969–1973*, Oct. 1973, xi, i (The Kilbrandon Report).

REPUBLIC OF IRELAND

Dáil Éireann. Minutes of Proceedings of the First Parliament of the Republic of Ireland, 1919–1921 (Dublin, n. d.).

Dáil Éireann. Minutes of Proceedings of the Second Dáil, 16–26 Aug. 1921 and 28 Feb.–8 June 1922, with Index (Dublin, n. d.).

Dáil Éireann. Minutes of Proceedings of the Private Sessions of the Second Dail, 18 Aug.–14 Sept. 1921 and 14 Dec. 1921 to 6 Jan. 1922 (Dublin, n. d.).

Dáil Éireann. Official Report: Debate on the Treaty Between Great Britain and Ireland, 14 Dec. 1921–10 Jan. 1922 (Dublin, n. d.).

Dáil Éireann Debates (Dublin, 1922–25).

Dáil Éireann: Official Correspondence Relating to the Peace Negotiations, June–Sept. 1921 (Dublin, 1921).

NORTHERN IRELAND

House of Commons Debates. First Series (Belfast, 1921–27).

PUBLISHED COLLECTIONS OF DOCUMENTS

Buckland, Patrick, ed. *Irish Unionism, 1885–1923: A Documentary History* (Belfast, 1973).

DeWolfe Howe, Mark, ed. *Holmes-Laski Letters: The Correspondence of Mr. Justice Holmes and Harold J. Laski*, 2 vols (Cambridge, Massachusetts, 1953).

Gilbert, Martin, ed. *Winston Churchill – Companion*: vol. IV, parts 1, 2, and 3 (London, 1977).

Gilbert, Martin, ed. *Winston Churchill – Companion*: vol. V, part 1 (London, 1979).

Hand, Geoffrey, J., ed. *Report of The Irish Boundary Commission: 1925* (Shannon, Ireland, 1969).

Moynihan, Maurice, ed. *Speeches and Statements by Eamon de Valera: 1917–73* (Dublin, 1980).

North-Eastern Boundary Bureau. *Handbook of the Ulster Question* (Dublin, 1923).

Self, Robert C., ed. *The Austen Chamberlain Diary Letters: The Correspondence of Sir Austen Chamberlain with His Sisters Hilda and Ida, 1916–1937* (Cambridge, 1995).

MEMOIRS, DIARIES AND CONTEMPORARY WORKS

Amery, Leo. *The Leo Amery Diaries*, vol. I: *1896–1929*, John Barnes and David Nicholson, ed. (London, 1980).

Amery, Leo. *My Political Life*, vol. II: *War and Peace, 1914–1929* (London, 1958).

Bayford, Lord (Robert Sanders). *Real Old Tory Politics: The Political Diaries of Lord Bayford, 1910–35*, John Ramsden, ed. (London, 1984).

Beaverbrook, Lord (Max Aitken). *The Decline and Fall of Lloyd George* (London, 1963).

Beaverbrook, Lord (Max Aitken). *Men and Power: 1917–1918* (New York, 1956).

Birkenhead, First Earl of (F. E. Smith). *Contemporary Personalities* (London, 1924).

Birkenhead, First Earl of (F. E. Smith). *Points of View*, vol. II (London, n. d).

Boothby, Robert. *I Fight to Live* (London, 1947).

Bridgeman, William. *The Modernisation of Conservative Politics: The Diaries and Letters of William Bridgeman, 1904–1935*. Philip Williamson, ed. (London, 1988).

Chamberlain, Austen. *Down the Years* (London, 1935).

Chamberlain, Austen. *Politics From Inside* (London, 1936).

Churchill, Winston S. *The Gathering Storm* (Boston, 1948).

Churchill, Winston S. *The World Crisis*, 5 vols (New York, 1929).

Collins, Michael. *The Path to Freedom* (Dublin, 1922).

Coote, Colin. *A Companion of Honour: The Story of Walter Elliot* (London, 1965).

Coote, Colin. *Editorial: The Memoirs of Colin R. Coote* (London, 1965).

Crawford, Earl of (David Lindsay). *The Crawford Papers: The Journals of David Lindsay, 27th Earl of Crawford and 10th Earl of Balcarres, 1871–1940, During the Years, 1892 to 1940*, John Vincent, ed. (Manchester, 1984).

Davidson, John Colin Campbell and Robert Rhodes James. *Memoirs of a Conservative: J. C. C. Davidson's Memoirs and Papers, 1910–37* (London, 1969).

Dove, John. *The Letters of John Dove*, Robert Henry Brand, ed. (London, 1938).

Fisher, H. A. L. *An Unfinished Autobiography* (London, 1940).

Grigg, P. J. *Prejudice and Judgment* (London, 1948).

Jones, Thomas. *A Diary with Letters: 1931–1950* (London, 1954).

Jones, Thomas. *Lloyd George* (Cambridge, Massachusetts, 1951).

Jones, Thomas. *Whitehall Diary*, 3 vols, Keith Middlemas, ed. (London, 1969–71).

Lloyd George, David. *Is It Peace?* (London, 1923).

Lloyd George, David. *The Truth About the Peace Treaties*, 2 vols (London, 1938).

Lloyd George, David. *War Memoirs* (London, 1933–36).

Lloyd George, Frances. *Lloyd George: A Diary by Frances Stevenson*, A. J. P. Taylor, ed. (New York, 1971).

Lloyd George, Frances. *The Years That are Past* (London, 1967).

Long, Walter. *Memories* (London, 1923).

Macmillan, Harold. *The Past Masters: Politics and Politicians, 1906–1939* (London, 1975).

Midleton, Lord (William St John Brodrick). *Records and Reactions: 1856–1939* (London, 1939).

Mosley, Oswald. *My Life* (London, 1968).

O'Brien, William. *The Irish Revolution and How It Came About* (Dublin, 1923).

Riddell, George Allardice. *Lord Riddell's Intimate Diary of the Peace Conference and After: 1919–1923* (London, 1933).

Riddell, George Allardice. *The Riddell Diaries: 1908–1923*, J. M. McEwen, ed. (London, 1986).

Roberts, Bechhofer [pseud., 'Ephesian']. *Lord Birkenhead* (London, 1926).

Scott, C. P. *The Political Diaries of C. P. Scott: 1911–1928*, Trevor Wilson, ed. (London, 1970).

Shakespeare, Geoffrey. *Let Candles Be Brought In* (London, 1949).

Shinwell, Emanuel. *I've Lived Through It All* (London, 1973).

Sylvester, A. J. *The Real Lloyd George* (London, 1947).

Thomas, J. H. *My Story* (London, 1937).

Winterton, Lord (Edward Turnour). *Orders of the Day* (London, 1953).

SECONDARY SOURCES

BOOKS

Addison, Paul. *Churchill on the Home Front: 1900–1955* (London, 1992).

Baldwin, A. W. *My Father: The True Story* (London, 1955).

Bardon, Jonathan. *A History of Ulster* (Belfast, 1992).

Beaslai, Piaras. *Michael Collins and the Making of a New Ireland*, 2 vols (Dublin, 1926).

Bell, Geoffrey. *Troublesome Business: The Labour Party and the Irish Question* (London, 1982).

Bennett, Richard. *The Black and Tans* (London, 1959).

Best, Geoffrey. *Churchill: A Study in Greatness* (London, 2001).

Blake, Robert (Introduction). *Ireland After the Union: Proceedings of the Second Joint Meeting of the Royal Irish Academy and the British Academy, London, 1986* (Oxford, 1989).

Blake, Robert. *The Unknown Prime Minister: The Life and Times of Andrew Bonar Law* (London, 1955).

Bond, Brian. *British Military Policy Between the Two World Wars* (Oxford, 1980).

Bowman, John. *De Valera and the Ulster Question: 1917–1973* (Oxford, 1982).

Boyce, D. G. *Englishmen and Irish Troubles* (London, 1972).

Boyce, D. G. *Ireland 1828–1923: From Ascendancy to Democracy* (Oxford, 1992).

Boyce, D. G. *The Irish Question and British Politics: 1886–1986* (London, 1988).

Bromage, Mary C. *Churchill and Ireland* (Notre Dame, Indiana, 1964).

Buckland, Patrick. *James Craig: Lord Craigavon* (Dublin, 1980).

Buckland, Patrick. *The Factory of Grievances: Devolved Government in Northern Ireland, 1921–39* (Dublin, 1979).

Callwell, C. E. *Field-Marshal Sir Henry Wilson, His Life and Diaries*, vol. II (London, 1927).

Campbell, John. *F. E. Smith: First Earl of Birkenhead* (London, 1983).

Campbell, John. *Lloyd George: The Goat in the Wilderness, 1922–31* (London, 1977).

Canning, Paul. *British Policy Towards Ireland: 1921–1941* (Oxford, 1985).

Carter, R. W. G. and A. J. Parker, ed. *Ireland: Contemporary Perspectives on a Land and Its People* (London, 1989).

Cattrell, Peter and Sean McDougall, *The Northern Ireland Question in British Politics* (London, 1996).

Chisholm, Anne and Michael Davie. *Beaverbrook: A Life* (London, 1992).

Churchill, Randolph S. *Lord Derby, 'King of Lancashire': The Official Life of Edward, Seventeenth Earl of Derby, 1865–1948* (London, 1959).

Coakley, John, ed. *Changing Shades of Orange and Green: Redefining the Union and the Nation in Contemporary Ireland* (Dublin, 2002).

Colum, Padraic. *Ourselves Alone! The Story of Arthur Griffith and the Origins of the Irish Free State* (New York, 1959).

Colvin, Ian. *The Life of Lord Carson*, vols II–III (London, 1934–36).

Coogan, Timothy Patrick. *Michael Collins: A Biography* (London, 1990).

Coogan, Timothy Patrick. *De Valera: Long Fellow, Long Shadow* (London, 1993).

Cowling, Maurice. *The Impact of Labour: 1920–1924* (Cambridge, 1971).

Cradden, Terry. 'Labour in Britain and the Northern Ireland Labour Party, 1900–70', in Cattrell, Peter and Sean McDougall, *The Northern Ireland Question in British Politics* (London, 1996).

Cross, J. A. *Sir Samuel Hoare: A Political Biography* (London, 1977).

Curran, Joseph M. *The Birth of the Irish Free State* (Mobile, Alabama, 1980).

Davis, Richard. *Arthur Griffith* (Dundalk, 1976).

Doherty, Gabriel and Dermot Keogh, ed. *Michael Collins and the Making of the Irish State*, (Dublin, 1998).

Drudy, P. J., ed. *Ireland and Britain Since 1922*, Irish Studies, vol. 5 (Cambridge, 1986).

Duggan, John P. *A History of the Irish Army* (Dublin, 1991).

Dutton, David. *Austen Chamberlain: Gentleman in Politics* (Bolton, 1985).

Dwyer, T. Ryle. *Michael Collins and the Treaty: His Differences With de Valera* (Dublin, 1981).

Dwyer, T. Ryle. *De Valera: The Man and the Myths* (Swords, Ireland, 1992).

Ellis, E. L. *T. J.: A Life of Dr Thomas Jones, CH* (Cardiff, 1992).

Ervine, St. John. *Craigavon: Ulsterman* (London, 1949).

Fanning, Ronan. *Independent Ireland* (Dublin, 1983).

Fanning, Ronan. *The Irish Department of Finance: 1922–58* (Dublin, 1978).

Farrell, Michael. *Arming the Protestants: The Formation of the Ulster Special Constabulary and the Royal Ulster Constabulary, 1920–27* (London, 1983).

Farrell, Michael. *Northern Ireland: The Orange State* (London, 1976).

Follis, Bryan A. *A State Under Siege: The Establishment of Northern Ireland, 1920–1925* (Oxford, 1995).

Foster, Robert Fitzroy. *Modern Ireland: 1600–1972* (London, 1988).

Fraser, T. G. *Partition in Ireland, India and Palestine* (New York, 1984).

Garvin, Tom. *1922: The Birth of Irish Democracy* (Dublin, 1996).

Gaughan, J. Anthony. *Austin Stack: Portrait of a Separatist* (Mount Merrion, County Dublin, 1977).

Gilbert, Martin. *Winston S. Churchill: World in Torment, 1917–1922*, vol. IV (London, 1975 [1990 edn]).

Gilbert, Martin. *Winston S. Churchill: 1922–1939*, vol. IV (London, 1976).

Grigg, John. *Lloyd George: From Peace to War, 1912–1916* (London, 1985).

Gwynn, Denis. *The History of Partition: 1912–1925* (Dublin, 1950).

Hammond, J. L. *C. P. Scott of the Manchester Guardian* (London, 1934).

Hand, Geoffrey J. 'MacNeill and the Boundary Commission', in Martin, F. X. and F. J. Byrne, ed. *The Scholar Revolutionary: Eoin MacNeill, 1867–1945, and the Making of the New Ireland* (Shannon, 1973).

Harkness, D. W. *The Restless Dominion: The Irish Free State and the British Commonwealth of Nations, 1921–1931* (London, 1969).

Hartley, Stephen. *The Irish Question as a Problem in British Foreign Policy, 1914–18* (London, 1987).

Hezlet, Arthur. *The 'B' Specials: A History of the Ulster Special Constabulary* (London, 1972).

Holt, Edgar. *Protest in Arms* (London, 1960).

Hopkinson, Michael. *Green Against Green: The Irish Civil War* (Dublin, 1988).

Hopkinson, Michael. *The Irish War of Independence* (Dublin and Montreal, 2002).

Hoppen, K. Theodore. *Ireland Since 1800: Conflict and Conformity* (London, 1989).

Hyde, H. Montgomery. *Carson* (London, 1953).

Hyde, H. Montgomery. *The Londonderrys: A Family Portrait* (London, 1979).

Jalland, Patricia. *The Liberals and Ireland: The Ulster Question in British Politics to 1914* (Brighton, 1980).

Jenkins, Roy. *Churchill: A Biography* (New York, 2001).

Kendle, John. *Walter Long, Ireland, and the Union, 1905–1920* (Montreal, 1992).

Kennedy, Dennis. *The Widening Gulf: Northern Attitudes to the Independent Irish State 1919–1949* (Belfast, 1988).

Kinnear, Michael. *The Fall of Lloyd George: The Political Crisis of 1922* (London, 1973).

Laffan, Michael. *The Partition of Ireland 1911–1925* (Dundalk, 1983).

Laffan, Michael. *The Resurrection of Ireland: The Sinn Féin Party, 1916–1923* (Cambridge, 1999).

Lavin, Deborah. *From Empire to International Commonwealth: A Biography of Lionel Curtis* (Oxford, 1995).

Lawlor, Shelia. *Britain and Ireland: 1914–1923* (Dublin, 1983).

Lawrence, R. J. *The Government of Northern Ireland: Public Finance and Public Services, 1921–1964* (Oxford, 1965).

Lee, J. J. *Ireland 1912–1985: Politics and Society* (Cambridge, 1989).

Lindsay, T. F. and Michael Harrington. *The Conservative Party: 1918–1979* (London, 1979).

Longford, Earl of (Frank Pakenham) and Thomas P. O'Neill. *Eamon de Valera* (London, 1970).

Lyman, Richard W. *The First Labour Government, 1924* (London, 1957).

Lyons, F. S. L. *Ireland Since the Famine* (London, 1971).

Macardle, Dorothy. *The Irish Republic* (New York, 1937 [1965 edn]).

MacDonagh, Oliver. *States of Mind: Two Centuries of Anglo-Irish Conflict, 1780–1980* (London, 1983 [1992 edn]).

Mackay, Ruddock F. *Balfour: Intellectual Statesman* (Oxford, 1985).

Mansergh, Nicholas. *The Unresolved Question: The Anglo-Irish Settlement and Its Undoing, 1912–1972* (New Haven, 1991).

Marquand, David. *Ramsay MacDonald* (London, 1977).

Martin, F. X. and F. J. Byrne, ed. *The Scholar Revolutionary: Eoin MacNeill, 1867–1945, and the Making of the New Ireland* (Shannon, 1973).

McColgan, John. *British Policy and the Irish Administration, 1920–22* (London, 1983).

McCoole, Sinead. *Hazel: A Life of Lady Lavery, 1880–1935* (Dublin, 1996).

McKittrick, David, Seamus Kelters, Brian Feeney, and Chris Thornton. *Lost Lives: The Stories of the Men, Women and Children who Died as a Result of the Northern Ireland Troubles* (Edinburgh, 2001).

McKittrick, David and David McVea. *Making Sense of the Troubles: The Story of the Conflict in Northern Ireland* (Chicago, 2002).

Middlemas, Keith and John Barnes. *Baldwin: A Biography* (London, 1969).

Middlemas, Robert Keith. *The Clydesiders: A Left Wing Struggle for Parliamentary Power* (London, 1965).

Miller, David W. *Queen's Rebels: Ulster Loyalism in Historical Perspective* (Dublin, 1978).

Mitchell, Arthur. *Revolutionary Government in Ireland: Dáil Éireann, 1919–22* (Dublin, 1995).

Morgan, Austen. *Labour and Partition: The Belfast Working Class, 1905–23* (London, 1991).

Morgan, Kenneth O. *Consensus and Disunity: The Lloyd George Coalition Government, 1918–1922* (Oxford, 1979).

Murphy, Brian P. *John Chartres: Mystery Man of the Treaty* (Blackrock, 1995).

Neeson, Eoin. *The Civil War 1922–1923* (Swords, Ireland, 1989).

Newsam, Frank. *The Home Office* (London, 1954).

O'Broin, Leon. *Michael Collins* (Dublin, 1980).

O'Carroll, John P. and John A. Murphy, ed. *De Valera and His Times* (Cork, 1983).

O'Halloran, Claire. *Partition and the Limits of Irish Nationalism* (Dublin, 1987).

O'Hegarty, P. S. *A History of Ireland Under the Union* (London, 1952).

O'Leary, Cornelius. *Irish Elections 1918–1977: Parties, Voters and Proportional Representation* (Dublin, 1979).

Pakenham, Frank (The Earl of Longford). *Peace by Ordeal* (London, 1935 [1972 edn]).

Petrie, Charles. *The Life and Letters of the Right Hon. Sir Austen Chamberlain*, 2 vols (London, 1939–1940).

Phillips, W. Allison. *The Revolution in Ireland: 1906–1923* (London, 1926).

Phoenix, Eamon. 'Michael Collins – The Northern Question, 1916–1922', in Doherty, Gabriel and Dermot Keogh, ed. *Michael Collins and the Making of the Irish State* (Dublin, 1998).

Phoenix, Eamon. *Northern Nationalism: Nationalist Politics, Partition and the Catholic Minority in Northern Ireland, 1890–1940* (Belfast, 1994).

Prager, Jeffrey. *Building Democracy in Ireland: Political Order and Integration in a Newly Independent Nation* (Cambridge, 1986).

Pringle, Dennis. 'Partition, Politics and Social Conflict', in Carter, R. W. G. and A. J. Parker, ed. *Ireland: Contemporary Perspectives on a Land and Its People* (London, 1989).

Pugh, Martin. *Lloyd George* (London, 1988).

Ramsden, John. *A History of the Conservative Party: The Age of Balfour and Baldwin, 1902–1940* (London, 1978).

Rhodes James, Robert. *The British Revolution 1880–1939* (New York, 1977).

Rhodes James, Robert. *Churchill: A Study in Failure, 1900–1939* (London, 1970).

Rhodes James, Robert. *Anthony Eden* (London, 1986).

Rowland, Peter. *David Lloyd George* (New York, 1975).

Ruane, Joseph and Jennifer Todd, ed. *After the Good Friday Agreement: Analysing Political Change in Northern Ireland* (Dublin, 1999).

Salvidge, Stanley. *Salvidge of Liverpool: Behind the Political Scene, 1890–1928* (London, 1934).

Searle, G. R. *Country Before Party: Coalition and the Idea of 'National Government' in Modern Britain, 1885–1987* (London, 1995).

Shannon, Catherine B. *Arthur J. Balfour and Ireland: 1874–1922* (Washington, 1988).

Skidelsky, Robert. *Oswald Mosley* (London, 1975).

Soames, Mary. *Clementine Churchill* (New York, 1981).

Stewart, A. T. Q. *The Narrow Ground: The Roots of Conflict in Ulster* (London, 1977).

Talbot, Hayden. *Michael Collins' Own Story* (London, 1923).

Taylor, A. J. P. *Beaverbrook* (London, 1972).

Taylor, A. J. P. *English History: 1914–1945* (Oxford, 1965).

Taylor, A. J. P., ed. *Lloyd George: Twelve Essays* (London, 1971).

Taylor, Rex. *Assassination: The Death of Sir Henry Wilson and the Tragedy of Ireland* (London, 1961).

Taylor, Rex. *Michael Collins* (London, 1958).

Tierney, Michael. *Eoin MacNeill: Scholar and Man of Action, 1867–1945* (Oxford, 1980).

Townshend, Charles. *The British Campaign in Ireland: 1919–1921* (London, 1975).

Townshend, Charles. *Political Violence in Ireland: Government and Resistance Since 1848* (Oxford, 1983).

Turner, John. *British Politics and the Great War* (New Haven, 1992).

Turner, John. *Lloyd George's Secretariat* (Cambridge, 1980).

Valiulis, Maryann Gialanella. *Portrait of a Revolutionary: General Richard Mulcahy and the Founding of the Irish Free State* (Dublin and Lexington, Kentucky, 1992).

Wall, Maureen. 'Partition: The Ulster Question (1916–1926)', in Williams, Desmond, ed., *The Irish Struggle* (London, 1966).

Watt, David, ed. *The Constitution of Northern Ireland: Problems and Prospects* (London, 1981).

Wheeler-Bennett, John W. *John Anderson, Viscount Waverley* (London, 1962).

White, Terence de Vere. *Kevin O'Higgins* (Tralee, 1966).

Williams, Desmond, ed. *The Irish Struggle: 1916–1926* (London, 1966).

Williamson, Philip. *Stanley Baldwin: Conservative Leadership and National Values* (Cambridge, 1999).

Wilson, Thomas, ed. *Ulster Under Home Rule: A Study of the Political and Economic Problems of Northern Ireland* (London, 1955).

Wilson, Trevor. *The Downfall of the Liberal Party: 1914–1935* (London, 1966).

Wrigley, Chris. *Arthur Henderson* (Cardiff, 1990).

Younger, Calton. *Arthur Griffith* (Dublin, 1981).

Zebel, Sydney H. *Balfour: A Political Biography* (Cambridge, 1973).

ARTICLES

Andrews, J. H. '"The Morning Post" Line', *Irish Geography*, vol. IV, no. 2, 1960.

Bew, Paul. 'A Protestant Parliament and a Protestant State: Some Reflections on Government and Minority in Ulster, 1921–1943', *Irish Historical Studies*, vol. XIV, 1983.

Boyce, D. G. 'British Conservative Opinion, the Ulster Question and the Partition of Ireland, 1912–21', *Irish Historical Studies*, vol. XVII, no. 65, 1970.

Boyle, Kevin. 'The Tallents Report on the Craig–Collins Pact of 30 March 1922', *The Irish Jurist*, vol. XII (N.S. part I), 1977.

Buckland, Patrick. 'Who Governed Northern Ireland? The Royal Assent and the Local Government Bill 1922', *The Irish Jurist*, vol. XV, 1980.

Close, David. 'Conservatives and Coalition After the First World War', *Journal of Modern History*, vol. 45, no. 2, 1973.

Costello, Francis. 'King George V's Speech at Stormont (1921): Prelude to the Anglo-Irish Truce', *Eire-Ireland*, vol. XXII, no. 3, 1987.

Costello, Francis J., Jr 'The Irish Representatives to the London Anglo-Irish Conference in 1921: Violators of Their Authority or Victims of Contradictory Instructions?', *Eire-Ireland*, vol. XXIV, no. 2, 1989.

Fanning, Ronan. '"Rats" versus "Ditchers": The Die-hard Revolt and the Parliament Bill of 1911', *Irish Historical Studies*, vol. XIV, 1983.

Harkness, David. 'Britain and the Independence of the Dominions: the 1921 Crossroads', *Irish Historical Studies*, vol. XI, 1978.

Hart, Peter. 'Michael Collins and the Assassination of Sir Henry Wilson', *Irish Historical Studies*, vol. XXVIII, no. 110, 1992.

Hopkinson, Michael. 'The Craig–Collins Pacts of 1922: Two Attempted Reforms of the Northern Ireland Government', *Irish Historical Studies*, vol. XXVII, 1990–91.

Jackson, Alvin. 'Unionist Myths, 1912–1985', *Past & Present*, no. 136, Aug. 1992.

Kendle, J. E. 'The Round Table Movement and "Home Rule All Round"', *Historical Journal*, vol. XI, no. 2, 1968.

Laffan, Michael. '"Labour Must Wait": Ireland's Conservative Revolution', *Irish Historical Studies*, vol. XV, 1985.

MacMillan, Gretchen. 'British Subjects and Irish Citizens: The Passport Controversy, 1923–24', *Eire-Ireland*, vol. XXVI, no. 3, 1991.

Mansergh, Nicholas. 'The Government of Ireland Act, 1920: Its Origins and Purposes; The Working of the "Official" Mind', *Irish Historical Studies*, vol. IX, 1974.

McColgan, John. 'Implementing the 1921 Treaty: Lionel Curtis and Constitutional Procedure', *Irish Historical Studies*, vol. XX, no. 79, 1977.

Neville, J., H. Douglas, and P. A. Compton. 'The Northern Ireland–Irish Republic Boundary', *Espace, Populations, Sociétés*, no. 2, 1992, pp. 215–26.

O'Halpin, Eunan. 'Sir Warren Fisher and the Coalition, 1919–1922', *Historical Journal*, vol. 24, no. 4, 1981.

Seedorf, Martin, F. 'Defending Reprisals: Sir Hamar Greenwood and the "Troubles", 1920–21', *Eire-Ireland*, vol. XXV, no. 4, 1990.

Staunton, Enda. 'The Boundary Commission Debacle, 1925: Aftermath & Implications', *History Ireland*, vol. 4, no. 2, 1996.

REFERENCE BOOKS

The Annual Register: A Review of Public Events at Home and Abroad: 1920–1925 (London, 1921–1926).

Butler, David and Jennie Freeman. *British Political Facts: 1900–1967* (London, 1968).

Dictionary of National Biography: 1931–1940 (London, 1949).

Dictionary of National Biography: 1941–1950 (London, 1959).

Dictionary of National Biography: 1951–1960 (London, 1971).

Dictionary of National Biography: 1961–1970 (London, 1981).

Dictionary of National Biography: 1971–1980 (London, 1986).

Doherty, J. E. and D. J. Hickey. *A Chronology of Irish History Since 1500* (Dublin, 1989).

Foote, Geoffrey. *A Chronology of Post War British Politics* (Beckenham, Kent, 1988).

Hickey, D. J. and J. E. Doherty. *A Dictionary of Irish History Since 1800* (Dublin, 1980).

Ramsden, John, ed. *The Oxford Companion to Twentieth-Century British Politics* (Oxford, 2002).

Who Was Who: 1916–1928 (London, 1929 [1992 edn]).

Who Was Who: 1929–1940 (London, 1941 [1967 edn]).

Who Was Who: 1941–1950 (London, 1952).

Who Was Who: 1951–1960 (London, 1961).

Who Was Who: 1961–1970 (London, 1972).

Who Was Who: 1971–1980 (London, 1981).

Who Was Who: 1981–1990 (London, 1991).

UNPUBLISHED WORKS

Dooher, John B. 'Tyrone Nationalism and the Question of Partition, 1910–25'. MA thesis, University of Ulster, 1986.

Freeman, Patricia. 'The Career of Michael Collins, With Special Reference to the Treaty of 1921'. MA thesis, University of Bristol, 1963.

Murphy, Richard. 'Walter Long and the Conservative Party, 1905–1921'. PhD thesis, University of Bristol, 1984.

Index